Thanks for Nothing

Thanks for Nothing

The Economics of Single Motherhood since 1980

NICHOLAS H. WOLFINGER
MATTHEW MCKEEVER

OXFORD
UNIVERSITY PRESS

Oxford University Press is a department of the University of Oxford. It furthers
the University's objective of excellence in research, scholarship, and education
by publishing worldwide. Oxford is a registered trade mark of Oxford University
Press in the UK and certain other countries.

Published in the United States of America by Oxford University Press
198 Madison Avenue, New York, NY 10016, United States of America.

© Oxford University Press 2024

All rights reserved. No part of this publication may be reproduced, stored in
a retrieval system, or transmitted, in any form or by any means, without the
prior permission in writing of Oxford University Press, or as expressly permitted
by law, by license, or under terms agreed with the appropriate reproduction
rights organization. Inquiries concerning reproduction outside the scope of the
above should be sent to the Rights Department, Oxford University Press, at the
address above.

You must not circulate this work in any other form
and you must impose this same condition on any acquirer.

Library of Congress Cataloging-in-Publication Data
Names: Wolfinger, Nicholas H., 1966– author. | McKeever, Matthew, author.
Title: Thanks for nothing : the economics of single motherhood since 1980 /
Nicholas H. Wolfinger and Matthew McKeever.
Description: New York, NY : Oxford University Press, [2024] |
Includes bibliographical references and index.
Identifiers: LCCN 2024013831 | ISBN 9780199324323 (hardback) |
ISBN 9780197790014 (epub)
Subjects: LCSH: Single mothers—United States. | Low-income mothers—United States. |
Motherhood—United States. | Equality—United States.
Classification: LCC HQ759.915 .W64 2024 | DDC 331.4/4—dc23/eng/20240615
LC record available at https://lccn.loc.gov/2024013831

DOI: 10.1093/oso/9780199324323.001.0001

Printed by Integrated Books International, United States of America

Matt dedicates this book to Susanna, single mother extraordinaire
Nick dedicates this book to Nick, who's the complete package

Contents

Preface	ix
Acknowledgments	xiii

1.	Introduction: The Original Mommy War	1
2.	Who Are These Mothers?	19
3.	Counting Change	44
4.	From Moynihan to Piketty	81
5.	Thirty-Nine Years in the Lives of Mothers	109
6.	Thirty-Nine Years of Counting Change	136
7.	Conclusion: Where Have We Been, and Where Should We Go Now?	153

Appendix A: Explaining the Growth of Single Motherhood	167
Appendix B: On Moynihan, the Enduring Fallout from his 1965 Report, and the Implications for Studying Single Motherhood	171
Appendix C: The Equivalence of Equivalence Scales	175
Appendix D: Data and Methods	177
Notes	183
References	223
Index	249

Preface

Despite raising three children as a single mother, she'd beaten the odds.

In 1981, Sara McLanahan was a young postdoc at the University of Wisconsin.* When she'd gotten divorced nine years earlier she hadn't even finished college. Like many women of her generation, she'd dropped out to get married. She'd managed to go back to school at the University of Houston, then finished her Ph.D. at the University of Texas in just five years. Now she found herself in a seminar at Madison. Among those present was Irv Garfinkel, soon to be her second husband and a lifelong collaborator.

The seminar was discussing a series of articles in the *New Yorker* by Ken Auletta, then near the start of a long career as a prize-winning author and journalist. He'd done a prodigious amount of research on what was then called the underclass, combining expert opinion with shoe-leather reporting. The Auletta articles offered bracingly strong evidence that family structure and poverty were inextricably linked. Single-mother families now constituted a large and growing portion of the underclass, and children were suffering as a result.

"Sara was stunned by Auletta's claims," wrote the sociologist Kathryn Edin, because they flew in the face of everything she'd learned about family structure. The prevailing academic wisdom in 1981 was that family structure didn't matter for children's well-being. This understanding had emerged in opposition to the Moynihan Report, written in 1965, and had incubated in the 1970s, a decade in which popular culture and elite discourse had valorized divorce and new family forms to a degree that seems jarring in modern times.

Sara McLanahan emerged from the seminar determined to prove Auletta wrong. Like so many pioneers, she was in the right place at the right time. Madison, which soon offered her a professorship, was filled with

---

*. This preface is based on Kathryn Edin's obituary for Sara McLanahan, a series of interviews conducted with Sara as a former president of the Population Association of America (PAA), and conversations with Kathy Edin and Ken Auletta. The obituary and interview transcripts are available via the PAA website, https://higherlogicdownload.s3.amazonaws.com/POPUL ATIONASSOCIATION/3e04a602-09fe-49d8-93e4-1dd0069a7f14/UploadedImages/Past_ PresidentInterviews/67_Sara_McLanahan.pdf.

demographers and econometricians to mentor her. She learned about the Panel Study of Income Dynamics, the first-ever nationally representative panel survey, and an ideal resource for testing Auletta's claims.

Five years later, Sara and Irv Garfinkel, now her husband, published *Single Mothers and Their Children: A New American Dilemma*, and had established once and for all that Auletta had been right in the first place about the connection between poverty, single-mother families, and children's well-being. Sara's ground-breaking scholarship set the stage for all future research on family structure.

Viewed in retrospect, Sara's encounter with Ken Auletta's articles seems like the precise moment where the entire post-Moynihan edifice began to crumble. For a generation, social scientists had denied that family structure mattered, but Sara's research set the academy straight. Her scholarship has been tremendously influential on our work; this book wouldn't exist had she not blazed the trail. We were saddened to learn that Sara passed away in December of 2021 at the age of 81, just as we were finishing this book.

Our book builds on the work Sara McLanahan started by studying the economics of single motherhood since 1980. We were motivated in part by a tent pole finding, a fact that's equal parts surprising and enduring: In 1980, single mother families were five times as likely to be poor as were two-parent married families. By 2020, the most recent data available, single mother families were *still* five times as likely to be poor. How can that be, given the economic progress women have made over the past 40 years? Our goal in this book is to answer that question.

Unlike Sara in 1981, we had a variety of excellent choices when it comes to data. We ended up choosing two national data sets that provide overlapping coverage of single mothers since 1980. The Census Bureau's Current Population Survey draws a new sample every year, so it lets us look at how the population of single mothers has changed over time. It's also a very large survey, so we can explore economic dynamics across the income distribution. The National Longitudinal Survey of Youth's 1979 cohort has followed the same women over the past 40-plus years with annual or biennial interviews, enabling us to understand how women become single mothers, and whether the consequences of single motherhood are persistent. Together these two data sources offer an in-depth portrait of the economics of single motherhood.

By the end of the book we've come full circle, right back to Daniel Patrick Moynihan and his momentous 1965 report. Moynihan was the first modern writer to emphasize the connection between family structure and inequality, drawing on themes that earlier generations of African American sociologists—W. E. B. Du Bois, Franklin Frazier, Ira De A. Reid—had first raised. Writing vividly about African American "pathology" in the heyday of the Civil Rights era, he sparked ferocious backlash that led family scholars astray in the 1970s. It was in that Wisconsin seminar room in 1981 that Sara McLanahan was inspired to get social science back on track with rigorous data analysis. In doing so, she learned that Ken Auletta—and before him, Moynihan—had gotten a great many things right. In 2015, she'd summed up the accomplishments of a very productive career in an article titled "Was Moynihan Right?"

Our analysis of two national data sets lends credence to Moynihan's basic insight in 1965: family structure matters. In the years to come, Moynihan developed a set of ideas about what the government might do in response to the challenges of single motherhood. Moynihan ultimately believed the government was good at redistributing income, but not much else when it came to the family. Our analysis of two national data sets ultimately led us to some of the same public policies once advocated by Senator Moynihan.

Single mothers are here to stay, and their economic challenges remain just as salient in 2024 as they did in the early 1980s, when Sara McLanahan started her career. Our book shows what's stayed the same, what's changed, and how we might best address this enduring American dilemma.

Acknowledgments

The origins of this book can be dated precisely to 1:30 p.m. on Tuesday, August 20th of 1996. We were both finishing up graduate school in sociology at UCLA and were in New York to give papers at the annual meeting of the American Sociological Association (ASA). Together we attended a small round table paper session, where one of two presenters was Richard Peterson, then at the Social Science Research Council. Peterson had just published a bombshell paper in *American Sociological Review*, the ASA's flagship journal. That paper had demolished the conventional wisdom about the economic consequences of divorce for women. At the time, the prevailing finding on the subject, endlessly repeated by politicians and the media, was that women lost 73% of their income upon divorce. Yet no one had looked too closely at this statistic, and Peterson had just shown it was a wild overestimate. Now we found ourselves in a paper session where Peterson was talking about his research. Afterwards, we turned to each other, and with the arrogance unique to grad students, figured we could do what Peterson had just done, only better.

Thus emerged a collaboration that produced papers in fits and starts, but took an unduly long time to produce this book. Our first look at never-married mothers was funded 20 years ago by the W. T. Grant foundation (#202080524). Around the same time Nick received generous support from the Bireley Foundation (and regrets having to wait 15 years to express his appreciation). We presented material from this book at more department colloquia and professional meetings than we can remember, including meetings of the ASA, the International Sociological Association Research Committee 28, and the Population Association of America.

Many colleagues and friends have given us suggestions over the years, including the late Suzanne Bianchi, Dave Brady, Tim Brown, Robert Emery, Jessie Fan, Renata Forste, Joe Hotz, Lori Kowaleski-Jones, Rebecca Maynard, Gary Sandefur, Brad Wilcox, and Zac Zimmer. Eanswythe Leicester Grabowski and Linda Keiter helped us get started with the Current Population Survey, while Steve McClaskie patiently answered our dumb questions about the National Longitudinal Survey of Youth. Our grad school

xiv ACKNOWLEDGMENTS

classmate Eric Kostello provided clutch aid with programming early on. Ken Auletta and Kathy Edin generously shared their time with us to help us understand Sara McLanahan's revelations about family structure when she was a University of Wisconsin postdoc in 1981. And finally, we thank our families, especially Joshua and Ethan, and the countless friends over the years who've patiently listened to us ramble on about this project, and in return reaffirmed the importance of understanding inequality and family structure.

Two people who are both colleagues and friends deserve their own paragraph. Our graduate school classmate Andy Roth has commented extensively on all of Nick's books, and has once more provided valuable feedback. Andy has a unique ability to look at a piece of writing you're convinced is polished and offer granular suggestions that improve its clarity and import. Any writer would be lucky to have his or her own Andy. Moving on, Pam Smock was the discussant the first time we presented some of our findings, way back in Toronto in 1997. She's been a source of friendly council ever since. Pam deserves special recognition for offering to review the manuscript at a time when no one else would.

Over the years, many research assistants have helped out, particularly with the library research in this project's early days. We convey our appreciation to Sonja Anderson, Angela Casady, Kylan Gould, Jackie Griffith, Amanda Grolig, Al Hernandez, Ann House, Emma Bin Liang, Kim Shaff, Shaleia Thompson, and Alta Williams for their difficult yet lightly remunerated work.

At Oxford, James Cook stayed with this project as we flaunted all deadlines, while Alexcee Bechthold made going to press a breeze. Copy editor Abigail Rothberg deserves a medal for working on a book with 64 pages of typo-ridden references. In India, Kavitha Yuvaraj handled the production and graciously fielded a lifetime's worth of emails from us.

1

Introduction

The Original Mommy War

In February 2020, right before the Coronavirus pandemic upended normal life, the Joint Economic Committee of the U.S. Congress met to discuss "improving family stability." In his introductory remarks, Senator Mike Lee (R-Utah) chronicled the challenges facing single parents and their children. Ignoring the economic dynamics of family structure, he instead pointed to the impact of cultural change:

> Well, the breakdown of the family is at least partly caused by cultural changes that have reverberated throughout our society, including changing romantic norms that led to greater relationship ambiguity, cultural individualism that too often emphasizes the desires of individuals over the well-being of the family, and the retreat from religion which is one of the strongest supports of marriage and family life.[1]

These arguments will sound familiar to anyone who's been paying attention to the public discourse on families in the past 40 years. One of the best-known examples is the Dan Quayle–Murphy Brown kerfuffle.

In 1992, incumbent president George H. W. Bush had been locked in a tight reelection contest against Bill Clinton. On the campaign trail, Vice President Dan Quayle gave a speech to the Commonwealth Club of California on May 19. Los Angeles had been wracked by the worst rioting in a major American city since the 1960s, and the vice president sought to attribute the unrest, at least in part, to single motherhood. Near the end of his speech, Vice President Quayle assailed the titular character of the TV sitcom *Murphy Brown* for opting to give birth out of wedlock: "It doesn't help matters when prime time TV has Murphy Brown—a character who supposedly epitomizes today's intelligent, highly paid, professional woman—mocking the importance of fathers, by bearing a child alone, and calling it just another 'lifestyle choice.'"[2] Probably to the vice president's surprise, this became the most memorable

---

Thanks for Nothing. Nicholas H. Wolfinger and Matthew McKeever, Oxford University Press.
© Oxford University Press 2024. DOI: 10.1093/oso/9780199324323.003.0001

moment of the speech, and perhaps even of his entire tenure in office. Even the president felt compelled to speak to Vice President Quayle's remarks.[3] A spate of published commentary only served to amplify the controversy.[4]

Senator Lee and Vice President Quayle were drawing attention to a demographic phenomenon that's grown far more prevalent in the U.S. over the past few decades. From the 1940s until the 1990s divorce had been the predominant reason for single motherhood.[5] Since then, more children live with a mother who has never been married than reside with a divorced mother. By 2018, 40% of American births were to unmarried mothers.[6] At the same time, divorce has continued to produce a substantial number of mother-headed families even as the divorce rate declined over the past few decades.[7] Currently, about one in four children will have experienced divorce by age twelve and the children of divorce most often live with their mothers.[8] All told, over fifteen million American children, or over one in five, now live with an unmarried mother.[9] The growth of single motherhood is shown in Figure 1.1.[10] The reasons for this growth are ultimately beyond the scope of this book, but we present an overview in Appendix A.

Washington heavyweights had been fretting about the purported demise of the family long before Vice President Quayle fulminated against a fictional TV character. The first decade of the twentieth century saw a wave of concern over single-parent families, buoyed by both politicians and academic researchers, that culminated in a 1909 White House conference.[11] "There is wide-spread conviction that the divorce laws are dangerously lax

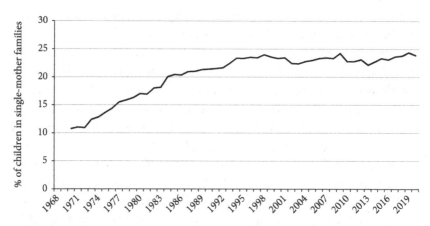

Figure 1.1. Children in Single-Mother Families.
Notes: N = 3,589,425.
Source: CPS 1968–2019.

INTRODUCTION   3

and indifferently administered," thundered Teddy Roosevelt in a message to Congress in 1905.[12] Daniel Moynihan wrote his famous (or infamous, depending upon your perspective) Report about the African American family for the Johnson administration in 1965.[13] The Kerner Commission report raised similar concerns in 1967.[14] And in the throes of the 1965–1980 divorce boom, President Jimmy Carter moralized to members of his administration soon after taking office: "We need a better family life to make us better servants of the people. So those of you living in sin I hope you'll get married. Those of you who have left your spouses, go back home."[15]

Despite these earlier rumblings, the federal paradigm for single-mother families essentially dates to the Reagan administration. The Heritage Foundation, a key source of public policy guidance for Ronald Reagan and subsequent GOP presidents, has set out the underlying logic most bluntly: "The collapse of marriage is the principal cause of child poverty in the United States."[16] Ever since, the federal government's response to the rising number of single mother families has been to promote marriage, with the ultimate goal of bettering children's lot by raising family incomes. The GOP has been the prime mover, although Democratic administrations have also gotten in on the action. The Department of Health and Human Services' Healthy Marriage and Responsible Fatherhood initiative gives grants to organizations "to help participants build and sustain healthy relationships and marriages, and to strengthen positive father-child interaction."[17] Launched in 2001, the initiative has spent over a billion dollars.[18] In its most recent iteration, this program has a five-year funding window, 2015–2020, with a budget of $150 million per year.

Marriage programs followed on the heels of attacks on the portions of the welfare state that redistribute money to single mothers. These attacks are inevitably justified by an enduring canard, as one of the authors of this book recently described:

> The favored narrative among conservatives—that generous welfare benefits undercut marriage by propping up single mothers—holds even less weight.[19] Government transfers were declining in the 1970s and 1980s, the same years when nonmarital fertility was rising the most quickly.[20] When studies do show effects of welfare policy, those effects tend to be small. Irwin Garfinkel and his colleagues, for instance, showed that declining welfare between 1980 and 1996 produced at best a 6 percent decrease in the number of nonmarital births.[21] A detailed review by economist Robert

4   THANKS FOR NOTHING

Moffitt arrived at a similar conclusion, as did a more recent study by Mark Rosenzweig.[22]

Perhaps even more convincingly, the 1996 welfare reform legislation failed to increase the number of two-parent families. In addition, a cross-national comparison of European countries showed an effect that was small at best.[23]

But politicians clearly haven't gotten the message. As the testimony from Senator Lee shows, many continue to echo Reagan's emphasis on culture. The 40th president had frequently attacked "welfare culture" as a cause of poverty, both on the campaign trail and while in office. The following passage, from his 1986 State of the Union address, is representative:

> In the welfare culture, the breakdown of the family, the most basic support system, has reached crisis proportions: female and child poverty, child abandonment, horrible crimes, and deteriorating schools. After hundreds of billions of dollars in poverty programs, the plight of the poor grows more painful. But the waste in dollars and cents pales before the most tragic loss: the sinful waste of human spirit and potential. We can ignore this terrible truth no longer.[24]

Echoing Charles Murray's landmark attack on the welfare state in *Losing Ground: American Social Policy, 1950–1980*, the president's remarks advanced several dubious narratives about state aid: it accelerated the formation of mother-headed families, weakened social institutions, bred a culture of poverty that reduced individual initiative, and juiced the crime rate.[25] Perhaps best remembered is Reagan's denunciation of an emblematic "welfare queen" in his 1976 presidential campaign: "She used 80 names, 30 addresses, 15 telephone numbers to collect food stamps, Social Security, veterans' benefits for four nonexistent deceased veteran husbands, as well as welfare. Her tax-free cash income alone has been running $150,000 a year."[26] The target of his denunciation was a career criminal, but the implication was that the American welfare state was rife with fraud and a wellspring of moral hazard.

Reagan's response to the growing number of single-mother families wasn't always so strident. On March 21, 1984, he proclaimed a National Single Parents Day: "I call on the people of the United States to recognize the contributions single parents are making, sometimes under great hardships, to the lives of their children, and I ask that they volunteer their help, privately

INTRODUCTION 5

or through community organizations, to single parents who seek it to meet their aspirations for their children."[27] In August of the same year he signed a bill that strengthened collection of unpaid child support.[28]

Republicans haven't had a monopoly on public aid polemics. Bill Clinton "ended welfare as we know it" with the 1996 Personal Responsibility and Work Opportunity Act, which placed lifetime limits on welfare receipt and devolved funding to block grants to states. A primary goal of the bill was to "end the dependence of needy parents on government benefits by promoting job preparation, work, and marriage."[29] Curtailing government transfers as a means to both help children and dispatch a hated government program had become centrist politics, not the right-wing invective of Reagan's campaign from 20 years earlier. Perhaps Clinton felt like he was staking out middle ground given how overheated some of the anti-welfare rhetoric had become. In 1992, for instance, political scientist Lawrence Mead deemed welfare dependence to be "an American crisis comparable to the Civil War, even as a threat to the basic values of Western civilization."[30]

While jeremiads like Mead's may no longer be at the forefront of the culture wars, family structure remains central to public debates on inequality and the welfare state.[31] The staying power of this debate is explained by one of the most enduring findings in the scholarly literature on families: both in 1980 and 2020, mother-headed families are over five times as likely as two-parent families to be poor.[32] In the wake of the Great Recession, the poverty rate for single-mother families ascended to heights not seen since the mid 1990s. It has declined somewhat, but as of 2018 remains at 25%; in the past, it had exceeded 50%.[33] Moreover, there is evidence that the proliferation of single-mother households has contributed to the growing gap between the rich and poor in modern America.[34] Family structure remains a key correlate of income; thus, the women who head these families and the children who are raised in them continue to find themselves at the bottom of the income distribution.

This book explores the economics of single motherhood since 1980. We follow mothers' incomes over nearly 40 years to find out who's doing well and who isn't in contemporary America. It's long been known that single mothers are disadvantaged compared to married mothers. Our research seeks to better understand the extent of this disadvantage by contrasting the attributes of married, divorced, and never-married mothers and their families. Our primary thesis is straightforward: *There are two very different kinds of single mothers in America today—divorced women and women who*

6 THANKS FOR NOTHING

give birth out of wedlock—and this can explain why the poverty gap between married and single mothers has held steady for so long. Divorced mothers look very much like married mothers with respect to their demographic and vocational attributes; the most significant difference is the absence of a spousal income. Never-married mothers are an entirely different population. These women, suffering from pervasive disadvantages that go far beyond their low incomes, often remain poor despite impressive gains in education and other labor market qualifications more broadly correlated with prosperity.

What Matters? Family Income

There are two fundamental considerations that inform our exploration of income and single motherhood. First, income is a family-level phenomenon insofar as it affects how family member's lives unfold. An individual's quality of life occurs as part of a family. Family income is what shapes how well family members eat, their opportunities for schooling, where they live, their access to healthcare, and whether they are able to own their own homes. This is recognized by public policy aimed at ameliorating the effects of poverty by providing food, income replacement, housing vouchers, and other benefits to families. Indeed, much of the debate over public assistance focuses on policies that are articulated at the family level. This is important to acknowledge, as family structure is such a strong predictor of family income.[35] All else being equal, families with only one adult, most obviously mother-headed families, will be at a disadvantage because they lack the potential for two incomes.

Second, income in the United States is primarily determined through individual participation in the labor market. The vast majority of Americans earn a living, so most research on the determinants of income focuses on the attributes of individuals that are valued in the labor market, such as education and job experience. These factors, along with demographic traits such as gender and race, determine how remunerative employment is for any particular individual. For these reasons we examine individual characteristics when attempting to understand variation in income, and how the relationship between these characteristics and income has changed over time.

It is only possible to understand American inequality, then, by focusing on the intersection of individual and family characteristics. In looking at families, we analyze how the characteristics of the adults in these families

INTRODUCTION 7

shape income. In doing so, we document how individual-level contributions to income are fundamentally contingent on family structure, thus underscoring the importance of taking both individual- and family-level characteristics into account when studying inequality. Not only are single-mother families deprived of two incomes, but the adults who head them often have less of the human capital it takes to make money by working. In contrast, women from the privileged social classes—those with the highest incomes and the most education—are the most likely to get married and stay married.[36] These women are also among the least likely to give birth out of wedlock.[37] Above and beyond invoking family structure as a basis for inequality, it's necessary to understand the complex interaction between family structure and labor force attributes.

Studying family income is a choice with explicit trade-offs. Some studies have focused on the poverty line, a ratio of needs to poverty levels, or one of more than fifty other "equivalence scales."[38] Many are artificial metrics that makes comparisons across predictors unwieldy, while an emphasis on poverty lines excludes the great majority of mothers.[39] We are interested in all parts of the income distribution, so we can learn which mothers are prospering and which have been left behind. What's more, there's less variation in family size than might be imagined. In the following chapter, Figure 2.4 shows that over 80% of mothers in the Current Population Survey (CPS) data have only one or two children. Thus there isn't substantial variation in the data that might be captured by equivalence scales.[40]

All the reassurances in the world are less convincing than data, so we present results based on different equivalence scales in Appendix C. The short answer is that they all show the same relative gaps between married mothers, divorced mothers, and never-married mothers that we observe by looking at family income.

Another option is to focus on consumption. Sociologists Kathryn Edin and Laura Lein have observed that single mothers often have multiple sources of income: wage labor, different kinds of public assistance, transfers from parents, boyfriends or girlfriends, and employment in the informal economy.[41] Consequently single mothers may be likely to under-report their incomes in comparison to married mothers.[42] Consumption entails studying how much money single mothers spend rather than how much money they take in. Looking at consumption rather than income suggests that single mothers are faring somewhat better economically.[43]

8   THANKS FOR NOTHING

There are clearly benefits to studying consumption, but it is not uniformly superior as a measure of living standards compared to family income. The nature of consumption has changed over time in ways not easily reducible to dollar figures. Almost no one had mobile phones or internet service providers in 1980, and no one without them felt deprived. In addition, consumption measures are not immune to misreporting in survey data. For example, if consumption far outstrips income from all sources (including in-kind transfers), it might imply not properly accounting for expenditures, or it might imply debt (which is a further complication). An inflated level of consumption today might signify lower consumption tomorrow. Finally, full measures of consumption aren't available in the data used here.

Single Mothers and Government Transfers

Any examination of family income and single mothers needs to account for the role of government transfers. These benefits have varied substantially, both among different kinds of single-mother families and over time, as the political mood has shifted. The history of federal family policy in the U.S. shows that family structure and economic support have been intertwined for well over a century, and this relationship has generally reflected changing morality and the deservedness of different groups of single mothers.

One early example is the pensions for Union widows of the Civil War. For most women of that era, widowhood meant losing the ability to maintain an independent household, so the government sought to relieve their predicament by providing direct cash benefits. These pensions provided the opportunity for many widows to establish comfortable households.[44] Unlike divorcées and bereaved women from the former Confederacy, Union widows were seen as "deserving" single mothers by federal lawmakers. Given the number of eligible women, the expenditures were in the long-run much higher than initially anticipated.[45] One consequence was to foment a backlash that served to delay the adoption of more wide-reaching reforms to assist other needy families of the time.[46]

As periodic economic crises of the latter nineteenth century swept over the country, reformers sought to expand social assistance programs to deal with poverty among single mothers who weren't war widows. Much of this owed to the work of urban reformers, such as those responsible for the Hull House movement in Chicago.[47] These reforms targeted widows more generally, as well as "abandoned" women left with children to raise.[48] Several local programs across the country paid cash benefits to single mothers.[49] In 1911, Illinois became the first state to do so, and by 1935, the year Aid to Families with Dependent Children (AFDC) became law, nearly all states provided aid to at least some single mothers.[50] These transfers were undoubtedly helpful to the families who qualified, but the payments were relatively small.

These programs continued the American tradition of setting conditions above and beyond mere single motherhood for receiving assistance. Aid was given only to "fit" mothers: those who maintained good homes, were citizens, and were raising their children in a suitable manner.[51] Women who had given birth out of wedlock or who had abandoned their husbands did not qualify.[52] African American mothers were often excluded from receiving benefits.[53] Some programs were innovative in that they did not set conditions on fitness. For example, starting in 1890 "mothers' aid" programs offered the first direct cash assistance given to single mothers no matter why they were single.[54] Most programs, however, maintained some distinction between deserving and undeserving women.

Debate about the propriety of cash payments to single mothers accompanied the New Deal policies enacted during the Great Depression. The Depression had worsened life for America's poor, especially its single mothers. Employees of the federal Children's Bureau, originally created in 1912 but expanded under the Roosevelt administration, helped to construct a new federal program to provide cash to single mothers, the Aid to Dependent Children program.[55] This was formally created as a separate fund by the Social Security Act of 1935. Under provisions of the Act, the federal government gave money to the states, and the states established provisions for disbursement to mothers. Later years saw the creation of anti-poverty programs such as food stamps, which also disproportionately benefited single-mother families.

As federal support expanded during the Great Society and the number of single mothers ballooned, most Americans disapproved.[56] Increasingly, politicians tapped into this disapproval, and argued that the growth of the number of these families was only exacerbated by social aid programs. The critique of state support of "undeserving" mothers perhaps reached its defining moment when Ronald Reagan denounced "welfare queens" in 1976.[57] As we have observed, it was argued that welfare provided a major disincentive for women to work or marry.

10 THANKS FOR NOTHING

Above and beyond claims of the unworthiness of certain mothers, allegations about the harmfulness of single parenting consistently worked their way into the political debate over welfare policies.[58] These claims often relied on evidence from academic studies demonstrating differences in both short- and long-term outcomes for children of married and non-married parents, as well as studies showing income differences that correlated with family structure.[59]

Although federally funded, AFDC was in effect a state-run program. In response to prevailing concerns about welfare in the 1980s, many states experimented with various limitations on aid. At the federal level, the critique of direct cash assistance was behind the most dramatic transformation of welfare programs for single mothers, the move from AFDC to Temporary Assistance for Needy Families (TANF) in 1996. The main features of the transition to TANF were the establishment of time limits on welfare receipt, and increased control given to individual states over welfare policy.[60] Prior to 1996, there were no limits on funds allocated to states; in other words, the federal government would provide benefits to all single mothers who met program requirements. Subsequently funds were allocated as block grants to states, many of which soon devised criteria for denying eligible mothers.[61] And while TANF added programs for transitioning women from welfare to employment, they fell far short of what the program's principal architect, economist David Ellwood, had originally envisioned.[62]

While the primary objective of the transition to TANF was to move women from welfare to work, its renewal in 2002 also highlighted marriage promotion. That year, President George W. Bush asserted "My administration will give unprecedented support to strengthening marriages."[63] Since marriage has been shown to be beneficial to both children and adults, why not drive down welfare roles by shifting the burden of poverty from the state to the individual?[64] Ultimately welfare reform meant that women raising children by themselves could count on diminishing assistance from the federal government.

Currently, there is a patchwork of policies aimed at helping impoverished parents. These include TANF, nutrition programs such as food stamps and subsidized lunches, Medicaid, the State Children's Health Insurance Program, and more. There is enormous variation in how much single mothers receive and as we will show, few receive enough to support their families. Over time, cash transfers to single parents have mattered less for

INTRODUCTION 11

determining a family's bottom line, as paid employment is now the primary source of income for single mothers.[65]

The Transformation of the Labor Market

The past 40 years witnessed not only growing numbers of mother-headed families and changes in public policy regarding supporting them, but also the transformation of the labor market. There are three related trends that have affected all families, but have been especially consequential to those families headed by single women. The first is the entry of women into the labor market in ever greater numbers; the second, the transition from a manufacturing-based economy to an economy where services comprise the bulk of employment; and third, the growing importance of education in achieving high wages, a trend that coincided with rising levels of education for women. We will discuss each of these developments in turn.

The modern nadir of women's labor market participation occurred in the 1950s, with only a third of women working.[66] During this era women had few rights in the labor market and women, especially wives and mothers, were excluded from most jobs.[67] Both authors of this book heard stories from their mothers and family friends of being forced out of jobs because they got married, had children, or simply because they were women. This all changed over the next few decades, and there continued to be a steady increase of women in the workforce. By 2009, over half of all women were working, with almost three-fourths of female employees working full-time.[68] The labor force participation of mothers grew even more remarkably. Despite the centurial rise in women's employment, mothers remained much more likely to stay home. This was especially true of women with young children. In 1980, only 57% of all mothers and just 47% of those with a child under six were working.[69] By 2018, 71% of mothers worked. This trend extended to women with young children, with 64% of them now employed.[70]

The two main explanations for these trends are the declines in men's real wages since the early 1970s and the growth of single-mother families over the same time period; a third, less tangible reason is the growing legal and social equality between men and women.[71] Over these years it became increasingly difficult for a single male wage earner to provide for a family as unions weakened and the basis of the economy shifted from manufacturing to the service and information sectors.[72] These industries require very different types

12 THANKS FOR NOTHING

of workers, are less likely to be unionized, and generally provide lower wages and fewer benefits. The information economy jobs that pay well generally require a college degree, if not an advanced education, something only a minority of Americans possess. Moreover, there are far fewer of these jobs than there were manufacturing jobs prior to the 1980s. What became more available were lower-status service sector jobs that don't require advanced training.

The shift from a manufacturing to service and information economy has expanded opportunities for female employment. Just like men, women now enter a labor market with vast variation in wages.[73] Some women, well-educated and finally able to enter professions previously closed to them, now earn high incomes as professionals. This has contributed to rising female wages; while the gender wage gap is larger for workers with college degrees, it's smaller among non-salaried women able to work longer and longer hours.[74] However, it was the expansion of the low-paid service sector that has provided the lion's share of employment for single mothers.[75] Consequently women's wages have not increased as quickly as might be expected given the growing representation of women in well-paying jobs.[76] The increased opportunities in a service and knowledge economy, some have argued, hold the possibility of higher incomes for some mother-headed families, but most mothers don't find themselves in the type of jobs that pay well.[77]

The third consequential change in the U.S. occupational structure has been the increasing importance of education for the employment and compensation of workers.[78] This has noteworthy repercussions for gender differences in wages, as women's educational attainment has risen more quickly than men's over the past 40 years. Today more women than men graduate from both high school and college.[79] This has helped to narrow the gender gap in earnings, as has the growing inequality in men's wages. Nonetheless, the gender gap remains: women still earn only 84 cents on the male dollar.[80] Wages have also grown more unequal for men and women alike. Still, as women's educational attainment has risen in an economy that places greater importance on credentials, the potential for higher incomes for some single mothers exists. This topic will be explored at length in these pages.

Teen Mothers and Welfare Reform as
Approximations of Single Motherhood

Who, exactly, has been counted as a single mother in previous studies? What specific populations have been the focus of research in this field? Although

INTRODUCTION 13

there is a good amount of research on income and inequality across different family types, much of it circumscribes family structure in crucial ways. Many studies have examined how divorce affects women's incomes, but this research includes many childless women. There has been comparably less research on women who give birth out of wedlock,[81] and even fewer studies have considered how the incomes of divorced and never-married mothers have changed over time.[82] Perhaps the main reason for this has been the tendency for researchers to either lump together all single mothers—as have most studies of welfare reform—or to focus on populations that include only a fraction of the population of single mothers (most notably, studies of teen motherhood).

Economists have long studied the economics of teenage childbearing. In particular, scholars have explored whether teenage fertility is a cause or consequence of poverty.[83] Characterized by formidable methodological innovation, this research has examined teenage childbirth within pairs of sisters, or compared teenage mothers with would-be mothers who miscarry, and contrasted the differences produced by single children and twins.[84] Taken together, this body of research shows that most of the apparent economic consequences of teenage childbirth are a product of sample selection: teenage mothers would be impoverished even had they remained childless. Additional evidence for this contention comes from the finding that women who grow up poor are disproportionately likely to give birth out of wedlock; thus, poverty is a cause as well as a consequence of nonmarital births.[85]

There are four problems with applying these studies of teenage childbearing to single motherhood in general. First, one out of ten teenage mothers is married, so research nominally devoted to teenage childbearing does not provide an accurate depiction of unwed teenage mothers, or unwed mothers in general.[86] Second, older women who give birth out of wedlock are neglected entirely. By 1995, only about 30% of never-married mothers were teenagers, and the rate has continued to decline.[87] Older women might become never-married mothers under different and perhaps more financially advantageous circumstances. Furthermore, unwed teenage mothers who avoid further nonmarital fertility fare better economically than women who continue to have children out of wedlock.[88] Third, divorced mothers are underrepresented. Few women get married, have kids, and get divorced all while still teenagers. Finally, none of the studies on teenage motherhood consider how the incomes of mothers have changed over time. This is a significant omission in an era when all women's labor force prospects

14 THANKS FOR NOTHING

have improved, potentially eroding the link between single motherhood and poverty.

A number of studies over the past 25 years have evaluated the incomes of women after welfare reform.[89] Initial studies were cautiously optimistic: welfare rolls were shrinking, incomes had increased modestly, and poverty rates had declined. However, this may have been a consequence of the bullish economy of the late 1990s rather than a product of changing welfare policy. Later research offered a more mixed assessment: many former welfare recipients had joined the workforce and were benefiting from an expanded earned income tax credit, but some had slipped through the cracks and were desperately poor.[90] Either way, these studies suffer from the limitation common to most work on single mothers: rarely are distinctions made between divorced women, whose welfare participation is inherently more likely to be transitory, and women who give birth out of wedlock.

Finally, many studies have been more concerned with the differences between one-parent and two-parent families than variation within the population of single mothers.[91] These studies have made valuable contributions to our understanding of inequality. Yet, as we suggest here, such an approach glosses over the profound differences between divorced mothers and women who give birth out of wedlock.

Our Approach to the Economics of Single Motherhood

This book examines how changes in family structure and mothers' attributes have affected the incomes of families headed by married, divorced, and never-married mothers.[92] These are by far the three most common living arrangements for mothers; together, they are raising 91% of American children.[93] Moreover, 96% of children living in mother-headed families reside with a separated, divorced, or never-married mother.[94] Youthful widowhood is uncommon today, with less than 4% of mother-only families headed by a widow according to CPS data. The other two kinds of mother-headed families measurable by national survey data are families headed by separated mothers and married families with a father who lives elsewhere. The latter have far more in common with married families than with single-mother families, while the former are not easily classified using survey data due to their changing personal and economic circumstances.[95]

INTRODUCTION 15

Should unwed mothers living with an unmarried partner be counted as single mothers? We believe that for the purposes of our study the answer to this question should be yes, for one simple reason: cohabitation is for most people in the United States a fundamentally unstable relationship, far more tenuous than marriage. Most cohabiting unions end quickly, whether through marriage or dissolution. After five years, just over 10% of cohabiting partners are still living together out of wedlock.[96] Having a child together doesn't change things. About four out of five cohabiting parents will have split up by their child's 15th birthday.[97] Moreover, stability does not increase in long-term relationships—irrespective of duration, any cohabiting relationship is equally likely to dissolve.[98] In some cases it's not even clear who's cohabiting and who's not.[99] At the same time, we recognize that cohabitation is important to understanding single motherhood. Sixty percent of unmarried mothers are living with their child's father at the time of birth, a figure that's risen considerably in recent decades.[100] Consequently one out of four American parents is unmarried.[101] Our solution to the issue of cohabitation is to treat it as one of many factors that may affect the incomes of divorced and never-married mothers.

Another of our objectives is to better understand one of the most prominent features of the modern American economy, the ever-increasing gulf between rich and poor.[102] Income inequality is of broad interest because of its many deleterious effects on individuals and society alike.[103] The proliferation of single-mother families can explain about one-fifth of the growth in American income inequality.[104] Furthermore, previous research has shown that income is distributed differently within different types of families, with greater overall inequality within the populations of divorced mothers and never-married mothers than for married mothers.[105]

The question of inequality among never-married mothers may be of particular interest for non-academic reasons. In the wake of the Dan Quayle–Murphy Brown hullabaloo, the stereotype arose of the professional woman, perhaps in her late 30s or 40s, opting to give birth out of wedlock.[106] This narrative drove the hope that perhaps never-married mothers were not as bad off as many people thought. Perhaps Murphy Brown mothers comprised a growing population. Indeed, nonmarital childbearing by women with four or more years of college had doubled between 1985 and 1994.[107] Although our previous research cast doubt on the prevalence of Murphy Brown mothers, more than 10 years has passed and the question remains of interest.[108] There is no such debate about divorced mothers—almost everyone

16 THANKS FOR NOTHING

agrees they are disadvantaged, although perhaps not as much as sometimes believed.[109] Still, are some single mothers getting ahead at the expense of others? Accordingly this book explores both median incomes and the position of married, divorced, and never-married mothers within the income distribution. Inequality affects the conditions of families today, but also the prospects of their children—and thus America's prospects for years to come.

Families are not static. Many single mothers marry (or remarry). Others will live with a partner out of wedlock. Some women will give birth out of wedlock, get married, and then divorce. Accordingly we will explore the economic consequences of moving in and out of single motherhood for individual women. This approach is motivated in part by the finding that many single mothers are economically disadvantaged before they ever give birth. Finally, we consider whether the economic consequences of single motherhood are transitory or persistent.[110]

It's an old joke in academia that economists worry about selection bias and try to model it away, whereas sociologists study it.[111] It's for this reason that much microeconomic research in recent years relies on instrumental variables and naturally occurring experiments, like the study that compared teenaged mothers with comparable women who miscarried.[112] We don't question the fundamental utility of this approach to quantitative research, although we do observe that it often relies on sensitive statistical assumptions.[113]

Our approach to the economics of single motherhood is fundamentally different. With the exception of some of the analysis in Chapter 6, we are interested in description rather than causal modeling. How does income vary by marital status and various individual attributes? How have the economics of single motherhood changed over the past 40 years? These are descriptive questions, not queries about causal relationships. Our statistical analysis isn't predicated on sensitive statistical models, but more fundamental techniques for describing data. Causal modeling has produced worthwhile results in the economics of single motherhood, but are largely irrelevant to the questions we seek to answer.

Finally, this is a book is about the economics of single motherhood, not its causes. In particular, we leave the cultural considerations to others. We do not claim that the growth of single-parent families is the exclusive product of economic factors. The economics of single motherhood cannot be understood without determining which women are likely to become single mothers, but this shouldn't be treated as a comprehensive explanation of the causes of single motherhood. Readers interested in why single motherhood increased so much in recent decades should consult Appendix A.

Plan of the Book

We examine the economics of single mothers and their families since 1979, and how they compare to married mothers. Our conclusions are based on two national data sets, the March Demographic Supplement of the CPS and the NLSY 1979 cohort.[114] The CPS, an annual cross-section of approximately 50,000 families, provides a look at how the economics of single motherhood have changed over historical time. Our analysis of the CPS begins in 1980 to capture changes effected by the Reagan presidency, often thought to herald a new economic regime.[115] Starting in with 1980 also provides comparability to the NLSY data.

The NLSY is a sample of 12,686 men and women aged 14 to 22 in 1979, the year of the first interview. Respondents were re-interviewed annually through 1994 and biennially thereafter. There are also recalled data on pre-interview characteristics, including union formation and dissolution prior to 1979, as well as information on respondents' families of origin. These data allow us to track mothers into middle age: by 2018, the most recent year of data we analyze, the NLSY respondents range in age from 53 to 61. By this time in their lives, virtually all fertility has been completed and respondents have reached peak earning power.[116] The NLSY data therefore facilitate a broad examination of the enduring economic consequences of single motherhood.

Together the CPS and the NLSY provide a wealth of data on single mothers, as is evidenced by the fact that this book has more than 100 figures and tables. This abundance of data is both by design and by necessity. From the beginning, our intention was to provide a resource that would enable readers to readily answer any question about the economics of single motherhood that can be addressed by quantitative data. In the course of writing this book, we learned that the differences between divorced mothers and never-married mothers are so wide-ranging that they appear across almost any measurable dimension. This accumulation of evidence in turn buttresses our conclusions.

Chapters 2, 3, and 4 are based on the CPS, while Chapters 5 and 6 draw on the NLSY. In Chapter 2, we consider how the economic, social, and demographic characteristics of single mothers have changed over the past 40 years. Chapter 3 is devoted to the predictors of median family income. We look at how the effects of individual and family attributes on income differ between married, divorced, and never-married mothers, and whether these differences have grown over the years of the study. Chapter 4 extends our inquiry beyond median income levels to changes across the entire income distribution. How does income inequality vary between married, divorced, and never-married mothers? Are a few pulling ahead at the expense of others? How has inequality increased over time? Chapter 5 contrasts the economic, social, and demographic characteristics of married, divorced, and never-married mothers as they move from youth into middle age. We explore the accumulation of human capital over the life course, and whether it differs by family structure. The characteristics of mothers' families of origins are contrasted. This chapter also explores the process of entering and exiting single motherhood. Chapter 6 considers how mothers' changing characteristics affect their incomes. Does the accumulation of human capital benefit never-married and divorced mothers to the same extent that it does married mothers? Chapter 7 provides a summary of our findings and a discussion of their implications for public policy.

2

Who Are These Mothers?

America has changed a lot in the past 40 years, so this is where we start our exploration of income and family structure. In this chapter, we explore the changing demographic and social characteristics of married, divorced, and never-married mothers. In short, mothers in 2018 look very different than mothers in 1980. Nowadays these women have more education, better jobs, give birth later, and have fewer children, and these differences have obvious implications for family income. Critically, many of these attributes have changed at different rates for married and single mothers.

Trends in Marital Status

The natural point of departure is the 40-year trend in family structure, shown in Figure 2.1—as well as a disclaimer about the limitations of cross-sectional data. Since 1980, rates of married motherhood have declined from just under 90% to about 75%. This decline has been offset by the rise in never-married motherhood, from 3% in 1980 all the way up to 16% over the past few years. Meanwhile, divorced motherhood has held steady at about 10% throughout this time period, though it dipped slightly in the past few years.

These numbers are hard to square with the received wisdom on modern family demography regarding divorce. In 1980, at the height of the divorce boom, weren't one out of two marriages breaking up?[1] Aren't 40% of children now born out of wedlock?[2] Isn't marriage in sharp decline?[3] These seeming discrepancies with the Figure 2.1 statistics highlight the difference between cross-sectional data like the CPS provide, and the longitudinal NLSY data we will examine in Chapters 5 and 6. Well over 10% of married mothers will dissolve their marriages, but many—perhaps over one-half—will remarry within a few years.[4] A smaller number will lose custody of their children. Many more will see their children turn eighteen. Either way, they cease to count as divorced mothers for economic purposes. Similarly, many women who give birth out of wedlock will eventually get married. The CPS is only a

Thanks for Nothing. Nicholas H. Wolfinger and Matthew McKeever, Oxford University Press.
© Oxford University Press 2024. DOI: 10.1093/oso/9780199324323.003.0002

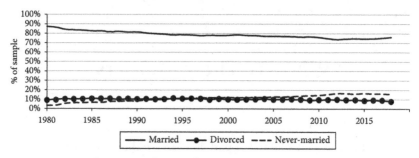

Figure 2.1. Trends in Marital Status for Mothers.
Notes: N = 681,144 (married) 85,105 (divorced) 87,480 (never married). Results are weighted.
Source: CPS 1980–2018.

snapshot of mothers at one moment in time, and therefore doesn't reflect the full incidence of divorce and nonmarital fertility.

The CPS data make it clear that married motherhood (and fatherhood) continues to represent the most common living arrangement for American children. At the same time, the growth in nonmarital fertility has considerably increased the number of children being raised by a single mother.

Trends in Fertility

One factor which greatly affects the ability of women to earn a good income is the age at which they become a mother, as economist Arthur Campbell famously pronounced in 1968: "The girl who has an illegitimate child at the age of sixteen suddenly has 90 percent of her life's script written for her."[5] It should come as no surprise to anyone with even a cursory understanding of income inequality that teenage fertility is strongly correlated with low earnings.[6] What's less commonly known is that there has been a steady decline in teenage births since the Baby Boom.[7] In the 1950s, the teen birth rate peaked at 96 births per 1,000 women aged 15 to 19. By 1980, it had fallen to below 60 births per 1,000, or about the level prior to the Boom. After a brief rebound in the late 1980s, the rate continued its long decline. By 2018, it stood at 17 per 1,000 teenaged women, the lowest in recorded history. Yet the broader downwards trend conceals dramatic differences by marital status, as Figure 2.2 shows[8] While teenage parenthood has declined across the board, never-married mothers remain far more likely to have their first children as teenagers than are married or divorced mothers.

WHO ARE THESE MOTHERS? 21

Figure 2.2. Teen Births by Marital Status.
Notes: N = 681,144 (married) 85,105 (divorced) 87,480 (never married). Results are weighted.
Source: CPS 1980–2018.

Many people think of women who give birth out of wedlock and teenage mothers as one and the same, but the data show that the great majority of unmarried mothers are now twenty or over when their first child is born. Throughout the 1980s almost 50% of women who gave birth outside of marriage were teenagers, but by 2000 this figure had dipped below 40%.[9] It now stands at 25%, or one in four. The decrease was particularly dramatic for births to unwed 15- to 17-year-olds, which have declined by approximately one-third since the start of the new millennium.[10]

These trends are consequential. First, older women are in almost every respect better equipped to cope with motherhood. Compared to teenagers they are more likely to have completed high school, and perhaps college.[11] They are almost certainly more mature, which increases their ability to be effective parents and wage earners. They are also more likely to have at least a modicum of job experience. Second, the rising age at which women give birth out of wedlock changes how we should think about nonmarital childbearing. Increasingly the designations "teenage childbearing" or "young unwed mothers" are no longer accurate. Although teenagers represent a notable number of unmarried mothers, they are no longer in the majority, and public policy aimed at unwed motherhood should take notice.

Rates of teen childbirth have also been uniformly lower for married and divorced mothers over the last 40 years. According to Figure 2.2, 24% of first births among divorced mothers and 15% for married mothers were to teenagers in 1980. Early marriage has long been one of the strongest predictors of divorce, so it's not surprising to see a higher rate of teenage births among women who eventually ended their marriages.[12] These

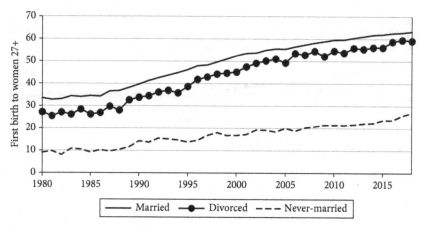

Figure 2.3. Percent of Births to Women 27 and Older by Marital Status.
Notes: N = 681,144 (married) 85,105 (divorced) 87,480 (never married). Results are weighted.
Source: CPS 1980–2018.

numbers converged over time, so by 2001 rates of teenage birth were around 10% for both sets of women. Early marriage continues to increase the likelihood of divorce, but teenage marriage (and childbirth) has become a far less common phenomenon.[13]

Married and divorced mothers are more similar in their chances of a later first birth. Figure 2.3 shows the percentage of women who first give birth at or after age 27.[14] Later births have become more common for all women, but especially for married and divorced mothers. Later births increased much more slowly for never-married mothers. By 2018, roughly one-quarter of these women had given birth to their oldest child at 27 or above, compared to about 60% of married and divorced mothers. Delayed childbirth is associated with greater educational attainment and work experience and is therefore consequential for earning potential.

Is the changing average age at which women give birth out of wedlock the product of a few much older unwed mothers, perhaps in their 30s or 40s, or does it reflect more uniform delays in fertility timing? Figures 2.4a and 2.4b compare the distributions of age at first birth for married, divorced, and never-married mothers at the beginning (1980–1984) and the end (2015–2018) of our time series. In both time frames, married and divorced women are quite similar in their distributions of birth timing; both differ substantially from never-married mothers. That said, over time all women are more likely to first become mothers at an older age.

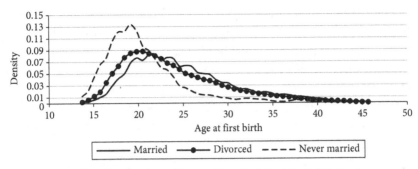

Figure 2.4a. The Distribution of Age at First Birth by Marital Status in 1980–1984.

Notes: N = 93,963 (married) 10,684 (divorced) 4,928 (never married). Results are weighted.
Source: CPS 1980–2018.

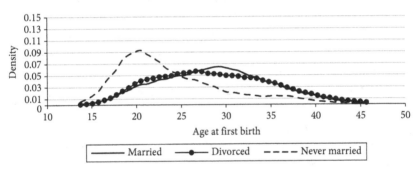

Figure 2.4b. The Distribution of Age at First Birth by Marital Status in 2015–2018.

Notes: N = 67,309 (married) 7,985 (divorced) 12,526 (never married). Results are weighted.
Source: CPS 1980–2018.

In the early 1980s, a substantial number of never-married mothers were teenagers. By 2015–2018, the proportion giving birth before 20 had decreased. Many married and divorced mothers also started having children early on in the 1980s, but back then there was a far greater range in age at first birth compared to never-married mothers. And while early birth was the norm for all mothers in the early 1980s, never-married mothers diverged from their ever-married counterparts in the 2015–2018 data. Married and divorced mothers by then had become most likely to first give birth in their late 20s—unsurprisingly, since by the 2010s most women were first marrying in their late 20s.[15]

24 THANKS FOR NOTHING

This demographic transformation has both positive and negative implications for family income. On the positive side, older unwed mothers have more education and more work experience than younger women who give birth out of wedlock. For instance, in 2018 12% of never-married mothers who first gave birth in their twenties had college degrees, compared to only 6% of those who had their first child as a teenager. This is a propitious consequence of the trend towards later fertility. On the other hand, later childbirth has repercussions for never-married mothers' marriage prospects. Past the median marriage age, now around 28 for women, marriage becomes increasingly unlikely.[16] Therefore, older women who give birth out of wedlock are probably less likely to wed—ever—than are their younger counterparts.

In both 1980 and 2018 married and divorced mothers had similar patterns of fertility. Teen birthrates for both groups were comparably low to begin with, so they didn't change much over the years of our study. On the other hand, far more women over 30 had given birth for the first time in 2018. In 1980, and to a lesser extent in 2018, divorced women were slightly more likely than married women to have been younger when first giving birth. Why is this the case? Given that youthful marriage is a powerful predictor of divorce, many of these women presumably wed early, soon after had children, and then dissolved their marriages.

Another dimension of fertility is family size. Each child a woman has incrementally decreases her wages, so we would expect women's improving financial prospects to coincide with smaller families.[17] Figure 2.5 plots the incidence of high fertility—three or more children—over time and by marital status. Over the past 40 years, married mothers have consistently had the highest levels of multiple fertility. At least 20% had three or more children, a figure that has remained essentially stable. Divorced and never-married mothers have smaller families, and the trend for both groups has been towards fewer children. Never-married mothers have experienced more variable fertility than have divorced mothers, with a period in the early 1990s where their incidence of multiple fertility hovered around 20%. Otherwise, rates have generally been just over 15%, while most years divorced mothers have been slightly under 15%.

These figures reflect complex trends for divorced and never-married mothers. Changing patterns of marriage or remarriage, and, in the case of divorced women, the timing of marital dissolution, could be responsible

WHO ARE THESE MOTHERS? 25

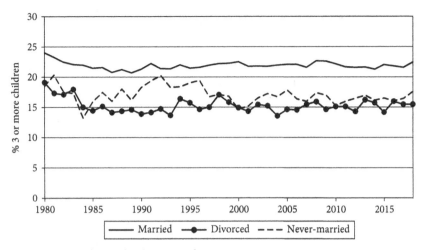

Figure 2.5. High Fertility by Marital Status.
Notes: N = 681,144 (married) 85,105 (divorced) 87,480 (never married). Results are weighted.
Source: CPS 1980–2018.

for the modest declines in the number of high-fertility households evident in Figure 2.5. For instance, women with multiple children are less likely to end their marriages in the first place, so they should be comparably underrepresented in our data.[18] More important, divorce rates declined over the years of our study.[19] This might have contributed to the declining number of divorced mothers with three or more children.

This cannot explain the decline in family size for never-married mothers. Multiple children make marriage less likely for women who give birth out of wedlock. (For divorcées, additional children do not seem to affect remarriage rates: the increased economic need for marriage may be offset by the decreased ability of women with many children to find candidates for remarriage.)[20] The lower marriage rate for never-married mothers with multiple children suggests that it's less likely that these women would eventually come to be measured as married in our sample. Indeed, this same pattern shows up in data that track never-married mothers from childbirth.[21] For this reason, we might expect women with large families to be overrepresented in the ranks of never-married mothers, but this has likely been offset by declining birthrates for all teens since 1991.[22] Collectively these strands of evidence help explain the trend towards smaller families for women who give birth out of wedlock.

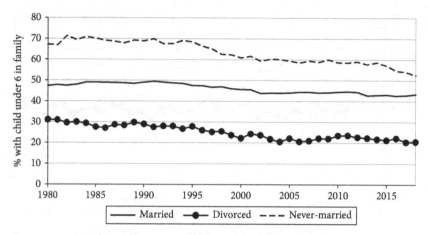

Figure 2.6. Families with Young Children by Marital Status.
Notes: N = 681,144 (married) 85,105 (divorced) 87,480 (never married). Results are weighted.
Source: CPS 1980–2018.

Finally, it's worth noting that multiple fertility for never-married mothers declined in the mid-1990s, when welfare reform was enacted, though the evidence cited in Chapter 1 suggests the impact of family policy is modest at best.

Another family characteristic that will impact a mother's ability to work is the presence of young children.[23] In particular younger children, those younger than six, mean women must choose between caring for them at home or finding and paying for childcare or preschool during working hours. Figure 2.6 shows that the proportion of families with children under six is much higher for never-married mothers, and lowest for divorced mothers. Again, the timing of childbirth and marriage formation or dissolution helps to explain these differences. The time it takes for married mothers to become divorced mothers means their children have aged. In contrast, never-married mothers who subsequently marry reduce the observed proportion of single mothers who have older children.

The overall decline in families with younger children is ultimately attributable to the trend of smaller families. Our data represent the tail end of a centuries-long decline in fertility, although the odds of three or more children haven't really changed since the start of the new millennium.[24] The economic consequences of declining fertility are obvious: smaller families and less time living with younger children should make it easier to provide a good living.

Age

A great deal of attention has been paid to another major trend in family demography: the retreat from marriage. Substantial increases in the median marriage age, combined with somewhat more modest declines in the overall marriage rate, means that younger Americans are much less like to be married than in the past.[25] And as we've seen, all mothers are now older when they first give birth. Consequently, all mothers in our study were on average older in 2018 than in 1980. This is shown in Figure 2.7.

In 1980, the mean age for both married and divorced mothers was about 35. In the early 1990s, this figure began creeping up, and by 2018 was around 40. There was a slight divergence over time, so that by the end of our time series married and divorced mothers had different mean ages, by about two years. We suspect this divergence is the product of changing patterns of post-marital union formation: divorced women are remarrying less and cohabiting more.[26]

Perhaps more unexpected is the clear upward trend for age of never-married mothers. For most of the 1980s, the mean age for women who gave birth out of wedlock (and hadn't subsequently married) hovered at or below 27. By 2018 it had steadily risen to just over 32. Mothers are increasingly older across all family structures.

The aging depicted in Figure 2.7 has both positive and negative implications for single mother's income: positive, in that older mothers have

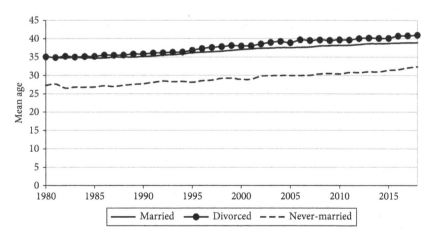

Figure 2.7. Age by Marital Status.
Notes: N = 681,144 (married) 85,105 (divorced) 87,480 (never married). Results are weighted.
Source: CPS 1980–2018.

stronger workforce qualifications; potentially negative, in that down the road marriage (or remarriage) is less likely.

Education, Work, and Income

Our findings on fertility have ambiguous implications for family income. Although many of the trends we have chronicled seem to favor the employment prospects of all mothers—married, divorced, and never-married alike—others likely reflect the retreat from marriage, which for most families means a drop in income due to fewer employed adults in the family. In contrast, the data on education and work broadly point toward economic progress for all mothers.

In recent years Americans in general have more schooling.[27] Married, divorced, and never-married mothers have all benefited from rising educational attainment. Figure 2.8 shows that in the early 1980s fewer than 60% of never-married mothers had even graduated from high school (or obtained equivalency certificates).[28] This consigned them to low-wage labor, given that even the majority of the worst paying jobs in twenty-first century America require a high school degree.[29] Over the last twenty years there has been steady progress in educational attainment for never-married mothers. By 2018, 88% of them had high school diplomas, on par with the population as a whole. This 30 percentage point gain is even more substantial after taking into account how marriage varies by education. Since educated women have higher marriage rates, out-of-wedlock mothers with more education are

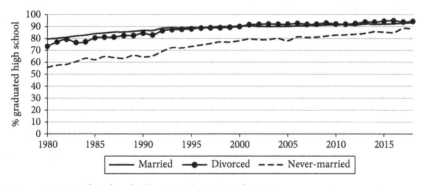

Figure 2.8. High School Education by Marital Status.
Notes: N = 681,144 (married) 85,105 (divorced) 87,480 (never married). Results are weighted.
Source: CPS 1980–2018.

WHO ARE THESE MOTHERS? 29

increasingly likely to have tied the knot and therefore selected themselves out of the data presented here.[30]

Married and divorced mothers are surprisingly similar in their high school graduation rates. From 1980 to 2018 the percentage of high school graduates in both groups rose from about just under 80% to almost 95% for both groups. Over the past 40 years, education has become a powerful predictor of marital stability, with educated Americans disproportionately likely to have stable marriages, so it's surprising that married and divorced mothers don't vary in their rates of high school completion.[31] Perhaps this can be explained by a change in the likelihood of remarriage for divorced mothers.

The bigger story concerning educational attainment has been the growing number of college graduates, increasingly the baseline requirement for prosperity in the United States.[32] Although all mothers are now more likely to be college graduates, a large divergence occurred over the years of our study. Figure 2.9 shows that in 1980 relatively few mothers of any kind obtained four-year college degrees. This included 14% of married mothers, 9% of divorced mothers, and under 4% of never-married mothers. By 2018, the comparable figures were 48%, 33%, and 14%. The gap between married and divorced mothers (48% vs. 33%) is almost as large as the gap between divorced and never-married mothers (33% vs. 14%). Married mothers are thus over three times more likely than never-married mothers to have college

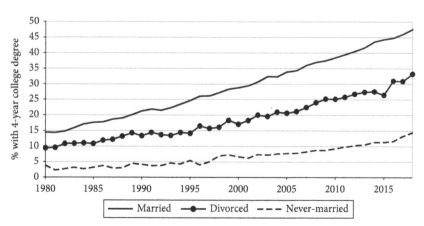

Figure 2.9. College Education by Marital Status.
Notes: N = 681,144 (married) 85,105 (divorced) 87,480 (never married). Results are weighted.
Source: CPS 1980–2018.

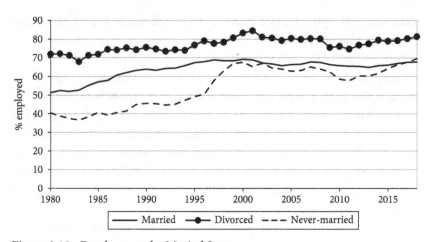

Figure 2.10. Employment by Marital Status.
Notes: N = 681,144 (married) 85,105 (divorced) 87,480 (never married). Results are weighted.
Source: CPS 1980–2018.

degrees (48% vs. 14%). By way of comparison, 35% of women in the population at large in 2018 are college graduates.[33]

There are two important points behind these trends. On the one hand, irrespective of marital status gains in education have been substantial. Millions of women now have better prospects for remunerative employment than they had in the past. Even never-married mothers, consistently last in education, have earned millions of college degrees over the past forty years. On the other hand, the growing disparity in college degrees represents dramatic differences in earning potential by marital status. Married mothers, who are in households with two adults with earning power, are presumably the least needy yet have improved their earning potential the most. Divorced and never-married mothers, traditionally among the poorest Americans and more likely to subsist on a single income, increasingly lag behind. These findings are strong evidence of the importance of marital status as a marker of prosperity in contemporary America.

Education can provide the skills and qualifications necessary to earn a good living, but it only matters if the degree holder is employed. Figure 2.10 shows how the percentage of mothers currently employed has changed over time, while Figure 2.11 shows trends in full-time employment. The two figures are similar, so we will focus on the overall employment numbers in Figure 2.10. Unlike with educational attainment, the trend has been convergence across marital status. In 1980, divorced women had the highest employment rate,

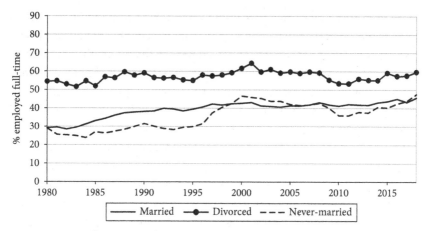

Figure 2.11. Full-time Employment by Marital Status.
Notes: N = 681,144 (married) 85,105 (divorced) 87,480 (never married). Results are weighted.
Source: CPS 1980–2018.

about 70%. In the same year, 40% of never-married mothers had jobs, and married mothers were at 51%. Over the next 20 years, rates rose for all three groups, becoming more similar in the process. Two years represent high-water marks in employment: 2001, with 84% of divorced mothers, 65% of never-married mothers, and 69% of married mothers working, and 2018 with 81%, 70%, and 68%, respectively. In between these years employment dipped modestly for all mothers. These declines were presumably a product of economic downturns. Since single as well as married women were affected, lower employment rates presumably cannot be explained by a voluntary trend towards "opting out" by married women (a narrative beloved by the media in recent years).[34]

The variation within single-mother households is considerable. Divorced and never-married mothers are both women raising children by themselves, but 30 percentage points separated their rates of employment in 1980. This disparity provides the most likely explanation for why never-married mothers have traditionally fared worse economically than their divorced counterparts, as well as raises important questions about their finances: With such low rates of employment, how are never-married mothers able to support themselves? We will return to this issue later in the book. In recent years, employment for never-married mothers increased twice as quickly as it did for other mothers, particularly in the 1990s, the decade of welfare reform and a major expansion of the Earned Income Tax Credit. Still, by 2018, it lagged more than 10% below the comparable figure for divorced mothers. This is some of the clearest evidence we've presented thus far that the two represent distinct populations of women. Divorced women likely already had some attachment to the labor force before their marriages ended, if not before they got married. Subsequent to divorce they became employed at even higher rates than married mothers in order to restore some of the income previously provided by their spouses. Never-married mothers, on the other hand, may not have relied on employment to make ends meet until fairly recently.

Of course, employment does not guarantee a good income. Traditionally many single mothers have been relegated to low-wage service sector jobs.[35] We explore whether mothers are getting better jobs by examining their Socio-Economic Index (SEI) scores.[36] SEI scores measure the prestige of an occupation on a scale from one to 100. These scores have proven to be remarkably stable over time.

Figure 2.12 plots median SEI scores since 1980 for employed mothers. As with educational attainment (Figures 2.8 and 2.9), the key distinction is between ever-married and never-married mothers. In general, the mean SEI score for the latter lags about six points below that of divorced mothers, and eight points below that of married mothers. And while all mothers' SEI scores have increased since 1980, the gains have not been equal: divorced and, especially, married mothers have pulled farther ahead of women who give birth out of wedlock. While never-married mothers have gone from an average score of 29 to 32 since 1990, married mothers have risen from 35 to 42, or more than twice as much. The larger SEI gains of married mothers make sense given their higher rates of college completion (Figure 2.9)—more education means better jobs. This trend also contributes to growing income inequality. Married mother families now benefit from multiple wage

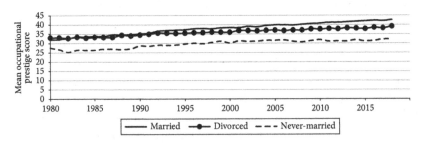

Figure 2.12. Occupational Prestige Scores by Marital Status.
Notes: N = 407,125 (married) 61,034 (divorced) 45,505 (never married). Results are weighted.
Source: CPS 1980–2018.

earners with better jobs. Single mothers are more likely to be reliant on their own wages, but have worse jobs. This includes divorced women, who over the years of our study were more likely to be working, but at worse jobs than married women. In general, the SEI data indicate a widening occupational divide among married and unmarried working women.

Changes in average SEI don't tell the whole story. More substantial has been the distributional shifts in SEI scores evident in density plots for 1980–1984 and 2015–2018 (Figures 2.13a and 2.13b). For both years, the starkest differences are between never-married mothers and their ever-married counterparts. Never-married mothers are overwhelmingly concentrated within a small range of low-SEI jobs. Their representation at the top of the career distribution is minimal. The density traces for married and divorced mothers are more alike, and both are flatter than for never-married

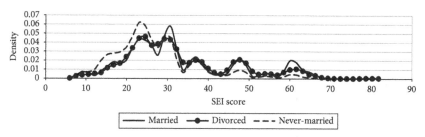

Figure 2.13a. The Distribution of Occupational Prestige Scores by Marital Status, 1980–1984.

Notes: N = 93,963 (married) 10,684 (divorced) 4,928 (never married). Results are weighted.
Source: CPS 1980–2018.

Figure 2.13b. The Distribution of Occupational Prestige Scores by Marital Status, 2015–2018.

Notes: N = 67,309 (married) 7,985 (divorced) 12,526 (never married). Results are weighted.
Source: CPS 1980–2018.

mothers: although most ever-married women fall into the left-hand side of the distribution, they occupy a wider range of SEI than do never-married mothers.

The distribution of all mothers in the early 1980s shows a clear pattern that places most of them in lower-status occupations. Although married women enjoyed slightly higher representation at the top of the distribution of occupations, few women held the best jobs. The story in 2015–2018 is more complex. Figure 2.13b shows that occupational inequality both increased and decreased. The overall distribution is flatter in 2018 than in 1980, indicating that women hold a broader variety of jobs. Fewer are concentrated in low-status employment. On the other hand, the contrast between never-married and ever-married mothers at the bottom of the distribution is much stronger in 2018 than in 1980. In other words, all women were more likely to hold low-status jobs in 1980, but by 2018 this niche is disproportionately occupied by never-married mothers. Finally, married women are now pulling ahead of their divorced counterparts with respect to their representation in high-SEI jobs. That is, while all mothers are getting better jobs than they used to, married mothers have achieved the most progress by increasingly obtaining the high-quality jobs that were disproportionately filled by men in years gone by.

Have better jobs translated into higher incomes? As shown in Figure 2.14, the answer is yes and no. Married mothers have seen substantial progress, their median incomes growing from $71,000 in 1980 to a high of $96,000 in 2018 (income is measured in 2018 dollars). Divorced mothers experienced the next fastest income growth over these years. Their median incomes rose from around $31,000 in 1980 to a high of $38,200 in 2003. This

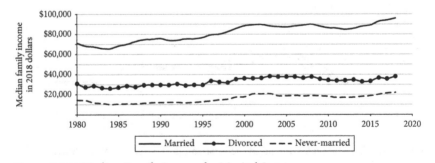

Figure 2.14. Median Family Income by Marital Status.
Notes: N = 681,144 (married) 85,105 (divorced) 87,480 (never married). Results are weighted.
Source: CPS 1980–2018.

figure dipped in the course of the Great Recession, but by 2018 had nearly recovered to 2003 levels. Never-married mothers have made the least progress. In 1980 their median income was just over $14,000. By 2018 they were at $22,000. This was just barely over the poverty line for a family of three—and well below it for four people.[37] Despite modest economic growth, many never-married mothers and their families continue to be desperately poor. Moreover, the income gap between married mothers and their unmarried counterparts has grown substantially over time. While divorced and never-married mothers remain about $16,000 apart in family income between 1980 and 2018, married mothers went from earning $40,000 and $57,000 more than their divorced and never-married counterparts, respectively, to $58,000 and $74,000 more by 2018.

Mounting income inequality by family structure is even more apparent at the margins of the income distribution. Figure 2.15 shows incomes by marital status for the lower quartile, that is, the bottom 25% of the income distribution. Two differences from the median income plot (Figure 2.14) are immediately apparent. First, both divorced and never-married mothers in the lower income quartile have seen almost no improvement over the last four decades. In 1980, the lower quartile income for never-married mothers was $8,600; by 2018, it was just under $9,000. The corresponding figures for divorced mothers are $17,300 and $18,000. Fluctuations across our 39 years of data are small for both groups: the standard deviation for divorced mothers is about $2,500. For never-married mothers, it's just over $1,000.

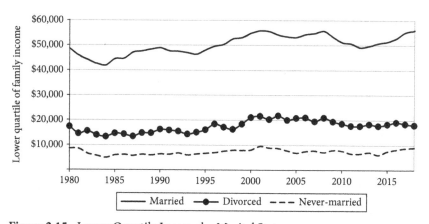

Figure 2.15. Lower Quartile Income by Marital Status.
Notes: N = 681,144 (married) 85,105 (divorced) 87,480 (never married). Results are weighted.
Source: CPS 1980–2018.

The income growth for single mothers in the lower income quartile is far lower than it is at any other part of the income distribution (i.e., the median and the upper quartile). Divorced and never-married mothers in the lower income quartile have been uniquely impervious to the social forces that have improved the lot of women in recent years. That rising tide that lifted so many boats over the past few decades? Thanks for nothing.

The second difference between the lower quartile and the median income plots concerns the difference between married and single mothers. Over all the years of our study, the gap between married and single mothers is proportionately larger at the bottom of the income distribution (Figure 2.15) than it is at either the median (Figure 2.14) or the upper quartile (Figure 2.16). Put another way, marriage is more important to a mother's economic prospects for the poor than for the middle or the wealthy. Furthermore, this marriage premium has grown over time. The median lower quartile married mothers gained about $8,000 in annual family income between 1980 and 2018, while divorced and never-married mothers essentially held steady.

Predictably, marriage also helps more for the upper income quartile—the most well-off 25% of the population—than it does for the median mother. Figure 2.16 shows how family incomes in the upper quartile changed between 1980 and 2018 for American mothers. Although married mothers made the most rapid progress, all mothers in this quartile have greatly improved their incomes since 1980.

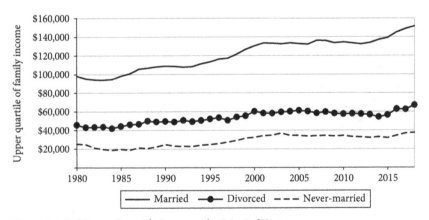

Figure 2.16. Upper Quartile Incomes by Marital Status.
Notes: N = 681,144 (married) 85,105 (divorced) 87,480 (never married). Results are weighted.
Source: CPS 1980–2018.

We will explore the reasons for these income trends in greater detail in subsequent chapters. For now, it is possible to draw inferences about *improvement* and *inequality*. With the exception of single mothers in the lower income quartile, all American mothers are faring better in recent years. However, this improvement must be qualified by an assessment of growing income inequality. It has already been well established that family structure is an important component of inequality in contemporary America. Our data show that the economic advantages of marriage have also grown. Yet the relationship between family structure and income is more complicated. On the whole, divorced women fare much better than do never-married mothers. They consistently have higher family incomes and, excepting the bottom quartile of the income distribution, have fared better since 1980. In addition, there is considerable inequality within specific family structures: across the board, the upper quartiles have seen greater improvement over time than at the median or at the lower quartiles.

Living Arrangements

A common trope of women who give birth out of wedlock is that they live in multigenerational (and often matriarchal) families: grandmothers, their adult daughters, and grandchildren all living together under one roof. Divorced women stereotypically move back in with their parents after their marriages end.[38] These perceptions raise questions about economic independence.[39] While such living arrangements are quite common in many countries around the world, our data suggest otherwise for the U.S.[40] Figure 2.17 shows that multigenerational living was never the norm, and has increasingly become less common over time. In the early 1980s, roughly 30% of never-married mothers were living with their parents or grandparents (or both). By 2018, this figure had declined to under 20%. Rates of parental co-residence for divorced mothers have held steady at between 6% and 9% for most years. There were predictable increases during tougher times, such as the recessions of the early 1980s and 2008, along with a noticeable decline between 1985 and 1995 that's consistent with our previous research.[41] Quite understandably, only about 1–2% of married respondents lived with their parents at any point during this period.[42] Note that these figures slightly underestimate true rates of parental co-residence, as they only capture living arrangements where the parent or grandparent is the householder; the CPS

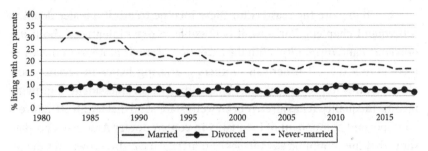

Figure 2.17. Co-residence with Parents by Marital Status.
Notes: N = 681,144 (married) 85,105 (divorced) 87,480 (never married). Results are weighted.
Source: CPS 1980–2018.

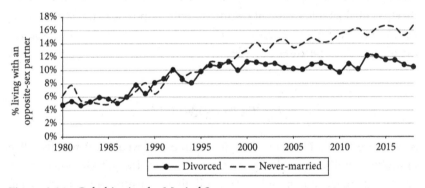

Figure 2.18. Cohabitation by Marital Status.
Notes: N = 85,105 (divorced) 87,480 (never married). Results are weighted.
Source: CPS 1980–2018.

does not allow for the detection of parents or other relatives living with an adult child householder or a more distant relative.[43]

Why are fewer single mothers moving back home? The obvious explanation is that more of these mothers are living on their own. However, the paltry income gains shown in Figure 2.14 cast doubt on this notion: many are probably not making enough money to support independent living. Another explanation is the growth in nonmarital cohabitation. Living with a partner out of wedlock has traditionally been common among previously married people, with several scholars attributing modest declines in the remarriage rate to the growth in cohabitation.[44] Figure 2.18 shows trends in nonmarital cohabitation computed using the adjusted Person of Opposite Sex Sharing Living Quarters (POSSLQ) measure.[45] Cohabitation rates rose

WHO ARE THESE MOTHERS? 39

dramatically for all Americans since 1980, but the growth for divorced and never-married mothers have been particularly noteworthy. In the early 1980s, about 5–6% of single mothers were living with partners out of wedlock. By 2018, this figure had risen to 10% for divorced mothers, and 17% for never-married mothers. Note that these increases approximately offset the declining number of never-married mothers living with their own parent or parents. The climbing cohabitation rate for divorced mothers, combined with relatively steady rates of intergenerational living, means that over time fewer divorced mothers are living with no one but their children.

Cohabiting relationships tend to be unstable.[46] This means that the estimates of cohabitation presented here are on the low side, since our numbers exclude the women who have just left, or are just about to enter, cohabiting unions. In addition, since an average of seven years has elapsed since the never-married mothers in our sample first gave birth out of wedlock, many who were probably cohabiting at birth were no longer doing so at the time they were interviewed for the CPS. At the end of the twentieth century about half of unmarried parents lived together at the time of childbirth.[47] A decade later this number was approaching 60%.[48]

Caveats aside, higher rates of nonmarital cohabitation have various implications for the well-being of divorced and never-married mothers, as well as their children. One obvious benefit is the financial contributions that cohabiting partners can provide. These cannot be properly measured with the CPS. Cohabiting partners share households with our respondents, but not families, so family income does not include these men's incomes.[49] Moreover, cohabiting households are less likely than married families to pool their income, or otherwise act as a cohesive economic unit.[50] Nevertheless, the presence of these partners often elevates the living standard of single mothers. The downside is the lack of stability of the additional income, given the high break-up rate of these relationships.

In other regards the implications of cohabitation are mixed. Ample research has shown that the presence of a cohabiting partner does not appear to benefit children; offspring in both cohabiting and single parent families fare worse on a variety of outcomes compared to children in two-parent biological families.[51] Apparently the greater incomes of cohabiting families do not offset their negative effects on offspring well-being. The other liability concerns economic dependence. Although a cohabiting partner may help support a single mother, he may also induce her to limit her labor force participation. Since cohabiting relationships are often short, a mother may

40 THANKS FOR NOTHING

be left in the financial lurch if she came to depend on an unmarried partner for her family's standard of living. What's more, it's harder to get child support from an unwed partner. We'll return to this topic in the next chapter.

Race and Ethnicity

Black Americans have had higher rates of mother-headed families since the nineteenth century, and the stereotype of single motherhood as an African American condition has long guided public opinion.[52] This stems in part from Daniel Patrick Moynihan's 1965 report, which indelibly linked single parenting, particularly out-of-wedlock childbirth, to African Americans in the minds of many people. We discuss the complex influence of the Moynihan Report in detail in Appendix B. Ronald Reagan's racially tinged attacks on welfare also shaped public opinion.[53]

Figure 2.19a, Figure 2.19b, and Figure 2.19c show the racial/ethnic breakdown of married, divorced, and never-married mothers since 1980. Married motherhood has become less common for all CPS mothers, with an especially steep decline for African Americans. For Whites and Latinas, the incidence of married motherhood declined about 10 percentage points since 1980 (Figure 2.19a). For Black mothers the decline is over 20 percentage points. However, we should note that the estimates for African American mothers for 1980 and 1981—showing higher rates of married motherhood and lower rates of never-married motherhood—are less reliable due to how the CPS measured race prior to 1982.[54]

Looking at divorced motherhood by race/ethnicity over time, as shown in Figure 2.19b, reveals trends that cannot be understood without reference to the concurrent trends in marriage and nonmarital motherhood. Divorced motherhood declined the most for African American women, in part because fewer of them were getting married. Otherwise, the trends in Figure 2.19b are largely unremarkable, although the rate of divorced motherhood did dip a bit for Latinas. For Whites, divorced motherhood held steady at about 10%. Readers should keep in mind that divorced motherhood tends to be a temporary status: many divorcées will remarry, while others will first empty the nest. This is why divorced mothers comprise a relatively small fraction of the total, even in the early 1980s, back when at least one in two marriages dissolved.[55]

Finally, never-married motherhood has increased for all women since 1980. As seen in Figure 2.19c, the growth is largest for African American

WHO ARE THESE MOTHERS? 41

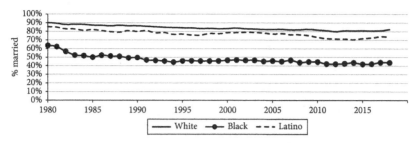

Figure 2.19a. Trends in Married Motherhood by Race/Ethnicity.
Notes: N = 681,144. Results are weighted.
Source: CPS 1980–2018.

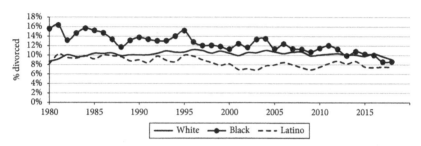

Figure 2.19b. Divorced Motherhood by Race/Ethnicity.
Notes: N = 85,105. Results are weighted.
Source: CPS 1980–2018.

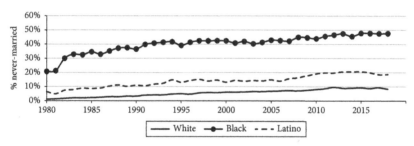

Figure 2.19c. Never-Married Motherhood by Race/Ethnicity.
Notes: N = 87,480. Results are weighted.
Source: CPS 1980–2018.

women, surging from 20% in the early 1980s to almost 50% by 2018. (As we noted previously, we suspect that the 1980 and 1981 estimates are artificially low due to data issues.) But never-married motherhood jumped more significantly for Latina and White mothers as a proportion of all families. In 1980, just 1% of White mothers headed families formed by premarital births.

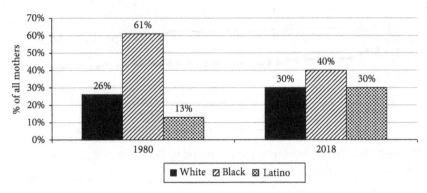

Figure 2.20. Trends in Never-Married Motherhood by Race/Ethnicity.
Notes: N = 681,144 (married) 85,105 (divorced) 87,480 (never married). Results are weighted.
Source: CPS 1980–2018.

By 2018, that figure had increased to almost 10%. For Latinas, the corresponding increase was from 6% to 19%.

Figure 2.19a, Figure 2.19b, and Figure 2.19c show racial/ethnic differences by family structure, but it's also instructive to look at it the other way around: How has the racial composition of never-married mothers changed over time? In 1980, closer to the publication date of the Moynihan Report than the present, African Americans composed over 60% of never-married mothers (Figure 2.20). By 2018, they reflected a plurality of 40%. Over the same years, the share of White never-married mothers grew, from 26% to 30%. The share of Latina never-married mothers increased even more, from 13% to 30%.

These numbers need to be viewed in the context of a diversifying United States.[56] In 1980, non-Hispanic Whites comprised 80% of Americans. By 2018, this number had declined to 60%. Over the same years, the African American share of the population more or less held steady, while the Latino proportion tripled, from 6% to 18%. Never-married motherhood increased across the board, and America's changing racial-ethnic composition means that nonmarital fertility is no longer concentrated in the African American community.

Conclusion

There are two main takeaways from the data presented here on the changing attributes of American mothers. First, there are clear differences between divorced and never-married mothers. Divorced mothers are generally more likely to resemble married mothers in many of the ways likely to benefit income. In contrast, never-married mothers have less education, lower-status jobs, and are more likely to have become mothers at a young age. The one area where single-mothers are more similar to each other than to married mothers is income itself. Nevertheless, never-married mothers remain much more likely to be deeply impoverished than divorced mothers.

The second takeaway is that the attributes of all mothers, married and single alike, have changed considerably over the past 40 years. All of these changes are in the general direction of greater earning power. Indeed, single mothers have realized some gains in median income (but not so much in the lower income quartile).

The descriptive statistics presented do not tell us the extent to which changes in the characteristics of mothers explain trends in income. To what extent has growing levels of human capital contributed to higher incomes? Do single mothers receive the same returns to their human capital that married mothers receive? The next chapter will address these questions.

3

Counting Change

The previous chapter showed that social, economic, and demographic attributes of married, divorced, and never-married mothers changed greatly over the past 40 years. Yet the economic returns to these changing attributes have been uneven. In this chapter, we consider the import of these trends for married, divorced, and never-married mothers. What do gains in labor market attachment and human capital mean for incomes since 1980?

The story we'll tell is that prosperity is about more than just a mother's measured attributes. Instead, we will explore two dynamics that condition the relationship between individual characteristics and income. First, the economic returns to individual attributes have, almost without exception, changed in the years since 1980. A college education pays more today than it did in 1980, whereas a high school degree pays less. Second, the economic returns to mothers' attributes vary by family structure in almost all cases. Coupled with the changing levels of individual attributes—mostly in the positive direction, as described in Chapter 2—these intersecting dynamics have had considerable implications for income.

The analysis in this chapter is primarily based on a series of median regression models of family income using the Current Population Survey (CPS) data.[1] Median regression is appropriate for dependent variables like income that are highly skewed. It also has the benefit of more easily interpreted results compared to a least squares analysis of logged income, a conventional approach to studying income. The results we present are based on separate models for married, divorced, and never-married mothers that include all the independent variables under consideration in this chapter. For example, we describe the impact of education on income that is net of family size, race, age, and other consequential differences between families. Finally, all results presented reflect statistically significant differences. Statistical inference is generally not a consideration given the large sample size of our multiyear sample of CPS data.

Thanks for Nothing. Nicholas H. Wolfinger and Matthew McKeever, Oxford University Press.
© Oxford University Press 2024. DOI: 10.1093/oso/9780199324323.003.0003

Education

The relationship between education and income is the foundation of modern stratification research, with education being the primary labor market qualification that allows people to get well-paying jobs.[2] In the United States today, the basic entry requirement for stable employment is a high school diploma or GED. Even most low-level service sector jobs now require a high school education.[3] Furthermore, completing high school is a prerequisite for pursuing higher education, which is increasingly necessary for even many mid-salary jobs. Recall from Chapter 2 that there has been substantial variation by family type in educational attainment over time. The gap in high school completion by marital status has collapsed, while the disparities in college completion have increased. In 1980, never-married mothers were around 20 percentage points less likely to be high school graduates than women who've ever been married. By 2018, the gap was just a few percent points. Over the same years, rates of college completion exploded for married mothers and, to a lesser extent, divorced mothers, but rose much more slowly for their never-married counterparts.

It is not surprising that high school and college completion rates have increased so much, nor that they would vary by marital status. More surprising is that economic returns to education also vary significantly by marital status, and have changed substantially over time. Figures 3.1a, 3.1b, and 3.1c show how income has changed since 1980 for mothers according to education and marital status. Two things are apparent. First, irrespective of family structure, incomes have only risen for mothers who possess four-year college degrees. Median incomes for all mothers with less education have remained essentially stable over time. Non-college-educated divorced mothers have incomes around $30,000 in 1980, 2018, and all the years in between. For never-married mothers without four-year degrees, median incomes have hovered between $15,000 and $20,000 throughout the nearly 40 years of our study. There is more variation for married mothers without college degrees. Some of this variation can be attributed to a second wage earner, and therefore more potential for a high income. More likely than not, spouses will have similar levels of education given that assortative mating based on education has only grown stronger over the years of our study.[4] Nevertheless, it's entirely likely that married mothers themselves receive greater financial returns to a junior college diploma than do single mothers. One possible explanation is the benefits of a spouse for sharing parenting duties, allowing both to increase their earnings.

46 THANKS FOR NOTHING

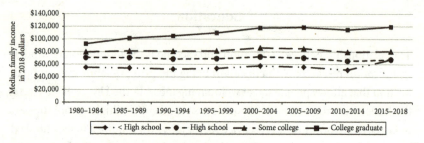

Figure 3.1a. Income by Education for Married Mothers.
Notes: N = 681,144. Results are weighted.
Source: CPS 1980–2018.

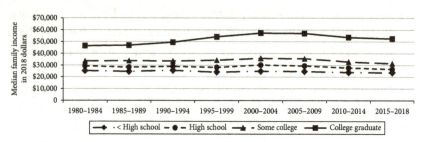

Figure 3.1b. Income by Education for Divorced Mothers.
Notes: N = 85,105. Results are weighted.
Source: CPS 1980–2018.

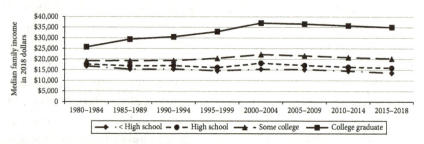

Figure 3.1c. Income by Education for Never-Married Mothers.
Notes: N = 87,480. Results are weighted.
Source: CPS 1980–2018.

Rising income for mothers with a college degree is a finding that shouldn't surprise anyone who has studied inequality in the past half-century. It's also not a huge surprise that the returns to a four-year college degree have increased the most for married women, changing from $93,000 to $118,000. College-educated wives usually have college-educated spouses, both of whom are reaping greater returns to their human capital in recent years.

COUNTING CHANGE 47

Indeed, the returns to higher education have grown larger for all Americans over time up to the Great Recession.[5] Incomes for college-educated single mothers have declined a bit since 2008, whereas incomes for college-educated married mothers have merely leveled off.

The second finding in Figures 3.1a, b, and c is that, irrespective of education, married mothers have higher incomes than do divorced mothers, who in turn have higher incomes than do women who give birth out of wedlock. Indeed, the differences across family structures are generally larger than the differences within family structures. Obviously some of the difference between married and unmarried families is due to the likelihood of two earners, but this isn't enough to account for the differences by family structure for college-educated mothers. Here's a thought experiment: cut income for college-educated married mothers in half—in other words, assume away half of their family income as their spouse's earnings—to make them more directly comparable to single mothers. This would give married mothers incomes of $46,500 between 1980 and 1984, and $59,000 by 2015 to 2018. This income gain of about $12,500 would reflect a larger growth in return to a college degree than single mothers received, and would produce a much larger family income as well.

Between 1980 and 1984, the median divorced mother with a college degree earned about $46,000 in 2018 dollars. Twenty years later, this figure hit a high-water mark of $57,000 before declining after the 2008 recession. Between 1980 and 1984 the median college-educated never-married mother earned about $26,000 in 2018 dollars. Twenty years later this figure had risen to $37,000, before declining to just over $35,000. Divorced and never-married mothers with four-year college degrees thus experienced similar income growth. However, college-educated never-married mothers earn about $20,000 less a year than do their divorced contemporaries despite having similar educational credentials. As we wrote a decade ago, never-married mothers have been singularly unable to convert their human capital into higher wages.[6]

Our results accord with the broader literature on income inequality and the changing American labor market. In the past there were many more high paying jobs that required only a high school diploma.[7] As a result of weakening labor unions, automation, monopoly growth, and, to a lesser extent off-shoring, real wages flatlined for everyone except the college-educated since the early 1970s.[8] College-educated workers saw notable income gains between 1980 and 2000, but stagnation since the start of the new millennium.[9] Our data show that the stagnation has been far more consequential for single mothers.

48   THANKS FOR NOTHING

Figures 3.1a, b, and c also depict a finding that is a mystery at the heart of this book: Why do never-married mothers get smaller returns to education than do their divorced contemporaries? After all, both are single mothers, and both are employed at similar rates since the start of the new millennium. This conundrum will be explored at length in Chapters 5 and 6. For now, we point out that the returns differential cannot be explained by fundamental social and demographic differences between respondents. Remember that the results presented in this chapter, based on multivariate analysis, control for differences in age, race, number of children, onset of fertility, and living arrangements. Other factors, not measurable with the CPS appear to be responsible for the higher economic returns received by divorced mothers.[10]

Employment

For most families the primary source of income is employment. Having job skills and experience is not remunerative unless it's converted into income in the labor force. Figures 3.2a, 3.2b, and 3.2c show how employment has generated income over the past 40 years for married, divorced, and never-married mothers. Employment is divided into part-time (1 to 34 hours a week) and full-time (35 or more hours weekly) categories.

These charts show that work pays: all mothers are much better off if engaged in full-time work. Married mothers benefit the least, which is presumably due to the chances that their spouses are their families' primary or exclusive earners.[11] Conversely, married mothers are less affected by their own unemployment. There was a slight dip in income for all married mothers since the Great Recession started in 2008, but only those who weren't working failed to see some recovery in the final years covered by our data. Married mothers may exit the labor force or shift to part-time employment when their spouse has a well-paying job, but this was less of an option during the recession.

Single mothers obviously don't have the luxury of counting on a spouse's earnings.[12] Figures 3.2b and 3.2c show that not working full-time has large impacts on their family income. Additionally, between 1980 and 2005 there was little difference between working part-time and not at all, especially for never-married mothers. More substantial differences emerged after 2005, and grew during the years of the Great Recession.

COUNTING CHANGE 49

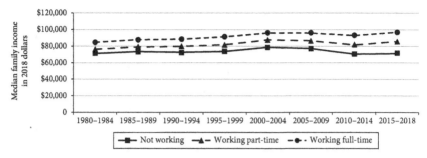

Figure 3.2a. Income by Employment for Married Mothers.
Notes: N = 681,144. Results are weighted.
Source: CPS 1980–2018.

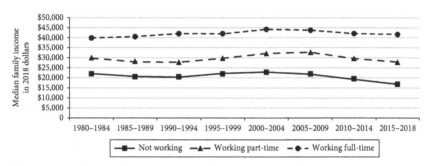

Figure 3.2b. Income by Employment for Divorced Mothers.
Notes: N = 85,105. Results are weighted.
Source: CPS 1980–2018.

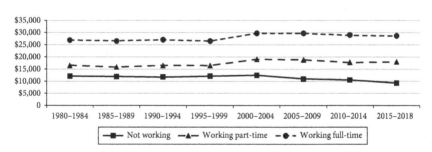

Figure 3.2c. Income by Employment for Never-Married Mothers.
Notes: N = 87,480. Results are weighted.
Source: CPS 1980–2018.

50 THANKS FOR NOTHING

The data also show large income differences between divorced and never-married mothers. Divorced mothers out of the labor force reported incomes of about $22,000 from 1980 to about 2005; the corresponding figure for never-married mothers is $12,000. Part of the difference between these figures—but nowhere close to all of it—can be explained by the higher rate at which divorced women receive income transfers from the fathers of their children (see Figure 3.20). The economic returns of non-work over this 25-year period also doesn't appear to be related to income transfers from the government, as the biggest declines in welfare receipt occurred after welfare reform in 1996. We return to the contributions of income transfers from the government and non-resident fathers later in this chapter.

After 2005, the costs of unemployment steadily grew for single mothers. Unemployed divorced mothers were bigger losers than unemployed never-married mothers. Some of this is due to the fact that never-married mothers had less to lose: they started at a much lower baseline, and have broadly weaker attachments to the labor force than do divorced mothers. But the main takeaway is clear: having a job has become more important for single mothers in recent years.

The data shed light on why the benefits of work vary by family structure, but don't provide much insight on why the income of non-working mothers stayed stable between 1980 and 2005, then declined after that. One possible explanation is that women in precarious employment over time can show up in the data as unemployed. Respondents are queried about whether they were employed in the past week, whereas income is reported as the previous year's income. Perhaps many women counted as out of the labor force have worked for pay in the year prior to the time of the survey, but their employment is sporadic. One example is seasonal labor that generates income but not stable employment. Another example is women working informally, or in the gig economy. Both offer the flexible scheduling single mothers usually need.[13] If this is happening for many of the women in our sample, then we'd expect sporadic employment to be reflected in these low incomes for nominally unemployed women.

Cohabitation

Two types of living arrangements, co-residence with parents and nonmarital cohabitation with an opposite-sex partner, have the potential to dramatically affect single mothers' incomes net of other demographic differences between respondents.[14] In both cases, having additional adults in a household who are invested in the family can result in additional income, through anything from childcare help to emotional support in navigating the labor market.[15] Chapter 2 described different trends in living arrangements for divorced and never-married mothers. More single mothers, especially never-married mothers, are living out of wedlock with male partners in recent years, while fewer live with their own parents—a drop that was especially marked for never-married mothers.

In theory, nonmarital cohabitation can either increase family income due to increased support for work, or reduce family income if single mothers have partners who can provide for them. Indeed, Figure 3.3 shows different impacts of cohabitation for divorce and never-married mothers. Across all years of our study, divorced women living with partners out of wedlock report lower incomes than do their contemporaries who live alone. The cost of cohabitation—in other words, the lower income associated with co-residence with a romantic partner—is not only substantial, but has risen over time. In the 1980s, cohabiting divorced women report family incomes between $5,000 and $6,000 lower than do divorced women who aren't living with their partners. By the first decade of the twenty-first century, the difference rose to over $10,000. These are meaningful shortfalls given that divorced mothers only report median incomes of between $25,000 and $40,000 since 1980. About three quarters of cohabiting divorcées work, so perhaps live-in partners merely allow women to work fewer hours, or opt for jobs that pay

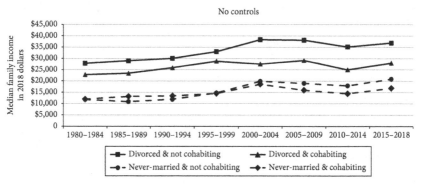

Figure 3.3. Income by Cohabitation and Marital Status.

Notes: N = 76,937 (divorced not cohabiting) 8,168 (divorced cohabiting) 75,546 (never married not cohabiting) 11,934 (never married cohabiting). Results are weighted.
Source: CPS 1980–2018.

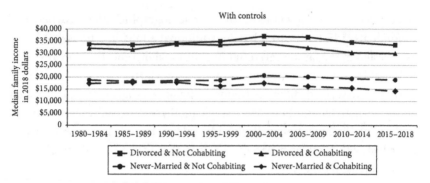

Figure 3.4. Income and Cohabitation and Marital Status.
Notes: N = 76,937 (divorced not cohabiting) 8,168 (divorced cohabiting) 75,546 (never married not cohabiting) 11,934 (never married cohabiting). Results are weighted.
Source: CPS 1980–2018.

less but are otherwise more desirable. In contrast, never-married mothers' incomes aren't much affected by cohabitation. Small differences emerged in the last 20 years, but these are much smaller than the disparities produced by cohabitation for divorced women.

The growing income gap between cohabiting single mothers and single mothers without live-in partners likely reflects the changing nature of cohabitation, and the kinds of people most likely to cohabit. Indeed, controlling for our suite of measured differences between respondents—age, race, education, employment status, and differences in family composition—explains much of the gap in income between cohabiting and non-cohabiting divorced mothers (Figure 3.4). Measured differences between respondents don't have the same effect on never-married mothers, a finding consistent with one of the primary arguments of this book: the low earnings of women who give birth out of wedlock cannot be explained by fundamental sociodemographic differences between women.

Previous research on cohabitation can help explain some of what is driving these findings. Sociologists Pamela Smock and Christine Schwartz found that the relationship between cohabitation and education has grown stronger since 1980: increasingly cohabiters are people with less education.[16] The CPS data reveal a more nuanced picture, as shown in Figure 3.5. For divorcées, the gap in four-year college degree attainment has indeed grown larger between cohabiting and non-cohabiting mothers over the past 40 years, mirroring the finding from Smock and Schwartz. Never-married mothers, in contrast, who have consistently lower rates of college graduation, have no difference in college education rates between those who cohabit and

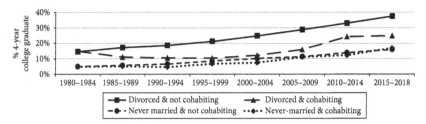

Figure 3.5. Four-year College Graduation Rates by Marital Structure and Living Arrangement.

Notes: N = 76,937 (divorced not cohabiting) 8,168 (divorced cohabiting) 75,546 (never married not cohabiting) 11,934 (never married cohabiting). Results are weighted.
Source: CPS 1980–2018.

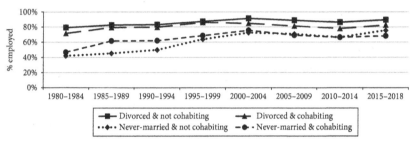

Figure 3.6. Employment Rates by Marital Structure and Living Arrangement.

Notes: N = 76,937 (divorced not cohabiting) 8,168 (divorced cohabiting) 75,546 (never married not cohabiting) 11,934 (never married cohabiting). Results are weighted.
Source: CPS 1980–2018.

those who do not. In 1980, 4% of all never-married mothers, cohabitating or not, had a college degree at the time they participated in the CPS. This figure rose to about 15% in 2018.

Other predictors of income and earning potential are largely unrelated to cohabitation, and this is true for divorced mothers as well as never-married mothers. Figure 3.6 shows employment rates for single mothers broken down by cohabitation status. Although cohabiting single mothers are a few percentage points less likely to work than are their peers who don't live with romantic partners, the difference hasn't been substantial since the mid-1990s. For divorced mothers, the employment gap between cohabiting and non-cohabiting women has increased modestly over the past 20 years. For never-married mothers, the gap was larger in the years prior to welfare reform in 1996. Between 1985 and 1990, women who give birth out of wedlock had employment rates that were almost 50% higher

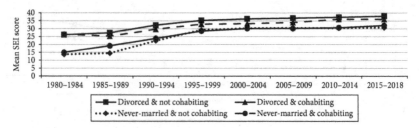

Figure 3.7. Occupational Status by Marital Structure and Living Arrangement.
Notes: N = 76,937 (divorced not cohabiting) 8,168 (divorced cohabiting) 75,546 (never married not cohabiting) 11,934 (never married cohabiting). Results are weighted.
Source: CPS 1980–2018.

if they weren't living with a romantic partner. Since then, there has been virtually no relationship between cohabitation and employment for never-married mothers.

An additional difference in earning ability between cohabiting and non-cohabiting mothers to consider: occupational prestige. While employment rates don't differ that much between cohabiting and non-cohabiting mothers, cohabitation might affect the types of jobs these women are able to get. A partner at home able to help out with childcare might make the difference between career employment and working in the gig economy. And as we saw in Chapter 2, never-married mothers have worse jobs than do divorced mothers. But this isn't affected by cohabitation, as Figure 3.7 makes clear. Divorced women who live with their partners have slightly worse jobs than do their peers who live alone, but the differences are small and except for one five-year stretch in the 1980s, cohabiting and non-cohabiting never-married mothers hold almost identical sorts of jobs. Clearly cohabitation is not associated with better or worse opportunities for good jobs.

In addition to gaps in education and work status, there are substantial demographic differences between cohabiters and non-cohabiters that might explain the income gap. For example, cohabiting divorcées are on average three years younger than those who are not living with romantic partners. By 2015, the age gap between cohabiting and non-cohabiting mothers had grown to four years. Other things being equal, older mothers have more job experience and therefore greater earning potential. As shown in Figure 3.8, this difference in particular explains a large portion of the income gap between divorced mothers with and without cohabiting partners. Indeed, this one difference between divorced women who live

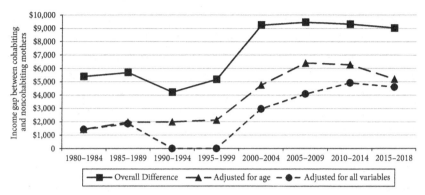

Figure 3.8. The Cost of Cohabitation for Divorced Women.
Notes: N = 85,105. Results are weighted.
Source: CPS 1980–2018.

with a partner and those who don't shrinks the economic cost of cohabitation almost by half.

The bottom line in Figure 3.8 accounts for not just age but also education and other demographic attributes. Age differences are an important part of the story, but the cost of cohabitation is even smaller for divorced mothers once we control for all differences between respondents. In other words: younger divorced women who have less education are especially likely to cohabit, and these are women who fare less well in the labor force. Cohabitation in and of itself has only minor economic implications for mothers, albeit implications that grew during the Great Recession. The same is true for never-married mothers, whose median incomes are the same whether or not key social and demographic attributes are held constant (as shown in Figures 3.3 and 3.4).

On the surface, these results don't appear to make much sense. The most obvious way an adult can subsist without an income is to depend on someone else's income, but that really doesn't seem to be the case with single mothers and cohabitation. Why? To be sure, there's less income sharing in cohabiting relationships than in marriage.[17] But the more important answer is the unstable nature of cohabiting relationships. Most are short-lived, culminating in either marriage or dissolution. Ten years down the road, only 6% of couples are still living together out of wedlock.[18] Most end much more quickly. The reality of cohabitation is probably even more fuzzy. In some cases, it's difficult to tell who's cohabiting and who isn't.[19] In the words of psychologist Scott Stanley, couples often "slide" into cohabitation rather than

56 THANKS FOR NOTHING

making a deliberate decision to live together.[20] One partner stays over a lot, so the would-be cohabiters reason that they might as well save money on rent while living together. Other couples in this situation may continue to maintain separate dwellings, and not get counted as cohabiting in surveys. Either way, it's not always an arrangement that leads a mother to count on her partner for the money to make ends meet. She may reduce her work hours, but will keep her job and her own source of income.

Of course, one reason some mothers move in with their partners is because they don't have enough money to live on their own. In these cases, neither partner is liable to be particularly well off, given the increasing trend towards assortative mating on education. According to a Pew Research study from 10 years ago, among adults without college degrees, the median household income of cohabiters ($46,540) is only slightly higher than that of comparable adults living alone ($45,033). College-educated adults fare much better, but they're less likely to be cohabiting in the first place.[21]

For all of these reasons, the relationship between cohabitation and income is fairly weak for single mothers, especially women who give birth out of wedlock. Even when cohabitation has more of an impact on income it's unlikely to make an enduring contribution. This is ultimately why we don't treat cohabitation as a full-fledged alternative to marriage in exploring the economics of single motherhood.

Living with Parents

Many people, single mothers included, move back in with their own parents. People often return home for financial reasons; in turn, living at home may lead to less incentive to earn a good wage. For others, increased family support might allow for more time to pursue job opportunities. We examine this issue by contrasting the overall difference in income between mothers who live with their parents and those who don't. Predictably, living with parents is associated with lower incomes across the board. This is shown in Figure 3.9.

This cost of living with one's own parents—the gap in income between mothers who live with their parents and those who don't—has steadily grown over the past 40 years, topping out at $40,000 by 2010 for married mothers. The cost is much lower for divorced mothers, although it's grown modestly over time. Over the 39 years of our data, the cost of living with parents has increased from about $9,000 to $14,000 for divorcées. For never-married

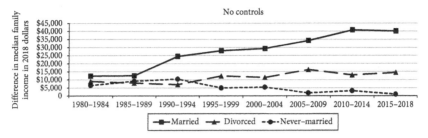

Figure 3.9. The Cost of Living with Parents, by Marital Status.
Notes: N = 681,144 (married) 85,105 (divorced) 87,480 (never married). Results are weighted.
Source: CPS 1980–2018.

mothers, the cost of parental co-residence has declined, falling from a height of $10,000 between 1990 and 1994 down to under $1,000 by 2018.

As we showed in Figure 2.16, the rate of parental co-residence for married mothers has remained stable and low over the past 40 years. What's changed over these years is selection into marriage: the average married mother (and her spouse) looks much different on paper today than she did in 1980. Back then, the correlation between marriage and economic factors was weak. Today, married mothers are disproportionately an educated and remuneratively employed segment of the population. Married mothers nowadays are also more likely to be the offspring of intact families; 40 years ago the correlation between family structure of origin and entry into marriage was weaker.[22] Finally, we'll take it as an article of faith that married parents are especially unenthusiastic about moving back into their own parent's home. Most will do so only when they lose their jobs and there are no other options.[23] All of this suggests that married parents only boomerang following a precipitous drop in income, and that the requisite drop should have become larger in recent years as marriages increasingly became related to prosperity.

This speculation is borne out by multivariate analysis. Figure 3.10a shows how parental co-residence is related to median family income after accounting for social and demographic differences between survey participants. Figure 3.9 showed a large and growing income disparity based on parental co-residence that topped out at $40,000 for married mothers. After adjusting for difference between respondents, the income gap between co-resident and non-co-resident married mothers is stable over time, and peaks at about $20,000. This difference confirms the conventional wisdom that married parents who are better prepared to make a good living tend to avoid returning to the nest.

58 THANKS FOR NOTHING

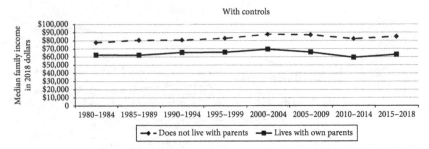

Figure 3.10a. Income by Co-residence with Parents, Married Mothers.
Notes: N = 681,144. Results are weighted.
Source: CPS 1980–2018.

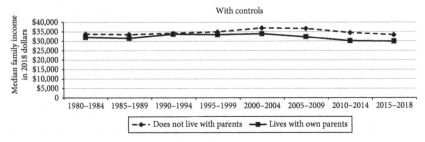

Figure 3.10b. Income by Co-residence with Parents, Divorced Mothers.
Notes: N = 85,105. Results are weighted.
Source: CPS 1980–2018.

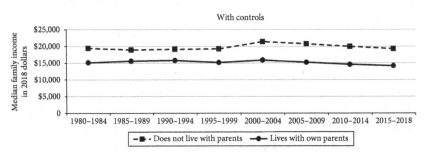

Figure 3.10c. Income by Co-Residence with Parents, Never-Married Mothers.
Notes: N = 87,480. Results are weighted.
Source: CPS 1980–2018.

This logic holds even more for divorced mothers: controlling for measurable differences between CPS participants effectively eliminates the income gap between mothers who live alone and mothers who live with their own parents. As shown in Figure 3.10b, at its largest the gap is several thousand dollars. In some years it declines to several hundred. As Chapter 2 shows, a fair number of divorcées do move back in with parents, and obviously they face greater financial pressure to do so than do most married mothers. However, measured attributes between respondents—education, age, and so on—figure more prominently here for divorced mothers than for their married contemporaries.

Figure 3.10c depicts the relationship between parental co-residence and income for never-married mothers. On the surface, it looks more similar to the corresponding figure for married women (Figure 3.10a) than the figure for divorced mothers (Figure 3.10b), albeit with smaller absolute values. After controlling for various differences between survey respondents, never-married mothers who live with their parents report incomes about $5,000 less a year than do those living on their own. However, since the mid-1990s the adjusted income gap shown in Figure 3.10c is larger than the zero-order difference shown in Figure 3.9. This stands in contrast to the corresponding results for married and divorced mothers, for whom the controls for age, education, employment, and other factors substantially attenuated the relationship between parental co-residence and income.

Viewed on its own, it's difficult to know what to make of this contrast: our control variables attenuate the relationship between income and parental co-residence for married and divorced mothers, but exacerbate it for never-married mothers. Like other young adults, divorced and married mothers without jobs (or without well-paying jobs, or spouses with jobs) sometimes move back in with their own parents. The decision to boomerang remains inversely related to economic prospects. Never-married mothers are an exception. This is more evidence for this book's thesis: divorced mothers and women who give birth out of the wedlock have very different demographic profiles, different relationships to the labor market, and, it seems, different relationships between their extended family arrangements and income. It's no coincidence that never-married mothers continue to be over twice as likely as divorced mothers to live with their own parents. Indeed, some of them have probably never have lived on their own.

This distinctive relationship between labor market participation, family life, and income for women who give birth out of wedlock has far-ranging consequences in many areas of life. Moving in with one's parents makes people depressed.[24] It reduces the incentive for labor market participation. Children who live with both a single mother and a grandparent fare even worse than do kids living with just a single parent, although this is presumably a consequence of selection bias: only the single mothers least prepared to care for their kids probably move back home.[25] On the other hand, a spell at home sometimes

60 THANKS FOR NOTHING

gives single parents a needed break. It may allow single mothers to spend more time with their children, or perhaps allow them to go back to school.

Teenage Mothers

In Chapter 2, we noted the consensus finding that teenage childbirth is strongly correlated with poverty. By 2018, teenage childbirth was less common and almost entirely relegated to never-married mothers. While less than half of teenage births occurred to never-married women in 1980, by the start of the new millennium this had risen to 80%.[26] By 2018, this figure was over 90%.[27] Is the poverty traditionally associated with a teenaged childbirth now just a product of family structure?[28] The reality is more complex.

Having a child as a teenager is clearly correlated with much lower incomes for married mothers. By 2015–2018, one-time teenage mothers who were married at the time the CPS data were collected had family incomes almost $50,000 a year lower than mothers who first had children after they were teenagers (see Figure 3.11a). This income penalty has grown considerably over time: back in the early 1980s, teen childbirth reflected a much smaller income gap of about $20,000. What changed was the kind of people who have children when they're teenagers. Forty years ago nearly twice as many married mothers had children as teenagers (see Figure 2.1). It had not been unusual to get married out of high school and start building a family. As teenage childbearing became less common, the kinds of people who became teen moms changed: as a population, teenaged mothers, even those who were married, increasingly reflected an economically marginalized group. This is why the median income of married women who first became mothers as teenagers flatlined at about $50,000 for four decades, even as the incomes of married women who became mothers later in their lives increased almost 50%, from about $71,000 in 1980–1984 to just under $100,000 by 2015.

This finding suggests that social and demographic differences between CPS participants have the potential to explain the substantial income gap between married women who first give birth as teenagers and those who have children later. This is fully borne out by our data analysis. After adjusting for differences in age, education, employment, and family size, the income gap between one-time teen mothers and older mothers is under $200 (result not shown). This comparison within the population of married mothers shows that there is nothing inherent to teenage motherhood

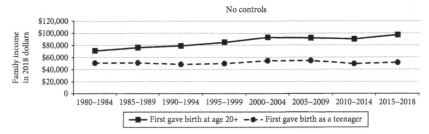

Figure 3.11a. Birth Age and Income for Married Mothers.
Notes: N = 612,143 (not teenage birth) 69,001 (teenage birth). Results are weighted.
Source: CPS 1980–2018.

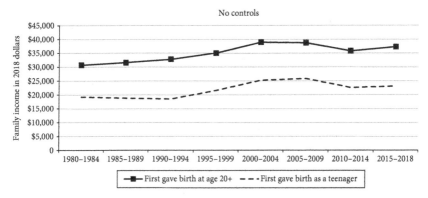

Figure 3.11b. Birth Age and Income for Divorced Mothers.
Notes: N = 73,607 (not teenage birth) 11,498 (teenage birth). Results are weighted.
Source: CPS 1980–2018.

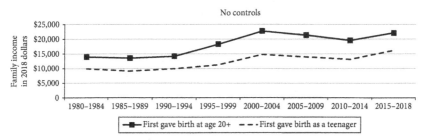

Figure 3.11c. Birth Age and Income for Never-Married Mothers.
Notes: N = 57,796 (not teenage birth) 29,684 (teenage birth). Results are weighted.
Source: CPS 1980–2018.

that reduces incomes. The story is similar for divorced and never-married mothers. For both groups, there are notable zero-order income gaps between teen mothers and older mothers (Figures 3.11b and 3.11c). In both cases, the disparities shrink to almost nothing after controlling for social and economic differences between mothers (result not shown). This finding is consistent with research by economist V. Joseph Hotz and his colleagues, who used causal models to examine the effects of a teenage birth on income.[29]

That having children while still a teenager doesn't in and of itself reduce incomes for women should not be a huge surprise. Although it's common fodder for policy debates, it's not like there are pay scales for jobs that explicitly penalize people based on when they become parents. Instead, teen mothers have various attributes that correlate with lower earnings. Our CPS data do not exhaust the full list of these attributes, but two examples will suffice to make the point about the differences between women who have their first children as teenagers, and those who wait. Figure 3.12 shows the lower rate of four-year college degrees for mothers who first gave birth as teenagers, while Figure 3.13 shows the gap in Socio-Economic Index (SEI) scores for

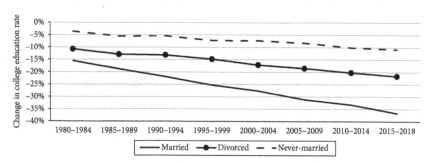

Figure 3.12. The College Completion Penalty for Having a Teenaged Birth.
Notes: N = 612,143 (married) 73,607 (divorced) 57,796 (never married). Results are weighted.
Source: CPS 1980–2018.

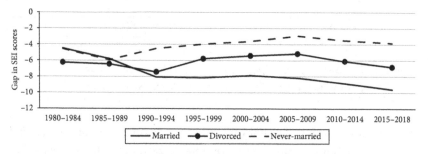

Figure 3.13. The SEI Penalty for Having a Teenaged Birth.
Notes: N = 612,143 (married) 73,607 (divorced) 57,796 (never married). Results are weighted.
Source: CPS 1980–2018.

teenaged mothers compared to women who first had children after the age of 20. Both figures indicate that those who became mothers first as teenagers are less likely to have college degrees and will have lower SEI scores, both strong correlates of a lower income. The penalties—in other words, the dips in education and job status associated with having a teenage first birth—have grown stronger in recent years. This occurred as teenage childbirth became less common and more associated with women from poor families, destined to be poor themselves. Finally, the teen birth penalties are strongest for married mothers, the women who've enjoyed the largest income growth over the past few decades. Conversely, the teenage childbearing penalties to education and SEI are weakest for never-married mothers, whose incomes are generally low to begin with.

Finally, we should note that the data we present on teenage childbearing are more influenced by selection bias than are other data in this chapter. Our analysis is based on women who are currently mothers of minor children; mothers whose children are all older than 17 are excluded. This means that one-time teenage mothers who did not have additional children must be 36 or younger to have been included our data. Our analysis of teenage childbearing is therefore biased towards younger women. It's also possible that some women had children as unwed teenagers, then subsequently got married. All of this may explain why a teenage childbirth has minimal net effects on income after controlling for social and demographic differences between respondents.

Family Size

It's well established that women's wages decline with each additional child, but previous research doesn't say much about how the child wage penalty has varied over time and marital status.[30] Sarah Avellar and Pamela Smock showed that the penalty has held constant over the past 30 years, but did not examine differences by marital status.[31] Conversely, Michelle Budig and Paula England explored the child wage penalty separately for married, divorced, and never-married mothers, but did not consider change over time.[32] We suspect that both historical period and family structure are important considerations in understanding the effects of children on women's incomes.

First and foremost, children reduce women's wages by hindering their ability to work. Mothers with multiple children will have spent more time out of the labor force, especially if their children are young, which in itself reduces earnings.[33] Multiple children should cause more complications for single mothers, who often lack partners to either assist with or pay for childcare. On the other hand, multiple children increase single mothers' entitlements to both child support and public assistance. Child support payments are generally larger than they used to be (and now get made more frequently), while public assistance has declined since welfare reform in 1996.[34] For all these reasons, it is worthwhile examining how the relationship between income and numbers of children varies both by family structure and over time.

Our findings show virtually no differences in income between having one and two children, but notably lower incomes for married and divorced women with three or more children. According to Figures 3.14a–3.14c, which show zero-order differences in income by family size, married mothers (Figure 3.14a) with three or more children report median incomes

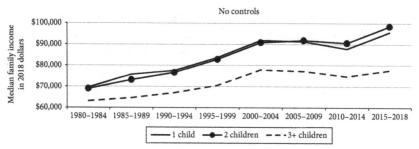

Figure 3.14a. Income and Family Size for Married Mothers.
Notes: N = 252,890 (one child) 272,703 (two children) 155,551 (three or more children). Results are weighted.
Source: CPS 1980–2018.

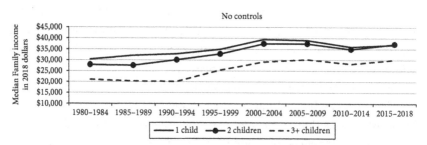

Figure 3.14b. Income and Family Size for Divorced Mothers.
Notes: N = 42,977 (one child) 28,699 (two children) 13,429 (three or more children). Results are weighted.
Source: CPS 1980–2018.

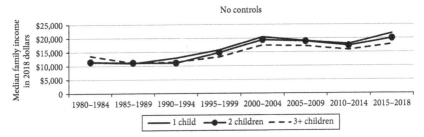

Figure 3.14c. Income and Family Size for Never-Married Mothers.

Notes: N = 48,281 (one child) 24,305 (two children) 14,894 (three or more children). Results are weighted.
Source: CPS 1980–2018.

about $20,000 less a year than do mothers with fewer kids. What's more, this disparity hasn't changed much over the 40 years of our study. With a lower starting baseline, divorced mothers (Figure 3.14b) have incomes about $5,000 less a year when they have three or more children. Never-married mothers (Figure 3.14c) have only a minimal child income penalty, albeit one that's grown slightly larger in recent years. Never-married mothers of course starting at such a low baseline that it's difficult for their incomes to fall too much. Still, every dollar counts when you don't have much to begin with.

For married and divorced mothers, the income penalty associated with having three or more children shown in Figures 3.14a, 3.14b, and 3.14c can be explained by measured differences between respondents. Controlling for variation in education, employment, age, race, and other factors reduces the differences in income by family size to insignificance (results not shown). In other words, the only reason that the married and divorced mothers of large families report lower median family incomes is due to various measured differences between survey respondents.

The opposite is true for never-married mothers: while there were minimal differences in income based on family size without controlling for additional factors, applying statistical controls reveals noteworthy differences in income. Figure 3.15 shows that multiple children increased mothers' incomes in the early 1980s. This makes sense given that the majority of never-married mothers used to obtain most of their income from public assistance (see Figure 3.19). By 2015, these mothers have lower median incomes than do never-married mothers with one or two children. This trend reflects the declining significance of state transfers and the growing importance of work. By the second half of the 1990s, only a minority

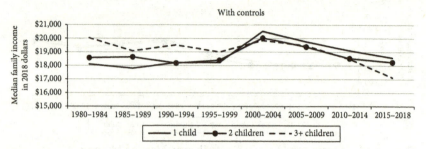

Figure 3.15. Income and Family Size for Never-Married Mothers.
Notes: N = 48,281 (one child) 24,305 (two children) 14,894 (three or more children). Results are weighted.
Source: CPS 1980–2018.

depended on public aid, and the labor market was more important in determining income. Single mothers with larger families almost inevitably find it more difficult to work in the paid labor force, yet somehow divorced mothers with three or more children aren't comparably affected. Consistent with the overarching theme of this book, never-married mothers have a uniquely tenuous relationship with the paid labor force that defies articulation using national survey data.

Finally, we examined the possible influence of having children under six, not old enough to be attending school. As shown in Chapter 2 (see Figure 2.6), there are large differences by marital status in the likelihood of having younger children, with single mothers especially likely to have them. That being said, our multivariate results show no relationship between income and the presence of young children (result not shown).

Race and Ethnicity

There continues to this day fiery debate about the extent to which higher rates of African American poverty are related to family structure, discrimination (both individual and structural), inherited economic inequality, or something else entirely.[35] The debate has been buoyed by two of the most well-known social science findings: African Americans have lower incomes and higher rates of single-parent families than do other population groups.[36]

Figures 3.16a, 3.16b, and 3.16c show the relationship of race, net of other social and demographic differences, to the incomes of married, divorce, and never-married mothers between 1980 and 2018.[37] Whites consistently have

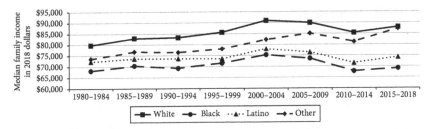

Figure 3.16a. Income by Race for Married Mothers.
Notes: N = 498,069 (White) 39,621 (Black) 102,643 (Latino) 40,801 (Other). Results are weighted.
Source: CPS 1980–2018.

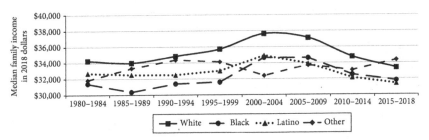

Figure 3.16b. Income by Race for Divorced Mothers.
Notes: N = 60,043 (White) 10,275 (Black) 11,335 (Latino) 3,452 (Other). Results are weighted.
Source: CPS 1980–2018.

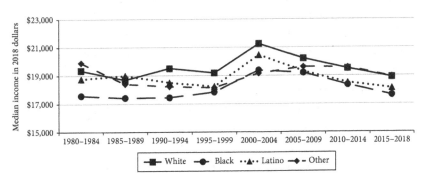

Figure 3.16c. Income by Race for Never-Married Mothers.
Notes: N = 31,079 (White) 33,156 (Black) 19,036 (Latino) 4,209 (Other). Results are weighted.
Source: CPS 1980–2018.

higher incomes than other mothers. However, the difference between Whites and others varies considerably by family structure. Married mothers are the most impacted by racial and ethnic inequality. Given that Black mothers are likely to have Black spouses, the race gap in earnings for married mothers is

68 THANKS FOR NOTHING

magnified by the lower incomes of African American men. What's more, the disparities in income by population group have grown over the past 40 years. In the early 1980s, the income gap between Whites, the highest earning racial group, and African Americans, the lowest earning group, was under $12,000. By 2015–2018, it was almost $14,000. This gap was fueled by rising incomes for White married couples; incomes for Black couples have essentially remained unchanged over the past four decades. So too has the racial wage gap for Americans more broadly.[38] Married Latino families have consistently higher incomes than Black families, but lower incomes than Whites or Americans who self-identify as being of some other ethnicity. Otherwise, incomes for married Latino families have followed a similar pattern as have Black families: growth between 1980 and 2005, then stagnation. The big winners have been married couples in the other category, predominantly Asian Americans. In the early 1980s, their incomes were similar to Latinos. By 2015–2018, they'd caught up to Whites.

The effect of race/ethnicity on divorced mothers' incomes has been consistently smaller, yet still important to account for in examining inequality across families. White mothers have had the highest incomes, at least until the past few years, but over most of the past 40 years the racial disparity has never been more than several thousand dollars a year. It was slightly higher in the mid aughts before abating, mostly as a product of declining incomes for White divorced mothers.

Race has had surprisingly minimal net effects on income for never-married mothers. Over the past 40 years, there has rarely been more than a difference of $1,000 between the incomes of White, Black, Latina, and other never-married mothers. These women have the weakest labor force attachment among the three family structures considered here, so there is presumably less opportunity for costly discrimination in the workplace. In other words, race makes little difference in low-level jobs because everyone is paid so poorly. The story is more about skills and experience than discrimination. In contrast, divorced mothers have stronger labor force attachments than do their counterparts who have never been married, so their incomes vary a bit more by race.

These findings speak to public discourse in ways that go beyond debate about race, income, and family structure. In recent years, references to *intersectionality* have been everywhere, eliciting both enthusiasm and criticism. The core tenet of intersectionality is that people have multiple identities or locations within the social structure that must be considered together in order to make sense of their opportunities and incomes. Legal scholar Kimberlé

Crenshaw, intersectionality's progenitor, wrote about race and gender as the key social categories, but other early works have emphasized race, gender, and social class as the big three.[39] More recent works have cast a wider net.[40]

Our findings indicate that the usual relationship between race/ethnicity and income, two critical identities in virtually every treatment of intersectionality, do not hold for women who give birth out of wedlock. Our results therefore imply that any treatment of intersectionality that neglects marital status is incomplete. Marital status is a crucial social location that belongs in any attempt at understanding inequality, as economist Melissa Kearney has noted recently.[41] Conversely, our results validate intersectionality as a useful construct for understanding the social world when it's combined with data analysis.[42]

Public Assistance Transfers

Up to this point, we have provided evidence that mothers are faring better over time with gains in specific characteristics, like education and employment rates, that directly affect their earnings. We now turn to the two primary sources of non-employment income for single mothers: public assistance and child support.

Public assistance to the needy has dominated popular and scholarly discussions of single mothers in a way no other issue has. In Chapter 1, we noted how the welfare queen shibboleth contributed to the bipartisan welfare reform bill signed into law by Bill Clinton in 1996. Public assistance to the poor, most notably the Temporary Assistance to Needy Families (TANF) program that replaced Aid to Families with Dependent Children (AFDC), remains a hot-button issue today. In 2018, 37% of Americans felt that the government was spending too much money on welfare. This was down from a high of 60% in 1995, but still represents a considerable lack of support for this program; only 22% thought more money should be spent.[43] The strength of popular sentiment and its long-run relevance to family policy over the years highlight the importance of examining the economic contributions made by public assistance. The question of child support, most notably with regard to deadbeat dads, has also featured prominently in public discourse on the family, albeit without generating the same level of fervor that public aid does.

The weak public support for cash welfare persists despite its continuing decline in relevance for single-mother families. Figure 3.17 shows that receipt

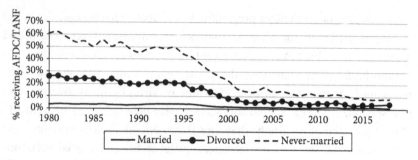

Figure 3.17. AFDC/TANF Receipt by Marital Status.
Notes: N = 681,144 (married) 85,105 (divorced) 87,480 (never married). Results are weighted.
Source: CPS 1980–2018.

of government income transfers via AFDC or TANF has greatly declined since 1980. In that year over 60% of never-married mothers and almost 30% of divorced mothers received transfer income. By 2015, fewer than 10% of all mothers got TANF funds. The largest decline occurred in the 1990s, corresponding to the 1993 expansion of the Earned Income Tax Credit and the 1996 welfare reform act. Receipt continued to decline through the start of the twentieth century and didn't even increase during the Great Recession in 2008 despite mounting need as unemployment peaked at 9.6%.[44] Kathryn Edin and Luke Shaefer were not far off the mark when they wrote in 2015 that cash welfare effectively no longer existed.[45] Over the past few decades the American safety net has increasingly been linked to employment, most notably in the form of the Earned Income Tax Credit, and in-kind benefits like food stamps in lieu of direct cash transfers.[46]

Never-married mothers have always been the most frequent recipients of cash welfare. As we have seen, they have persistently lower incomes and weaker attachment to the paid labor force than do divorced mothers. Furthermore, as we'll see in Chapter 5, divorced mothers have higher incomes in the years immediately prior to becoming single mothers. This may well depress their rates of AFDC/TANF receipt, insofar as they are unfamiliar with the welfare bureaucracy. In recent years, this became a self-fulfilling prophecy for all single mothers: since federal income transfers seem so unattainable, no one bothers applying for them.[47]

Over the same time that fewer single mothers received AFDC and then TANF, the typical payment size also declined. Figure 3.18 shows the median annual transfer size in 2018 dollars over the past 40 years. In 1980, the median single mother received almost $9,000 a year. That same year

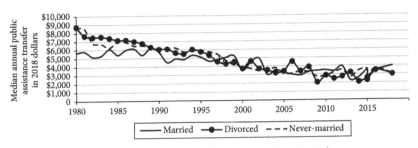

Figure 3.18. Annual Size of AFDC/TANF Transfers by Marital Status.
Notes: N = 681,144 (married) 85,105 (divorced) 87,480 (never married). Results are weighted.
Source: CPS 1980–2018.

married mothers averaged about $6,000. The past 40 years saw almost linear decline for all mothers. By 2018, the median single mother only received $3,000 a year—or about a third of what she got in 1980—while married mothers pulled down $4,000. In other words, single mothers used to get transfers that were 50% larger than married mothers received. Now their awards are only three-fourths the size of married mother's. Finally, over the past 40 years, there has been little difference between divorced and never-married mothers in the size of the median cash award they've received.

Do married couples deserve larger TANF checks than single mothers? Here are several considerations. First, few mothers of any kind still receive cash transfers, and that's especially true for those who are married: since 2000, only 1% have received TANF. Yet the need among this population is surely much greater: in 2013, the Urban Institute estimated that only 12% of eligible married couples received TANF funds (the corresponding figure for single-parent families is 28%).[48] Second, some readers might conclude that single-parent families are especially deserving of larger TANF remittances, because they contain only one potential wage earner (and one caretaker of children). That is true, but of course it doesn't mean that any adult in the married family is actually earning a wage. For many married families, support comes because both of the adults are unable to earn a wage. While on average two-parent families have more income due to more adults who can work, at the lower end of the income distribution these families also have multiple adults who need support from TANF. On these grounds, it's perfectly reasonable that married mothers receive larger transfers in the unlikely event they are the beneficiaries of public aid.

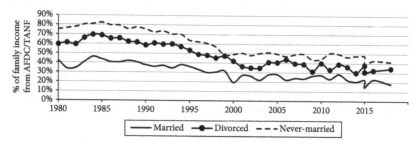

Figure 3.19. The Share of Income Provided by AFDC/TANF by Marital Status.
Notes: N = 681,144 (married) 85,105 (divorced) 87,480 (never married). Results are weighted.
Source: CPS 1980–2018.

We have established that few mothers still receive federal cash transfers, and when they do the awards are relatively small. Nevertheless, they represent a vital source of income for recipients. Figure 3.19 shows the proportion of income provided by AFDC or TANF for all CPS participants receiving federal cash transfers. In other words: if you're an aid recipient, what percentage of your overall family income is provided by AFDC/TANF? The short answer: a lot. Prior to welfare reform in 1996, AFDC provided the majority of income for its recipients. Not surprisingly, never-married mothers were more reliant on federal income transfers than were divorced mothers in the years prior to welfare reform. In the mid-1980s, it comprised 80% of the income for the half of never-married mothers who received it. Over the same years, far fewer divorced mothers received AFDC, but it was no less significant to their wallets. All this started changing after the 1996 welfare reform act. Nowadays, it provides only half the family income for the ever declining number of single mothers who receive it at all. In the past 40 years, "welfare" has shifted from a program that supported a large number of single mothers to an income supplement for a small minority of families. Never-married mothers remain somewhat more likely to receive public aid, and remain somewhat more dependent on it for their family income, but it's become a distinction without a difference in an era when cash aid has diminished to insignificance for most needy parents.

Child Support

The more common source of transfer income for single mothers is child support; less often, mothers receive alimony (hereafter we'll speak of "child support" as shorthand that includes alimony and, rarely, palimony).[49] Figure

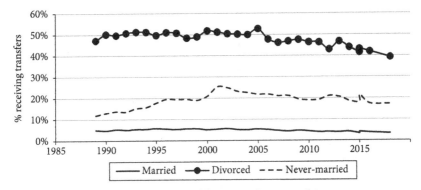

Figure 3.20. Receipt of Alimony/Child Support by Marital Status.
Notes: N = 681,144 (married) 85,105 (divorced) 87,480 (never married). Results are weighted.
Source: CPS 1980–2018.

3.20 shows how receipt of transfers from fathers has changed for married, divorced, and never-married mothers since 1989 (earlier years of data aren't directly comparable). Over the past 30 years, divorced mothers have been at least twice as likely as never-married mothers to receive child support payments. This disparity represents, most conspicuously, the legal status that accords to dissolving a marriage: any divorce that involves minor children will result in a child support order. Compliance with that order is a different question: according to the most recent Census Bureau report on the subject, in 2015 over a third of custodial parents with child support orders did not receive any payment. Just under half (44%) of parents with support orders received payment in full.[50]

Unmarried single parents have a legal right to child support, but face far more roadblocks to getting it. Without a court involved, a single mother must make her own provisions to obtain cash payments from her former partner. If the parents cannot reach an agreement on their own, a custodial mother faces steep legal hurdles. She'll have to hire an attorney, file a court order, participate in a pretrial hearing, and convince the court to order genetic testing if the (presumed) father disputes paternity. Only when paternity is established can she then pursue a new court order for support. Most single mothers don't have the money to do all this. For many, it won't be worth the time or the effort.

Figure 3.20 shows that child support receipt rates for never-married mothers more than doubled in the 1990s, even as they stagnated at around 50% for divorced moms. It's hard to know what to make of these two different

74 THANKS FOR NOTHING

trends. Three different pieces of federal legislation were intended to increase compliance with support orders. The Brady Amendment, enacted in 1986, instituted automatically triggered liens for deadbeat dads. The 1992 Uniform Interstate Family Support Act sought to reduce jurisdictional confusion over support orders. Finally, the 1996 Personal Responsibility and Work Opportunity Reconciliation Act (aka welfare reform) required custodial parents to pursue support orders in order to receive TANF funds. While this should have raised the proportion of support payments for all single mothers, it's not clear why never-married mothers benefited but divorced moms did not. One possibility is the low starting rate for never-married moms—they simply had more ground to make up. Conversely, divorced moms may have already hit the ceiling for child support—the theoretical maximum proportion of men both inclined to comply with support orders and sufficiently well-off to do so. Indeed, many fathers simply can't afford to make court-stipulated payments, but instead furnish in-kind aid to their children.[51]

Child support receipt began stagnating for all mothers after the first few years of the twenty-first century. The CPS data don't offer an explanation, but the Great Recession was surely a big reason. Another contributing factor may have been the growing number of single mothers who lived with their partners out of wedlock. Between 1990 and 1995, just over one-third (38%) of unwed parents were living together at the time of childbirth. This figure increased to 62% by 2006 to 2013.[52] Obviously live-in fathers provide in-kind aid to their partners and children in lieu of cash transfers to support children they live with.[53] Perhaps rising rates of births to cohabiting unions reduced child support payments to never-married mothers since the start of the twenty-first century. But this dynamic can't explain the much steeper decline in child support receipt among divorced mothers over these same years. Furthermore, the number of CPS participants in cohabiting relationships at any given time is low (see Figure 2.18). The recent decline in support payments thus cannot be explained away by other demographic changes, but it's obviously affecting incomes for single mothers.

For most mothers, the size of the median support payment hasn't changed much over time, as shown in Figure 3.21. Divorced mothers, by far the more common recipients of child support payments, saw their median remittances rise about a thousand dollars in the first years of the new millennium before falling back down to 1980s levels. Married mothers saw even fewer changes. Only never-married mothers have seen their child support benefits persistently increase over the past 40 years. Their median payments doubled between 1980 and 2005, from $2,000 to $4,000, before falling back down to

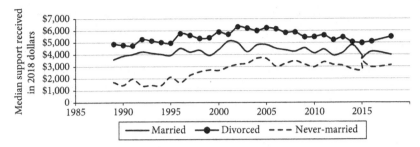

Figure 3.21. Annual Median Alimony/Child Support Payments, by Marital Status.
Notes: N = 681,144 (married) 85,105 (divorced) 87,480 (never married). Results are weighted.
Source: CPS 1980–2018.

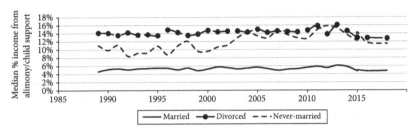

Figure 3.22. The Percentage of Income Provided by Alimony/Child Support by Marital Status.
Notes: N = 681,144 (married) 85,105 (divorced) 87,480 (never married). Results are weighted.
Source: CPS 1980–2018.

$3,000 in the past few years. This increase accords with the declining stigma of a nonmarital birth, coupled with changing laws and a growing judicial willingness to order support for unwed mothers.[54]

These dollar figures are all low, and most fall short of the full stipulated awards. Yet they comprise a meaningful fraction of total family income, especially for divorced and never-married mothers. Figure 3.22 shows the fraction of family income provided by child support. For both divorced and never-married mothers, it's held steady over the past 40 years at between 10% and 15% of total family income. The figure for married mothers is predictably lower.

Age

Age and income have a well-known curvilinear relationship. People make more as they get older and advance in their careers When retirement looms, they both work less and stop moving up the job ladder and so their earnings decline. Younger workers gain job experience more quickly than older ones, so age will have a greater impact for workers earlier in their careers. The relationship between age and income for women is more complicated, given their frequent moves in and out of the labor force in conjunction with childbearing and parenting.[55] Unfortunately the CPS lacks data on employment history, so we will look at age as a proxy.

How do these dynamics vary by marital status? We foresaw two possibilities. First, single mothers will spend less time out of the paid labor force, given that they can't rely on a spousal income when they're not working. Indeed, in Chapter 2, Figure 2.10 suggests this might especially be the case for divorced mothers, who are consistently employed at higher rates than other mothers. We would therefore expect faster income growth as divorcées age, even as they start out from a lower baseline. The other possibility is that the advantages of married motherhood prevail here. By virtue of spousal income and assistance with the responsibilities of parenthood, married mothers will enjoy stronger income growth across the life course. Finally, we expect a stronger relationship between age and income in recent years as women continued to hold better jobs.

Figure 3.23 shows that our second conjecture is correct: with age, income increases much more quickly for married women, and there's been no appreciable change in this relationship over the past 40 years. All young mothers, irrespective of marital status, have lower incomes. By the time women hit age 50, when they (and if married, their spouses), are at the peak of their earning power, married mothers are pulling in over $120,000 a year. In contrast, a 50-year-old, divorced mother is only bringing in a median $40,000; never-married mothers' incomes are in the mid-$30,000s. Moreover, there is no appreciable change in this pattern over the past years—the relationships depicted in Figures 3.23a and 3.23b are virtually identical.

It is worth noting the potential role of sample selection in these results. Divorce is more common among less prosperous couples, which purges the ranks of lower-income married mothers. Moreover, women who have minor children at home at age 50 reflect disproportionately late childbirth. Conversely, younger mothers are more likely to have children out of wedlock (Figure 2.2), while older mothers tend to be married (Figure 2.3). Therefore, the large income difference at age 50 would be smaller if all these forms of selection were taken into account.

Figure 3.23a. Income by Age in 1980–1985 by Marital Status.
Notes: N = 93,963 (married) 10,684 (divorced) 4,928 (never married). Results are weighted.
Source: CPS 1980–2018.

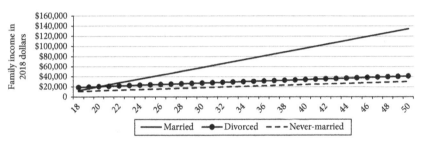

Figure 3.23b. Income by Age in 2015–2018 by Marital Status.
Notes: N = 67,309 (married) 7,985 (divorced) 12,526 (never married). Results are weighted.
Source: CPS 1980–2018.

Counterfactual Income Distributions

So far, in this chapter, we have relied on what we might think of as model-based predictions of income: based on our 39 years of CPS data we generated separate estimates for married, divorced, and never-married women to understand how changing levels of education, employment, and other individual characteristics affect income. But this approach doesn't offer insight on the changing returns to individual attributes. For instance: Is a college degree equally remunerative for divorced mothers in 1980 and 2018? To what extent are growing incomes the product of increases in human capital, as opposed to higher returns to human capital? We answer these questions via regression decomposition, which allows us

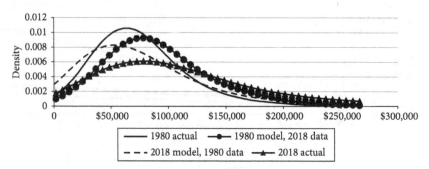

Figure 3.24. Actual and Counterfactual Income Distributions for Married Mothers.
Notes: N = 681,144. Results are weighted.
Source: CPS 1980–2018.

to ask what incomes in 1980 might have looked like if women back then had the individual attributes that women possessed in 2018 (or, conversely, if women in 2018 received the pecuniary returns to individual attributes that women received in 1980).[56]

Figure 3.24 shows counterfactual comparisons for married women.[57] Each of the lines represents the distribution of income. The actual predicted incomes for 1980 and 2018 are shown, along with two counterfactual distributions. The first, the solid line with circle markers, shows what incomes would have looked like in 1980 if married mothers had 2018 levels of education and other attributes. The second, the dashed line, offers the alternate contrast: hypothetical estimates based on 1980 attributes but 2018-level returns to attributes. By comparing real and hypothetical distributions, we can see what matters more in predicting income today: growing levels of human capital, or growing returns to human capital.

The results show that if married mothers in 1980 had 2018 levels of education and other labor market resources, their incomes would have gone slightly up but the overall shape of the distribution wouldn't change much. The other counterfactual, 1980 individual attributes but 2018 economic returns, suggests a more polarized income distribution with expanded populations of both poorer and wealthier women, and fewer in the middle. But this future was never realized, as by 2018 women had more education, better jobs, and more broadly scored better on the attributes that correlate with prosperity. The economy changed, but married women's attributes changed along with it. Both are responsible for the greater prosperity married mothers enjoy now compared to in 1980.

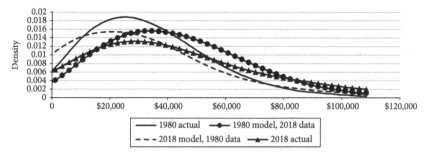

Figure 3.25. Actual and Counterfactual Income Distributions for Divorced Mothers.
Notes: N = 85,105. Results are weighted.
Source: CPS 1980–2018.

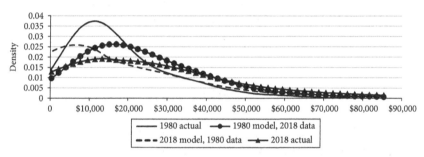

Figure 3.26. Actual and Counterfactual Income Distributions for Never-Married Mothers.
Notes: N = 87,480. Results are weighted.
Source: CPS 1980–2018.

Figure 3.25 shows the same comparisons for divorced mothers. Generally speaking, the results are similar to the findings for married women (Figure 3.24), albeit with lower incomes across the board. A mother's attributes—as opposed to the economic returns to those attributes—continue to be more responsible for higher incomes over time. For example, there is a range of income for these mothers, middle class incomes between approximately $45,000 and $75,000, that was only available to certain women in 1980. The counterfactual distribution of women with 2018 levels of human capital but 1980 returns shows that as more of these women achieved higher levels of human capital, they were able to attain higher family incomes.

Figure 3.26 shows these comparisons for never-married mothers. The difference between the two years is again substantial. Never-married mothers were more likely to be located higher in the income distribution in 2018, as a decrease in the mode at the lower income level resulted from a shift of respondents into higher levels of income. The difference between 1980 incomes, and what incomes would have been if they had similar characteristics to 2018 never-married mothers, is equally notable. Looking at the hypothetical distribution, if these women had similar labor market characteristics in 1980 as in 2018, they would have had much higher incomes. As with the previous comparisons, having the same labor market characteristics as 1980 in a 2018 income model would have resulted in lower incomes for this population of mothers. That is, while all mothers appear to be doing what it takes to raise their family incomes—gaining more education, participating in the labor market, having smaller families—the labor market in 2018 was less likely to reward them for this. Without those gains in human capital, many never-married mothers would have had even lower incomes, which is noteworthy given how low their incomes already are.

Conclusion

The story about the economics of single motherhood is that there is no one story. The findings in this chapter show that both individual variation and historical context matter. Family structure remains inextricably related to income, but the link is not so simple as commonly portrayed. First, the variation within family structures is sometimes nearly as great as the gap between married and unmarried mothers. College-educated divorced mothers, for instance, have family incomes almost as high as do married mothers without high school diplomas. We'll further explore this issue in the next chapter, which focuses more on variation within family type.

Second, the world is a much different place than it was 40 years ago. As was shown in Chapter 2, individual attributes have changed considerably, but equally important is how the economic returns to these attributes have also changed—and how this dynamic varied by marital status. In particular, we've continued to find evidence that never-married mothers differ from their ever-married contemporaries in ways that transcend either family structure or variation in human capital and other measured attributes.

4

From Moynihan to Piketty

One of the most familiar stories about America's economy is the growth in income inequality: the skyrocketing gap between rich and poor over the past 40 years.[1] The American labor market has changed dramatically, with employment shifting from production to services and information-based work. One result has been a burgeoning gender difference in inequality: since the early 1970s, for men only the real wages of the college-educated have increased substantially. Women's wages have increased over these years, at least partially at the expense of less educated men.[2] This is an understandable development: women's wages were low compared to men's because of systematic gender differences, including (but not limited to) discrimination. As women entered the workforce in greater numbers they moved into many traditionally male realms of employment. To a certain extent men's losses were women's gains.

These grand economic shifts created a new standard for prosperity in America. Over time the norm for a comfortable life became a household with two employed spouses. This puts single parents at a substantial and irremediable disadvantage, leading some scholars to designate single-mother families as the new underclass for the end of the twentieth century.[3] As we discussed in Chapter 1, single motherhood has long held a privileged position in the political discourse on rising inequality, with many conservative writers embracing a facile association between the growth of single parent families, their high poverty rate, and the growth of inequality in America more generally. "The biggest reason for income inequality," writes economist and former Mitt Romney advisor Avik Roy, "is single parenthood."[4]

This is an overstatement. It cannot be denied that the growth of single-mother families has replaced families with two potential workers—or one worker and one childcare provider—with single-earner families. In the 1980s, approximately 23% of the increase in childhood poverty resulted from the proliferation of mother-headed families.[5] Yet sociologist Bruce Western's

Thanks for Nothing. Nicholas H. Wolfinger and Matthew McKeever, Oxford University Press.
© Oxford University Press 2024. DOI: 10.1093/oso/9780199324323.003.0004

82   THANKS FOR NOTHING

authoritative analysis shows that the proliferation of single-mother families only accounts for about one-fifth of the growth in American inequality.[6] Moreover, it's a mistake to assume causality only runs in one direction, with single mothers *causing* inequality. Studies have shown that a regional lack of economic opportunity decreases the marriage rate (and thereby leads to more single-mother families).[7] Finally, marriage isn't an economic panacea: many two-parent families are struggling.[8]

Inequality has many causes besides the proliferation of single-mother families. The decline of labor unions has played a big part.[9] So too has growing labor market concentration and monopsony.[10] The tax code changed significantly, with top marginal tax rates slashed.

Other changes in the regulation of labor markets have helped to increase inequality. In recent years the requirement for occupational licensing has skyrocketed to such a ridiculous extent that Louisiana requires florists to be licensed (and pass a written test; a hands-on test was dropped a few years back).[11] Massachusetts licenses fortune tellers, while Minnesota licenses frog sellers.[12] Occupational licensing create cartels that allow license holders to exclude competitors that might drive profits down. What's more, almost one-fifth of American workers are covered by noncompete agreements, which depress their ability to shop around for a higher-paying job.[13] Over on Wall Street, the financial sector is growing like kudzu, enriching its employees while choking out growth in other sectors of the economy.[14] Finally, the rise of the gig economy has had more equivocal effects on inequality, but a large sector of poorly paid service-sector jobs—in food delivery, ride share apps, and the like—has created a growing sphere of the economy that's appealing to single mothers and others with unpredictable schedules.[15]

This isn't meant to be a comprehensive overview of what's causing inequality. Our aim is to cast doubt on the notion that single mother families are primarily responsible. The proliferation of single motherhood has played its part, but as Western's research has shown it's only a small portion of the story. It's not a simple case of single motherhood leading to impoverishment.

In this chapter, we focus on inequality *within* the population of single mothers. As we have seen, single mothers are disproportionately likely to lack the credentials, like education, necessary to make a living wage, and it's difficult for households with only one poorly compensated worker to do well. In bygone years, having only one working parent in the household would have been fine. For example, having only one adult employed in the 1950s or 1960s, perhaps in manufacturing or heavy industry, would by itself

FROM MOYNIHAN TO PIKETTY   83

provide for a comfortable middle-class lifestyle. Although there were fewer single mothers then, they were disadvantaged in not being able to hold well-compensated "male" jobs.[16] Now the trends are reversed. There are fewer barriers to entry into occupations for women, but fewer jobs that can, by themselves, provide adequate incomes to support a family.

Still, single mothers are not a unitary segment of the workforce. Are some faring better in recent years? The past 30 years have seen the birth of the archetype of the middle-class professional women who opts, perhaps while in her 30s or 40s, to have a nonmarital birth. The analog for divorcées is the successful single mother who feels no need, economic or otherwise, to remarry. The trope first arose in the wake of Dan Quayle's 1992 speech condemning sitcom character Murphy Brown's nonmarital pregnancy.[17] Since then, the notion of the successful middle-class single mother has persisted despite the fact that, as we show in Chapter 2, very few of these women actually exist.[18]

That so few single mothers earn middle-class incomes remains a surprising result, because never-married and especially divorced mothers have achieved such striking gains in labor force credentials over the past 40 years. Perhaps gains for some have resulted in sufficient inequality within the overall population of single mothers that broad averages are misleading. In this chapter, we first consider overall levels of inequality within different populations of mothers. Then, we examine how trends in labor force characteristics have differentially affected married, divorced, and never-married mothers at different parts of the income distribution.

Inequality within Marital Status

A common measure of inequality is the Gini coefficient, a statistic that ranges from zero to one. A Gini of zero means that income is distributed equally throughout a population, while a Gini of one means that a single person receives all income. Of 176 countries ranked by the World Bank, the United States checks in with a Gini coefficient of .41, making it the 53rd most unequal country in the world.[19] Inequality has risen substantially in the past 40 years: back in 1979, America's Gini coefficient was .35.[20] America, in short, is an increasingly unequal country, and that inequality has baleful consequences for individuals, their communities, and the nation as a whole.[21]

Most scholars of inequality do not examine inequality specifically within the population of mothers. One notable exception is sociologist Molly Martin's 2006 study.[22] She found that inequality was highest among never-married mothers, who experienced rapid growth in inequality in the 1980s. Divorced mothers had lower levels of inequality, with married and cohabiting mothers experiencing the least.

Although her results only extend to 2000, our analysis shows that these findings continue to hold. Figure 4.1 shows annual Gini coefficients for married, divorced, and never-married mothers.[23] Like Martin, we find the greatest inequality among never-married mothers, the least among married mothers, with divorced mothers somewhere in the middle. And while inequality for all mothers has increased over time, differences in inequality across family structure have decreased: in recent years the gap in Gini coefficients between married, divorced, and never-married mothers have declined even as incomes became more unequal for everyone.

These Gini coefficients are all high by international standards, and demonstrate that there are substantial differences across marital status. What these statistics don't show is the nature of the underlying inequality that is boosting the Gini values. Are they driven by a few women high in the income distribution, for example, or a burgeoning upper-middle class? To answer this question, we will explore the income distribution for mothers separately by marital status.

The CPS data suggest that inequality amongst single mothers isn't a function of a few prosperous mothers at the top—a common explanation for

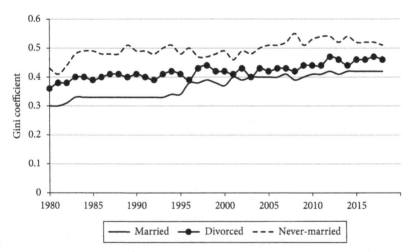

Figure 4.1. Trends in Income Inequality for Mothers by Marital Status.
Notes: N = 681,144 (married) 85,105 (divorced) 87,480 (never married). Results are weighted.
Source: CPS 1980–2018.

inequality in the U.S. as a whole, and truer for married mothers—but instead the product of how low incomes are for most single mothers. Figures 4.2a,

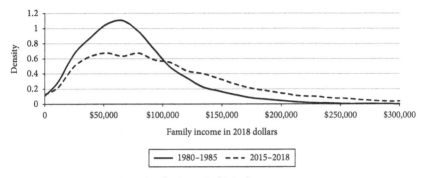

Figure 4.2a. Income Density for Married Mothers.
Notes: N = 93,963 (1980–85) 67,309 (2015–2018). Results are weighted.
Source: CPS 1980–2018.

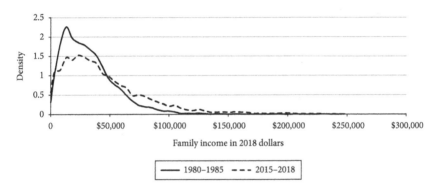

Figure 4.2b. Income Densities for Divorced Mothers.
Notes: N = 10,684 (1980–1985) 7,985 (2015–2018). Results are weighted.
Source: CPS 1980–2018.

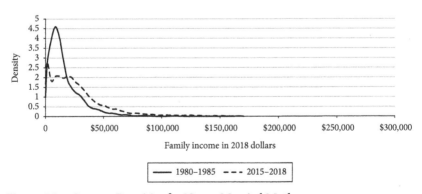

Figure 4.2c. Income Densities for Never-Married Mothers.
Notes: N = 4,928 (1980–1985). 12,526 (2015–2018). Results are weighted.
Source: CPS 1980–2018.

4.2b, and 4.2c show density plots of income for married, divorced, and never-married mothers. All show flattening distributions and thus a growth in inequality, since 1980. Between 1980 and 1985, far more of these women's incomes were similar to each other, falling into a big bulge near the lower end of the distribution. By 2015–2018, there were larger numbers of Americans with higher-than-typical incomes than in 1980–1985, thus producing more inequality. The size of this group, the right tail of the income distribution, is predictably much larger for married mothers and extends to much higher incomes than it does for single mothers. This is a group of extremely high income families that substantially increase overall inequality for this population. In contrast, the right tail of the income distribution for divorced and never-married mothers approaches zero much more quickly, even in recent years. There are not only vanishingly few high-income single mothers in comparison to married mothers, but also less of a broad middle class.

This difference between married and single mothers becomes even more apparent if we consider the top of the income distribution: incomes at the 90th percentile (in other words, 90% of the population makes less money, while 10% makes more). In theory, the top 10% of incomes reflect self-evident privilege, a society's most prosperous citizens. But as Figure 4.3 shows, this really only holds for married mothers: the levels of income for the top decile of single mothers remain low, only surpassing $100,000 for divorced women in the past few years. For never-married mothers, incomes in the top 10% of the distribution haven't increased much over time, and barely cracked $50,000 by 2018. Put another way, a never-married mother in the top income decile makes less per year than the median American family.

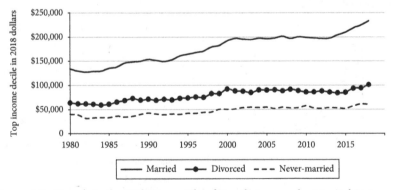

Figure 4.3. Trends in the 90th Percentile of Family Income by Marital Status.
Notes: N = 68,117 (married) 8,510 (divorced) 8,748 (never married). Results are weighted.
Source: CPS 1980–2018.

Income "privilege" looks very different for single mothers than it does for married Americans. What's more, the idea of a burgeoning population of Murphy Brown mothers—prosperous professional women who choose to have children out of wedlock—is clearly a myth.

In one sense, the trends in 90th percentile incomes shown in Figure 4.3 don't readily accord with the Gini coefficients shown in Figure 4.1. The Gini coefficients suggest rising income inequality, but shrinking gaps in inequality between married, divorced, and never-married mothers. Yet the top decile incomes suggest that a few privileged married mothers are pulling far ahead of single mothers, so we have to look elsewhere to fully understand the growth in inequality among American mothers. The answer can be found in looking at the other end of the income distribution. Figure 4.4 shows income data from the bottom decile, the 10% of married, divorced, and never-married mothers with the lowest incomes. The data show that bottom decile incomes have remained relatively stable for married and divorced women since 1980. Put another way, things haven't been going well, but at least they haven't gotten any worse for the least prosperous American mothers. The exception is for never-married mothers, whose bottom decile incomes have *declined* over the past 20 years. Since 2008 and the start of the Great Recession, the income for never-married mothers at the 10th percentile has effectively been zero. In other words, 10% of never-married mothers have no reported income from any source.[24]

This result is consistent with the well-known finding from Kathryn Edin and Luke Shaefer about extreme poverty in the United States.[25] In documenting the inequality that emerged from welfare reform in 1996, they find that while many single mothers have fared better on account of joining

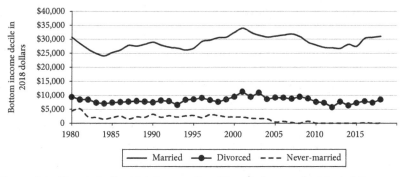

Figure 4.4. Trends in the 10th Percentile of Family Income by Marital Status.
Notes: N = 68,117 (married) 8,510 (divorced) 8,748 (never married). Results are weighted.
Source: CPS 1980–2018.

88 THANKS FOR NOTHING

the workforce and benefiting from the Earned Income Tax Credit, some have fallen through the cracks. They've been pushed off the welfare rolls, and are either unable or unwilling to work. Consequently, their incomes fell and they joined the ranks of the extreme poor depicted in Figure 4.4. Our analysis shows that the population of single mothers without income is primarily comprised of women who give birth out of wedlock, not divorcées.

Our initial inspection of inequality by family structure, based on Gini coefficients (Figure 4.1), suggested increasing similarity across marital statuses. Subsequent analysis reveals more complex income dynamics. Greater inequality for married mothers resulted from a few having pulled far away from the pack, but that hasn't happened for single mothers. Instead, low median incomes, the lack of a noteworthy middle-income population, and declines in income for the lowest earning never-married mothers have raised the Gini coefficients. The observed inequality reflects a worsening income situation for some single mothers, versus the economic gains enjoyed by some married women.

We now turn to data analysis to reveal which individual and family characteristics are most responsible for movements into the fringes of the income distribution. To do so, we use regression methods that allow us to examine the top quartile, or 75th percentile, and the bottom, or 25th. This allows us to better understand the impacts of personal attributes of these women across the income distribution.

Education

Over the years of our study, higher education increasingly became a prerequisite for decent wages. In earlier chapters, we showed how this represented a far greater hurdle for divorced and especially never-married mothers than it did for their married counterparts. Single mothers are less likely to have college degrees, and receive smaller economic returns when they do have them. Paradoxically this reinforces the benefits of having a high school degree for single mothers. Figure 4.5 addresses the question of the importance of a high school degree, at each end of the four decades we study, for mothers at different points of the income distribution. Most broadly, the returns to a high school degree for single mothers have changed little over time. For both divorced and never-married mothers, those with high school degrees have very similar expected levels of income at each end of this time period. These might appear small at times—for example, only roughly $10,000 for

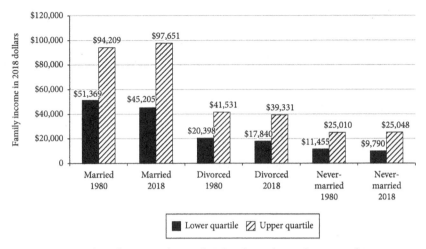

Figure 4.5. Predicted Income for High School Graduates by Marital Status, Year, and Income Quartile.

Notes: N = 20,589 (married 1980) 15,820 (married 2018) 2,125 (divorced 1980) 1,759 (divorced 2018) 749 (never married 1980) 2,798 (never married 2018). Results are weighted.
Source: CPS 1980–2018.

never-married mothers in the bottom quartile—but are important in relation to overall average earnings for these groups of mothers. In addition, the differences between quartiles have changed very little for either group. The differences between quartiles are substantial—roughly $15,000 for never married mothers and $20,000 for divorced mothers—but this difference has not changed much since 1980. The declining value of these returns for nearly all single mothers lead us to conclude that the absence of a high school education is not the most crucial reason for the growing economic divide in these groups. It matters, but it takes more than simply the presence or absence of a high school diploma to explain difference in the incomes of single mothers.

For married women, high school degrees can mean a great deal, particularly among families with the highest incomes: on average it means much more income—over $40,000—for those in the top quartile compared to the bottom. By 2018, a high school degree was worth less than it was in 1980 in the lower quartile, but somewhat more for the upper quartile. These findings reflect the growing inequality of wages among married women. That a high school diploma provided less economic benefit in the lower quartile than in the upper is also a reflection of wage compression among lower-income adults in the contemporary United States.

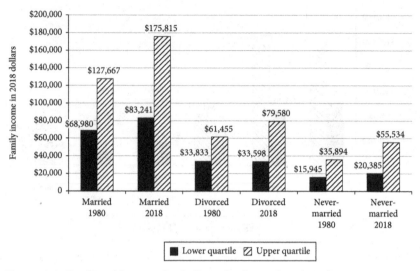

Figure 4.6. Predicted Income for College Graduates by Marital Status, Year, and Income Quartile.

Notes: N = 20,589 (married 1980) 15,820 (married 2018) 2,125 (divorced 1980) 1,759 (divorced 2018) 749 (never married 1980) 2,798 (never married 2018). Results are weighted.
Source: CPS 1980–2018.

Chapter 3 showed that the economic returns to a college education differ appreciably between married, divorced, and never-married mothers. Figure 4.6 shows the expected income for those women with a college degree by marital status, year, and income quartile. Here the effects of education vary substantially by quartile and over time.

The gap between quartiles is smallest for single mothers in 1980, suggesting that college-educated single mothers used to have more difficulty converting their degrees into income. These differences are not negligible, considering overall income levels for these mothers. For example, in 1980, divorced mothers were much more likely to be employed full-time than were their married or never-married counterparts (see Figure 2.10), and their educational qualifications are subsequently very important for the upper income quartile. The difference between quartiles for married mothers, though, are much more substantial in 1980 than for other mothers.

The bigger story here is that for all mothers the distance between quartiles in the incomes for college degree holders grew between 1980 and 2018. Predictably, the biggest gap between quartiles belongs to married mothers. By 2018, married mothers with a college degree had family incomes of $83,000 in the lower quartile and $176,000 in the upper. We would expect married mothers to benefit more from college degrees. A college education contributes to their own earnings and makes it likely that mothers have educated spouses. The sheer size of the gap between quartiles reveals the greater inequality for married mothers, especially in recent years.

Although the interquartile range grew for single mothers over time, the gap between quartiles remained under $50,000. Inequality has thus grown among single mothers, but it is more modest at least insofar as it is produced by educational attainment. Predictably the gap between quartiles is larger for divorced mothers than it is for never-married mothers. Divorced women have been more successful in converting their credentials into income, but only at the upper quartile. Unique among the mothers depicted in Figure 4.6, lower quartile divorced women receive the same returns to a college degree in 2018 that they did in 1980.

Work

The previous chapter showed that employment, net of other factors, makes a big difference to the incomes of single mothers, especially divorcées. We now consider how much employment contributes to income heterogeneity. In other words, is the mere fact of employment associated with a wide range of incomes for mothers?

Figure 4.7, which shows predicted income for mothers in part-time employment by survey year and quartile, reaffirms that the impact of work varies across family structures. The most noteworthy difference remains the

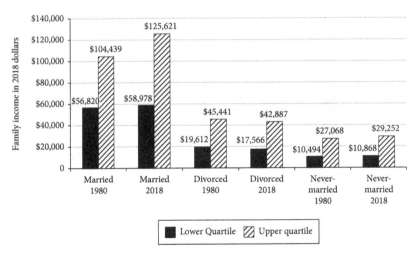

Figure 4.7. Expected Income for Part-Time Workers by Year, Marital Structure, and Income Quartile.

Notes: N = 20,589 (married 1980) 15,820 (married 2018) 2,125 (divorced 1980) 1,759 (divorced 2018) 749 (never married 1980) 2,798 (never married 2018). Results are weighted.
Source: CPS 1980–2018.

gap between single and married mothers. Even at the lower quartile, married mothers have higher incomes when working part-time than do other women. Married women, particularly those in the upper quartile, often have spouses with comparably high incomes, and higher family incomes might simply reflect the latitude to select well-paying part-time jobs. Otherwise, the results in Figure 4.7 mostly reflect the type of inequality consistently depicted in this book. Divorcées receive larger returns to part-time employment than do their never-married counterparts. Interestingly, the economic returns to employment have not changed over time. With the exception of married mothers in the top quartile, the differences between time period are under $2,000, and even decrease for divorced mothers at the lower quartile.

For full-time employment, as shown in Figure 4.8, there are again substantial differences between married and unmarried mothers. The family income levels for those working full-time vary by quartile for single mothers, and the gap between never-married and divorced mothers grew between 1980 and 2018. The gap between single and married mothers is substantially larger, though, and only grew over time, particularly at the upper quartile. For all mothers, employment exerts a substantial impact on inequality among families with children. This underscores a basic fact about the economics of family structure: to become well-off, single mothers must work.

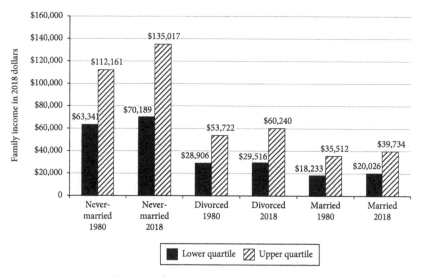

Figure 4.8. Expected Income for Full-Time Workers by Year, Marital Structure, and Income Quartile.

Notes: N = 20,589 (married 1980) 15,820 (married 2018) 2,125 (divorced 1980) 1,759 (divorced 2018) 749 (never married 1980) 2,798 (never married 2018). Results are weighted.
Source: CPS 1980–2018.

These results might be viewed as supportive of aims of the 1996 welfare reform legislation, which sought to move single mothers from welfare to work. Even at the bottom of the income distribution and net of other differences, any employment by single mothers is associated with substantially higher incomes. The issue, of course, is their ability to work given their responsibility to their children.

Age

Figures 4.9, 4.10, and 4.11 show how income varies by age and marital status for the lower and upper income quartiles. For single mothers, there is virtually no change within quartile over the past 40 years. The prospect of economic security in the United States rests on the assumption that workers will improve their career prospects as they get older. But this doesn't appear to be the case for single mothers in the lower income quartile. It's not a surprise that growing older yields stronger income gains in the upper quartile than in the lower quartile; in other words, inequality increases with age. Yet the gains for the lowest quartile are noteworthy for their paltriness. Between ages 18 and 50, divorced mothers' income for the lowest quartile only increases about $10,000, from around $15,000 to $25,000 (Figure 4.10). The income gains for never-married mothers at the lower quartile are even smaller, from around $9,000 to $15,000 (Figure 4.11).

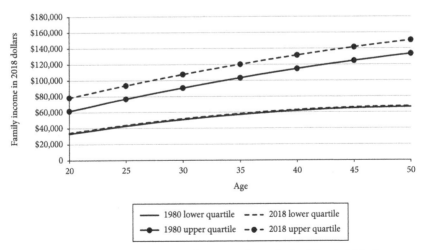

Figure 4.9. Income by Age, Year, and Income Quartile for Married Mothers.
Notes: N = 5,147 (1980) 3,955 (2018) per quartile. Results are weighted.
Source: CPS 1980–2018.

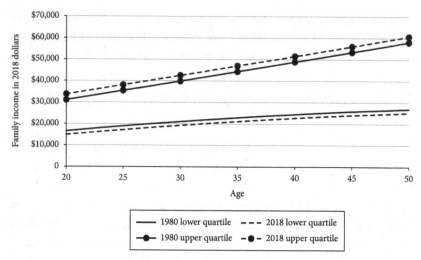

Figure 4.10. Income by Age, Year, and Income Quartile for Divorced Mothers.
Notes: N = 531 (1980) 440 (2018) per quartile. Results are weighted.
Source: CPS 1980–2018.

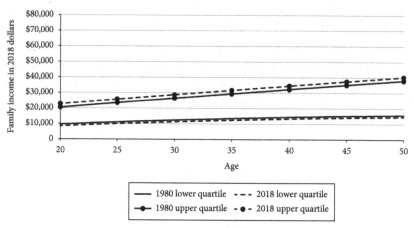

Figure 4.11. Income by Age, Year, and Income Quartile for Never-Married Mothers.
Notes: N = 187 (1980) 700 (2018) per quartile. Results are weighted.
Source: CPS 1980–2018.

The story for married mothers, shown in Figure 4.9, is a little more complex. As we saw for single mothers, upper-quartile married mothers have fared much better than their contemporaries in the lower income quartile. Women in the upper income quartile are also the only mothers depicted in Figures 4.9–4.11 to enjoy substantially higher income growth in 2018 than in 1980: from ages 18 to 50, the upper quartile premium is about $20,000. What

FROM MOYNIHAN TO PIKETTY   95

is also different for these women is that even at the lower quartile married mothers do much better as they get older, with their incomes approximately doubling, from about $33,000 to $66,000.

Taken together, Figures 4.9–4.11 demonstrate multiple layers of inequality, based on age, marital status, position in the income distribution, and change over historical period. Unsurprisingly, married women in the upper income quartile, the privileged population called the "dream hoarders" by Brookings Institute scholar Richard Reeves, are the only population who've benefited from the changing economic currents since 1980.[26] In contrast, single mothers are seeing smaller gains over time and age. This is especially the case for never-married mothers in the lowest quartile, who barely experience any income gains as they age. Their paltry returns imply a weak attachment to the labor force, and run counter to the received wisdom about working your way up the income ladder.

These findings should be tempered by the acknowledgement of the multiple ways that sample selection is driving the results. Fifty-year-old mothers represent women who had children late, which as we've shown in Figures 2.2–2.4 is most common for married mothers. Conversely, motherhood at age 20 is uncommon for all save never-married mothers (Figure 2.2) and has only become less common in recent decades. Moreover, marriage and divorce now both reflect social class distinctions. That wasn't the case in 1980. In short, the dimensions of age-related income growth by position in the income distribution are informed by many cross-cutting sociological dynamics.

Children

The previous chapter showed that youthful childbirth is a strong correlate of income: irrespective of family structure, women who first gave birth as teenagers had substantially lower incomes than did would-be mothers who waited. Subsequent analysis established that the relationship between birth timing and income can be explained by other differences between respondents, notably work and age. Does this still hold true when looking at income differences across quartiles? It's easy to imagine that the benefits of delayed childbirth are more consequential for women who've had greater success in converting their human capital into income.

The short answer to this question is no: there aren't substantial differences when looking across income quartiles. Figures 4.12 and 4.13 show predicted

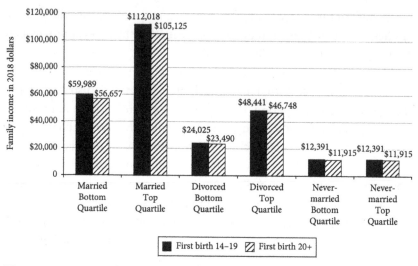

Figure 4.12. Income by Teenage Birth, Marital Structure, and Income Quartile, 1980.

Notes: N = 20,589 (married 1980) 15,820 (married 2018) 2,125 (divorced 1980) 1,759 (divorced 2018) 749 (never married 1980) 2,798 (never married 2018). Results are weighted.
Source: CPS 1980–2018.

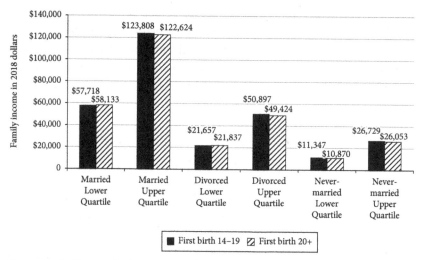

Figure 4.13. Income by Teenage Birth, Marital Structure, and Income Quartile, 2018.

Notes: N = 20,589 (married 1980) 15,820 (married 2018) 2,125 (divorced 1980) 1,759 (divorced 2018) 749 (never married 1980) 2,798 (never married 2018). Results are weighted.
Source: CPS 1980–2018.

income by quartile and marital status in 1980 and 2018 for women who first gave birth as teenagers. Teen births are predictably more consequential for the top 25% of incomes, but not in the expected direction. In 1980,

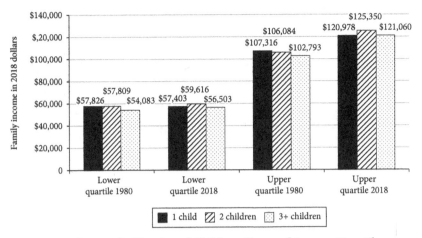

Figure 4.14. Income by Number of Children, Year, and Income Quartile, Married Mothers.

Notes: N = 20,589 (1980) 15,820 (2018). Results are weighted.
Source: CPS 1980–2018.

upper-quartile married mothers who gave birth as teens have somewhat higher income than those who didn't, almost $7,000. By 2018, this had shrunk to just over $1,000.

Contrary to public perceptions, the economic impact of having first given birth as a teenager is negative for only two groups, divorced women and married women in the bottom income quartile in 2018. However, the differences are trivial. After adjusting for other differences between these women, the effects of a teenaged birth largely disappear.

Family size is another way that children affect income. Figure 4.14, which displays average predicted family income across both survey year and income quartiles, shows married women with three or more children have lower family incomes than do those with fewer kids. The exception is at the upper income quartile in 2018, where mothers of only children have the lowest incomes. But the income differences here are again small, only on the order of $2,000–$5,000.

At the lower income quartile for divorced mothers, we would expect that multiple children would increasingly attenuate income; this sector of the economy has been largely immune to wage growth. Figure 4.15 indicates that the income penalty associated with multiple children has indeed increased over time for divorced mothers. In 1980, those with three children had the highest income, whereas by 2018 those with two children experienced slightly higher incomes than other divorced mothers. Note also that the child support payments most divorcées now receive do not offset the lower wages

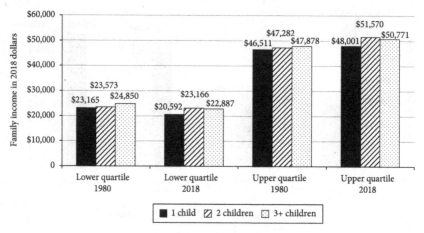

Figure 4.15. Income by Number of Children, Year, and Income Quartile, Divorced Mothers.

Notes: N = 2,125 (1980) 1,759 (2018). Results are weighted.
Source: CPS 1980–2018.

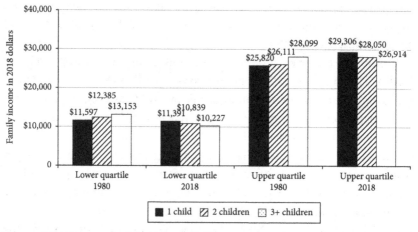

Figure 4.16. Income by Number of Children, Year, and Income Quartile, Never-Married Mothers.

Notes: N = 749 (1980) 2,798 (2018). Results are weighted.
Source: CPS 1980–2018.

for women with three or more children.[27] All of this aside, the main story is that the differences by family size remain small, particularly in 2018.

In 1980, most never-married mothers made ends meet with public assistance, not work. As a result, children were an economic asset: more kids meant more welfare income (see Chapter 3). As Figure 4.16 shows, this held true even in the upper income quartile. Never-married mothers used to make so little money that even the upper income quartile derived the balance of their incomes from public assistance. By 2018, state transfers had declined drastically and the majority of never-married mothers were working, so multiple children had become an economic liability. This was particularly the case in the upper quartile. At this point in the income distribution, never-married mothers are now likely to have good jobs that may be more affected by childcare responsibilities than are the jobs that produce lower quartile incomes. These differences remain small, but are proportionately larger given the lower overall family incomes for this group of mothers.

Multiple children makes it more difficult for mothers to work. So too does having children under six: mothers with kids who are not yet school-aged must pay for childcare, arrange for help from friends or relatives, or stay home to do it themselves. As Figures 4.17, 4.18, and 4.19 show, for single mothers, having any children under six is associated with somewhat lower incomes. The differences between predicted incomes are similar in size for both divorced and never-married mothers, although proportionately the effect is larger for never-married mothers given their lower overall incomes. There is no cost of having a young child for married women: those with a child under six have slightly higher predicted

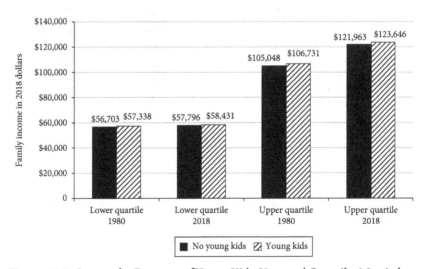

Figure 4.17. Income by Presence of Young Kids, Year, and Quartile, Married Mothers.

Notes: N = 20,589 (1980) 15,820 (2018). Results are weighted.
Source: CPS 1980–2018.

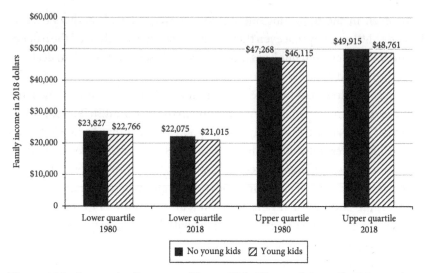

Figure 4.18. Income by Presence of Young Kids, Year, and Quartile, Divorced Mothers.

Notes: N = 2,125 (1980) 1,759 (2018). Results are weighted.
Source: CPS 1980–2018.

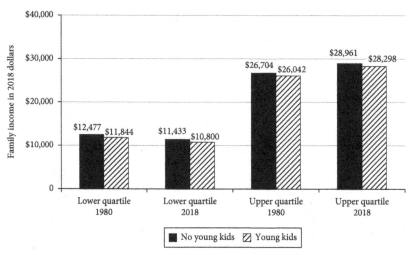

Figure 4.19. Income by Presence of Young Kids, Year, and Income Quartile, Never-Married Mothers.

Notes: N = 749 (1980) 2,798 (2018). Results are weighted.
Source: CPS 1980–2018.

incomes. In addition, the impact of a young child does not change noticeably over the time period of our study. Finally, for all mothers the cost of a child under six is much higher at the higher income quartiles. Irrespective of family structure, most well-off mothers in contemporary

America earn a living by working, and young children make working more difficult. Compared to other factors, however, the overall impact from any differences related to children are small.

Race and Ethnicity

In Chapter 3, we observed that race and ethnicity mattered most to inequality between married mothers. White, African American, Latina, and other-category mothers had significantly different incomes when married, but negligible differences when divorced or, especially, never-married. We now turn to the question of whether these differences hold for both the top and the bottom of the income distribution. We speculated that race should make more of a difference at the top than the bottom. Here's why: married mothers are most likely to be well off, and race has the most substantial effects on their incomes. Divorced and never-married mothers are less well off, and race should make less difference for them. By extension, race shouldn't matter much at the bottom of the income distribution, either.

This idea isn't entirely supported by the data. Holding other factors constant, race has minimal effects on income for mothers who have never been married at both the bottom (Figure 4.20) and the top (Figure 4.21) of the income distribution. Similarly, the effects of race on divorcées' incomes are

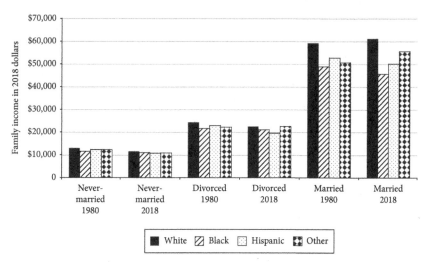

Figure 4.20. Income by Marital Structure, Race, and Year, Lower Income Quartile.
Notes: N = 20,589 (married 1980) 15,820 (married 2018) 2,125 (divorced 1980) 1,759 (divorced 2018) 749 (never married 1980) 2,798 (never married 2018). Results are weighted.
Source: CPS 1980–2018.

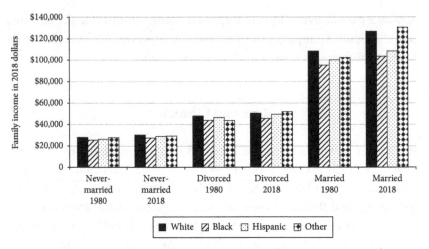

Figure 4.21. Income by Marital Structure, Race, and Year, Upper Quartile.
Notes: N = 20,589 (married 1980) 15,820 (married 2018) 2,125 (divorced 1980) 1,759 (divorced 2018) 749 (never married 1980) 2,798 (never married 2018). Results are weighted.
Source: CPS 1980–2018.

modest at best, with almost no change over time. There's simply little story to tell for unmarried mothers here beyond family structure.

That's not the case for married mothers. In 1980, married White women had the highest incomes in both the lower and the upper quartile. By 2018, mothers in the other category—neither White, African American, nor Hispanic—had moved ahead. This shift reflects the rise of Asian Americans as a high-earning group in contemporary America.[28] As shown in Figure 4.20 (see also Figure 3.16a), there are substantial differences between Whites, African Americans, Latinas and others, differences that have only grown larger in the past 40 years. In 1980, White married mothers in the lower quartile had incomes about $10,000 higher than did Black mothers or mothers in the other category, and about $6,500 higher than their Latina peers. By 2018, married African American and Latina mothers in the lower quartile had slightly lower incomes than in 1980, while White and other married mothers in the same quartile had slightly higher incomes. Consequently, the racial income gap for married mothers in the lower income quartile has increased since 1980.

The story for married mothers in the upper quartile is broadly similar, although none saw their predicted income decline. The disparities are also, understandably, much larger. In 1980, White married upper quartile mothers out-earned their African American peers by $13,000. By 2018, the gap was $23,000. The racial disparity is similar for Whites and Latinas, expanding from $8,000 to $18,000. In 2018, upper-quartile mothers in the other category pulled in about $4,000 a year *more* than their White contemporaries. These findings further demonstrate the usefulness of looking at the intersection of family structure and race for understanding income inequality in the United States.

Living Arrangements

Chapter 3 revealed substantial differences between divorced and never-married mothers in the effects of living arrangements on income. Nonmarital cohabitation substantially reduces incomes for divorced mothers but has little effect on incomes for their peers who have never been married. The story gets more complicated when we consider the changing effects of nonmarital cohabitation across the income distribution. Figure 4.22 shows zero-order effects of cohabitation on income. Consistent with the Chapter 3 results, cohabitation lowers income more for divorced mothers than their never-married contemporaries. When we turn from medians to income

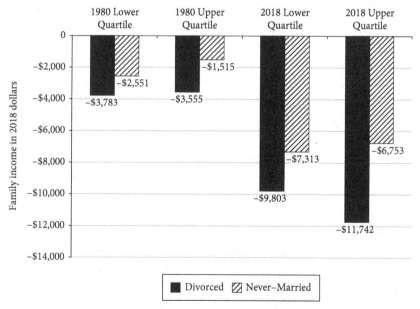

Figure 4.22. Zero-Order Income Penalties for Cohabitation.

Notes: N = 2,125 (divorced 1980) 1,759 (divorced 2018) 749 (never married 1980) 2,798 (never married 2018). Results are weighted.
Source: CPS 1980–2018.

104 THANKS FOR NOTHING

quartiles, the results reveal the growth in inequality related to cohabitation. Back in 1980, the effect of cohabitation on income was almost the same in the lower and upper quartiles. This result stands out both in the context of this book and in thinking about inequality in the U.S. more generally—since when is just about *anything* the same for the bottom and the top of the income distribution? To be sure, there was less income inequality 40 years ago, but that still can't account for the minimal difference in between quartiles in the (negative) economic effect of a cohabiting partner.

Since 1980, the economic penalty associated with cohabitation has increased. By 2018, the biggest contrast is for divorcées in the top quartile, where cohabiting single mothers were making thousands of dollars a year less than women who were not living with a partner out of wedlock. This suggests that there could be a growing reliance on a cohabiting partner's wages over time. Alternately, it could reflect the changing population of mothers who opt for cohabitation. For instance, cohabiters with less education are decreasingly likely to get married, so the population of cohabiting adults disproportionately represents less educated parents.[29] For never-married mothers there are smaller (and declining) income penalties over time, and curiously little difference between the upper and lower quartiles. In both 1980 and 2018, the difference between quartiles was less than $1,000. Finally, it's noteworthy that the differences between quartiles are relatively small, especially compared to the inter-quartile differences described elsewhere in this chapter. At the bottom end of the distribution, cohabitation produces a $2,000 to $4,000 income shortfall; at the top of the distribution, the corresponding range is $7,000 to $12,000. None of these differences are irrelevant for struggling mothers, yet they make it abundantly clear that cohabitation does not have the ability to lift mothers into the middle class.

Figure 4.23 shows the relationship between cohabitation and income after controlling for various social and demographic differences between respondents. The relationship between cohabitation and income is to a great extent explained by differences between mothers. The economic penalties associated with cohabitation are about half the size in Figure 4.23 as they are in Figure 4.22. The exception to this pattern is upper quartile never-married mothers in 2018. For these women, adjusting for differences in education, employment, and other characteristics has a negligible effect of about $600 on the relationship between cohabitation and income ($6,753 in Figure 4.22, $6,122 in Figure 4.23). Upper quartile women still reduce their earnings

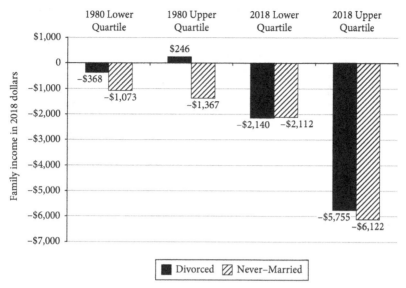

Figure 4.23. Regression Based Income Differences for Cohabitation.
Notes: N = 2,125 (divorced 1980) 1,759 (divorced 2018) 749 (never married 1980) 2,798 (never married 2018). Results are weighted.
Source: CPS 1980–2018.

when living with a partner, but this cannot be explained simply because of their relationship to the labor market.

Figure 4.23 also shows that controlling for differences between respondents makes divorced and never-married mothers more alike in their financial relationship to cohabitation. Absent controls, cohabitation was consistently more consequential for divorced mothers: cohabitation reduced their incomes to a greater extent than it did for never-married mothers. With controls in place, the economic costs of cohabitation are fairly similar for divorced and never-married mothers.

Finally, this analysis shows the increasing cost of cohabitation for divorcées. As shown in Chapter 3, cohabiting divorcées always have lower incomes than their counterparts who live alone. As shown in Figures 4.22 and 4.23, this is even more true in 2018 as it was in 1980. Since more divorced women are living with partners out of wedlock by 2018, this has greatly increased the overall levels of inequality related to cohabitation for these mothers. What's more, a cohabitation-based divide has grown within the income distribution. In 1980, the relationship between cohabitation and

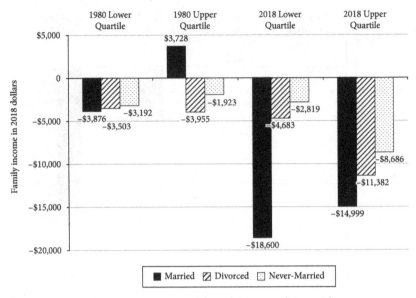

Figure 4.24. Zero-Order Income Penalties for Parental Coresidence.
Notes: N = 20,589 (married 1980) 15,820 (married 2018) 2,125 (divorced 1980) 1,759 (divorced 2018) 749 (never married 1980) 2,798 (never married 2018). Results are weighted.
Source: CPS 1980–2018.

income was fairly similar between the lower and the upper income quartiles. By 2018, cohabitation was far more consequential at the upper quartile.

A second form of economic dependence is living with one's parents. Chapter 2 showed that far fewer never-married mothers are now living with their own parents than had been the case in years gone by. Chapter 3 indicated that the economic consequences of parental co-residence are consistently negative: living with a parent reduces a single mothers' independent income. Figure 4.24 shows that the consequences of living with one's parents have changed over time. For both the bottom and top income quartile the effect of moving back home (or never leaving) in 1980 was limited to a few thousand dollars, for married, divorced, and never-married mothers alike. At the lower income quartile in 1980, there were minimal differences related to family structure. At the upper quartile, married mothers distinguished themselves by having uniquely higher incomes when they lived with parents.[30] Presumably for these mothers, parental co-residence provided childcare that allowed for more remunerative labor force participation. Still, the lack of major differences between quartiles is surprising. Mothers at the top of the income distribution should presumably have parents who can provide greater economic assistance.

All this had changed by 2018. Parental co-residence now produced substantially lower incomes for most mothers, but with a wide range of effects across family structures. Married mothers in the lower quartile were the biggest economic losers, with their incomes dropping over $18,000 when they lived with their parents. In contrast, the economics of parental co-residence for lower quartile single mothers in 2018 weren't that much different than they were back in 1980. Although the same small number of married mothers lived with their parents in 1980 and in 2018 (see Figure 2.16), it has clearly become a bigger deal in recent years, likely a last resort in hard times. For the upper income quartile, a return to the nest for married women produced a mildly smaller but still substantial income decline of $15,000. The upper quartile income penalty for moving back home also increased noticeably for divorced and never-married mothers.

Figure 4.25 shows the income penalties for parental co-residence after controlling for a host of measured differences between mothers. This has little overall effect: these results don't differ substantially from the zero-order results shown in Figure 4.24. In short, the economic consequences of living with one's own parents don't depend on employment status, education, or other basic differences between respondents.

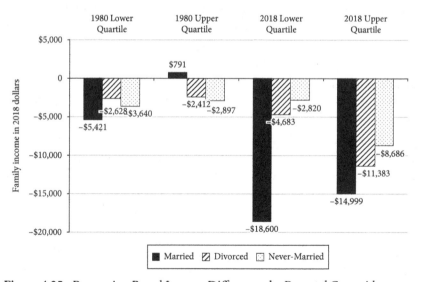

Figure 4.25. Regression Based Income Differences by Parental Co-residence.
Notes: N = 20,589 (married 1980) 15,820 (married 2018) 2,125 (divorced 1980) 1,759 (divorced 2018) 749 (never married 1980) 2,798 (never married 2018). Results are weighted.
Source: CPS 1980–2018.

The general trend here is a bit surprising. Living with parents could theoretically provide for greater ability to retain a job, and thus earn more money. Instead, it increasingly signifies a substantial drop in family income, especially for married mothers. It's tempting to think of the lower incomes for single mothers as indirect evidence of the fact that women who give birth out of wedlock may themselves be products of unstable, impoverished families.[31] However, married mothers have even lower incomes after moving back home. The smaller effects for single mothers, especially in the lowest quartiles, is partially reflective of the lower incomes for these households in general. Married households in both quartiles have more to lose; alternately, perhaps things have become really bad before married mothers will move into their parent's home. Either way, these findings suggest that moving in with parents is a strategy of removing oneself from paid employment, and increased reliance on parental support.

Conclusion

We started this chapter by documenting that while inequality for all mothers has increased over time, differences in inequality across family structure have decreased. The analysis in the rest of the chapter shows that the reasons behind these trends in inequality are complex, and differ by marital status. For married mothers, a subset of families is lifting up the income distribution and thus increasing overall inequality. For single mothers, inequality is driven by stability at the lower end of the income distribution for divorced mothers and declines for never-married mothers at the bottom of the distribution.

We also explored the reasons for these shifts. We found that overall education and employment greatly impact inequality. Increasingly, having a college education and working full-time have become requirements for attaining higher family income across family types. In contrast, family timing and size have little role in explaining inequality. Other respondent attributes depict a more complicated relationships to inequality. Age can matter, but primarily for respondents in the highest income quartile. Cohabitation has small, mostly negative, effects across family type and year, while living with parents has consistent and substantial implications on family income, most especially for married respondents. Finally, we found that respondent race was associated with the greatest differences in income for only married mothers. It's therefore necessary to account for the interaction of race and marital status in accounting for their impact on growing inequality in the United States.

5

Thirty-Nine Years in the Lives of Mothers

As the previous chapters have made clear, incomes grew steadily for all families in the decades prior to the Great Recession, but the strongest gains belonged to married parents. Having two incomes rather than one goes a long way towards explaining prosperity. Another part of this story is the human capital enjoyed by married mothers. While all mothers have more education and job experience than they used to, Chapter 2 shows that married mothers continue to enjoy a strong advantage in labor market qualifications. As established in Chapters 3 and 4, these resources translate into higher incomes, but not equally. Married and divorced mothers reap relatively similar levels of returns to their demographic and social characteristics, while never-married mothers fare far worse.

The differences by family structure are substantial. Women who give birth out of wedlock suffer from pervasive disadvantage that cannot be explained by their basic social and demographic attributes.[1] They work less. When they do work, they make less money. A high school or college education provides lower economic returns than it does for married or divorced mothers. Never-married mothers' incomes increase more slowly with age. Even the impact of children, although modest for all mothers, is less strongly related to income than it is for married and divorced mothers.

Previous chapters are based on the Current Population Survey (CPS), which offers a series of snapshots of motherhood in America. These data show how motherhood is changing as new generations of women become parents. Since the CPS interviews new respondents with every survey cycle, it cannot tell us about the long-term effects of divorce and out-of-wedlock birth on individual women's incomes. In other words, the CPS does not allow us to determine whether specific individual mothers have bettered themselves economically, or instead, if different kinds of women are now becoming single mothers.

Chapters 5 and 6 seek to answer these questions using data from the National Longitudinal Survey of Youth's (NLSY) 1979 cohort. The NLSY

Thanks for Nothing. Nicholas H. Wolfinger and Matthew McKeever, Oxford University Press.
© Oxford University Press 2024. DOI: 10.1093/oso/9780199324323.003.0005

110 THANKS FOR NOTHING

allows us to follow a sample of young women as they became mothers, and thereafter into middle age. By tracking women over time—and, notably, approximately over the same years as the CPS participants we looked at in earlier chapters—we can learn whether differences between married, divorced, and never-married mothers persist as these women move from young adulthood into their 30s and 40s. We also hope to learn more about why never-married mothers receive poor returns to their human capital. The NLSY allows us to track women before they become mothers, so we can explore the possibility that single mothers suffer disadvantages throughout their lives.

A brief reminder about the NLSY sample: our analysis is based on the slightly over 4,000 mothers or future mothers between the ages of 14 and 22 initially interviewed in 1979. They were polled annually through 1994 and biennially thereafter. The last year of data analyzed here was collected in 2018. At that point, 57% of the original sample was still participating in the survey.

We start off by looking at income differences among the mothers in our sample, then explore issues related to family formation and dissolution, such as the age at which women first became mothers. We then examine characteristics of the parents of mothers, to see if there are systematic differences in the types of families in which married and single mothers were raised. Finally, we examine the characteristics of these women themselves, including education, other measures of cultural capital, and living arrangements.

The Poverty of Single Motherhood Is Persistent

To examine changes over time, we classify mothers as married, divorced, or never-married in each year of NLSY data available to us. We also rely on information collected in the inaugural 1979 survey to ascertain whether women married or became mothers in earlier years.[2] We employ two different measures of family structure: current marital status and one-time marital status. Current status refers to the marital status of mothers in any particular year. This allows us to examine the characteristics of, say, all mothers in the data set who are married in 1990. One-time status lets us identify women who have ever been married, divorced, or never-married mothers, even if their marital status subsequently changes. Unless otherwise noted, having ever been a never-married mother supersedes married and divorced motherhood. In other words, a woman who gives birth out of wedlock before marrying is identified as a never-married mother. She is still characterized as a never-married mother even if she eventually gets divorced. Similarly, a woman who marries, has children, and then dissolves her marriage is treated as a divorced mother. Chapter 6 explores these transitions at greater length.

We start by looking at income. Figures 5.1a and 5.1b contrast median family incomes in 2018 dollars both by current family structure (Figure 5.1a) and according to whether women have ever been married, divorced, or never-married mothers (Figure 5.1b).[3] As would be expected, married mothers have by far the highest incomes, followed by divorced and then never-married mothers. This is true across all survey years. The Great Recession aside, all mothers make more money as they get older, but the age gradient is much steeper for married mothers than for their divorced and never-married contemporaries. Married mothers, who started out with median family incomes of around $20,000 in 1979, experienced nearly continuous growth and they broke six figures in 2010. It is generally assumed that job experience and tenure will produce higher incomes as people move from

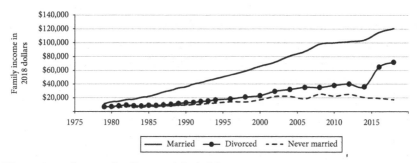

Figure 5.1a. Income by Current Marital Status.

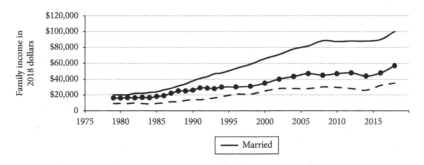

Figure 5.1b. Income by One-Time Marital Status.

Notes: Average annuals Ns = 1,420 (married) 810 (divorced) 869 (never married). Results are weighted.
Source: NLSY 1979–2018.

112   THANKS FOR NOTHING

young adulthood into middle age, but our results show that this assumption really only holds for married mothers.

Divorced mothers had incomes somewhat lower than married mothers in 1979, but by 2010 they were only making around $38,000. Subsequent large income gains may be the product of more selective samples. The youngest NLSY mothers in 2010 are 45 years old, and mostly have older offspring at home—who are less likely to make it difficult for their mothers to work.

Never-married mothers also experienced income gains in the early 2000s, nearly catching up to divorced mothers, but these evaporated with the Great Recession. Over the 40 years of NLSY data, these mothers have achieved only modest income growth. The story begins early on, given the low incomes in the early years of the NLSY for women classified as never-married mothers.

Looking at current marital status only tells part of the story, given the conditions under which women enter and exit motherhood. Few women become married or divorced mothers as teenagers. In addition, the women who remain mothers in the most recent survey waves aren't typical either: they had children later in life. For some women, especially married mothers, this reflects delaying childbearing until out of school and ensconced in careers. And given that most women who have children out of wedlock do so while relatively young means that never-married mothers in 2018 are highly atypical.

For these reasons, we turn to the relationship between one-time marital status and income shown in Figure 5.1b. For both divorced and never-married mothers, the similarities between current family structure and ever having experienced single motherhood are striking. Incomes are consistently lower for women who are currently single mothers (Figure 5.1a), which accords with the results presented in previous chapters, but these data show only slightly higher incomes, gains of about ten or fifteen thousand dollars higher, *if they have ever been divorced or never-married mothers* (Figure 5.1b). Having been a single mother has lasting effects on a woman's income as she moves from adolescence and young adulthood into middle age. There is no comparable disparity for married mothers, as usually the only way they can stop being married mothers—without becoming divorced mothers—is by emptying the nest. This is what ultimately explains the higher income peak for married mothers in Figure 5.1a ($120,000) compared to Figure 5.1b ($100,000). Women who are still married mothers in 2018 are a selective group who had their children later in life.

It's also worth looking at the extent to which lifetime income differences between married, divorced, and never-married mothers persist at different parts of the income distribution. Due to its smaller sample size, the National Longitudinal Survey of Youth is less useful here than the CPS. Still, the NLSY sample is large enough to contrast married, divorced, and never-married mothers at the lower (Figure 5.2a) and upper (Figure 5.2b) quartiles. Generally speaking, this figure looks quite similar to Figure 5.1b. In both panels married mothers have far higher incomes than divorced or never-married mothers. Similarly, these income disparities grow as women age out of adolescence and young adulthood.

Two trends in Figures 5.2a and 5.2b are worth noting. The first concerns the relative advantage of married motherhood for women in the lower income quartile. Although the absolute difference in income between married and divorced mothers is similar in the upper and lower quartiles, the

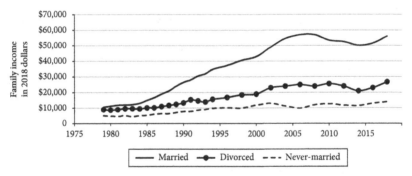

Figure 5.2a. Lower Quartile Income by One-Time Marital Structure.
Notes: Average annual Ns = 1,420 (married) 810 (divorced) 869 (never married). Results are weighted.
Source: NLSY 1979–2018.

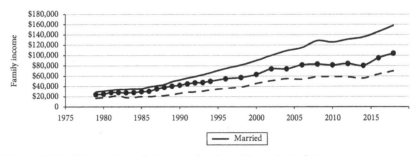

Figure 5.2b. Upper Quartile Income by One-Time Marital Structure.
Notes: Average annual Ns = 1,420 (married) 810 (divorced) 869 (never married). Results are weighted.
Source: NLSY 1979–2018.

114 THANKS FOR NOTHING

difference represents a much larger proportional income boost for lower quartile married mothers. Marriage, therefore, produces a bigger income premium among less well-off women; higher up in the income distribution, everyone is a little more alike.

The second noteworthy pattern in Figures 5.2a and b concerns the faltering finances of married mothers in the lower quartile. Their incomes peaked in 2005 and have since declined, experiencing more precipitous losses than any of the other mothers in the sample. Divorced and never-married mothers didn't experience big losses in the wake of the Great Recession. Nor did the better-off mothers in the upper income quartile. There is some recovery post-recession for lower quartile married mothers, and perhaps more years of data collection would produce a return to their original income trajectory. Finally, we note the substantial difference in how lower and upper quartile families experienced the Great Recession.

Why do one-time single mothers remain comparably impoverished? This chapter overviews the individual and family characteristics associated with marital status over the life course. Perhaps most noteworthy is the lack of human capital for single mothers. Even as they get older and sometimes marry or remarry, single mothers have less education, and in the case of never-married mothers, less job experience. These women also come from less advantaged families. Furthermore, unmarried mothers suffer from lasting disadvantages paradoxically related to marriage. Women who give birth out of wedlock have disproportionately low rates of marriage and, if they do marry, high rates of divorce.[4] While remarriage is one way for single mothers to lift their incomes, divorce rates are notoriously higher for second marriages.[5] Thus, even if single mothers get married, they are less likely to stay married. Moreover, unmarried mothers are likely to remain unmarried mothers as they get older. Past a certain point, the odds of marriage for all women, single mothers included, only decline.[6]

A final point to consider here involves sample selection: is there a similar reason for why women both become single mothers and earn less money? If so, these women would have less money even had they not become mothers. There is substantial research that shows these outcomes are indeed linked. Marriage is now most likely among women with good incomes and accumulated wealth.[7] However, the extent to which this relationship applies to single mothers is less clear. For example, previous studies have offered conflicting results on the impact of education on the likelihood that never-married mothers subsequently get married, with some finding that it lowers the likelihood for marriage, while others find no impact.[8] Neither education nor employment appear to have any impact on remarriage rates for White divorcées, although they do increase remarriage likelihood for Blacks.[9] (Though African American single mothers in general have lower marriage rates.[10]) As we will see in this chapter, unwed mothers have other characteristics that keep them both unmarried and cash-strapped over the long haul. Chapter 6 explores this sample selection issue in greater detail.

Starting and Ending Motherhood

By following a single cohort for 40 years, the NLSY provides an excellent opportunity for observing when in their lives women become married or single mothers, how long they remain married or single, and how this relates to income. It should be stressed at the outset that married motherhood remains the most common family status for these mothers. As Figure 5.3 indicates, over two-thirds of the women in the sample will become married mothers over the years of our study. In contrast, slightly less than one in four will experience either divorced or never-married motherhood (and only 8% will

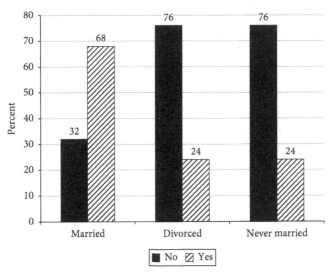

Figure 5.3. Overall Marital Structure Prevalence Rates.
Notes: N = 6,242. Results are weighted.
Source: NLSY 1979–2018.

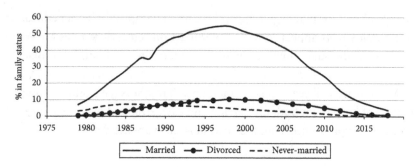

Figure 5.4. Marital Status over Time.
Notes: Annual N = 4,593. Results are weighted.
Source: NLSY 1979–2018.

experience both types of single motherhood). Across their lives, married motherhood remains the norm for most women in the U.S., although a noteworthy minority will experience some form of single motherhood. It is also worth noting that divorced and never-married motherhood, the two forms of single motherhood examined in this book, are almost equally likely among the NLSY women. This is more evidence that it doesn't make sense to speak of either divorced or never-married mothers as representative of single mothers as a whole. Single mothers comprise approximately equal numbers of two very different populations; the CPS data presented in Chapter 2 show that over time never-married mothers compose more of the population of single mothers, but by no means are the overwhelming majority.

The lifetime prevalence figures offered by Figure 5.3 conceal substantial annual differences in family structure. Figure 5.4 shows the percentage of women who are married, divorced, or never-married mothers in each survey year. As expected, the number of married mothers annually outstrips the figures for divorced and never-married motherhood. The differences are smaller at the beginning of the survey, when fewer women had formed families. By the mid-1990s the differences are quite large, at which point roughly half of all mothers are married.

Thereafter, married motherhood becomes less common as children start to reach adulthood and fertility rates slow down. At this point, rates of divorced motherhood continue to increase as more married couples call it quits. Only in the last 10 years of the survey do rates of divorced motherhood decline. By this time, the majority of marriages likely to end in divorce will have already done so; it should be kept in mind that divorce rates decline steadily after a few years of marriage.[11] By the end of

Figure 5.5. Age of Entry onto Married, Divorced, and Never-Married Motherhood.

the sample, respondents are in their late 40s or mid-50s and have mostly become empty nesters.

Never-married motherhood peaks around 1985, much earlier than married motherhood. This can be explained by the fact that unwed motherhood usually starts much earlier in life. This is apparent in Figure 5.5, which shows the distribution of ages at which women become married, divorced, or never-married mothers. The most common time women become never-married mothers is in their late teens, a result that aligns with both the findings presented in Chapter 2 and earlier research.[12] Married and divorced motherhood peak a little later, when the NLSY women are in their mid-20s. Divorced mothers tend to be a bit older—primarily because they first have to be married before they get divorced. Entrance into motherhood continues, particularly for married women, into the mid-30s and even the early 40s. By this time almost no women give birth out of wedlock.

We should keep in mind that family composition can change in two primary ways. (Our estimates of leaving motherhood also reflect less common developments, such as loss of custody or the death of a child or a spouse.)[13] First, women exit motherhood when all children at home turn 18. This removes the legal obligation for material support, and it's for this reason we only study mothers living with their minor children. Second, women's marital status may change: married mothers divorce, or unmarried mothers acquire spouses. Any of these transitions has profound consequences for income. Mothers who empty the nest no longer have to support their children,

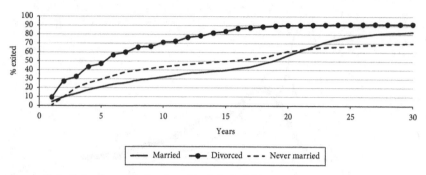

Figure 5.6. Exits from Motherhood by Marital Status.
Notes: N = 4,180 (married) 1,483 (divorced) 1,483 (never married). Results are weighted.
Source: NLSY 1979–2018.

while single mothers who marry can generally count on substantially larger incomes.[14] Conversely, married mothers who divorce must suddenly make do with far less money.[15] For these reasons, we view any change in family status as noteworthy.

Over the 40 years of NLSY data presented here, the vast majority of all respondents we follow exited motherhood. This is shown in Figure 5.6.[16] Married motherhood shows the slowest exit rate at first, but with increasing rates after around 20 years. Of course this includes exits from both divorce and emptying the nest. The former predominate at first, given that the exit rate is highest within a few years after the start of married motherhood. This corresponds to the fact that divorce rates are highest in the first few years of marriage.[17] Thirty-one percent of women identified as married mothers at some point during the NLSY are subsequently classified as divorced mothers.[18] By the end of the time series, there are few married mothers left in the data. Most have emptied the nest; the remainder dissolved their marriage.

Overall, the lowest exit rate is for never-married mothers. Fewer than 80% of these women will exit never-married motherhood over the course of our 39 years of NLSY data. Initially, their exit rate is higher than that for married mothers, although within a few years their exit rate declines steadily. This is further shown in Figure 5.7, which displays marriage/remarriage rates for single mothers. Twenty percent of never-married mothers will marry within two years of a nonmarital birth. Indeed, marriage (or remarriage, for divorced mothers) is most likely to occur within a couple of years after single motherhood starts. Sixty-six percent of never-married mothers in our NLSY data will at some point be classified as married mothers.

This profusion of early exits from single motherhood represents women who get married soon after a nonmarital birth, perhaps before the "magic

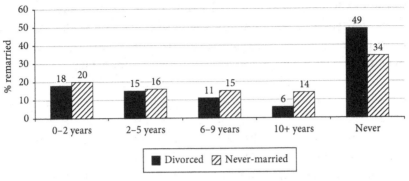

Figure 5.7. (Re)marriage Timing for Single Mothers.
Notes: N = 1,460 (divorced) 1,482 (never married). Results are weighted.
Source: NLSY 1979–2018.

moment" of childbirth gives way to the realities of childrearing.[19] Yet even at this point marriage rates for never-married mothers are surprisingly low. In research based on the Fragile Families and Child Wellbeing Study, Wolfinger and W. Bradford Wilcox found that less than 15% of never-married mothers married the father of her child within one year of a nonmarital birth.[20] Sociologist Daniel Lichter and his colleagues offer a similar finding drawing on a different data set.[21]

Divorced mothers are the most likely to experience a family structure change, either upon remarriage or having their children turn eighteen. The life table estimates shown in Figure 5.6 indicate that all divorced mothers will at some point stop being divorced mothers during the 30 years of data considered. Per Figure 5.7, about half will remarry, a somewhat lower estimate than was calculated based on roughly contemporaneous data from National Survey of Families and Households.[22] For both divorced and never-married mothers, the odds of remarriage decline with years spent in single motherhood.

Based on these results, how can movement into and out of married, divorced, and never-married motherhood be characterized? First, most women become mothers in their 20s. Never-married mothers differ substantially from their ever-married counterparts with respect to family formation. The typical never-married mother in the NLSY is in her late teens when she first gives birth. Ever-married motherhood generally begins a few years later. We expect this difference to have profound implications for income given the relationship between birth timing, education, and employment. Second, most unwed mothers will eventually marry (or remarry, in the case of divorced women). Single motherhood, and its immediate consequences for income, generally does not last forever. Third, transitions from single to married motherhood are most likely to occur with a few years of becoming a single mother. Thereafter the likelihood of marriage declines. Transitions to single motherhood often carry the impetus to start a new relationship. Married mothers may divorce their spouses to start new relationships (indeed, some may already have a potential replacement in mind).[23] Unwed parents may want to raise their child within wedlock, or may simply marry in response to the magic moment of new parenthood. Finally, almost all women transition out of motherhood over the years of our study. The exception is never-married mothers, about one-fifth of whom remain unmarried with minor children at home thirty years after first becoming mothers.

Early Advantages and Disadvantages

Despite the mythology of America as a land where people create their own destiny, social science has repeatedly demonstrated the role of family origins in determining how far one gets in life.[24] With this in mind, there are various reasons to believe that married mothers enjoy myriad advantages even before they become mothers. Sociologists Peter Blau and Otis Dudley Duncan showed decades ago that educational attainment is correlated across generations.[25] In turn, education is positively correlated with marriage, while negatively correlated with divorce and nonmarital fertility.[26] Family structure is also inherited. People from divorced families themselves have higher divorce rates.[27] Women born out of wedlock are disproportionately likely to become unwed mothers.[28] Parental divorce increases nonmarital fertility, while unmarried parentage increases the chances of someday ending one's own marriage.[29] Furthermore, people from nonintact families do not go as far in school,[30] and they make less money as adults.[31] All of these trends have adverse implications for the economic prospects of divorced and never-married mothers.

Another factor that affects children's prospects is whether their parents were employed. Most obviously, employment produces a more prosperous upbringing. An employed parent also serves as a role model, instilling in children the quotidian rhythms of employment—rising in the morning and heading off to work—as well as professional capital: how to find work, how to get along with a supervisor and resolve disputes on the job, and so on.[32] This knowledge should prove beneficial to children when it becomes time for them to get jobs of their own.

THIRTY-NINE YEARS IN THE LIVES OF MOTHERS   121

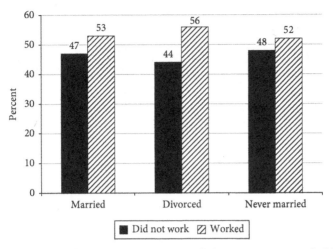

Figure 5.8. At Age 14, Was Mother or Other Adult Woman in Household Employed?
Notes: N = 2,273 (married) 1,150 (divorced) 1,285 (never married). Results are weighted.
Source: NLSY 1979–2018.

For the NLSY sample, married, divorced, and never-married mothers report similar levels of parental employment. Figure 5.8 shows employment rates for mothers when married, divorced, or never-married mothers were 14; Figure 5.9 shows employment data for the fathers of NLSY respondents.[33] For respondents' mothers, rates of employment extend from 52% to 56%; for fathers, levels of employment range from 89% to 95%. Never-married mothers are only a few percentage points less likely to have had an employed father at age 14. Given the broad range of disadvantages associated with being a divorced or, especially, a never-married mother, it is unexpected that rates of parental employment are so similar across family structures. The most obvious explanation is the simplest: most men work. So too did many women who were raising teenagers in the late 1970s, when the NLSY commenced.[34] Although the divorced and never-married mothers in our study experience many disadvantages, parental unemployment is not one of them: their parents had similar levels of employment to those of the women who went on to be married mothers.

In contrast to parental employment, there are large differences in parental education for NLSY mothers. Figures 5.10a and 5.10b show the percentage of fathers of NLSY respondents who have graduated from,

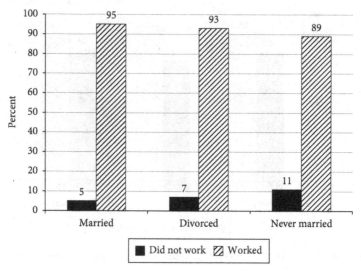

Figure 5.9. At Age 14, Was Father or Other Adult Man in Household Employed?

Notes: N = 2,001 (married) 982 (divorced) 838 (never married). Results are weighted.
Source: NLSY 1979–2018.

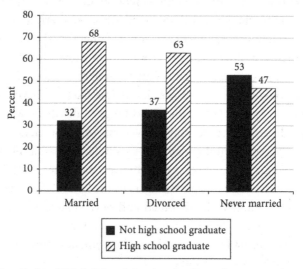

Figure 5.10a. Fathers' High School Graduation Rates by Respondent Marital Status.

Notes: N = 2,083 (married) 1,035 (divorced) 958 (never married). Results are weighted.
Source: NLSY 1979–2018.

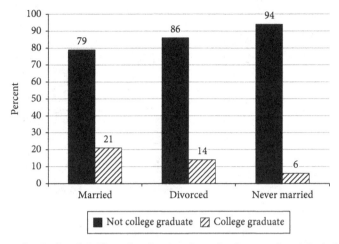

Figure 5.10b. Fathers' College Graduation Rates by Respondent Marital Status.
Notes: N = 2,083 (married) 1,035 (divorced) 958 (never married). Results are weighted.
Source: NLSY 1979–2018.

respectively, high school and college. Sixty-eight percent of married mothers have fathers who graduated from high school, compared to 63% of divorced mothers and just 47% of never-married mothers. The differences are just as stark for rates of four-year college graduation. Just over a fifth of married mothers have fathers with college degrees; the comparable figures for divorced and never-married mothers are 14% and 6%. Keep in mind that all these figures represent an era when average educational attainment was much lower than it is now.[35]

Turning to mothers of NLSY respondents' mothers, Figures 5.11a and 5.11b show even larger differences. Rates of high school graduation for the mothers of married, divorced, and never-married mothers are 71%, 65%, and 43%, respectively (Figure 5.11a). Figure 5.11b shows that 11% of married mothers have mothers who themselves graduated from college, compared to 8% for divorced-mothers and just 3% of never-married mothers. All in all, married mothers enjoy a substantial advantage by virtue of their comparably well-educated parents.[36] This provided early-life benefits, long before they became mothers themselves, and shaped the way they subsequently experienced family formation.

Of course these data don't illustrate the full relationship between parental education and women's experience with married, divorced, or never-married parenthood later on. Here there are several possibilities. First, the

124 THANKS FOR NOTHING

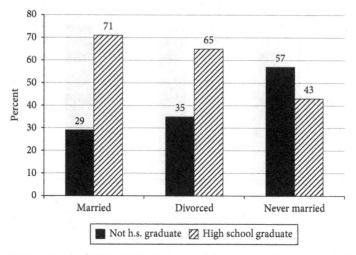

Figure 5.11a. Mother's High School Graduation Rates by Respondent Marital Status.

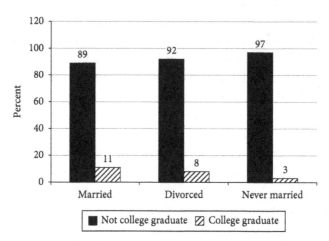

Figure 5.11b. Mother's College Graduation Rates by Respondent Marital Status.

Notes: N = 2,196 (married) 1,132 (divorced) 1,209 (never married). Results are weighted.
Source: NLSY 1979–2018.

THIRTY-NINE YEARS IN THE LIVES OF MOTHERS   125

relationship between parental education and offspring family structure reflects the transmission of family structure across generations.[37] Less educated mothers are less likely to be married, and so the women in these families are more likely to be children in single-parent families. This in turn increases the likelihood that these NLSY respondents eventually become single mothers. Second, the findings shown in Figures 5.10 (a and b) and 5.11 (a and b) may reflect the inheritance of educational attainment: less educated parents are not able to help their own daughters stay in school, which in turn made them more likely to become single mothers.[38] Both explanations are supported by existing research, although sociologists Kelly Musick and Robert Mare have shown that the intergenerational transmission of poverty and family structure occur through separate pathways (although we should keep in mind that poverty and low education are not the same thing).[39] Finally, there are other benefits of parental education. Educated parents provide various forms of social or cultural capital that ultimately help offspring make more money.[40] No matter the cause, the substantial gap in parental education means that divorced and especially never-married mothers are at a disadvantage right out of the starting gate, long before they started their own families.

The National Longitudinal Survey of Youth provides simple measures for examining the cultural capital mothers received in their families of origin. We consider two commonly used variables: 1) Did anyone in your household regularly get a newspaper? 2) Did anyone in the house have a library card? Both inquire about respondents' households at age 14. Newspapers and library cards are fairly insignificant in and of themselves, but are good indicators of both early literacy and academic engagement that might help mothers excel in high school, college, and subsequently their work lives.

Figure 5.12 shows household newspaper subscriptions for married, divorced, and never-married mothers, while Figure 5.13 shows figures for library card ownership. As has been the story for most of this chapter, there are big differences by marital status. Married mothers had the most experience with libraries and newspapers in childhood, while never-married mothers had the least. The differences are not as dramatic as many of the findings presented elsewhere in this chapter, but still noteworthy. Newspaper receipt ranges from 86% to 67%, while library card possession varies from 79% to 66%. For both measures of cultural capital, married and divorced mothers are more similar to each other than to never-married mothers.

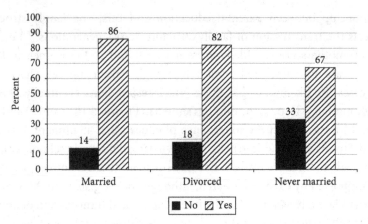

Figure 5.12. At Age 14, Did Anyone in Your Household Regularly Get a Newspaper?
Notes: N = 2,306 (married) 1,173 (divorced) 1,312 (never married). Results are weighted.
Source: NLSY 1979–2018.

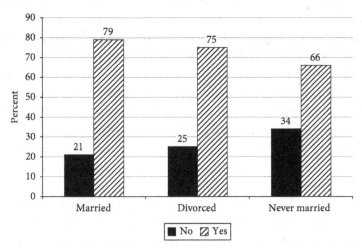

Figure 5.13. At Age 14, Did Somebody in the House Have a Library Card?
Notes: N = 2,305 (married) 1,174 (divorced) 1,312 (never married). Results are weighted.
Source: NLSY 1979–2018.

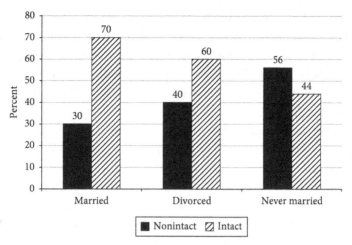

Figure 5.14. Family Structure of Origin by Respondent Marital Status.
Notes: N = 1,975 (married) 1,078 (divorced) 1,196 (never married). Results are weighted.
Source: NLSY 1979–2018.

The final component of family background that we examine is the family structure mothers grew up in. Given what we know about the intergenerational transmission of family structure, it should come as little surprise that married mothers are far more likely to hail from intact families than are divorced and never-married mothers. Still, the difference is striking in its magnitude, as Figure 5.14 reveals. Seventy percent of married mothers lived with both biological parents to age 18, compared to 60% of women who were ever, at any point during their participation in the NLSY, divorced mothers. Only a minority of never-married mothers lived with both parents to age 18, 44%. This is a full 26 percentage points lower than the number for married mothers. Living with two parents provides children with numerous advantages, including a higher standard of living, cultural capital, lessons about marriage, and support for higher education.[41] Given the substantially lower incomes of divorced and never-married mothers, it's understandable that fewer of them have benefited from two continually married parents. The differences shown in Figure 5.14 are also more evidence that family structure is frequently inherited.

Taken as a whole, the data presented on family background (Figures 5.8–5.14) show that divorced and especially never-married mothers have backgrounds that often put them at a material disadvantage compared to married mothers while growing up, long before becoming single mothers.

Divorced and never-married mothers in the NLSY have less educated parents, are less likely to reach age 18 in a household with both biological parents, and enjoy less cultural capital in their families of origin. Future single mothers are also less likely to grow up with employed parents (or stepparents), although these differences are not large. These results collectively suggest that single mothers would be at a disadvantage when it comes to earnings even had they not become single mothers. This is consistent with research showing endogeneity in the relationship between family structure and poverty for teenage mothers and divorced women—in other words, these women would have ended up poor even had they never become teenage mothers or divorced women.[42] These findings imply complex relationships between family background, current family structure, and poverty that will be further explored in Chapter 6.

Employment

Chapter 2 showed that employment rates for all mothers increased from the early 1980s until 2000. Thereafter, employment declined somewhat. Married and divorced mothers have more in common with each other than with never-married mothers. As Figure 5.15 shows, this pattern holds for the NLSY data as well as the CPS. Divorced mothers have consistently higher employment rates than do married and never-matter mothers. Employment rates for divorced mothers have always exceeded 70%, and since about 1990 have been over 80%. Presumably in response to less favorable economic conditions,

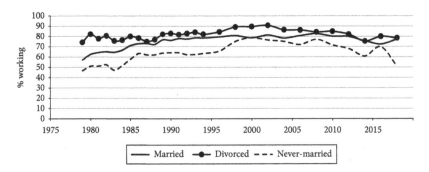

Figure 5.15. Employment Rates by Current Marital Status.
Notes: Average N = 1,327 (married) 253 (divorced) 383 (never married). Results are weighted.
Source: NLSY 1979–2018.

this figure dips starting in 2006, reaching a low point of 75% in 2014 before slowly recovering. The figures are similar for married mothers, but not their never-married contemporaries. Although never-married mothers are more likely to be employed as they move from adolescence into adulthood, they have worked less than other mothers. Throughout the early years of the NLSY, never-married mothers have almost always had employment rates at least 10 percentage points lower than mothers who have ever been married. At times, most notably the early 1980s and the early 1990s, the difference grew close to 20 percentage points. In more recent years the gap closed somewhat, then expanded in the wake of the Great Recession as employment rates for never-married mothers dropped more quickly than for others.

It's hardly a surprise that divorced mothers are more likely to be employed than are married mothers. After dissolving a marriage, women who had been relying on their spouse's income must fend for themselves. For never-married mothers, the employment data reflect in part the Personal Responsibility and Work Opportunity Reconciliation Act (PRWORA) of 1996 (i.e., welfare reform), which placed lifetime limits on public aid income transfers. Employment rates shot up in the wake of the Earned Income Tax Credit expansion of 1993, PRWORA, and the bull market of the late 1990s (and as we'll see in Chapter 6, all mothers have become less likely to receive public aid). Many of these women then left the labor market as the economy cooled in the aughts. Still, this dynamic cannot account for the steep decline in employment for never-married mothers from a high in 2000 of 79% to a low in 2018 of 51%. The recession also hit the employment rates of other mothers, but they had recovered by 2018. One possibility is that unemployment is both consequence and cause: it's well established that not working makes later-life employment less likely.[43] Never-married mothers in their late 40s and early 50s thus dropped out of the workforce when the economy cooled, and were unwilling or unable to rejoin as employment picked up.

We will return to the disparity in employment later in this chapter. For now, it's easy to see its consequences: less work means less income for this chronically disadvantaged population.

Education

Much has been written about the relationship between education and marital status. It has long been known that people with more formal education divorce less often.[44] The same holds true for education and the likelihood of a nonmarital birth—and conversely, a nonmarital birth makes further schooling less likely.[45] These findings are corroborated by the results presented in Chapter 2. Although divorced and never-married mothers are more likely to be high school or college graduates than in the past, they still lag behind married mothers. To what extent are gains in education the product of cohort replacement—in other words, new survey respondents becoming mothers—as opposed to the same women acquiring more education as they get older? In conjunction with findings from Chapter 2, the NLSY data allow us to address this question.

Figure 5.16 looks at high school graduate rates for women who ever spent time in married, divorced, or never-married motherhood. By 1984 the youngest National Longitudinal Survey of Youth respondents are old enough to have graduated from high school. Eighty-eight percent of married mothers had done so, compared to 82% of divorced mothers and just 68% of never-married mothers. Over time, never-married mothers gradually made up much of the difference, so that by 2014 86% had a high school degree, compared to 94% for married mothers. Divorced mothers are more similar to their married contemporaries. In their teens and 20s, divorced mothers are slightly less likely to have completed high school, but by their 40s and 50s, the disparity vanished.

Figure 5.16. The Percentage of Respondents Who Are in High School Graduates by Marital Status.

Notes: Average N = 1,389 (married) 263 (divorced) 389 (never married). Results are weighted.
Source: NLSY 1979–2018.

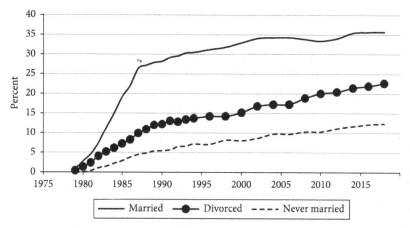

Figure 5.17. The Percentage of Respondents with a Four-Year College Degree by Marital Status.
Notes: Average N = 1,389 (married) 263 (divorced) 389 (never married). Results are weighted.
Source: NLSY 1979–2018.

The differences are far greater with respect for four-year college degrees. By the late 1980s, when the NLSY respondents were in their 20s, about 27% of married mothers had graduated from college, compared to 10% of divorced mothers and less than 4% of never-married mothers (Figure 5.17). These figures represent normative college completion: women who attended college right after high school and finished in a timely fashion. This creates such a large gap in education that single mothers never close the distance. By 2014, 34% of married mothers were college graduates, compared to 22% of divorced mothers and 11% of never-married mothers. Clearly the educational disadvantage associated with single motherhood occurs early in life. Although unmarried mothers close some of the distance as they age, they continue to lag far behind married mothers.[46] Based on the research cited earlier, low educational attainment is both a cause and a consequence of single motherhood.

The results presented here shed light on the findings offered in Chapter 2, which depicts a smaller disadvantage in education for single mothers. The new generation of divorced mothers, women born after the NLSY respondents, includes more women who presumably completed college before divorcing. This accounts for why recent CPS data shows that 20% of divorced mothers are college graduates, compared to only 15% of the NLSY women.

Race and Ethnicity

The publication of the Moynihan Report in 1965 cemented the notion that unmarried mothers are disproportionately women of color.[47] Although still true, it's less true than it used to be. When it comes to race and ethnicity, perhaps the most noteworthy finding of Chapter 2 is the declining percentage of never-married mothers who are African American, a trend produced by the growing number of White and non-White/non-Black mothers. Given that the NLSY respondents all came of age in the late 1970s and early 1980s, before many of the changes documented in Chapter 2 occurred, there is strong reason to suspect that the unwed mothers in this dataset are mostly non-White. Figure 5.18, which measures whether White, African American, and Latino women were married, divorced, or never-married mothers at any time during the NLSY, shows that the reality is a little more complicated.[48] White mothers are by far the most likely to be classified as married, at 62%, compared to 20% for African Americans and 44% for Latinos. These differences are largely explained by the equally large differences in never-married motherhood: 62% for Black women, compared to 24% for Latinos and 9% for Whites. The gap is smaller for divorce, with White and Latino mothers relatively equal at 29% and 32% respectively, but African Americans at only 14%. Why is this figure so low, given higher overall divorce rates for African Americans?[49] These mothers are less likely to have gotten married in the first place. Keep in mind also that never-married motherhood trumps

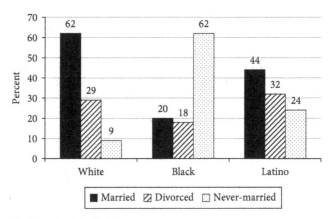

Figure 5.18. Race by Marital Structure.
Notes: N = 4,816. Results are weighted.
Source: NLSY 1979–2018.

divorced motherhood in our family structure typography, so it is possible that Black never-married mothers have also married and divorced.

The racial/ethnic breakdown of NLSY respondents, first interviewed in 1979, looks very different than exists in the U.S. today. This has clear implications for income given the way racial differences affect labor market returns.

Fertility

As we have noted earlier in this book, children have two effects on income. On the one hand, they typically reduce wages by limiting women's ability to work; on the other hand, they increase income transfers from public aid and child support, particularly for single mothers. Given our findings on labor force participation and public aid receipt, we would anticipate that never-married mothers are especially likely to have several children. Figure 5.19 confirms this prediction: 50% have three or more children, compared to 35% of married mothers and 38% of divorced mothers. Indeed, "three or more children" is the most common category for women who give birth out of wedlock, but not for other mothers. Married and divorced mothers have more in common when it comes to fertility. Relatively few mothers have

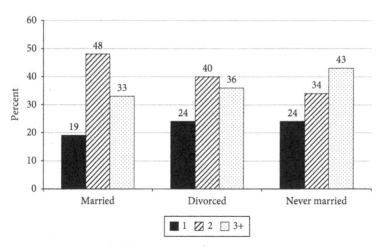

Figure 5.19. Number of Children by One-Time Marital Status.
Notes: N = 4,816. Results are weighted.
Source: NLSY 1979–2018.

134　THANKS FOR NOTHING

only one child; two is more common for divorced and, especially, married mothers. Finally, we should note that these findings on fertility are at odds with those presented in Chapter 2, which suggests that married mothers are the most likely to have large families. This discrepancy is likely the product of differences between cross-sectional and longitudinal data. The CPS data presented in Chapter 2 only include women who are never-married mothers at the time of the survey, typically a young population who may not be finished with having children. Additionally, those data capture multiple eras, and not simply women coming of age in the early 1980s.

Conclusion

The National Longitudinal Survey of Youth's 1979 cohort offers an excellent resource for following mothers from adolescence into middle age. With almost 40 years of data, we gain insight into how and when marital status changes for married, divorced, and never-married mothers. We also have the opportunity to learn about how the social and economic circumstances of mothers unfold as they get older. This is particularly informative when it comes to never-married mothers. Most are young when they first give birth, and many will subsequently get married, so they are not easily identified by the cross-sectional CPS data. Finally, we explore how the family backgrounds of married, divorced, and never-married mothers differ, information not available in the CPS.

Our findings are largely consistent with those presented in earlier chapters. Married mothers have the highest incomes, followed by divorced mothers and then never-married mothers. Married and divorced mothers have more in common with each other when it comes to basic labor market attributes, like employment or a high school education, than either population does with never-married mothers. Furthermore, the longitudinal nature of the National Longitudinal Survey of Youth reveals that many of the disadvantages of single motherhood are persistent. Women who have once been divorced or never-married mothers remain poorer through middle age, no matter how their family structure subsequently changes. Many of the correlates of income also follow this trend. Even as they enter middle adulthood, single mothers are far less likely to have college degrees, and, in the case of never-married mothers less likely to have a high school diploma or even be employed.

THIRTY-NINE YEARS IN THE LIVES OF MOTHERS 135

Why are single mothers at such a disadvantage? The next chapter will address this question via multivariate analysis. One answer is already clear: many divorced and, especially, never-married mothers experienced profound disadvantage even before they became mothers. Single mothers come from less educated families. They benefit less from different forms of cultural capital in their families of origin. Finally, single mothers are themselves more likely to come from nonintact families. All of these disadvantages may play a role in explaining the economic misfortunes of single mothers. These results are consistent with the findings of economists like Jeff Grogger and V. Joseph Hotz, who suggest that teenage mothers would have been poor even had they not become teenage mothers, and with Kelly Bedard and Olivier Deschênes, who report the same finding for divorced women.[50]

These data also demonstrate that, in the long run, the economic outlook for children is more positive than it might initially appear. First, the majority of mothers in our sample are married mothers. Marriage, and married motherhood, remains the modal family experience. Second, we note that most single mothers do not stay single mothers. About two-thirds of divorced mothers remarry; the number is almost as high for never-married mothers. Single mothers also cease being single mothers when their children leave home. Given that each child typically costs its parents more than $10,000 a year, emptying the nest represents a significant decline in a mother's economic burden.[51]

6

Thirty-Nine Years of Counting Change

The previous chapter documents pervasive differences by family structure for the women in the NLSY panel. Married mothers have substantially higher incomes than divorced and, especially, never-married mothers. These differences are persistent: any time spent as a single mother is associated with consistently lower incomes later on, even if followed by marriage.

How can these disparities in income by family structure be explained? Broadly speaking, there are three possibilities. The first is the most obvious and the most easily measured: spouses. Men continue to be the primary wage earner in the majority of heterosexual marriages.[1] Marriage doesn't ensure prosperity—indeed, the majority of low-income families are headed by couples—but as we've seen having two wage earners is a big help.[2]

The second explanation for the relative poverty of single-mother families lies in the large differences in human capital and other resources documented in Chapters 2 and 5. In Chapter 3, we saw how human capital is related to income in a series of cross-sections spanning almost 40 years. In the current chapter, we will explore whether many of the same measures of human capital affect individual women as they move from their teenage years to middle age.

The third and final explanation is that unmeasured differences between women produce the large observed differences by family structure. We will address this possibility as well. What exactly do social scientists mean when they speak of "unmeasured differences?" When writing for scholarly journals, we often use the terms *sample selection* or *endogeneity* to describe particular differences between individuals that are correlated with income yet not reflected in the measures of human capital or family background considered in this book. As we have noted in earlier chapters, this is the possibility that married, divorced, and never-married mothers may differ in ways that are difficult to identify or describe. One possibility is a spurious correlation between family structure and income. If this is the case, single mothers might have ended up poor even if they had never had children, or if they had otherwise not become single mothers.

Thanks for Nothing. Nicholas H. Wolfinger and Matthew McKeever, Oxford University Press.
© Oxford University Press 2024. DOI: 10.1093/oso/9780199324323.003.0006

Perhaps these unmeasured differences could be detected with the kinds of in-depth data that don't make it into the national surveys analyzed in this book. Some of this information might be gleaned from in-depth interviews, ethnography, psychometric instruments, or twin studies. Some of it is difficult to measure with any social science research methodology. Unmeasured characteristics, we will conclude, matter much more for women who give birth out of wedlock than they do for married and divorced mothers. Although we obviously can't measure the immeasurable, we can show that unmeasured differences go a long way towards explaining how marital status and income are related.

Family Structure Trajectories and Income

Chapter 5 suggests that the single mothers of the NLSY's 1979 cohort have persistently lower incomes even if they subsequently marry. This also is clear from Figure 6.1, which shows how lifetime income growth varies for several different sequences of family structure.

The Figure 6.1 numbers reflect income both before and after childbirth. Women who have all their children within the bonds of matrimony and stay married start out with the highest incomes in 1979, before many of them even became married mothers and experience far greater income growth as they age into midlife. Women who have their children while married but subsequently divorce also start out with higher incomes, but experience little income growth: their family incomes hover around $50,000 (in 2018 dollars)

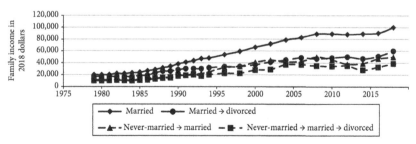

Figure 6.1. How Single Motherhood Affects Lifetime Earnings for Married Mothers.

Notes: N = 2,245 (married) 1,019 (married -> divorced) 568 (never married -> married) 349 (never married -> married -> divorced). Results are weighted.
Source: NLSY 1979–2018.

after the start of the new millennium, dipping during the Great Recession and then slowly rising again. It's important to note that these numbers are averages that combines divorcées who remarry—and reap the associated financial benefits—and women who remain single.

Women who give birth out of wedlock start out with much lower incomes. They experience modest income growth if they get married, but not if these marriages end in divorce. A few women, not shown in Figure 6.1, have children out of wedlock but never marry. As we showed in the previous chapter, these mothers have persistently low incomes.

Figure 6.1 suggests both direct and selection effects of family structure on income. How so? First, continually married mothers and, to a lesser extent, women who had children while married but subsequently divorced, start out with much higher incomes than do women who had children out of wedlock. Keep in mind that few women in the sample were married in 1979, when the NLSY was first administered. In that year respondents were between the ages of 14 and 22. Most were still living with their parent(s). As they grew up, our sample of women who would become and remain married mothers experienced income growth both before and after marriage. The evidence for a direct effect of family structure on income is the fact that a married mother's income increases with age, whether or not her children were born in wedlock. The disadvantage associated with a nonmarital birth substantially reduces but doesn't fully depress future income growth.

The economic costs of single motherhood are enduring, but they are most acute right at the time women first become single mothers. Figure 6.2 shows family incomes for the five years before and after women become single

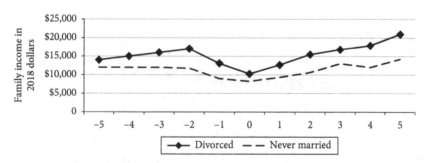

Figure 6.2. Median Income before and after the Transition to Single Motherhood.

Notes: Annual Ns = 340 (divorced) 231 (never married). Results are weighted.
Source: NLSY 1979–1994.

mothers.[3] For both divorced and never-married mothers, income dips before single motherhood begins. This should be interpreted differently for the two groups. Divorced women generally separate before formally ending their marriages; this probably explains the precipitous drop in income in the year before single motherhood officially starts.[4] Incomes rebound a few years after divorced motherhood begins, but never entirely, as both Figure 5.1 and Figure 6.1 suggest. What's more, divorce sets a woman's income back several years. The decline in income is less severe for never-married mothers, but even five years down the road it has not risen much beyond the levels attained several years prior to a nonmarital birth.[5] That is, despite being 10 years older, these women are barely receiving more income. This makes sense in the context of the low lifetime incomes we have observed for never-married mothers.

The decline in income before never-married motherhood begins likely has a couple of different sources. Unlike divorced motherhood, never-married motherhood begins with childbirth. Some mothers work less when they're expecting, although less so than they used to.[6] Some of the prenatal income declines might be explained by cohabitation, which, in Chapter 3, we showed reduces unmarried mothers' family incomes.[7] Perhaps unmarried women who move in with their partners while pregnant work less, and since their boyfriends' incomes do not count towards their own family income they appear to have less money.

Although Figure 6.1 reveals broad divergences in income, it doesn't account for the correlates of family structure so crucial to income, most notably education and employment. We therefore turn to multivariate analysis of the NLSY's 1979 cohort to examine the extent to which we can understand income differences as related to the different characteristics of these women.

Peak Lifetime Earnings

Studying lifetime earnings is more complex than it might first seem. An analysis of people's highest lifetime earnings might reflect periods of fleeting good fortune rather than a sustained trajectory of income growth. For this reason, we measure peak earnings as the median of survey respondents' three most prosperous years. These models are useful for examining the impact of individual attributes and family background on income. Later in this chapter we will report on statistical models that exploit panel data. These latter models afford greater insight into causality, but limit our ability to explain income differences on the basis of observed respondent characteristics.

Figure 6.3 summarizes our analysis of peak family income. It depicts income differences between various family structure configurations, then shows how these differences are attenuated by adjusting for a variety of covariates.[8] We caution against drawing strong causal conclusions given the structure of the data. Family structure transitions typically come early in life, prior to the time when people attain their highest incomes. With this analytic design, we cannot be certain that family transitions are anterior to income. The same holds true for some of the other variables included in the analysis. We exclude certain variables like employment history because their causal relationship to income would be ambiguous.

The baseline model in Figure 6.3, adjusting for race/ethnicity, reproduces the zero-order differences shown in Figure 6.1. Continuously married mothers have the highest median lifetime incomes, over three times the corresponding figure for women who give birth out of wedlock and never get

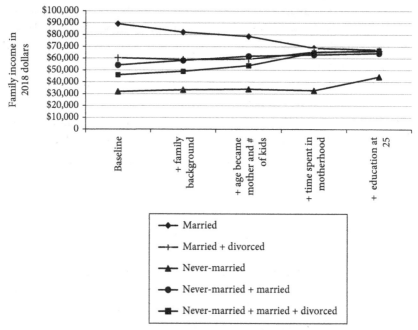

Figure 6.3. Peak Lifetime Income by Family Structure and Other Factors.
Notes: N = 3,624. Results are weighted.
Source: NLSY 1979–2018.

married. These differences are only slightly attenuated by adjusting for a variety of measures of family background, tapping parental social capital, socioeconomic status, and whether mothers hail from intact families. In other words, broad racial income disparities and the intergenerational transmission of family structure and socioeconomic status cannot explain the strong relationship between marital status and income.[9] Nor can the timing of motherhood or the number of children in a family.

Adjusting for time spent in married, divorced, or never-married motherhood greatly diminishes the broader economic consequences of current family structure. Each year spent as a married mother produces a higher median lifetime family income, but time spent in never-married motherhood has no impact on family income—simply being a never-married mother is more than enough to result in a lower income. Finally, education at age 25 has a generally modest effect on income variation by family structure. Only for continuously never-married mothers is there any shift in the impact of family structure, showing that education is the only measured characteristic which has even modest effects on peak lifetime income for these mothers.

What's the big takeaway from Figure 6.3? The most important explanation for the effect of family structure on peak income is the time spent as a married or divorced mother. Married motherhood affords an opportunity for career advancement (or fostering a spouse's career advancement) that's not available to single mothers, an opportunity that pays dividends even if one becomes a single mother later on. Conversely, the economic consequences of never-married motherhood persist over time. Only education boosts these mothers' peak earnings, but nowhere near as high as ever-married mothers' income. Finally, these results seem to point to sample selection; in other words, the existence of unmeasured differences between ever-married and never-married mothers. Accordingly, we'll explore these dynamics below.

Statistical Models for Sample Selection

Longitudinal data like the NLSY offer more insight into causality than do repeated cross-sectional designs such as the Current Population Survey (CPS). Most notably, the NLSY offers information on women before they become mothers. This can help explain whether family structure is directly affecting income, as opposed to only being indirectly related due to mother's unmeasured characteristics.

To explore sample selection, we report results based on fixed effects models (FEM).[10] FEM essentially allow each survey respondent to become her own control. Multiple years of data on each respondent mean that all individual time-invariant differences between individuals are factored out of the model. This is also a downside of FEM: time-invariant attributes like race and parental attributes cannot be included.[11]

Figure 6.4 shows the results of the fixed effects analysis of family income.[12] There are three noteworthy findings. First, consistent with other analysis presented in this book, married mothers have much higher incomes than unmarried mothers. (The dollar amounts shown in the table are low because they emphasize the years women first became mothers, not the years of peak earning power.) Second, predicted incomes for divorced and never-married mothers are relatively similar, especially compared to married mother's incomes. Third, adding controls for education, employment, nonmarital cohabitation, and numbers of children, makes little difference in the income disparity between married and single mothers.

The income gap between married and single mothers is substantial. Looking back at Figures 6.1 and 6.3, we see that married mothers have incomes more than twice what's sustaining single mothers. The fixed effects models show that the income gap is not only large, but also not affected by a mother's employment or education, two things we know are broadly associated with prosperity. The most likely explanation is also the simplest: married mothers have two incomes, single mothers have one. Stripping away all the unmeasured confounds leaves us with a simple story.

This analysis does offer a finding that's at odds with the rest of this book: higher incomes for never-married mothers than for divorced mothers. How can that be? Chapter 5 showed that divorced and never-married

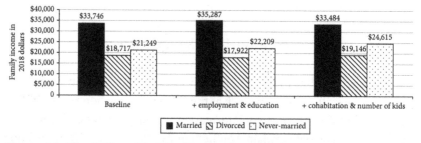

Figure 6.4. Fixed Effects Models of Income by Marital Structure.
Notes: N = 4,790; 47,906 person-years. Results are weighted.
Source: NLSY 1979–2018.

mothers look much different on paper: never-married women are less likely to have educated parents, more likely to hail from nonintact families themselves, and enjoy less social capital growing up. Yet as Figure 6.4 suggests, collectively these measured disadvantages can't explain why never-married women have such low incomes. These differences only grow between the baseline fixed effects model and those that control for education, employment, family size, and cohabitation.

The answer to understanding these results lies in the unmeasured (and stable) differences between the two groups. These populations must differ in ways that are manifestly difficult to measure, factors not in the data yet associated with income. The measured differences are only compounded by the unmeasured differences captured by the fixed effects models. Chapter 3 showed that even when never-married mothers manage to graduate from college they receive smaller pecuniary returns to their degrees than do divorced mothers. What's more, there are probably long-term causal effects of a premarital childbirth that aren't captured by the simple measures of labor force qualifications. For example, educational attainment may suffer, but even when it does not lag quantitatively there might be qualitative differences that are being captured in the fixed effects.[13]

These difficult-to-measure differences likely compound the correlates of nonmarital fertility that we know are associated with lower incomes. For instance, the previous chapter showed that never-married mothers were especially likely to have three or more children—and there has been extensive research demonstrating that each child a woman has cumulatively reduces her wages.[14] And as we have noted, women who give birth out of wedlock have lower marriage rates, which in turn results in lower incomes down the line. In short, the lower incomes for never-married mothers are explained by both measured and immeasurable factors.

Relying on Others, or the Government

Chapter 5 has described lower levels of human capital for single mothers and remarkably low employment rates for women who give birth out of wedlock. How do single mothers make ends meet with low-paying jobs, or no jobs?[15] One obvious place to look for an answer is public aid. The stereotypical single mother has long relied on the direct cash payments first introduced as part of the Social Security Act in 1935, income transfers that were specifically intended

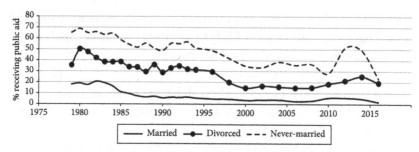

Figure 6.5. Public Aid Receipt by Current Marital Status.
Notes: Average annual N = 1,439 (married) 275 (divorced) 416 (never married). Results are weighted.
Source: NLSY 1979–2016.

for single mothers. Even more women benefit from non-cash help transfers, like the Supplemental Nutrition Assistance Program (SNAP/food stamps).[16]

As expected, Figure 6.5 shows that never-married mothers have the highest public aid receipt rates in our sample, with divorced mothers somewhat lower, and married mothers by far the lowest.[17] Furthermore, welfare receipt has fallen for all mothers over time. This goes beyond the secular declines in government transfers reported in Chapter 2: Figure 6.5 suggests that all mothers receive less public aid as they get older. Receipt had been steadily declining even before the landmark expansion of the earned income tax credit in 1993 and welfare reform in 1996.

In 1980, the disparity in aid receipt by marital status was considerable. Almost 70% of never-married mothers received some sort of public assistance, compared to half of divorced mothers and about one in five married mothers. After 2000, these numbers were much closer, with 40% of never-married mothers, 20% of divorced mothers, and 5% of married mothers getting assistance. It's not surprising that married mothers have the lowest level of aid receipt, but the difference between divorced and never-married mothers is substantial. Divorced women aren't used to getting public assistance available to single mothers, so they may feel daunted by the application process, or simply be ashamed that they need help.[18] This holds less true for never-married mothers, who may well have been born into families receiving Aid to Families with Dependent Children.[19]

By 2000, when survey respondents were in their mid-30s to early 40s, only a minority of mothers were receiving aid. For many, age brings work experience and therefore greater financial security. At the same time, the children in single mother families are turning 18, thereby decreasing family size and therefore the need (and eligibility) for public aid. Finally, some single mothers may be reaching lifetime limits for receipt of public assistance cash.

It's worth reiterating that the trends reported in Chapter 5, Figure 5.20, don't seem heavily affected by welfare reform in 1996. Rates of aid receipt started declining around 1990, and continued to decline after 1996, but it's not simply that mothers have aged out of federal aid. Welfare reform reduced cash transfers, but not in-kind benefits like SNAP. Since non-cash aid is included in the Figure 6.5 data, the effect of welfare reform on overall rates of aid receipt is muted.[20]

The relationship of marital status to public aid receipt is persistent. Figure 6.6 shows how aid receipt has changed over time based upon whether women have ever been married, divorced, or never-married mothers. As was the case for Figure 6.5, based on current marital status, receipt has declined for all mothers as they grow older. Nevertheless, any time spent as a single mother is associated with consistently higher rates of public aid receipt into middle adulthood. Between 1985 and 1995 rates of public aid receipt ranged from 35% to 40% for women who had ever been never-married mothers (or, less likely, would become never-married mothers later on). During the same years, aid receipt was around 20% for women who had been or would become divorced mothers and under 10% for married mothers. By 2002, the gap had narrowed considerably, with aid receipt at 22% for never-married mothers, 11% for divorced mothers, and 5% for married mothers. Nevertheless, we should not lose sight of the fact that any experience with single motherhood is associated with ongoing receipt of public assistance.

Public aid makes a big difference. While only a minority of mothers receive welfare, it constitutes a large proportion of total income for its recipients.

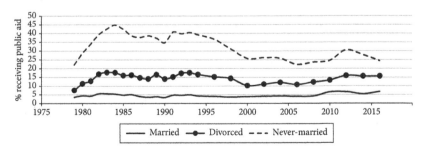

Figure 6.6. Public Aid Receipt by One-Time Marital Status.
Notes: N = 1,754 (married) 995 (divorced) 1,105 (never married).
Source: NLSY 1979–2018.

146 THANKS FOR NOTHING

Figure 6.7. Median Public Aid by Marital Status.
Notes: Average annual N = 163 (married) 89 (divorced) 259 (never married). Results are weighted.
Source: NLSY 1979–2010.

Figure 6.7 shows the median cash value of aid received by those getting any of these funds, in 2018 dollars.[21] This figure also shows the percentage of family income comprised of public aid in for a subset of years. Keep in mind that family income may reflect the incomes of other family members: spouses in the case of married mothers, or parents.

There are several conclusions to draw from these calculations. First, public aid isn't exclusive to single mothers; all kinds of families benefit from it. Second, the value of government transfers peaked around 1990, when the NLSY cohort ranged in age from 25 to 33. It was declining even before welfare reform in 1996. This mirrors the broader trend of the real dollar value of welfare payments, which has lessened substantially over time.[22] Finally, aid is an important source of revenue for single mothers, especially those who've never been married, constituting at times a very high proportion of their family incomes. The high-water mark was again in 1990, when public aid made up 90% of family income for the approximately 60% of never-married mothers who received it. Given their comparably low rates of employment (see Chapters 2 and 5), it's not surprising that never-married mothers were more reliant on government transfers. Over time, the proportion of never-married mothers receiving public aid declines, but for those still getting any it comprises the majority of their income throughout the years of our study. Indeed, this helps explain flatlining incomes for never-married mothers: they are heavily reliant on government income transfers, but these transfers are smaller than they used to be.

A moderate number of single mothers, especially if divorced, receive income transfers from the fathers of their children.[23] Figure 6.8 shows receipt of child support and, far less often, alimony over time by current

THIRTY-NINE YEARS OF COUNTING CHANGE 147

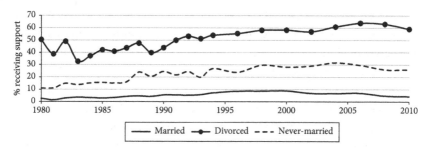

Figure 6.8. Child Support/Alimony Receipt by Marital Status.
Notes: Average annual N = 1,588 (married) 298 (divorced) 464 (never married). Results are weighted.
Source: NLSY 1979–2010.

marital status.[24] Divorced mothers are about twice as likely as never-married mothers to be receiving support, despite the fact that never-married mothers are more likely to need the money. A consistently small percentage of married mothers receive aid by virtue of a previous marriage. Women are more likely to receive support payments as they age, up until the final years of data. By 2000, when the NLSY respondents were between 35- and 43-years-old, almost three in ten never-married mothers and almost six in ten divorced mothers were receiving child support. Older women have had more time to accumulate both children and the commensurate eligibility for support payments.

Figure 6.9 shows the size of the median child support payment; the percentages represent the proportion of total income that any such payments provide. None of the NLSY mothers ever received more than about half of their family incomes as cash transfers from the fathers of their children,

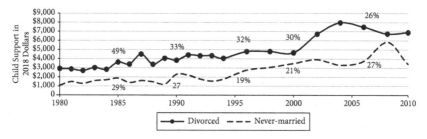

Figure 6.9. Median Annual Child Support Receipt by Marital Structure.
Notes: Average annual N = 142 (divorced) 88 (never married). Results are weighted.
Source: NLSY 1979–2010.

and most years they received far less than that. The size of the typical remittance is indeed small. For example, among women in these data receiving transfers from the fathers of their children in 2010, the median married mother and the median divorced mother received $6,900, while the median never-married mother took in $3,450. Payment size has gradually increased over time, with divorced mothers consistently receiving larger remittances than never-married mothers. As we've suggested, this reflects the reality that women who have been married are in a better position to receive child support by virtue of their divorce decrees.[25] The percentages shown in Figure 6.9 are also shaped by the fact that many women do not receive the support promised to them, or receive only a fraction of what they are due.[26]

Living Arrangements

Another way for any single person to make ends meet is to live with a romantic partner. About 60% of never-married mothers live with the fathers of their children at the time their children are born, a figure that's increased considerably over time.[27] Subsequent to the "magic moment" of childbirth, the cohabitation rate declines somewhat.[28] And for their part, divorced women have long had disproportionately high rates of cohabitation compared to women who haven't been married.[29] Turning to the NLSY, Figure 6.10 reveals somewhat uneven trends in cohabitation for unmarried mothers. The broad trend is of declining cohabitation rates as women age, especially as they reach their 40s and 50s, but there is considerable variation prior to that, which reflects both personal choices and, presumably, welfare reform

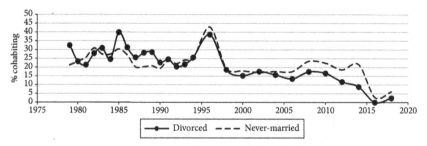

Figure 6.10. The Percent of Mothers Currently Cohabiting by Marital Status.
Notes: Average annual N = 239 (divorced) 321 (never married). Results are weighted.
Source: NLSY 1979–2018.

in 1996. Between 1980 and 1995 cohabitation rates vary from between 20% and 40%. This corresponds to the years of late adolescence and early adulthood, a common time for union formation (and dissolution). By the early 1990s, cohabitation rates have dropped to near 20%, but in 1996, the year welfare reform was enacted, rates spike up to 39%. Thereafter, they continue to decline. By 2006, about 15% or fewer single mothers are cohabiting. At this point, we assume that the majority of single mothers are entering more permanent relationships. The number of cohabiting never-married mothers rises again in the last few years of data, although few women are still custodial mothers with minor children by this time. Throughout most years of the NSLY, divorced and never-married mothers have very similar levels of cohabitation, with the latter cohabiting just slightly more than the former.

Most cohabiting relationships end quickly, whether by marriage or dissolution.[30] This can explain why rates of cohabitation are relatively low across the years of the NLSY despite the overall likelihood that young adults spend at least some time living out of wedlock with a romantic partner. The transitory nature of cohabitation in the U.S. is why we treat it as a temporary form of economic dependence rather than a more permanent departure from single motherhood.

Another way unmarried mothers can save money is live with their own parents.[31] As Figure 6.11 suggests, this is a common option for unwed mothers in their younger years, but becomes less likely over time. In the early 1980s, over 30% of divorced mothers and up to 50% of never-married mothers are living with a parent or parents. These are years in which some NLSY mothers are still minors, so it is natural that they would be living at home. Divorced

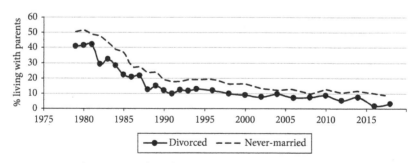

Figure 6.11. The Percent of Mothers Living with Their Own Parents by Marital Status.

Notes: Average annual N = 265 (divorced) 401 (never married). Results are weighted.
Source: NLSY 1979–2018.

150 THANKS FOR NOTHING

mothers have already lived elsewhere while married. This likely explains why they are not moving home at similar rates to never-married mothers (who may have never left home in the first place.) For most of the 1990s rates of co-residence with parents are lower, about 20% for never-married mothers and around 10% for divorced mothers. By 2005, when the NLSY mothers have reached middle age, only about 10% of single mothers are living with their parents. Above and beyond the broadly acknowledged awkwardness of moving home in middle age, it is increasingly likely that parental death forecloses the opportunity to do so.

Conclusion

This chapter has provided some indication of why single mothers have so much lower incomes than do their married contemporaries. For divorced mothers, the single most important explanation is the absence of a second income. Divorced mothers have high rates of employment and low rates of public aid receipt. A majority receive income transfers from their ex-spouses, but the payments tend to be small. And as we saw in Chapter 5, divorced mothers have less human capital than do married mothers, but it doesn't seem to be making as much of a difference as one might reasonably expect. After accounting for these factors, what remains is the difference between one and two incomes.

The data presented here tell a very different story for women who give birth out of wedlock. Many had low incomes and other forms of measurable disadvantage even before becoming mothers, yet fixed effects models show that it's *unmeasured* disadvantage that make the biggest difference. Were it not for this disadvantage, never-married mothers would have slightly higher incomes than divorced mothers. Never-married mothers are thus burdened by reliance on a single income, low levels of human capital, and hard-to-measure disadvantage.

The other key factor that affects income is time spent as a married mother. Each year of married motherhood raises family income, even if the respondent has once been a divorced or never-married mother. Marriage allows one or both spouses to cultivate careers in a way that's remunerative in the long run. Conversely, time spent as a single mother helps account for their comparably low incomes. In other respects, our results are counterintuitive. Take the role of education, one of the most important predictors of income. Both the CPS and NLSY show that all mothers have higher incomes when they have more formal education. The data also indicate that never-married mothers complete fewer years of school than women who've been married. Yet these differences in education don't explain the income gap between never-married mothers and their peers who've been married.

Many years ago we first looked at never-married mothers' incomes using data from the CPS. At the time, we wrote the following:

> Viewed more broadly, our results do not accord with the conventional story of stratification and poverty. The conventional story is that many Americans are poor because of their relationship to the labor market: they lack the skills and the jobs necessary to earn higher wages. Certainly this has been the case when attempting to explain the economics of marital disruption. Higher earning power, the result of both education and better jobs, appears to be the reason for divorcées' rising incomes [over time]. Although never-married mothers have achieved comparable educational and professional gains, economic returns have not followed suit. Even well-educated never-married mothers who struggle to work might find themselves thinking "thanks for nothing" as they survey their family's bottom line.[32]

The 35 years of longitudinal data from the NLSY ultimately yield the same conclusion: never-married mothers have lower incomes than divorced women for reasons that are impossible to discern with conventional survey data. They can be explained away in a statistical analysis, but not identified. There's less mystery when accounting for the broader income gap between married and unmarried mothers: two incomes are always better than one.

Finally, we explore a number of ways that single mothers rely on others: government transfers, child support payments, co-residence with parents or a romantic partner. All outside support helps, but none of it allows for most of the single mothers in our study to live well. Never-married mothers get more help from the government, while divorced mothers are more likely to be receiving support from the fathers of their children. For some families, income transfers comprise the bulk of their income. The high-water mark for government support was around 1990, when three out of five never-married mothers got 90% of their money from Uncle Sam. That same year about two fifths of divorce mothers relied on the government for a majority of their income. At the same time, the absolute dollar amount was

152 THANKS FOR NOTHING

never high enough to allow these families to escape the bottom of the income distribution. Furthermore, public aid fell for all mothers after this point, both in terms of the proportion of women receiving aid and the dollar value of that aid.

Unlike the other forms of economic dependence considered here, child support (and far less often, alimony) receipt has increased over time. Other things being equal, older mothers are better equipped to solicit and compel payment, while older fathers are more likely to afford it. Still, never more than 60% of divorced mothers and 30% of never-married mothers get aid in any given year. And compared to public aid, child support never provides more than half of a mother's income. The dollar value of child support payments is generally even lower than the value of income transfers from the state.

Finally, as young women, many single mothers will live with their parents. A declining percentage continues to do so over time. Between 1990 and 2000, when NLSY respondents ranged in age from 25 to 43, about one in five never-married mothers and one in ten divorced mothers resided with their parents. Over these same years between 20% and 40% of single mothers were living with a partner in any given year. The number spiked to almost 40% in 1996, the year of welfare reform, but thereafter tended to decrease. After that, these mothers were on their own.

7

Conclusion: Where Have We Been, and Where Should We Go Now?

> Power has only one duty—to secure the social welfare of the people.
>
> Benjamin Disraeli

In this book, we've offered a straightforward argument on the economics of motherhood in the U.S. over the past 40 years. Family structure remains a key component of both economic inequality and popular narratives about inequality. Our reasoning is simple: wages are earned by individuals, but they're converted into living standards that affect all family members. For most families, individual adults' participation in the labor market is the primary source of income. Like previous researchers, we've documented decades of low incomes for single-mother families. Fundamentally, this isn't surprising, given their reliance on a single wage earner. Transfers from nonresident parents and the state are directly related to family structure, but this income rarely makes up for the absence of a spousal wage.

We've repeatedly shown that single-mother families aren't created equal. The data from both the Current Population Survey (CPS) and the National Longitudinal Survey of Youth's (NLSY) 1979 cohort align on the basic facts. Divorced mothers generally resemble married mothers in many of the attributes associated with higher family incomes. Their relative poverty is directly the product of relying on a single wage. In contrast, never-married mothers have less education, lower-status jobs, and are more likely to have become mothers at a young age. Consequently, never-married mothers remain much more likely to be deeply impoverished than divorced mothers. In addition, they have lower incomes than divorced women for reasons that are impossible to discern with national survey data. These reasons can be

---

Thanks for Nothing. Nicholas H. Wolfinger and Matthew McKeever, Oxford University Press.
© Oxford University Press 2024. DOI: 10.1093/oso/9780199324323.003.0007

154   THANKS FOR NOTHING

explained away in a statistical analysis that controls for unmeasured individual attributes, but not identified. Never-married mothers thus differ from their ever-married contemporaries in ways that transcend either family structure or variation in human capital.

Our data show that America has changed considerably over the past 40 years. Today all mothers have more education, delay having children, have smaller families, and are more likely to work. All these developments reasonably lead to expectations of greater earning power. Single mothers have indeed made modest gains in median income (but less so in the lower income percentiles). These overall gains obscure growing inequality within the populations of married, divorced, and never-married mothers. Variation within any particular marital status is sometimes large enough to approach the income gap between married and unmarried mothers. College-educated divorced mothers, for instance, have family incomes almost as high as do married mothers without high school diplomas. It's therefore necessary to consider both average differences and increasing inequality within family structure.

These trends can be explained by variation across four distinct dimensions: 1) trends in single motherhood and the kinds of women who become single mothers; 2) rising levels of education and other individual attributes that predict employment income; 3) changes in the returns to individual attributes over the past 40 years; and 4) differences in both attributes and returns to attributes related to marital status. Many single mothers have found themselves in a labor market that fails to reward their human capital even as they've worked to improve it. Consequently, we must resist efforts to draw conclusions about single mothers that fail to account for both individual attributes and historical period, or that fail to distinguish divorced and never-married mothers.

Our analysis also demonstrates that many of the disadvantages of single motherhood are persistent. Divorced and never-married mothers remain poorer through middle age, even if they subsequently get married. Moreover, the data show that many divorced and, especially, never-married mothers experienced considerable disadvantage even before they became mothers. They come from less educated families, and benefit less from various forms of cultural capital in their families of origin. Single mothers are more likely to get public aid, although rates of receipt have plummeted over the years of our study. They're also more likely to receive transfers from the fathers of their children, although receipt has largely held steady over the past 40 years and only a minority of mothers are recipients. Finally, single mothers are themselves more likely to come from nonintact families. All of these disadvantages play a role in explaining the economic challenges facing single mothers.

Income and Children's Well-Being

Our analysis makes clear that family structure is a key component of childhood poverty and opportunity. Economic hardship experienced by children is a direct consequence of the families they are raised in, so this book is ultimately an appraisal of child poverty. Furthermore, it's important to remember that our analysis is within the context of a country that has actively shifted the burden of poverty onto mothers and children during the past 50 years.

Take the elderly as a comparison. Before the creation of social security in 1935, half of senior citizens lived in poverty.[1] In 1966, the year after Medicare was signed into law, 30% of the elderly were poor. Today, it's under 10%.[2] An even starker example can be found in the benefits of the 2021 American Rescue Plan. A team of Columbia University researchers anticipated a 31% decline in the poverty rate, from 12.3% to 8.5%, an all-time low.[3] In contrast, the child poverty rate in 2019, the last year before the COVID pandemic, was 15.7%.[4] After COVID-era income transfers expired, child poverty duly rebounded to 17%.[5] Finally, we can look to our contemporaries in Canada and Western Europe. American children are more likely to live with a single parent than in any other country in the world and the income gap between married and single mothers is larger in the United States than in Canada, the UK, Germany, and other European nations.[6] Poverty, in short, is in large part a policy choice.

Children's poverty is directly related to family structure because of how income is distributed to families—and most children in single-mother families, especially those headed by women who have never been married, will experience material hardship. As we point out in Chapter 1, today's single-mother families remain five times more likely to experience poverty than two-parent families, and over seventeen million American children—or about one in five—now live with an unmarried mother. As these mothers encounter economic hardship, their children do too. Furthermore, we are not just speaking of transitory poverty.[7] Our analysis of the NLSY indicates that single motherhood tends to be associated with enduring economic disadvantage for

156 THANKS FOR NOTHING

women and their children. Consistent poverty—as opposed to transitory poverty—is particularly bad for kids.[8]

The effects of childhood deprivation are not subject to dispute: growing up in an impoverished family has myriad enduring consequences for children.[9] For example, children who experience economic deprivation at earlier ages have lower academic achievement, both in terms of performance in school and educational attainment.[10] They are more likely to drop out of high school and are less likely to go to college. And growing up with fewer economic resources on average results in poorer physical health and cognitive ability as an adult.[11] Newer research has described poverty as a "bandwidth tax," so consuming that it sucks up the cognitive resources that might otherwise be spent on, perhaps, trying to escape poverty.[12]

Childhood poverty leads to lasting psychosocial challenges. Children raised in poverty have more challenging physical and psychological development.[13] They have more emotional problems and less self-esteem.[14] They are more likely to experience psychiatric disorders.[15] And these challenges sometimes endure into early adulthood.

All of these disadvantages will redound for children in terms of their long-term prospects in the labor market. Part of this is related to lower educational attainment, which is obviously crucial to making a good living. Children raised in poverty are less likely to maintain steady employment as adults.[16] When they do work, they are more likely to be in lower status jobs and have worse pay.[17] All in all, children who grow up in poor families are more likely to end up poor as adults.[18]

Poverty isn't destiny, of course. There are exceptions to every rule and American popular culture has always cherished the narrative of plucky heroes and (less often) heroines who transcend humble beginnings to prosper as adults. Still, the reality is that children raised poor are far more likely to end up as poor adults compared to children born to privilege. All things considered, it's always better to not grow up poor.

It's also important to recognize that the broad economic outlook for children is more positive than it might initially appear. As our data show, the majority of mothers in our sample are married mothers. Marriage, and married motherhood, remains the modal family experience. Moreover, most single mothers do not stay single mothers. About two-thirds of divorced mothers remarry; the number is almost as high for never-married mothers.[19] Single mothers also cease being single mothers when their children leave home. Finally, some single mothers, particularly those who are divorced, are able

CONCLUSION 157

to maintain high standards of living for their families. This has led some to claim that work is a better defense against poverty than marriage for single mothers.[20] We reject this thinking as Procrustean. Most women don't consciously choose one or the other as an anti-poverty strategy—they focus on caring for their family, something that often conflicts with employment.

Why Family Structure?

America is a polarized nation and scholars of the family are no exception. This has manifested itself in debates over the importance of family structure. Some researchers and activists identify family structure as the single most important component of inequality and view marriage as the crucial bulwark against poverty. Others have questioned family structure as a meaningful analytic distinction. We believe that both extremes are inconsistent with the facts.

The family structure maximalists are represented in the Chapter 1 epigraph from U.S. Senator Mike Lee (R-UT). This determinist view identifies family structure as the cardinal source of child poverty in modern America. This perspective has been prominent in policy debates at the federal level, most notably in attempts to reduce poverty by promoting marriage.[21] We see several problems with the maximalist view. First, it fails to heed the fact that marriage is often not enough to lift adults and children out of poverty.[22] Second, it represents efforts to push the burden of caring for the poor from the state, with its great wealth of resources, to individuals.[23] Finally, marriage promotion has been attempted for decades and has not succeeded.[24] It's a fine aspirational ideal to encourage marriage among the less fortunate, but there's little evidence that anyone is listening.

Others have minimized the importance of family structure in response to the maximalists.[25] These scholars point to the abundance of poor married families, the sorry track record of marriage promotion, and the relatively modest contribution of single-mother families to growing American inequality. To understand inequality amongst families, they argue, one must look primarily elsewhere. Single motherhood is only one factor among many that accounts for poverty—and only in the United States is the relationship between family structure and income so profound.[26]

We reject both absolutist positions, with a caveat. Our results show that family structure interacts with labor market qualifications to determine

158 THANKS FOR NOTHING

income. Moreover, the differences between divorced and never-married families highlight the unique role of family structure. As we have seen, never-married mothers are challenged for reasons that go beyond their labor market characteristics. And while it can be reasonably argued that these reasons are not purely caused by nonmarital fertility, this is a distinction without a difference when it comes to public policy.

The caveat is that we broadly agree with the minimalists on the subject of public policy. The United States has a history of conditioning benefits for children on family structure. This doesn't need to be the case, as programs like SNAP (food stamps), CHIP (children's health insurance), and the EITC (earned income tax credit) show. Support for children should not be determined by family structure alone. Still, all of these benefits are family specific: even when qualification is solely based on children, such as the child tax credit, money is sent to the parents. Consequently, it makes no sense when devising government programs aimed to help children to ignore family structure, which is likely to remain a determinant of income.

Our final plea for the consideration of family structure is scholarly and goes out to a discipline that hasn't given it enough serious thought over the past 40 years. This is the community of scholars who study inequality and social stratification and are primarily focused on income, occupation, and their transmission between generations. These scholars typically study individuals and their earnings, not families. Our book highlights the fact that people are all part of families. Individuals make money, but they do so in the context of families, and it's family income that determines quality of life. For this reason, it's important to look at both family structure and labor market returns. If you only look at family structure, it's easy to descend into arguments about choice and culture. If you only look at individuals and their earnings, it's easy to think that family structure is irrelevant. Our book has sought to demonstrate that both family structure and labor force attributes are integral to understanding economic well-being for a population that so often relies on income transfers to make ends meet.

What Would Help

Over the past 40 years, there have been large policy shifts that have led to the growing inequality among families we document in Chapter 4. The transition from Aid to Families with Dependent Children (AFDC) to Temporary

CONCLUSION 159

Assistance for Needy Families (TANF) is one case in point: it was created with the explicit aim of reducing support to children from the government, and increasing reliance on the labor market. Another modern innovation is marriage promotion, which is based on the idea that parents can be convinced to marry and rely on each other, as if it's entirely the case that the right mindset leads people to tie the knot. Policies like these tend to prevail because they rely on dogma about abundant opportunity, and that people just need the right motivation to pursue it. But economic opportunity isn't a cultural good, and insofar as marriage has become less ubiquitous, it's not going to be revivified with an ad campaign. Instead, let us return to a more direct role for the government.

That the government should help impoverished single mothers isn't a novel suggestion. We don't have to create a tranche of policy recommendations out of whole cloth because a leading policy expert who understood family structure and poverty outlined what's necessary decades ago.[27] Daniel Patrick Moynihan's approach to poverty and single motherhood, first formed in the Johnson and Nixon White Houses, comes down to three points:

- Family structure affects children and is a rightful topic of public concern.
- Government is chiefly effective at taxing and redistributing money.
- Government efforts aimed at reshaping the family are unlikely to be successful. Instead, government should help the neediest families and create the economic conditions that will allow families to support themselves (which in turn will boost marriage rates).

These insights help us understand how much of the family policy enacted at the federal level in the past 40 years has played out and where we might go from here. (We review the intellectual history of the Moynihan Report and its implications for social policy at length in Appendix B.) First and foremost, is the legacy of the 1996 welfare reform legislation.[28] Moynihan, by then a United States senator (D-NY), vehemently opposed the Clinton-era bill, deeming it the "most retrograde proposal in social policy in this century."[29] Children would be "put to the sword" and relegated to "sleeping on grates."[30]

Was Moynihan right? We contend that his understanding of family and government offered an accurate prediction of how things turned out for *some* families and children in the wake of welfare reform. Initially, it seemed that reform was benefiting many single mothers. By the time welfare reform

160 THANKS FOR NOTHING

arrived, the American economy was enjoying one of its strongest expansions in the past half-century, with commensurate wage growth.[31] In addition, the EITC, greatly expanded under President Clinton in 1993, aided lower income families with working adults.[32] It was under these conditions that the initial appraisals of welfare reform were guardedly optimistic.[33] Welfare rolls declined, employment rose, and the poverty for single mothers fell over the next few years. But it was only a brief respite: the poverty rate started rising again subsequent to the dotcom crash at the end of the millennium.[34] By 2008, when the Great Recession first hit, poverty rates were just as high as they'd been in the early 1990s, before federal welfare reform.[35]

Had nothing really changed? Our analysis of the Current Population Survey (CPS) in Chapters 2–4, shows that the story is more complex. From 1980 to about 2000, incomes gradually improved for the median single mother, although few had attained what we might think of as middle-class incomes. After that, single mothers' incomes essentially stagnated for the next 20 years. Moreover, even positive trends in income obscured growing inequality among single mothers, anchored by the bottom 25% of never-married mothers, a class of women who've experienced no income growth since 1980. For the past 40 years, their incomes have been stuck below $10,000 in 2018 dollars (Figure 2.15). Even worse off are the bottom 10% of never-married mothers, whose incomes have fallen from about $5,000—supplied mostly by AFDC—in 1980, to essentially nothing by 2005 (Figure 4.4). Here we find the children sleeping on grates, in Moynihan's words, or the more familiar $2 a day poverty described by Kathy Edin and Luke Schaeffer.[36] Thus the move from welfare to work has succeeded for a number of women, but too many are still languishing in penury.[37]

Our findings show that a living wage from employment will never be a viable goal for some never-married mothers under current economic conditions. Throughout the book we've observed their comparably low rates of labor force participation, their low human capital, and—more important—the lower economic returns to their human capital. We should therefore accept that not all mothers can make ends meet by transitioning from welfare to work. Moreover, the results presented in Chapters 5 and 6 suggest that the economic woes single mothers face are likely to persist for decades. This holds especially true for women who give birth out of wedlock. Indeed, some of the challenges they contend with would appear to be intergenerational (Figures 5.8–5.14). Some mothers are just unlikely to ever do better than minimum wage jobs.

CONCLUSION 161

Policy makers have traditionally looked to fathers for greater support for single mothers. Increasing transfers from fathers was a component of the 1996 welfare reform. These transfers remain a crucial source of support for many mothers. Could fathers give more money? We are skeptical. As we observed in Chapter 3, federal legislation in the 1980s and 1990s greatly increased rates of compliance with support orders. We may be at the upper limits of what nonresidential fathers can actually afford, so larger support orders and beefed-up compliance mechanisms might be seeking blood from a stone.[38] Nonresident fathers should certainly pay what they can, but there's little reason to believe it will ever be enough: contrast the largest median support payments shown in Figure 3.21, about $4,000–6,000 a year, with the average annual expenditure per child of just under $10,000 a year as of 2015. And that last figure is just for households with incomes under $59,200. High income families spend twice as much.[39]

Finally, as the accumulated evidence has shown, marriage promotion hasn't succeeded as an anti-poverty measure. For decades, governments and pundits alike have urged single mothers to tie the knot (indeed, one of us has been among those pundits). It hasn't worked out. At this point policy makers should concede the obvious: telling people to get married won't make them get married.

Moynihan anticipated the failure of government marriage promotion, as well as the casualties of welfare reform. His proposed remedy remains the best at hand: direct cash transfers to poor mothers. Think this isn't a viable option in our polarized, post-AFDC politics? Think again. In 2019, Senators Michael Bennet (D-CO) and Mitt Romney (R-UT) introduced bipartisan legislation that would essentially fund a universal basic income for kids.[40] Parents would receive a baseline of "a guaranteed $1,500 in cash every year per child under the age of 6, no matter their income, and $1,000 per child aged 6 to 17 in the form of a fully refundable child tax credit (CTC), with additional benefits accruing for parents in accordance with existing statutes.[41] The subsidies would be funded by eliminating stepped-up basis, a provision that greatly decreases the tax liability for inherited property. The primary benefits of Romney–Bennet would be universal, paid to all parents regardless of income. This obviously increases the overall cost, but also creates a much larger base of potential support.[42] Universal transfers do carry a greater risk of inflation, but this is avoidable and therefore not a reason to forego direct transfer to families.[43] Moynihan himself proposed a basic income, the famed "negative income tax," that came tantalizingly close to passing, clearing the

162 THANKS FOR NOTHING

House of Representatives by a wide bipartisan margin before bogging down in the Senate.[44]

An even more ambitious plan than Romney–Bennet, President Joe Biden's Build Back Better (BBB) legislation, came within two Senate votes of becoming law in 2021.[45] BBB would have extended the fully refundable 2021 child tax credit included in the pandemic-inspired American Rescue Plan by providing $300 a month for each child under six and $250 a month for older kids. We have already seen how these payments temporarily reduced poverty rates. What's more, the usual doomsayers were proven wrong. The American Rescue Plan CTC didn't reduce employment.[46] Over 90% of CTC funds to low-income recipients were spent on food, shelter, and other necessities (but not alcohol, recreational drugs, or cigarettes).[47] And it's far from a sure bet that the American Rescue Plan and other COVID-inspired income transfers are entirely responsible for inflation.[48]

None of this should be seen as evidence that we're anti-work or anti-marriage. Far from it. Although social scientists avoided studying marriage for a generation in the wake of the Moynihan report, Sara McLanahan's work led the way towards a consensus on the benefits of married parents, gay or straight, for children's well-being.[49] Accordingly, there should be no financial disincentives to marriage. The tax code shouldn't penalize partners who choose to tie the knot, nor should there be benefits cliffs that impel mothers to avoid marriage or employment. As the liberal Senator Sherrod Brown (D-OH) frequently hammers home, there is—or should be—dignity in work.

Single mothers, to reiterate, don't get married just because politicians or academics tell them to do so. Moynihan indeed foresaw the failure of this sort of social engineering. But it's become clear that the government can do something to help marriage, and that's raise the prosperity of single men and women. In 2015, sociologist Daniel Schneider reviewed a number of experiments that boosted subjects' economic prospects.[50] Doing so, showed Schneider, increased the chances that women (but not men) would get married.

This finding scrambles the usual politics of marriage. In contemporary America, marriage is generally identified as a conservative priority, while bolstering the welfare state is a liberal goal. But it doesn't have to be that way. The modern welfare state was the brainchild of Germany's Otto von Bismarck. Chancellor Bismarck, by all rights deeply conservative, introduced pensions and disability insurance in the 1880s in order to keep the German economy humming while undermining the appeal of the leftist

CONCLUSION 163

Social Democratic Party.[51] The Iron Chancellor anticipated twenty-first-century American politics when he scolded the Reichstag in 1881: "Call it socialism or whatever you like. It is the same to me."[52]

We think pundits should be less worried about the threat of creeping socialism if they share Bismarck's desire for stability. More financial support for single mothers turns them into better consumers, and boosts their chances of marriage. These are worthy objectives, and are aligned with conservative priorities. And just as we implore conservatives to rethink their opposition to social democracy, we urge progressives to think of marriage as a social good. It's vexing to us that some social scientists think otherwise, despite the overwhelming majority of Americans who are married or aspire to marriage, and view the institution of marriage as beneficial for society.[53]

It's just such a convergence of ideological imperatives that's led to the successes of what Ronald Reagan once called "the best anti-poverty, the best pro-family, the best job creation measure to come out of Congress," the EITC.[54] Oren Cass, a conservative think tanker and domestic policy advisor to Mitt Romney's 2012 presidential campaign, has gone further, proposing that the EITC should be raised to the status of a full-fledged wage subsidy.[55] This would entail monthly payments from the government, rather than the annual rebate the EITC currently provides. An annual payment gets treated as a windfall, whereas regular payments let recipients pay their bills.[56]

All of this heeds Moynihan's advice about what government is singularly good at: redistributing income. At this point, it's very clear that the government is not good at changing minds about marriage. Decades of marriage promotion programs haven't made a dent in the declining marriage rate. Indeed, the only thing that would make a difference in raising the marriage rate would be giving money to poor people or getting them well-paying jobs, given the role that structural factors have played in the growth of single-mother families in the United States.[57] It's within the power of government to redistribute income, but not to change culture. Moynihan foresaw this almost 60 years ago and history has only proved him right.

While it's important that states should have some room to innovate, we hold up the 1996 welfare reform as a cautionary tale for an excessive embrace of federalism. This legislation converted a federal entitlement into block grants to states. Subsequently, many states spent their TANF funds on things that had nothing to do with needy families, such as their general budgets. By 2014, only about a quarter of TANF funds were actually being transferred to needy families.[58] Another quarter went to childcare and other expenses related to moving low-income mothers into the labor force. Some of the programs funded by the remaining 50% are no doubt worthwhile, but there's little doubt that some states have made it harder for deserving mothers to get help.[59] This reality evokes one of Moynihan's criticisms of Great Society programs: they enrich middle-class social workers at the expense of poor single mothers—who are in a better position anyway to determine what sort of help they need.[60] Indeed, this is one of the tenets of the movement for a universal basic income.[61]

The broader lessons of the past few decades lead us to believe that transferring money to single-mother families is the best way the government can help. It also seems like a not completely implausible notion in our current political climate given its bipartisan support and recent senatorial near miss.

Our findings highlight the importance of making sure that work pays—that mothers who are able to invest the time and effort to get a job are adequately compensated for doing so. Consider that long-standing redoubt of single-mother employment: minimum wage jobs in the service sector. Seven states, all but one in the south, rely on the federal minimum wage; perhaps not coincidentally, these southern states have among the highest rates of female-headed households in the nation.[62] Yet the federal minimum wage of $7.25 an hour hasn't been raised since 2009, and it's now worth 27% less after adjusting for inflation. It's now at a 66-year low in real value.[63] Even a modest hike in the federal minimum wage would help many single-mother families.

A related piece of federal legislation that we feel strongly about is the PRO Act, which would roll back many provisions of the noxious 1947 Taft–Hartley Act and make it easier for workers to organize. "Unionization," shows sociologist David Brady and his colleagues, "reduces working poverty for both unionized and non-union households and does not appear to discourage employment."[64] The decline in organized labor has contributed significantly to income inequality in the United States, while the reemergence of a strong labor movement would boost incomes in a way that accords with Moynihan's tenets on family structure.[65] Higher incomes would result from work, not government intervention, and would therefore incentivize employment.[66] Unions also represent local action and have the potential to rebuild civil society from the ground up. This may be particularly valuable for single mothers given the unique constraints on their time and other challenges to fully participating in civic life.[67]

We end this section on policy recommendations with a plea to dispense with tired shibboleths about "dependence," the enduring notion that giving

CONCLUSION 165

single mothers money will condition them to be work adverse and marriage adverse. Studies conducted in the late 1980s and early 1990s, the heyday of cash welfare, all showed that the majority of recipients didn't spend a long time on the rolls.[68] And we've already summarized a large body of research establishing that welfare doesn't create single mothers. Indeed, it's the other way around: experimental evidence suggests that raising women's incomes makes them more, not less, likely to get married.[69] What's more, a study of 23 nations across Europe and North America revealed no association between welfare generosity and single mothers' employment.[70] And to the extent women choose welfare over work, it's because it makes more sense for them to spend time with their kids rather than in a lousy job.[71] They might feel otherwise if work pays a decent wage. Finally, if some women become dependent on welfare, then so what? We might despair of the iniquity of a few lazy mothers, but should remember that the ultimate beneficiaries of a child tax credit are their children. "Dependence" might seem more tolerable if it produces a generation of healthier, better-adjusted Americans.

In Closing

Single motherhood—and, more broadly today, single parenthood—is here to stay.[72] Social policy should not reflect a wishful desire to reestablish nuclear families with married parents as the universal experience for children.[73] There's no good reason to think we'll ever return to 1950s levels of two-parent families, a historical anomaly that emerged from a ruinous depression and a ruinous world war.[74] Despite women's strong gains in education, the labor force, and all other areas of American life, single-parent families will always face unique economic challenges in a society where two working adults are required for prosperity.

The challenge ahead is how to best support these families, given that the labor market hasn't proved to be a viable solution for every single mother. The quarter-century since the 1996 welfare reform legislation has laid this issue bare. Work has paid off for many single mothers, but others were never going to fare well once off government aid. A return to pro-family policies would pay dividends for future generations, so it's merely a question of when the political will to support these families will finally emerge.

APPENDIX A

Explaining the Growth
of Single Motherhood

This is a book about the economics of single motherhood, and how they've changed over the past 40 years. We explore the correlates of income, and how they differ for married, divorced, and never-married mothers. As we'll see, many of these correlates are apparent before women become mothers, or single mothers.

We can't understand the economics of single motherhood without considering the differences between women before they become single mothers, but this line of inquiry shouldn't be mistaken for an account of *why* women become single mothers, or why the number of single mothers has grown over the past few decades. These are important questions, but are well beyond the scope of our book. Accordingly, we will point interested readers in the right direction.

Like so much in American culture, this is a deeply polarized (and polarizing) academic literature. Liberals have long argued that the ranks of single mothers have swelled largely due to structural factors, most conspicuously deindustrialization and the concomitant decline in male wages. Some progressives will even question the need for a book about single mothers. Conservatives are more likely to attribute the growth in single mothers to a combination of cultural change in conjunction with feckless welfare policies.

We address (and largely dismiss) the role of welfare in Chapters 1 and 7, as this has bearing on our policy prescriptions. Otherwise, we believe that there are both cultural and structural forces that have shaped both the growth and the composition of the population of single motherhood. Wolfinger's book, *Soul Mates: Religion, Sex, Love and Marriage among African Americans and Latinos*, coauthored with W. Bradford Wilcox, used data from three different national surveys to explore the effects of structure and culture on the different family dynamics that lead to single motherhood.[1] These include nonmarital childbirth, getting married, and getting divorced. Wilcox and Wolfinger cast a wide net: the economic forces they measured included education, work history, income, and wealth, while their cultural measures included attitudes towards sex, pregnancy, and single parenting, along with media consumption, contraceptive use, delinquency, sexual behavior, and whether respondents hail from single- or two-parent families. Although the effects of these predictors vary somewhat on the different outcomes—nonmarital fertility, marriage, divorce—the underlying pattern does not: both cultural and structural factors help explain who ends up as a single mother.

Other studies have offered in-depth looks at the social forces responsible for single- and two-parent families. Two of the most important are a paper by economists Janet Yellen and George Akerlof—respectively the Biden administration's Treasury secretary and a Nobel laureate—and a book by sociologists Kathryn Edin and Maria Kefalas, *Promises I Can Keep: Why Poor Women Put Motherhood Before Marriage*.[2]

The Yellen and Akerlof piece shows that the development of effective birth control in the 1960s played a pivotal role in the rise of nonmarital births. Prior to the 1960s, sex

168   APPENDIX A

outside of wedlock wasn't uncommon, but the consequences were very different than they are today.[3] Back then an out-of-wedlock childbirth was deeply stigmatizing; this was the era when pregnant teenage girls were "sent away" to have their "bastards" so the neighbors wouldn't know. But that was an infrequent outcome. Most of the time, the man "did the right thing" and married his pregnant girlfriend. If he wavered, his future father-in-law might theoretically threaten him to insure he came to the alter—in other words, a shotgun wedding.

Effective birth control changed all that, Yellen and Akerlof argue, by releasing men of their obligation to do the right thing. If a women became pregnant, her paramour could now walk away. It was her own damn fault she got pregnant, because she didn't use birth control. If she really didn't want to become a mother, she was now free to get an abortion. Of course, many women kept their babies and became single mothers.

Why did they increasingly make this choice? Edin and Kefalas provide the answer. Nonmarital fertility has always been more common among less educated and less prosperous couples. Moreover, the rate of nonmarital fertility started to skyrocket in the 1970s and 1980s, as the good job opportunities for less educated men started to evaporate. Simultaneously, women's economic prospects were rising. This created a population of men unable to secure the kind of good jobs that might support a family.[4] Women might feel the same way, especially because some of them now felt like they could support themselves. Yet many of them didn't foresee great economic prospects. Since their marital prospects now looked equally dim, they turned to a more readily available source of fulfillment: motherhood. Men and women still aspired to marriage, but it just seemed unattainable or, at best, something to pursue after they were finally ensconced in jobs or careers with decent economic prospects.[5]

This is a thumbnail sketch of a well-developed argument from Edin and Kefalas, but it provides a cohesive explanation for how cultural and structural trends functioned together to drive up the rate of nonmarital fertility.

The other main way women become single mothers is through divorce. The divorce rate skyrocketed between 1965 and 1980 in what scholars have come to call the divorce boom.[6] Since 1980, the divorce rate has trended downwards in what's become the most sustained decline in divorce ever recorded. Yet the divorce rate remains well above pre-boom levels.

The American economy was thriving through the 1960s and into the early 1970s, so we must look elsewhere to explain the origins of the divorce boom. The causes are complex. In part, they reflect the unusual demographic conditions of the 1950s, but most fundamentally stem from a growing sense of individual rights. The 1960s gave rise to the notion of the right to be happy in one's marriage. This developed in accordance with a burgeoning spirit of equality between the sexes. Men and women alike now felt free to leave marriages that were unhappy, or even marriages that were simply unfulfilling.[7] And as the divorce rate increased, divorce came to beget more divorce. It turned out that divorce is socially contagious: people are more likely to divorce when they know more divorced people.[8]

Macroeconomic factors started to juice the divorce rate as the 1960s turned into the 1970s; the economy tanked and the divorce boom kicked into overdrive. Women joined the workforce in far greater numbers. At first, many did so due to a preference for work, but as male wages stagnated women were forced to work simply to make ends meet. This contributed to the growing divorce rate as dual-career marriages induced hitherto unknown domestic conflict. It's also true that women's newfound financial independence

APPENDIX A   169

allowed them to leave bad marriages, but this is less important a cause of divorce than was the emergent conflict over housework, childcare, and the collision of traditional and modern gender roles.[9]

In time, marriage changed from a near universal right of passage to a status good for elites.[10] Forty years ago there were virtually no difference in the marriage or divorce rates based on social class. Today, prime marriage-age adults aged 35–45 are over 20 percentage points more likely to be married if they have four-year college degrees.[11] Thus the marriage rate has declined only modestly among the college educated. Just like earlier generations, they're likely to get married, have children, and stay together. It's among the less educated that marriage rates have dropped way off. These trends have been well documented by the sociologist Andrew Cherlin and others. And to be sure, rates of nonmarital fertility have increased among college educated women. But they've grown much more for women with less education.

Here's one thing that didn't increase the population of single-mother families: no-fault divorce laws. California governor Ronald Reagan signed the first modern no-fault law on January 1, 1970, simply because divorce cases were clogging the courts in his state.[12] How do we know the move to no-fault didn't raise the divorce rate? The divorce rate was already rising in states that adopted no-fault laws early, in the first few years of the 1970s. Afterwards divorce rates continued to rise at the same rate. In contrast, divorce rates were already falling in states that adopted no-fault laws late, in the 1980s. After their adoption divorce rates continued to fall.[13] Divorce rates are now at a 50-year low.[14]

Finally, it's worth noting the implicit comparison that runs through treatments of how the family has changed in recent decades. Most accounts of *rising* divorce rates or *falling* marriage rates reference the 1950s, implicitly or explicitly.[15] This reflects the presumption that the 1950s were a normal decade, when in reality no decade is more normal than any other. The 1950s was a time of early marriage, low divorce, and almost no premarital fertility, and so many find it strategic to use as a baseline from which the modern family developed.

The 1950s were anomalous, however, first and foremost, by coming on the heels of the Great Depression and World War II.[16] Fertility declined during the Depression, which meant an unusually small birth cohort came of age in the early 1950s. This meant a scarcity of workers, which lifted wages, and a paucity of alternative partners, which reduced divorce. Demobilization after World War II produced big spikes in both marriage—which kick-started the baby boom—and divorce. The post-war surge in divorce purged troubled marriages from the overall pool, resulting in an artificially low divorce rate for the next few years.

Long-run trends also left an imprint on the 1950s family. Into the 1930s, more than one in two hundred American women died in childbirth.[17] Indeed, the number of single-parent families produced by divorce only surpassed those produced by bereavement in the 1940s.[18] Parental death was therefore in full retreat by the 1950s. Rates of nonmarital fertility were also low.

All of this helped produce the lowest median marriage ages and the highest marriage rates in American history, leading to a (White) workforce paid well enough to support children and a stay-at-home wife. To be sure, women's labor force participation increased in the 1950s, but there were still many more single-earner families than there are today. At the time it was legal for employees to discriminate on the basis of marital status, and female employment was simply not a cultural preference. Ultimately the 1950s witnessed the longest sustained decline in divorce then on record. The result was a decade in which

170 APPENDIX A

more children were raised in two-parent families than at any other time in American history.

Although it makes sense to describe the modern American family as something that emerged out of the 1950s, we should hardly consider that decade a baseline. It was more of a way station, emerging as a product of myriad unique dynamics.

APPENDIX B

On Moynihan, the Enduring Fallout from his 1965 Report, and the Implications for Studying Single Motherhood

Daniel Patrick Moynihan (1927–2003) cuts a unique figure in United States history as a scholar-politician. He was appointed to four successive presidential administrations, an unparalleled feat of public service, before serving four terms as a Democratic senator from New York. In between spells of government service, he was a tenured professor at Harvard, and authored 19 books. Woodrow Wilson may have risen from academia to the presidency, but Moynihan was a much more productive scholar and spent many more years in government service.

Today Moynihan is perhaps most remembered for his 1965 report, "The Negro Family: The Case for National Action."[1] Written while the author was Assistant Secretary of Labor under President Lyndon Johnson, the report was never intended for public release. Moynihan's name never appeared on it. The Report was a piece of serious social science, buttressed with pages of tables and citations. But unlike most social science, the Report's prose was often baroque, and sometimes overheated. This is evident in its most famous passage:

> At the center of the *tangle of pathology* is the weakness of the family structure. Once or twice removed, it will be found to be the principal source of most of the aberrant, inadequate, or antisocial behavior that did not establish but now serves to perpetuate the cycle of poverty and deprivation (emphasis added).[2]

Presumably the intent of language like this was to motivate the Johnson administration to pay attention, but it's probably what led to someone leaking the report a few months after it was submitted.

For our purposes the Report's arguments can be boiled down to three points:

- There's a crisis in Black America that relates to the high number of single-parent families.
- The African American crisis has its roots in racism and discrimination, both contemporary and historical.
- America must undertake financial investment in African American employment and education in order to become a fair and equitable nation.

Soon after the Report's publication, Moynihan wrote these ideas into Lyndon Johnson's soaring commencement address at Howard University. It articulated a vision of a vastly expanded Civil Rights Movement that was soon to tragically founder on the shoals of the Watts riot and the Vietnam War.

The response to the leaked Report fell somewhat short of soaring. Harvard psychologist William Ryan penned the best-known contemporary critique, lacerating the Report

172   APPENDIX B

for its language of disintegration, pathology, sexism, and dependence in single-mother families.[3] Moynihan was "blaming the victim," a turn of phrase coined by Ryan in reference to the Report and later expanded into a full-length book.[4] This interpretation of the Moynihan Report had legs, enduring to the present day. Celebrated author Ta-Nehisi Coates is just one of many to assail the Report.[5] Less often, the Report has been criticized from its economic left, most notably by the Civil Rights hero Bayard Rustin.[6] Yet Rustin also had praise for the Report. So too did Martin Luther King, Jr.—but only in private in conversation with Moynihan.[7]

As we observed in the preface, the Ryan-esque misreading of the Moynihan Report had a pernicious effect on social science in the 1970s, with scholars disavowing, or at least ignoring, the importance of family structure for all families, not just African Americans.[8] These intellectual currents found purchase in popular culture, arriving in an era of skyrocketing divorce rates, oil crises, stagflation, Vietnam, Watergate, malaise, and perhaps most important, a thoroughgoing suspicion of social institutions.[9] And while many left-leaning intellectuals were rejecting or ignoring the Moynihan report, it acquired conservative supporters. Some of Moynihan's friends, colleagues, and collaborators dating back to the era of the Report were the intellectuals later identified as the progenitors of neoconservatism, including Daniel Bell, Nathan Glazer, and Irving Kristol. These associations probably scared many academics away from the social science of the report, while greasing the skids for conservative admirers.

Perhaps no conservative endorsement has been more emblematic than the Manhattan Institute's Kay Hymowitz's, in a sneering 2005 article "The Black Family: 40 Years of Lies."[10] Like most of Moynihan's conservative supporters, Hymowitz is appropriately critical of those who called the report racist, and those who minimize the importance of family structure. But Moynihan's conservative admirers, then and now, tend to give short shrift to vital components of the Report.[11] Moynihan, a self-avowed liberal all his life, placed the blame for the condition of African American families squarely on racism, articulated the relationship between family structure and the labor market, and called for federal investment in Black communities.

The liberal rejoinder to the Moynihan detractors started in the 1980s with Sara McLanahan's work. Scholars came to recognize that the Report offers a structural explanation for poverty and inequality, focusing on the labor market determinants of both inequality and the intergenerational transmission of disadvantage.[12] William Julius Wilson, perhaps the foremost public sociologist of the past half-century, challenged liberal taboos surrounding the Moynihan Report in his 1987 book, *The Truly Disadvantaged*.[13] Wilson, who is himself Black, channeled Moynihan by linking African American family structure to economic disadvantage. He subsequently would describe the Report as a "prophetic document."[14] By 2015, Sara McLanahan and another senior scholar, Sandy Jenks, rehabilitated Moynihan even more explicitly, in an article entitled "Was Moynihan Right?"[15] Also answering this question in the affirmative was Barack Obama, in his 2006 book *The Audacity of Hope*.[16]

We've provided this thumbnail history of Moynihan and his 1965 Report to diffuse preconceptions. Some readers may have only a vague knowledge of Moynihan, above and beyond some murky understanding of a dead White guy who wrote something racist and sexist long ago. Others may be wholly unfamiliar with the Report, a pivotal document that's shaped public and academic consideration of family structure and single motherhood. As we suggest in Chapter 7, this is regrettable. Daniel Patrick Moynihan greatly contributed to our understanding of family structure—not to mention his insight into the

APPENDIX B 173

poisonous legacy of slavery and Jim Crow—and showed the way forward to a better social policy for single motherhood (and indeed, for all underprivileged Americans).

To commemorate the 50th anniversary of the Moynihan Report in 2015, the *Atlantic* reprinted it with annotations from the historian Daniel Geary.[17] His introduction establishes its continuing relevance amidst ideological tensions:

> Fifty years later, the Moynihan Report is still a contested symbol among American thinkers and policymakers, cited by everyone from Barack Obama to Paul Ryan. Earlier this month, New York City's police commissioner and mayor publicly sparred over the report with the former calling it "prescient" and the latter dismissing it as outdated. Liberals and conservatives alike praise the report's analysis, but it is still anathema to many on the Left.[18]

It shouldn't be. William Julius Wilson was right on the money when he called the Moynihan Report a prophetic document. It was the first modern federal study that examined the relationship between the labor market, race, family structure, and inequality. Back in 1965, Moynihan had the perspicacity to argue about how these were linked to opportunity and child well-being. Over the following years, he continued to advance the themes of the Report, even as both social scientists and politicians looked elsewhere for explanations and solutions. Moynihan also understood the limits of government power long before George W. Bush squandered hundreds of millions of dollars on marriage promotion, and conceived of a universal basic income decades before the phrase "universal basic income" meant anything.

In short, Moynihan knew both what the problem was, and what we should do about it. Politicians on both the left and the right have often failed to heed the call and the result has been the income disparities described in this book.

APPENDIX C

The Equivalence of Equivalence Scales[1]

In Chapter 1, we set out several reasons why we choose to focus on family income rather than per capita income or one of a number of alternatives. First, family income is what determines quality of life. Second, all equivalence scales are ratios and therefore are not acceptable dependent variables for regression analysis. Third, some equivalence scales are based on the poverty line and therefore aren't suitable for looking at more well-off mothers. Finally, we contend that it doesn't matter anyway since the majority of American mothers now have only one or two children.

But seeing is believing, so here we present results based on three equivalence scales: 1) per capita income, chosen because it's the simplest and most familiar such scale; 2) Census supplemental poverty-adjusted income, because the Census uses it; 3) income divided by the square root of family size, used by the Organization for Economic Cooperation and Development, the Congressional Budget Office, and others.[2]

The first thing to note from Figures C.1–C.3 is that the absolute dollar values are different in each. For instance, for married mothers in 2018, median adjusted incomes were at about $25,000 for per capita income (Figure C.1), $45,000 for Census supplemental poverty-adjusted income (Figure C.2), and $50,000 for square root-adjusted income (Figure C.3). A case can be made for each of the three equivalence scales, but none provide the intuitive insight into quality of life that family income offers.

More important, all three figures tell the same story about relative income that family income does: married mothers have by far the highest income and never-married mothers have the lowest, with divorced mothers in the middle. What's more, divorced and never-married mothers are closer to one another than to married mothers, a pattern that holds throughout this book in our analysis of family income. Finally, the three scales tell more or less the same story about trends over the past 40 years.

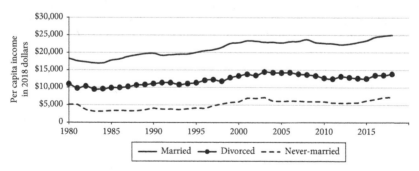

Figure C.1. Per Capita Income by Marital Status.
Notes: N = 681,144 (married) 85,105 (divorced) 87,480 (never married). Results are weighted.
Source: CPS 1980–2018.

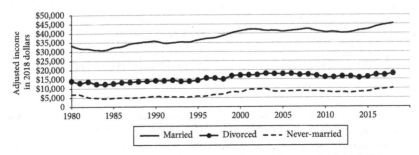

Figure C.2. Census Supplemental Poverty-Adjusted Income by Marital Status.
Notes: N = 681,144 (married) 85,105 (divorced) 87,480 (never married). Results are weighted.
Source: CPS 1980–2018.

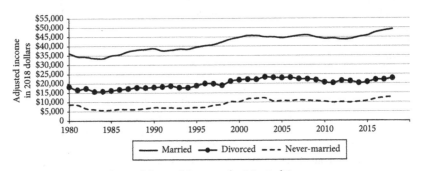

Figure C.3. Square Root-Adjusted Income by Marital Status.
Notes: N = 681,144 (married) 85,105 (divorced) 87,480 (never married). Results are weighted.
Source: CPS 1980–2018.

These observations make clear that we're not missing anything important by focusing on family income rather than income based on one of myriad equivalence scales. Indeed, given the data shown here it seems easier to justify our use of family income than choosing one equivalence scale over another.

APPENDIX D

Data and Methods

Chapter 1 briefly discusses the two datasets we use in the book, both of which provide a wealth of evidence on the incomes and other attributes of single mothers in the United States. This Appendix provides further details.

Part I. The Current Population Survey

The March Demographic Supplement of the Current Population Survey (CPS) is a cross-sectional survey of about 50,000 households collected annually by the Census Bureau and the Bureau of Labor Statistics.[1] The CPS data are nationally representative and contain detailed information on income and other participant characteristics. We use CPS data from 1980 through 2018, inclusive. We use the version of the data that have been made uniform by the Center for Economic and Policy Research, 2021, CPS ORG Uniform Extracts, Version 1.1. Washington, DC.

On Measuring Single Mothers

The CPS provides a roster of all residents in a household. We first exclude all households without minor children present. Families that include children who are not related to the householder are also excluded.[2] While these do potentially include a distinct population of single mothers, they also comprise various living arrangements that are hard to describe as child-rearing families. More important, we have no information on the mothers of these children. This initial winnowing of the sample leaves a representative set of families where children are being raised by person(s) who are either their parents or legal guardians.

After these sample restrictions, about 95% of CPS households contain only one family. Furthermore, the overwhelming majority of those households consist of what we usually think of as a nuclear family: one or two parents and their children. There are a relatively small number of more complex family arrangements, and we were able to use the family rosters to capture this complexity. Parents who live with their own parents are one such example. For many of these households, the grandparents are listed as the householder, but for some households the mothers we're studying are so designated. In both cases, it's possible to capture the presence of a three-generation household using the household roster, information on each person's relationship to the householder, and the presence of a subfamily in the household. Finally, we exclude respondents who are missing information on family relationships, as it's impossible to know what sort of families they are living in.

These coding decisions result in a sample of 807,715 families, 83% married mothers, 9% divorced mothers, and 8% never-married mothers, from a total CPS sample of just over 6.7 million participants. One implication of such a large sample is the irrelevance of

178   APPENDIX D

statistical inference. Accordingly we don't present the results of significance tests in our analysis of CPS data.

Other Variables and Analysis

Except where noted, we analyze family income.[3] The CPS measures pre-tax income from various sources. Some sources of income, such as capital gains or lump sum payments are excluded, as are nonmonetary benefits such as food subsidies. Money that family members bring in from wages, income from self-employment, government transfers, interest from investments, pensions, and transfers from people outside of the family (such as child support) are all included in the income total. Extremely high family incomes are top-coded in the CPS so that individual families cannot be identified.

As discussed in Chapter 3, we use median regression models to explore the correlates of income. These models are more robust than ordinary least squares (OLS) regression, and permit the use of skewed measures like income as dependent variables. One consideration with quantile regression is how to calculate the standard errors. Compared to OLS, median regression entails statistically complex estimation of the variance-covariance matrix. A common solution is to bootstrap standard errors. We did so, and obtained identical results.[4] For Chapter 4 we use quantile regression models that predict income at the 25th percentile and 75th percentile.

The quantile regression models include the following independent variables: race (White, African American, Latina, other); education (not a high school graduate, high school graduate, some college, four-year college graduate); employment (working 35 or more hours a week, working 1 to 34 hours a week, not working); number of children (one, two, three or more); whether there are children under age six present; whether mothers first gave birth as teenagers; whether mothers are living with their own parent(s) or grandparent(s); whether mothers are living with an opposite-sex partner; age and its square. Number of children is top-coded at three since fewer than 7% of American mothers have more than three minor children. The presence of a partner is measured using adjusted Person of Opposite Sex Sharing Living Quarters, or POSSLQ, as the CPS only started measuring cohabitation directly in 1995.[5] In addition, direct measures of cohabitation are themselves not always accurate due to the informal nature of some cohabiting relationships. (Some readers might attest to spending a lot of time at a significant other's house, then offering a qualified answer about one's place of residence.)[6] Finally, survey year is measured at five-year intervals to allow for reduced volatility in measuring changes over time, and to provide adequate sample sizes for estimating quantile regression models. All statistically significant interactions between survey year and other independent variables were retained in the models.

Part II. The National Longitudinal Survey of Youth 1979 Cohort

The National Longitudinal Surveys (NLS) are a series of panel surveys collected by the United States Bureau of Labor Statistics, a division of the Department of Labor. We analyze data from the longest running NLS panel, the National Longitudinal Survey of Youth's 1979 cohort (NLSY79).[7] NLSY79 began with a nationally representative sample of 12,686 men and women first interviewed in 1979, when respondents were ages 14 to 22. The original survey included over-samples of Hispanics, "economically disadvantaged non-blacks and non-Hispanics," and respondents in the military (these over-samples were discontinued over the next decade.)[8] Respondents were re-interviewed annually until 1994 and biennially thereafter.

Our analysis uses NLSY data collected through 2018, giving us 28 waves of data. We opt not to use the 2020 data because they would take us far afield: 2020 data are uniquely affected by COVID. Moreover, by 2020 NLSY respondents are between 55 and 63 years old. Just 5% of female respondents still had minor children at home in 2018, and therefore qualified as mothers for purposes of our book.

The data are weighted to make them nationally representative. To account for design effects and the inflated standard errors induced by the weights, we conduct significance tests based on robust standard errors.[9] Missing data are deleted listwise unless missing substantial numbers of cases. In these instances we rely on mean imputation and missing data dummy variables. More sophisticated means of handling missing data, such as multiple imputation, do not perform appreciably better.[10]

Identifying Mothers

For each survey wave, we identify mothers living with minor children, then distinguish them by marital status: married, divorced, never-married (there are too few widows to analyze.)[11] NLSY79 does contain an alternative: annual retrospective data on marriage, divorce, and fertility would permit us to narrow down motherhood and marital status to the month. But doing so comes with two tradeoffs. First, measurement error is far greater than with marital status and fertility ascertained at the time of data collection. Second, almost all of our independent variables are measured annually. For these reasons we used the annual data.

There is one exception: women who became married, divorced, or never-married mothers prior to the first wave of data collection in 1979. These items reveal a limited amount of family formation occurring as far back as 1971, when the oldest NLSY79 respondents were 13 years old. These data are primarily used to ascertain whether respondents were never-married, divorced, or married mothers. These data are often incomplete due to survey limitations; for instance, there is no way to identify women who exited divorced motherhood—in other words, they first got married, had children, got divorced, and then remarried, all before ages 14–22—prior to the first survey wave in 1979. Fortunately, there are very few women who fall into these complex patterns of family formation and dissolution prior to the start of the survey. For instance, there were a total of three women in the sample who first had children out of wedlock and then got married, all prior to 1979. For the most part, the retrospective data are sufficient for the simpler task of determining which women became married, divorced, or never-married mothers prior to the first survey wave.

Most of our data analysis measures motherhood and marital status annually, but in a few instances we compute a lifetime measure. For this item, never-married motherhood trumps divorced motherhood, which in turn trumps married motherhood. Thus a women who gives birth out of wedlock and subsequently gets married is identified as a never-married mother, whether or not her marriage eventually ends. Elsewhere we examine sequences of family formation, looking at mothers with more complex

180 APPENDIX D

marital histories. Other analyses explore the timing of entry into and exits from married, divorced, and never-married motherhood.

Other Variables

We examine how family structure is correlated with a number of respondent attributes, including income, education, employment, family size, age of entry into motherhood, time spent as a married, divorced, or never-married mother, and race/ethnicity. Here and elsewhere in the book, "income" refers to net family income measured in 2018 dollars to account for inflation; we explore alternate measures of income in Appendix C. Other analyses look at mothers' own families of origin. Here we measure family structure, maternal and paternal employment, maternal and paternal education, and two measures of social capital: at age 14, did a respondent's family have a newspaper delivered, and whether anyone in a respondent's family have a library card. We also explore respondents' living arrangements, ascertaining whether they live with either their own parents or with a romantic partner. Finally, we look at transfer income, from both the government and from former spouses and romantic partners. Our measure of government aid includes both in-kind benefits like SNAP (Supplemental Nutrition Assistance Program, i.e., food stamps) and cash transfers (e.g., "welfare," Aid to Families with Dependent Children and Temporary Aid to Needy Families).

Analysis

Chapter 5 is based entirely on bivariate and trivariate statistics, while Chapter 6 reports the results of multivariate analysis. Figure 6.2 relies on OLS regression to predict the natural logarithm of peak family lifetime income, calculated as the mean of the three largest annual measures of family income. We acknowledge that this is an imperfect statistical model. Ordinary least squares regression is rarely appropriate for panel data, and this model makes a muddle of causal order. Readers are cautioned to interpret these results accordingly. We include the results of this regression model because it permits the inclusion of covariates that cannot be used in the fixed effects regression described here.

Figure 6.2 reflects five nested regression equations. The baseline model measures marital status (married, divorced, never-married), race/ethnicity (White, African American, Latina, other), and a measure of panel attrition: the last year a mother participated in the NLSY79 survey. The second model adds measures of mothers' own families of origin, including mother's education, father's education, whether a respondent was raised in an intact family, father's employment, and the aforementioned items concerning newspapers and library cards. The third model adds measures of fertility, including a mother's age at first birth and how many children she'd had by 2000, when the NLSY79 mothers ranged from 35 to 43 years old. The fourth model adds three variables measuring the number of years each respondent had spent in married motherhood, divorced motherhood, and never-married motherhood. The fifth and final model adds respondent education at age 25, a time by which most Americans have completed their formal schooling. Here and elsewhere, education is measured with a five-category dummy variable classification: didn't graduate from high school, high school graduate, some college, four-year college graduate, advanced degree.

APPENDIX D   181

Chapter 6 also reports the results of a causal model. We estimate fixed effects models predicting annual log-family income, a more appropriate estimator for panel data than the aforementioned OLS model. A fixed effects model essentially uses multiple waves of panel data to treat each respondent as her own control.[12] This accounts for all differences between mothers that don't change over time. The flipside is that only time-varying covariates can be included as independent variables in a fixed effects model. We conducted Hausman tests to determine that fixed effects models rather than random effects models best fit our data.[13]

We conducted three nested fixed effects models. The first model includes only marital status, age and its square, and a measure of panel attrition.[14] The second adds measures of work and education, measured annually. Employment is measured as current employment status, the number of jobs a mother has held and its square, and hours worked. The third model adds the number of children a mother has, its square, and whether a mother is living with a romantic partner.

Notes

Chapter 1

1. "Joint Economic Committee. 2020. "Improving Family Stability for the Well Being of American Children." Hearing before the Joint Economic Committee, Congress of the United States, 2020, 2. Available at https://www.govinfo.gov/content/pkg/CHRG-116jhrg40561/pdf/CHRG-116jhrg40561.pdf. A disclaimer: the last clause of the quote from Senator Lee, about religion and family, reflects research conducted by one of the current authors with one of the witnesses at the Joint Economic Committee hearing. Wilcox, W. Bradford and Nicholas H. Wolfinger. 2016. *Soul Mates: Religion, Sex, Love and Marriage among African Americans and Latinos.* New York: Oxford University Press.

2. Quayle, Dan. 1992. "On Family Values." Address to the Commonwealth Club of California, May 19. Available at http://www.vicepresidentdanquayle.com/speeches_StandingFirm_CCC_1.html.

3. Wines, Michael. 1992. "Views on Single Motherhood Are Multiple at White House." *The New York Times*, May 21. Available at https://www.nytimes.com/1992/05/21/us/views-on-single-motherhood-are-multiple-at-white-house.html.

4. Perhaps the most prominent was Whitehead, Barbara Dafoe. 1993. "Dan Quayle Was Right." *The Atlantic*, April. Available at http://www.theatlantic.com/magazine/archive/1993/04/dan-quayle-was-right/7015/; see also Blankenhorn, David. 1995. *Fatherless America: Confronting Our Most Urgent Social Problem.* Scranton, PA: HarperCollins Publishers.

5. See Table C3 in United States Census Bureau. 2010. "America's Families and Living Arrangements: 2010." Washington, DC: United States Government Printing Office; on changes in the relative number of children living with divorced and never-married mothers, Rawlings, Steve W. and Arlene F. Saluter. 1994. *Household and Family Characteristics: March 1994.* Current Population Reports, 20–483. Washington, DC: United States Government Printing Office. Available at https://citeseerx.ist.psu.edu/viewdoc/download?doi=10.1.1.204.322&rep=rep1&type=pdf; on the historical importance of divorce as a source of single parenthood, Bumpass, Larry L. and James A. Sweet. 1989. "Children's Experience in Single-Parent Families: Implications of Cohabitation and Marital Transitions." *Family Planning Perspective* 21: 256–260.

6. Martin, Joyce A., Brady E. Hamilton, Michele J. K. Osterman, and Anne. K. Driscoll. 2019. *Births: Final Data for 2018.* National Vital Statistics Reports; vol 68, no 13. Hyattsville, MD: National Center for Health Statistics. See specifically Table 9. Available at https://www.cdc.gov/nchs/data/nvsr/nvsr68/nvsr68_13-508.pdf. This figure includes births to previously married women. In the past few years, the rate of nonmarital fertility has declined a bit, most likely due to expanded access to long-acting birth control. Schneider, Daniel and Alison Gemmill. 2016. "The Surprising Decline in the Nonmarital Fertility Rate in the United States." *Population and Development Review*: 627–649.

7. Wang, Wendy. 2020. "The U.S. Divorce Rate Has Hit a 50-Year Low." Institute for Family Studies. Available at https://ifstudies.org/blog/the-us-divorce-rate-has-hit-a-50-year-low.

8. On rates of children experiencing divorce, Wilcox, W. Bradford. 2011. *Why Marriage Matters: Thirty Conclusions from the Social Sciences*, 3rd ed. Broadway Publications, figures 1 and 2; on rates of maternal custody after divorce, Cancian, Marcia and Daniel R. Meyer. 1998. "Who Gets Custody?" *Demography* 35: 147–157; Cancian, Maria, Daniel R. Meyer, Patricia R. Brown, and Steven T. Cook. 2014. "Who Gets Custody Now? Dramatic Changes in Children's Living Arrangements After Divorce." *Demography* 51: 1381–1396.

9. United States Census Bureau. 2020. *America's Families and Living Arrangements: 2020.* Available at https://www.census.gov/data/tables/2020/demo/families/cps-2020.html. See Table C.2. Many more children, perhaps up to 50%, will have experienced single parenting by the time they turn 18. Bumpass, Larry L. 1984. "Children and Marital Disruption: A Replication and Update."

184   NOTES TO PAGES 2–3

Demography 21: 71–82; Bumpass, Larry L. and R. Kelly Raley. 1995. "Redefining Single-Parent Families: Cohabitation and Changing Family Reality." *Demography* 32: 97–109. A more recent estimate puts this figure slightly lower, at about 47%. Zill, Nicholas. 2021. "Growing Up with Mom and Dad: New Data Confirm the Tide Is Turning." *Institute for Family Studies*, June. Available at https://ifstudies.org/blog/growing-up-with-mom-and-dad-new-data-confirm-the-tide-is-turning#:~:text=The%20proportion%20of%20children%20living,between%20 4%20and%205%20percent

10. United States Census Bureau. 2023. "Historical Living Arrangements of Children," Table CH-1, 2021. Available at https://www.census.gov/data/tables/time-series/demo/families/children. html. See Table CH-1.

11. O'Neill, William L. 1967. *Divorce in the Progressive Era*. New Haven: Yale University Press. Perhaps one in seven marriages at the turn of the century ended in divorce, an all-time high. Many more children lived in single-parent families on account of the high death rate at the time.

12. Holbrook, Evans. 1910. "Divorce Laws and the Increase of Divorce." *Michigan Law Review*: 386–395. Available at https://repository.law.umich.edu/cgi/viewcontent.cgi?article=2093&context= articles.

13. Moynihan, Daniel Patrick. 1965. *The Negro Family: The Case for National Action*. Washington, DC: U.S. Department of Labor, Office of Policy Planning and Research. Available at https:// www.dol.gov/general/aboutdol/history/webid-moynihan.

14. Kerner, Otto, et al. 1968. *Report of the National Advisory Commission on Civil Disorders*. Washington, DC: United States Government Printing Office. Available at https://belonging. berkeley.edu/sites/default/files/kerner_commission_full_report.pdf?file=1&force=1.

15. Carroll, Peter N. 1982. *It Seemed Like Nothing Happened: America in the 1970s*. New Brunswick, NJ: Rutgers University Press, 279.

16. Rector, Robert and Melissa Pardue. 2004. "Understanding the President's Healthy Marriage Initiative." Washington, DC: Heritage Foundation. Available at https://www.heritage.org/ marriage-and-family/report/understanding-the-presidents-healthy-marriage-initiative; on the role of the Heritage Foundation as Reagan's policy shop, Blasko, Andrew. 2004. "Reagan and Heritage: A Unique Partnership." Washington, DC: Heritage Foundation. Available at: https:// www.heritage.org/conservatism/commentary/reagan-and-heritage-unique-partnership.   In 1980, Heritage provided President-Elect Reagan's team with an 1,100-page briefing book. The Reagan administration subsequently implemented or attempted two-thirds of the 2,000 specific recommendations floated in the book.

17. Office of the Administration for Children & Families, Office of Family Assistance. "About Healthy Marriage & Responsible Fatherhood." U.S. Department of Health and Human Services. Available at https://www.acf.hhs.gov/ofa/programs/healthy-marriage/about.

18. Reyes, Emily A. 2014. "Federal Funds to Foster Healthy Marriage Have Little Effect, Study Finds." *Los Angeles Times*, February 9; see also Manning, Wendy. D., S. L. Brown, K. K. Payne, and H. S. Wu. 2014. "Healthy Marriage Initiative Spending and U.S. Marriage & Divorce Rates, A State-level Analysis (FP-14-02)." National Center for Family & Marriage Research. Available at http://www.bgsu.edu/content/dam/BGSU/college-of-arts-and-sciences/NCFMR/docume nts/FP/FP-14-02_HMIInitiative.pdf.

19. The ur-text purporting to support this claim is Murray, Charles. 1984. *Losing Ground: American Social Policy, 1950–1980*. New York: Basic Books.

20. Ellwood, David.T. and Lawrence H. Summers. 1985. *Poverty in America: Is Welfare the Answer or the Problem?* NBER, Working paper 1711, National Bureau of Economic Research, Cambridge, MA.

21. Garfinkel, Irwin, C-C. Huang, S. S. McLanahan, and D. S. Gaylin. 2003. The Roles of Child Support Enforcement and Welfare in Nonmarital Childbearing. *Journal of Population Economics*. 16: 55–70.

22. Wolfinger, Nicholas H. 2023. "Family Change in the Context of Social Changes in the United States." Pp. 97–118 in *The Oxford Handbook of Family Policy Over The Life Course*, edited by Mary Daly, Birgit Pfau-Effinger, Doug Besharov, and Neil Gilbert. Oxford: Oxford University Press; Moffitt, Robert A. 1992. Incentive Effects of the U.S. Welfare System: A Review. *Journal of Economic Literature* 30 (No. 1): 1–61, Rosenzweig, Mark R. 1999. "Welfare, Marital Prospects, and Nonmarital Childbearing." *Journal of Political Economy* 107 (S6): S3–32. There's also cross-cultural evidence: countries with generous benefits for single mothers don't have more of them. Brady, David, and Rebekah Burroway. 2012. "Targeting, Universalism, and Single-mother Poverty: A Multilevel Analysis across 18 Affluent Democracies." *Demography* 49: 719–746.

NOTES TO PAGES 4–5   185

23. González, Libertad. 2007. "The Effect of Benefits on Single Motherhood in Europe." *Labour Economics* 14: 393–412.
24. The text of all State of the Union addresses is archived at The American Presidency Project. University of California, Santa Barbara. Available at https://www.presidency.ucsb.edu/docume nts/address-before-joint-session-congress-the-state-the-union .
25. Murray, Charles. 1984. *Losing Ground: American Social Policy, 1950–1980.* New York: Basic Books. On the lasting import of Murray's work, see Fremstad, Shawn, Sarah Jane Glynn, and Angelo Williams. 2019. "The Case Against Marriage Fundamentalism: Embracing Family Justice for All." *Family Story.* Available at https://familystoryproject.org/case-against-marriage-fundamentalism/. On the history of these ideas, see Somers, Margaret R. and Fred Block. 2005. "From Poverty to Perversity: Ideas, Markets, and Institutions over 200 Years of Welfare Debate." *American Sociological Review* 70: 260–87.
26. *The New York Times.* 1976. "'Welfare Queen' Becomes Issue in Reagan Campaign," *The New York Times,* February 15. Available at https://www.nytimes.com/1976/02/15/archives/ welfare-queen-becomes-issue-in-reagan-campaign-hitting-a-nerve-now.html?auth=login-google1tap&login=google1tap; On the story behind the "welfare queen," see Demby, Gene. 2013. "The Truth Behind the Lies of the Original 'Welfare Queen'" National Public Radio. All Things Considered, December. Available at https://www.npr.org/sections/codeswitch/2013/ 12/20/255819681/the-truth-behind-the-lies-of-the-original-welfare-queen. Reagan's attacks on welfare were often couched in racial dog whistles. Haney-Lopez, Ian. 2014. "The Racism at the Heart of the Reagan Presidency." *Salon,* January. Available at https://www.salon.com/2014/ 01/11/the_racism_at_the_heart_of_the_reagan_presidency/. Indeed, anti-Black attitudes are deeply rooted in White disapproval of welfare. Gilens, Martin. 1995. "Racial Attitudes and Opposition to Welfare." *The Journal of Politics* 57: 994–1014. Food stamps, confided Reagan to voters, allowed "some young fellow ahead of you to buy a T-bone steak." While campaigning in the South, "some young fellow" became a "strapping young buck." In the lexicon of Southern racists, "buck" was often coupled with a notorious racial slur to identify a male African American. Donald Bogle. 1989. *Toms, Coons, Mulattoes, Mammies, and Bucks: An Interpretive History of Blacks in American Films.* New York: Continuum.
27. The American Presidency Project. University of California, Santa Barbara. Available at: https:// www.presidency.ucsb.edu/documents/proclamation-5166-national-single-parent-day-1984.
28. Pear, Robert. 1984. "Reagan Signs Bill Forcing Payments for Child Support." *The New York Times,* August. Available at https://www.nytimes.com/1984/08/17/us/reagan-signs-bill-forc ing-payments-for-child-support.html.
29. Office of the Administration for Children & Families, Office of Family Assistance. "About TANF." U.S. Department of Health and Human Services. Available at https://www.acf.hhs.gov/ ofa/programs/tanf/about.
30. Mead, Lawrence M. 1992. *The Nonworking Poor in America.* New York: Basic Books. The quote is from Dennis H. Wrong's review of Mead's book: Wrong, Dennis H., 1992. "Why the Poor Get Poorer." *The New York Times,* April 19. Available at https://www.nytimes.com/1992/04/19/ books/why-the-poor-get-poorer.html. If nothing else, Mead has proven himself to be consistent. In 2020, he landed in hot water for writing the following: "The seriously poor are mostly blacks and Hispanics, and the main reason is cultural difference. *The great fact is that these groups did not come from Europe.* Fifty years after civil rights, their main problem is no longer racial discrimination by other people but rather that they face an individualist culture that they are unprepared for (italics in original)." Mead, Lawrence M. "Poverty and Culture." *Society,* July 21, 2020. The article was ultimately retracted after popular outcry. It can be found on the National Association of Scholars blog, https://www.nas.org/academic-questions/34/1/poverty-and-culture.
31. On growing acceptance towards single mother families, Thornton, Arland and Linda Young-DeMarco. 2001. "Four Decades of Trends in Attitudes toward Family Issues in the United States: The 1960s through the 1990s." *Journal of Marriage and Family* 63: 1009–1037.
32. DeNavas-Walt, Carmen, Bernadette D. Proctor, and Jessica C. Smith. 2011. *Income, Poverty, and Health Insurance Coverage in the United States: 2010.* United States Census Bureau, Current Population Reports, Washington, DC: United States Government Printing Office. See, Table 4 60–239. Available at http://www.census.gov/prod/2011pubs/p60-239.pdf. This figure probably underestimates the relative poverty of single-mother families, as it includes all households headed by women. For older data, Garfinkel, Irwin and Sara S. McLanahan. 1986. *Single Mothers and Their Children: A New American Dilemma.* Washington, DC: The Urban Institute Press.

186   NOTES TO PAGES 5–7

Further downward bias results from the 172,000 (as of late 2023) currently incarcerated women, who would disproportionately be impoverished single mothers were they not imprisoned. Desmond, Matthew. 2023. *Poverty, by America*. New York: Crown Publishing Group.

33. Bleiweis, Robin, Diana Boesch, and Alexandra Cawthorne Gaines. 2020. "The Basic Facts About Women in Poverty." Center for American Progress. Available at https://www.americanprogr ess.org/issues/women/reports/2020/08/03/488536/basic-facts-women-poverty/. A higher raw figure can be found in Semega, Jessica, Melissa Kollar, Emily A. Shrider, and John F. Creamer. 2020. *Income and Poverty in the United States: 2019*, United States Census Bureau, Current Population Reports, 60–270. Washington, DC: United States Government Printing Office, 2020. See Table B-2. Available at https://www.census.gov/content/dam/Census/library/publications/ 2020/demo/p60-270.pdf.

34. Eggebeen, David J. and Daniel T. Lichter. 1991. "Race, Family Structure, and Changing Poverty among American Children." *American Sociological Review* 56: 801–17; Martin, Molly A. 2006. "Family Structure and Income Inequality in Families with Children, 1976 to 2000." *Demography* 43: 421–45; Western, Bruce, Deirdre Bloome, and Christine Percheski. 2008. "Inequality among American Families with Children, 1975 to 2005." *American Sociological Review* 73: 903–920. Western et al. perhaps offering the strongest evidence, concluding that the proliferation of single-mother families explains about 20% of the increase in income inequality over the past few decades.

35. Important, but not exclusive: many married Americans are also under the poverty line. Fremstad, Shawn. 2016. "Partnered but Poor." Center for American Progress. Available at https://www.americanprogress.org/issues/poverty/reports/2016/03/11/131968/partnered-but-poor/.

36. Getting married: Goldstein, Joshua R. and Catherine T. Kenney. 2001. "Marriage Delayed or Marriage Foregone? New Cohort Forecasts of First Marriage for U.S. Women." *American Sociological Review* 66: 506–519; Schneider, Daniel. 2011. "Wealth and the Marital Divide." *American Journal of Sociology* 117: 627–667; Sweeney, Megan M. 2002. "Two Decades of Family Change: The Shifting Economic Foundations of Marriage." *American Sociological Review* 67: 132–147; staying married, Raley, R. Kelly and Larry Bumpass. 2003 "The Topography of the Divorce Plateau: Levels and Trends in Union Stability in the United States after 1980." *Demographic Research* 8: 245–260. In recent years, divorce rates have declined the most for women with college degrees. Institute for American Values and The National Marriage Project. 2010. *When Marriage Disappears: The New Middle America*. The State of Our Unions: Marriage in America. Available at http://www.virginia.edu/marriageproject/pdfs/Union_11_12_10.pdf.

37. Upchurch, Dawn M., Lee A. Lillard, and Constantijn W. A. Panis. 2002. "Nonmarital Childbearing: Influences of Education, Marriage, and Fertility." *Demography* 39: 311–329; Wu, Lawrence L. 1996. "Effects of Family Instability, Income, and Income Instability on the Risk of a Premarital Birth. *American Sociological Review* 61: 386–406.

38. Reeves, Richard V. and Christopher Pulliam. 2019. "Tipping the Balance: Why Equivalence Scales Matter More Than You Think." Brookings, April 17. Available at https://www.brookings. edu/articles/whats-in-an-equivalence-scale-maybe-more-than-you-think/.

39. Unwieldy: any regression equation with a ratio variable like per capita income or the ratio of income to the poverty line is mis-specified because it implies interactions between the denominator of the dependent variable and every independent variable in the model. Consider: $a/b = \beta_0 + \beta_1 \rightarrow b^*(a/b) = b^*(\beta_0 + \beta_1) \rightarrow a = b^*\beta_0 + b^*\beta_1$. This immutable fact means that any regression performed on a ratio variable is, to put it politely, garbage.

40. Figure 2.4 shows that married mothers are always about five percentage points more likely than their divorced or never-married contemporaries to have three or more children. This means that married mothers' family incomes are biased downward, a topic we return to in Chapters 2 and 3.

41. Edin, Kathryn and Laura Lein. 1997. *Making Ends Meet: How Single Mothers Survive Welfare and Low-Wage Work*. New York: Russell Sage Foundation.

42. Meyer, Bruce D. and James X. Sullivan. 2008. "Changes in the Consumption, Income, and Well-Being of Single Mother Headed Families." *American Economic Review* 98: 2221–2241.

43. Han, Jeehoon, Bruce D. Meyer, and James X. Sullivan. 2021. "The Consumption, Income, and Well-Being of Single Mother Headed Families 25 Years After Welfare Reform." Unpublished paper. Available at https://voices.uchicago.edu/brucemeyer/files/2017/05/Han_Meyer_S ullivan_NTJ_text_v2.5.pdf; Meyer, Bruce D. and James X. Sullivan. 2008. "Changes in the Consumption, Income, and Well-Being of Single Mother Headed Families." *American Economic Review* 98: 2221–2241.

NOTES TO PAGES 7–9   187

44. Garfinkel, Irwin and Sara S. McLanahan. 1986. *Single Mothers and Their Children: A New American Dilemma*. Washington, DC: The Urban Institute Press; Skocpol, Theda. 1992. *Protecting Soldiers and Mothers: The Political Origins of Social Policy in the United States*. Cambridge, MA: Harvard University Press. Even before the payments to Union widows was relief to Confederate widows paid during the Civil War. Lepore, Jill. 2018. *These Truths: A History of the United States*. New York: Norton, 303.

45. The costs were also more enduring than expected: the last pensioned Union widow didn't pass away until 2003 (an unpensioned widow survived to 2020). Coggan, Philip. 2011. "Falling Short." *The Economist*, April 9. As of 2016, the government was still paying pensions to the spouses of the Spanish-American war. Curt Mills. "U.S. Still Paying a Civil War Pension." *U.S. News and World Report*, August 8, 2016, available at https://www.usnews.com/news/articles/2016-08-08/civil-war-vets-pension-still-remains-on-governments-payroll-151-years-after-last-shot-fired#:~:text=Since%20the%20Civil%20War's%20conclusion,in%201914%20am ong%20European%20parties.

46. Skocpol, Theda. 1992. *Protecting Soldiers and Mothers: The Political Origins of Social Policy in the United States*. Cambridge, MA: Harvard University Press; Abramovitz, Mimi. 1988. *Regulating the Lives of Women: Social Welfare from Colonial Times to the Present*. Boston: South End Press; Reese, Ellen. 2005. *Backlash Against Welfare Mothers: Past and Present*. Berkeley: University of California Press.

47. Jansson, Bruce S. 1992. *The Reluctant Welfare State: A History of American Social Welfare Policies*, 2nd ed. Belmont, CA: Wadsworth.

48. Gordon, Linda. 1994. *Pitied but Not Entitled: Single Mothers and the History of Welfare, 1890–1935*. New York: Free Press.

49. Skocpol, Theda. 1992. *Protecting Soldiers and Mothers: The Political Origins of Social Policy in the United States*. Cambridge, MA: Harvard University Press.

50. Gordon, Linda. 1994. *Pitied but Not Entitled: Single Mothers and the History of Welfare, 1890–1935*. New York: Free Press.

51. Brush, Lisa D. 1997. "Worthy Widows, Welfare Cheats: Proper Womanhood in Expert Needs Talk about Single Mothers in the United States, 1900 to 1988." *Gender & Society* 1: 720–74; Grogger, Jeffrey T. and Lynn A. Karoly. 2005. *Welfare Reform: Effects of a Decade of Change*. Cambridge, MA: Harvard University Press; Skocpol, Theda. 1992. *Protecting Soldiers and Mothers: The Political Origins of Social Policy in the United States*. Cambridge, MA: Harvard University Press.

52. Jansson, Bruce S. 1992. *The Reluctant Welfare State: A History of American Social Welfare Policies*, 2nd ed. Belmont, CA: Wadsworth; Garfinkel, Irwin and Sara S. McLanahan. 1986. *Single Mothers and Their Children: A New American Dilemma*. Washington, DC: The Urban Institute Press; Abramovitz, Mimi. 1986. *Regulating the Lives of Women: Social Welfare from Colonial Times to the Present*. Boston: South End Press; Segal, Elisabeth. 2006. *The Promise of Welfare Reform: Political Rhetoric and the Reality of Poverty in the Twenty-First Century*. New York: Routledge. Morgan, Kimberly J. 2006. *Working Moms and Welfare State*. Stanford: Stanford University Press.

53. African American women were also frequently unable to receive Civil War pensions. Gorman, Kathleen L. 2010–2023. "Civil War Pensions." Virginia Center for Civil War Studies at Virginia Tech. Available at https://www.essentialcivilwarcurriculum.com/civil-war-pensions.html.

54. Gordon, Linda. 1994. *Pitied but Not Entitled: Single Mothers and the History of Welfare, 1890–1935*. New York: Free Press; United States Children's Bureau. 1933. "Mothers' Aid, 1931." Bureau Publication No. 220, Washington, DC: United States Government Printing Office. Available at https://archive.org/details/mothersaid193100unit.

55. Skocpol, Theda. 1992. *Protecting Soldiers and Mothers: The Political Origins of Social Policy in the United States*. Cambridge, MA: Harvard University Press.

56. On the relative approval of different family forms, Veroff, Joseph, Elizabeth Douvan, and Richard A. Kulka. 1981. *The Inner American: A Self Portrait from 1957–1976*. New York: Basic Books. On attitudes towards welfare for families, Reese, Ellen. 2005. *Backlash against Welfare Mothers: Past and Present*. Berkeley: University of California Press.

57. New York Times. 1976. "'Welfare Queen' Becomes Issue in Reagan Campaign," *The New York Times*, February. Available at https://www.nytimes.com/1976/02/15/archives/welfare-queen-becomes-issue-in-reagan-campaign-hitting-a-nerve-now.html?auth=login-google1tap&login=google1tap.

188   NOTES TO PAGES 9–11

58. Usdansky, Margaret. 2009. "A Weak Embrace: Popular and Scholarly Depictions of Single-Parent Families, 1900–1998." *Journal of Marriage and Family* 71: 209–225.
59. Perhaps the most prominent study in support of this point remains McLanahan, Sara S. and Gary Sandefur. 1994. *Growing Up with a Single Parent: What Hurts, What Helps.* Cambridge, MA: Harvard University Press.
60. Meyer, Bruce D. and Dan T. Rosenbaum. 2001. "Welfare, the Earned Income Tax Credit, and the Labor Supply of Single Mothers." *The Quarterly Journal of Economics* 116: 1063–1114.
61. Edin, Kathryn and H. Luke Shaefer. 2015. *$2.00 a Day: Living on Almost Nothing in America.* Boston, MA: Houghton Mifflin Harcourt.
62. Ellwood, David. 2001. "Welfare Reform as I Knew It: When Bad Things Happen to Good Policies." *The American Prospect.* Available at https://prospect.org/economy/welfare-reform-knew-it-bad-things-happen-good-policies/.
63. U.S. Department of Health and Human Services, Administration for Children & Families. 2012. "Premarital and Marriage Education." The Healthy Marriage Initiative.
64. On the marriage promotion goals of welfare reform, Edin, Kathryn. 2000. "What Do Low-Income Single Mothers Say about Marriage?" *Social Problems* 47: 112–133; Fagan, Patrick F., Robert W. Patterson, and Robert E. Rector. 2022. "Marriage and Welfare Reform: The Overwhelming Evidence that Marriage Education Works." The Heritage Foundation Backgrounder No. 1606, October 25, 2002. Available at https://www.heritage.org/welfare/report/marriage-and-welfare-reform-the-overwhelming-evidence-marriage-education-works. On the benefits of marriage for adults, Lichter, Daniel T., Deborah Roempke Graefe, and J. Brian Brown. 2003. "Is Marriage a Panacea? Union Formation Among Economically Disadvantaged Unwed Mothers." *Social Problems* 50: 60–86; Waite, Linda J. and Maggie Gallagher. 2000. *The Case for Marriage: Why Married People are Happier, Healthier, and Better off Financially.* New York: Doubleday; Wilcox, W. Bradford. 2024. *Get Married: Why Americans Must Defy the Elites, Forge Strong Families, and Save Civilization.* New York: HarperCollins. on the benefits of marriage for children, McLanahan, Sara S. and Gary Sandefur. 1994. *Growing Up with a Single Parent: What Hurts, What Helps.* Cambridge, MA: Harvard University Press. On marriage promotion as a strategy for shifting the responsibility for poverty, Moon, Dawne and Jaye Cee Whitehead. 2006. "Marrying for America." Pp. 23–45 in L. Kowaleski-Jones and N. H. Wolfinger *Fragile Families and the Marriage Agenda.* New York: Springer; Sigle-Rushton, Wendy, and Sara McLanahan. 2002. "For Richer or Poorer? Marriage as an Anti-poverty Strategy in the United States." *Population* 57: 509–526.
65. For divorced mothers, McKeever, Matthew and Nicholas H. Wolfinger. 2006 "Shifting Fortunes in a Changing Economy: Trends in the Economic Well-Being of Divorced Women." Pp. 127–157 in L. Kowaleski-Jones and N. H. Wolfinger *Fragile Families and the Marriage Agenda.* New York: Springer; for never-married mothers, McKeever, Matthew and Nicholas H. Wolfinger. 2011. "Thanks for Nothing: Income and Labor Force Participation for Never-married Mothers since 1982." *Social Science Research* 40: 63–76.
66. United States Census Bureau. 1961. *Statistical Abstract of the United States: 1961,* 81st ed. Washington, DC: United States Government Printing Office. Table 268.
67. Collins, Gail. 2009. *When Everything Changed: The Amazing Journey of American Women from 1960 to the Present.* New York: Little, Brown.
68. United States Department of Labor. 2010. "Women in the Labor Force: A Databook." Washington, DC: Bureau of Labor Statistics. Available at http://www.bls.gov/cps/wlf-databook-2010.pdf. See Tables 1, 20.
69. United States Census Bureau. 2012. *Statistical Abstract of the United States: 2012,* 132nd ed. Washington, DC: United States Government Printing Office. Calculations from Table 599.
70. United States Census Bureau. 2012. *Statistical Abstract of the United States: 2012* 132nd ed. Washington, DC: United States Government Printing Office.
71. For an excellent account of the move towards equality of the sexes, Collins, Gail. 2009. *When Everything Changed: The Amazing Journey of American Women from 1960 to the Present.* New York: Little, Brown.
72. Chevan, Albert and Randall Stokes. 2000. "Growth in Family Income Inequality, 1970–1990: Industrial Restructuring and Demographic Change." *Demography* 37: 365–380. Treas, Judith. 1987. "The Effect of Women's Labor Force Participation on the Distribution of Income in the United States." *Annual Review of Sociology* 13: 259–288.
73. This didn't used to be the case back when women were largely relegated to "women's jobs." On variation in female wages, Morris, Martina and Bruce Western. 1999. "Inequality in Earnings at the Close of the Twentieth Century." *Annual Review of Sociology* 25: 623–657.

NOTES TO PAGES 11–13   189

74. Day, Jennifer Cheeseman. 2019. "College Degree Widens Gender Earnings Gap." United States Census Bureau. Available at https://www.census.gov/library/stories/2019/05/college-degree-widens-gender-earnings-gap.html; Cha, Young-Joo and Kim A. Weeden. 2014. "Overwork and the Slow Convergence in the Gender Gap in Wages." *American Sociological Review* 79 (3): 457–84.

75. Peterson, Janice, Xue Song, and Avis Jones-DeWeever. 2002. "Life after Welfare Reform: Low-Income Single Parent Families, Pre- and Post-TANF." Research-in-Brief D446. Washington, DC: Institute for Women's Policy Research. Available at http://citeseerx.ist.psu.edu/viewdoc/download?doi=10.1.1.15.6994&rep=rep1&type=pdf.

76. Morris, Martina and Bruce Western. 1999. "Inequality in Earnings at the Close of the Twentieth Century." *Annual Review of Sociology* 25: 623–657.

77. A good example of single-mother hagiography is Hertz, Rosanna. 2006. *Single by Chance, Mothers by Choice: How Women Are Choosing Parenthood Without Marriage and Creating the New American Family*. New York: Oxford University Press.

78. Fischer, Claude S. and Michael Hout. 2006. *Century of Difference: How America Changed in the Last One Hundred Years*. New York: Russell Sage Press.

79. United States Census Bureau. 2011. *Statistical Abstract of the United States: 2011* 131st ed. Washington, DC: United States Government Printing Office.

80. On the gender wage gap, Barroso, Amanda and Anna Brown. 2021. "Gender Pay Gap in U.S. Held Steady in 2020." Pew Research Center. Available at https://www.pewresearch.org/fact-tank/2021/05/25/gender-pay-gap-facts/. The gap has narrowed appreciably in recent years and is now at 93% for women ages 25 to 34. For more on the sources of the gap, American Association of University Women. 2017. *The Simple Truth about the Gender Pay Gap*. Available at https://web.archive.org/web/20170224051057/https://www.aauw.org/aauw_check/pdf_download/show_pdf.php?file=The-Simple-Truth. Much—but not all—of the gap can be explained by differences in employment sector and work experience. On the relationship between polarization in men's wages and the gender wage gap, see Bernhardt, Annette, Martina Morris, and Mark S. Handcock. 1995. "Women's Gains or Men's Losses? A Closer Look at the Shrinking Gender Gap in Earnings." *American Journal of Sociology* 101: 302–328.

81. For a review of studies on the economics of divorce, McKeever, Matthew and Nicholas H. Wolfinger. 2001. "Reexamining the Economic Consequences of Marital Disruption for Women." *Social Science Quarterly* 82: 202–217; McKeever, Matthew and Nicholas H. Wolfinger. 2006 "Shifting Fortunes in a Changing Economy: Trends in the Economic Well-Being of Divorced Women." Pp. 127–157 in L. Kowaleski-Jones and N. H. Wolfinger *Fragile Families and the Marriage Agenda*. New York: Springer; for never-married mothers, McKeever, Matthew and Nicholas H. Wolfinger. 2011. "Thanks for Nothing: Income and Labor Force Participation for Never-married Mothers since 1982." *Social Science Research* 40: 63–76.

82. Divorce: McKeever, Matthew and Nicholas H. Wolfinger. 2006 "Shifting Fortunes in a Changing Economy: Trends in the Economic Well-Being of Divorced Women." Pp. 127–157 in L. Kowaleski-Jones and N. H. Wolfinger *Fragile Families and the Marriage Agenda*. New York: Springer; Smock, Pamela J. 1993. "The Economic Costs of Marital Disruption for Young Women over the Past Two Decades." *Demography* 30: 353–71; never-married mothers, McKeever, Matthew and Nicholas H. Wolfinger. 2011. "Thanks for Nothing: Income and Labor Force Participation for Never-married Mothers since 1982." *Social Science Research* 40: 63–76. Another study examines changing poverty rates for women who give birth out of wedlock: Wu, Lawrence L. and Miodrag Stojnic. 2007. "Poverty among the Poorest-Poor in the United States: Trends for Never-Married Women and Their Children." Paper presented at the inaugural conference, Center for Research on Inequalities and the Life Course, Yale University. Finally, sociologist Molly Martin has considered changing income inequality for divorced and never-married mothers, Martin, Molly A. 2006. "Family Structure and Income Inequality in Families with Children, 1976 to 2000." *Demography* 43: 421–45.

83. For a review, Hoffman, Saul D. 1998. "Teenage Childbearing Is Not So Bad After All . . . Or Is It? A Review of the New Literature." *Family Planning Perspectives* 30: 236–239, 243.

84. Sisters: Geronimus, Arline T. and Sanders Korenman. 1992. "The Socioeconomic Consequences of Teen Childbearing Reconsidered." *Quarterly Journal of Economics* 107: 1187–1214; Hoffman, Saul D., Michael E. Foster, and Frank F. Furstenberg, Jr. 1993. "Reevaluating the Costs of Teenage Childbearing." *Demography* 30: 1–13; miscarriage: Fletcher, Jason M. and Barbara L. Wolfe. 2009. "Education and Labor Market Consequences of Teenage Childbearing Evidence Using the Timing of Pregnancy Outcomes and Community Fixed Effects." *Journal of Human Resources* 44: 303–325; Hotz, V. Joseph, Susan Williams McElroy, and Seth G. Sanders.

190 NOTES TO PAGES 13–14

2002. "Teenage Childbearing and Its Life Cycle Consequences: Exploiting a Very Natural Experiment." *Journal of Human Resources* 40: 683–715; twins: Grogger, Jeff T. and Stephen Bronars. 1993. "The Socioeconomic Consequences of Teenage Childbearing: Findings from a Natural Experiment." *Family Planning Perspectives* 25: 156–161, 174. Bronars, Stephen G. and Jeff Grogger. 1994. "The Economic Consequences of Unwed Motherhood: Using Twin Births as a Natural Experiment." *American Economic Review* 84: 1141–1156." This last study is the only one to focus explicitly on nonmarital childbearing rather than teen childbearing.

85. Wu, Lawrence L. 1996. "Effects of Family Instability, Income, and Income Instability on the Risk of a Premarital Birth. *American Sociological Review* 61: 386–406.

86. Calculated from Tables 3 and 9 in Martin, Joyce A., Brady E. Hamilton, Michele J. K. Osterman, and Anne K. Driscoll. 2019 "Births: Final Data for 2018." National Vital Statistics Reports; vol 68, no 13. Hyattsville, MD: National Center for Health Statistics. Available at https://www.cdc.gov/nchs/data/nvsr/nvsr68/nvsr68_13-508.pdf. Three decades ago, one out of four teen-aged moms was married. Foster, E. Michael, Damon Jones, and Saul D. Hoffman. 1998. "The Economic Impact of Nonmarital Childbearing: How are Older, Single Mothers Faring?" *Journal of Marriage and the Family* 60: 163–174.

87. The 30% figure is from Wu, Lawrence L., Larry L. Bumpass, and Kelly Musick. 2001. "Historical and Life Course Trajectories of Nonmarital Childbearing." Pp. 3–48 in Lawrence L. Wu and Barbara Wolfe *Out of Wedlock: Causes and Consequences of Nonmarital Fertility.* New York: Russell Sage Foundation; on subsequent declines, McKeever, Matthew and Nicholas H. Wolfinger. 2011. "Thanks for Nothing: Income and Labor Force Participation for Never-married Mothers since 1982." *Social Science Research* 40: 63–76.

88. Foster, E. Michael, Damon Jones, and Saul D. Hoffman. 1998. "The Economic Impact of Nonmarital Childbearing: How are Older, Single Mothers Faring?" *Journal of Marriage and the Family* 60: 163–74; Saul D. Hoffman and E. Michael Foster. 1997. "Non-Marital Births and Single Mothers: Cohort Trends in the Dynamics of Non-Marital Childbearing." *The History of the Family* 2: 255–75.

89. Blank, Rebecca M. 2002. "Evaluating Welfare Reform in the United States." Working paper 8983, Cambridge, MA: National Bureau of Economic Research; Grogger, Jeffrey T. and Lynn A. Karoly. 2005. *Welfare Reform: Effects of a Decade of Change.* Cambridge, MA: Harvard University Press.

90. Edin, Kathryn and H. Luke Shaefer. 2015. *$2.00 a Day: Living on Almost Nothing in America.* Boston, MA: Houghton Mifflin Harcourt.

91. Perhaps the best known example is Garfinkel, Irwin and Sara S. McLanahan. 1986. *Single Mothers and Their Children: A New American Dilemma.* Washington, DC: The Urban Institute Press.

92. While it might be interesting to examine differences between never-married mothers based on whether fertility was planned, the CPS doesn't allow us to measure birth intentions. Moreover, these intentions cannot always be measured cleanly, given the large number of semi-planned pregnancies. Over 40% of pregnancies in the United States are unplanned. Rossen, Lauren M., Brady E. Hamilton, Joyce C. Abma, Elizabeth C. W. Gregory, Vladislav Beresovsky, Addriana V. Resendez, Anjani Chandra, and Joyce A. Martin. 2023. "Updated methodology to esti-mate overall and unintended pregnancy rates in the United States. National Center for Health Statistics." *Vital Health Stat* 2(201). Available at https://www.cdc.gov/nchs/data/series/sr_02/sr02-201.pdf.

93. Calculated from Table C3 of United States Census Bureau. 2020. *America's Families and Living Arrangements: 2020.* Available at https://www.census.gov/data/tables/2020/demo/families/cps-2020.html.

94. United States Census Bureau. 2020. *America's Families and Living Arrangements: 2020.* Available at https://www.census.gov/data/tables/2020/demo/families/cps-2020.html. This calculation excludes married families in which the spouse is absent (as opposed to separated).

95. Typically, data for these families reflect current marital status but the previous year's income, a time when the mother was presumably married, not separated.

96. On the five-year duration of cohabiting relationships, see Table 5 in Bumpass, Larry L. and Sheela Kennedy. 2008. "Cohabitation and Children's Living Arrangements: New Estimates from the United States." *Demographic Research* 19: 1663–1692.

97. Reeves, Richard V. and Eleanor Krause. 2017. "Cohabiting Parents Differ from Married Ones in Three Big Ways." Brookings Institute. Available at https://www.brookings.edu/research/cohabiting-parents-differ-from-married-ones-in-three-big-ways/.

NOTES TO PAGES 14–15   191

98. Wolfinger, Nicholas H. 2001 "The Effects of Family Structure of Origin on Offspring Cohabitation Duration." *Sociological Inquiry* 71: 293–313; Wolfinger, Nicholas H. 2005. *Understanding the Divorce Cycle: The Children of Divorce in Their Own Marriages.* New York: Cambridge University Press.

99. Brown, Susan L. and Wendy D. Manning. 2009. "Family Boundary Ambiguity and the Measurement of Family Structure: The Significance of Cohabitation." *Demography* 46: 85–101; Manning, Wendy D. and Pamela J. Smock. 2005. "Measuring and Modeling Cohabitation: New Perspectives from Qualitative Data." *Journal of Marriage and Family* 67: 989–1002.

100. Wu, Huijing. 2017. "Trends in Births to Single and Cohabiting Mothers, 1980–2014." Family Profile No. 04, National Center for Family & Marriage Research (NCFMR), Bowling Green State University. Available at https://www.bgsu.edu/ncfmr/resources/data/family-profiles/wu-trends-births-single-cohabiting-mothers-fp-17-04.html#:~:text=The%20share%20of%20bir ths%20to%20cohabiting%20mothers%20has%20more%20than,born%20into%20a%20coh abiting%20union.

101. Livingston, Gretchen. 2018. "The Changing Profile of Unmarried Parents." Pew Research Center. Available at https://www.pewsocialtrends.org/2018/04/25/the-changing-profile-of-unmarried-parents/.

102. This is a predictably voluminous literature. For overviews, Morris, Martina and Bruce Western. 1999. "Inequality in Earnings at the Close of the Twentieth Century." *Annual Review of Sociology* 25: 623–57; Hacker, Jacob S. and Paul Pierson. 2010. *Winner-take-all Politics: How Washington Made the Rich Richer—and Turned Its Back on the Middle Class.* New York: Simon and Schuster; Mechanic, Michael. *Jackpot: How the Super-Rich Really Live—And How Their Wealth Harms Us All.* Simon and Schuster, 2021. Reich, Robert B. 2020. *The System: Who Rigged It, How We Fix It.* New York: Vintage; Stiglitz, Joseph E. 2012. *The Price of Inequality: How Today's Divided Society Endangers Our Future.* New York: W. W. Norton; Noah, Timothy. 2012. *The Great Divergence: America's Growing Inequality Crisis and What We Can Do About It.* Camden: Bloomsbury Publishing USA.

103. See, for example, Frank, Robert H. 2007. *Falling Behind: How Rising Inequality Harms the Middle Class.* Berkeley: University of California Press; Johnston, David Cay, ed. 2015. *Divided: The Perils of Our Growing Inequality.* The New Press; Kevine, Adam Seth, Robert H. Frank, and Oege Dijk. 2010 "Expenditure Cascades." *Social Science Research Network.* Working paper. Available at http://ssrn.com/abstract=1690612; Stiglitz, Joseph E. 2012. *The Price of Inequality: How Today's Divided Society Endangers Our Future.* New York: W. W. Norton.

104. Western, Bruce, Deirdre Bloome, and Christine Percheski. 2008. "Inequality among American Families with Children, 1975 to 2005." *American Sociological Review* 73: 903–920.

105. Martin, Molly A. 2006. "Family Structure and Income Inequality in Families with Children, 1976 to 2000." *Demography* 43: 421–45.

106. See, for example, Hertz, Rosanna. 2006. *Single by Chance, Mothers by Choice: How Women Are Choosing Parenthood without Marriage and Creating the New American Family.* New York: Oxford University Press; Whitehead, Barbara Dafoe. 1993. "Dan Quayle Was Right." *The Atlantic*, April. Available at http://www.theatlantic.com/magazine/archive/1993/04/dan-quayle-was-right/7015/.

107. Usdansky, Margaret L. and Sara McLanahan. 2003. "Looking for Murphy Brown: Are College-Educated, Single Mothers Unique?" Working paper # 03-05-FF, Center for Research on Child Wellbeing, Princeton University. Available at https://citeseerx.ist.psu.edu/viewdoc/downl oad?doi=10.1.1.584.7060&rep=rep1&type=pdf.

108. McKeever, Matthew and Nicholas H. Wolfinger. 2011. "Thanks for Nothing: Income and Labor Force Participation for Never-married Mothers since 1982." *Social Science Research* 40: 63–76.

109. In the 1980s, Lenore Weitzman published an influential book that suggested that divorce cost women 73% of their incomes. This estimate was later shown to be wildly inflated. See Peterson, Richard R. 1996. "A Re-Evaluation of the Economic Consequences of Divorce." *American Sociological Review* 61: 528–536; Weitzman, Lenore J. 1985. *The Divorce Revolution: The Unexpected Social and Economic Consequences for Women and Children in America.* New York: The Free Press. Psychologist Sanford Braver has also argued that the economic consequences of divorce are milder than is customarily believed. Braver had better measures of income transfers and differential tax burdens than most scholars, but his findings are based on a random sample drawn just from Maricopa County, Arizona. Braver, Sanford L.

192 NOTES TO PAGES 15–17

1999 "The Gender Gap in Standard of Living after Divorce: Vanishingly Small." *Family Law Quarterly* 33: 111; Braver, Sanford L. and Diane O'Connell. 1998. *Divorced Dads: Shattering the Myths.* New York: Tarcher.

110. According to the U.S. Census, about one in six mothers has had children by two or more men. This book doesn't look at the effect of multi-partner fertility (MPF) on income for two reasons. The first and more important is data limitations: neither the CPS nor the NLSY permit us to accurately measure MPF. Second, we examine the economics of women with resident children; whether they receive support from one or more father is less relevant to our study than the level of income for the family. On the prevalence of MPF, Monte, Lindsay, 2017. *Multiple Partner Fertility Research Brief.* Current Population Reports, P70BR-146. Washington, DC: United States Census Bureau. Available at https://www.census.gov/content/dam/Census/library/publications/2017/demo/p70br-146.pdf. On the difficulty of measuring MPF using NLSY 1979 data, Dorius, Cassandra. 2012. "Measuring Maternal Multi-Partnered Fertility with the NLSY79." Paper presented at the annual meeting of the American Sociological Association. Denver, CO.

111. We refer readers interested in sample selection bias to income resulting from movement into and out of married, divorced, and never-married motherhood to consult our published papers, where we explore this issue at length. McKeever, Matthew and Nicholas H. Wolfinger. 2001. "Reexamining the Economic Consequences of Marital Disruption for Women." *Social Science Quarterly* 82: 202–217; McKeever, Matthew and Nicholas H. Wolfinger. 2006 "Shifting Fortunes in a Changing Economy: Trends in the Economic Well-Being of Divorced Women." Pp. 127–157 in L. Kowaleski-Jones and N. H. Wolfinger *Fragile Families and the Marriage Agenda.* New York: Springer; McKeever, Matthew and Nicholas H. Wolfinger. 2011. "Thanks for Nothing: Income and Labor Force Participation for Never-married Mothers since 1982." *Social Science Research* 40: 63–76.

112. Hotz, V. Joseph, Susan Williams McElroy, and Seth G. Sanders. 2002. "Teenage Childbearing and Its Life Cycle Consequences: Exploiting a Very Natural Experiment." *Journal of Human Resources* 40: 683–715.

113. There's no shortage of primers on instrumental variable models. Here's one that details some of the assumptions these models require. Labrecque, Jeremy and Sonja A. Swanson. 2018. "Understanding the Assumptions Underlying Instrumental Variable Analyses: A Brief Review of Falsification Strategies and Related Tools." *Current Epidemiology Reports* 5: 214–220. Available at https://www.ncbi.nlm.nih.gov/pmc/articles/PMC6096851/. For a debate on model specification relevant to this book, Fletcher, Jason M. and Barbara L. Wolfe. 2009. "Education and Labor Market Consequences of Teenage Childbearing Evidence Using the Timing of Pregnancy Outcomes and Community Fixed Effects." *Journal of Human Resources* 44: 303–325.

114. Current Population Survey: Annual Social and Economic Supplement. Washington, DC: United States Census Bureau. Available at https://www.census.gov/programs-surveys/saipe/guidance/model-input-data/cpsasec.html; we use Version 1.1 data from the Center for Economic and Policy Research. 2019, March CPS Uniform Extracts, Version 1.1. The National Longitudinal Surveys are a product of the Bureau of Labor Statistics, available at http://www.bls.gov/nls/nlsy79.htm. Data are accessed via the NLS Investigator portal, available at https://www.nlsinfo.org/investigator/pages/login.

115. Kymlicka, B. B. and Jean V. Matthews. 1988. *The Reagan Revolution?* Chicago: Dorsey Press; Robert Lekachman, Robert. 1982. *Greed is Not Enough.* New York: Pantheon Books.

116. On low fertility rates among older women, Osterman Michelle J. K., Brady E. Hamilton, Joyce A. Martin, Anne K. Driscoll, and Claudia P. Valenzuela. 2022. "Births: Final Data for 2020." National Vital Statistics Reports; vol 70 no 17. Hyattsville, MD: National Center for Health Statistics. Available at https://dx.doi.org/10.15620/cdc:112078.

Chapter 2

1. Martin, Teresa Castro and Larry L. Bumpass. 1989. "Recent Trends in Marital Disruption." *Demography* 26: 37–51.

2. Martin, J. A., B. E. Hamilton, M. J. K. Osterman and A. K. Driscoll. 2021. Births: Final Data for 2019. National Vital Statistics Reports; vol 70 no 2. Hyattsville, MD: National Center for Health Statistics. Available at https://www.cdc.gov/nchs/data/nvsr/nvsr70-02-508.pdf.

3. Bloome, Deirdre and Shannon Ang. 2020. "Marriage and Union Formation in the United States: Recent Trends Across Racial Groups and Economic Backgrounds." *Demography*

NOTES TO PAGES 17–20 193

57: 1753–1786; Martin, Steven P., Nan Marie Astone, and H. Elizabeth Peters. 2014. "Fewer Marriages, More Divergence: Marriage Projections for Millennials to Age 40." Urban Institute; Goldstein, Joshua R. and Catherine T. Kenney. 2001. "Marriage Delayed or Marriage Foregone? New Cohort Forecasts of First Marriage for U.S. Women." *American Sociological Review* 66: 506–519.

4. Livingstone, Gretchen. 2014. "The Demographics of Remarriage." Pew Research Center. Available at https://www.pewresearch.org/social-trends/2014/11/14/chapter-2-the-demog raphics-of-remarriage/; Smock, Pamela J. and Christine R. Schwartz. 2020. "The Demography of Families: A Review of Patterns and Change." *Journal of Marriage and Family* 82: 9–34; also useful is Martinson, Brian C. 1994. "Postmarital Union Formation: Trends and Determinants of the Competing Roles of Remarriage and Nonmarital Cohabitation among Women in the United States." Unpublished doctoral dissertation. Department of Sociology, University of Wisconsin-Madison.

5. Campbell, Author A. 1968. "The Role of Family Planning in the Reduction of Poverty." *Journal of Marriage and Family* 30: 236–245, 238.

6. For a review, Miller, Brent C., Rayna A. Sage, and Bryan Winward. 2005. "Teen Childbearing and Public Policy." Pp. 47–72 in L. Kowaleski-Jones and N. H. Wolfinger *Fragile Families and the Marriage Agenda*. New York: Springer. Individual studies of note include Fletcher, Jason M. and Barbara L. Wolfe. 2009 "Education and Labor Market Consequences of Teenage Childbearing Evidence Using the Timing of Pregnancy Outcomes and Community Fixed Effects." *Journal of Human Resources* 44: 303–325; Geronimus, Arline T. and Sanders Korenman. 1992. "The Socioeconomic Consequences of Teen Childbearing Reconsidered." *Quarterly Journal of Economics* 107: 1187–1214; Grogger, Jeff T. and Stephen Bronars. 1993. "The Socioeconomic Consequences of Teenage Childbearing: Findings from a Natural Experiment." *Family Planning Perspectives* 25: 156–161, 174; Hoffman, Saul D., Michael E. Foster, and Frank F. Furstenberg, Jr. 1993. "Reevaluating the Costs of Teenage Childbearing." *Demography* 30: 1–13; Hotz, V. Joseph, Susan Williams McElroy, and Seth G. Sanders. 2002. "Teenage Childbearing and Its Life Cycle Consequences: Exploiting a Very Natural Experiment." *Journal of Human Resources* 40: 683–715. Not surprisingly, research in this area has diminished as the rate of teenage childbirth continued its long descent. Finally, it's worth noting that when teenage childbirth was common and predominantly marital, it portended a higher family income. Lang, Kevin and Russell Weinstein. 2015. "The Consequences of Teenage Childbearing before Roe v. Wade." *American Economic Journal: Applied Economics* 7: 169–197.

7. Livingston, Gretchen and Deja Thomas. 2019. "Why is the Teen Birth Rate Falling?" Pew Research Center. Available at https://www.pewresearch.org/fact-tank/2019/08/02/why-is-the-teen-birth-rate-falling/.

8. It's important to remember that we are examining families with children who are currently living with their mothers. For this reason, our estimate of teenaged motherhood is a conservative measure. If a mother has multiple children and their first child is over 18 and doesn't currently live with them, we would be measuring her age of becoming a mother based on the timing of her second child. This means the real rate of teenage childbearing is probably somewhat higher than what the CPS shows.

9. Wu, Lawrence L., Larry L. Bumpass, and Kelly Musick. 2001. "Historical and Life Course Trajectories of Nonmarital Childbearing," Pp. 3–48 in Lawrence L. Wu and Barbara Wolfe *Out of Wedlock: Causes and Consequences of Nonmarital Fertility*. New York: Russell Sage Foundation.

10. "America's Children Key National Indicators of Well-Being 2004." 2004. ChildStats.gov, Federal Forum on Child and Family Statistics, 2004. Available at https://www.childstats.gov/pdf/ac2 004/ac_04.pdf.

11. National Conference of State Legislatures. 2013. "Postcard: Teen Pregnancy Affects Graduation Rates." Available at https://www.ncsl.org/research/health/teen-pregnancy-affects-graduat ion-rates-postcard.aspx; Perper, Kate, Kristen Peterson, and Jennifer Manlove. 2010. "Diploma Attainment among Teen Mothers. Child Trends, Fact Sheet," Publication #2010-01. Washington, DC: Child Trends. Available at https://cms.childtrends.org/wp-content/uploads/2010/01/child _trends-2010_01_22_FS_diplomaattainment.pdf.

12. Bumpass, Larry L., Teresa Castro Martin, and James A. Sweet. 1991. "The Impact of Family Background and Early Marital Factors on Marital Disruption." *Journal of Family Issues* 12: 22–42; Wolfinger, Nicholas H. 2015. "Want to Avoid Divorce? Wait to Get Married, but Not Too Long." *Institute for Family Studies*. Available at https://ifstudies.org/blog/want-to-avoid-divo

194   NOTES TO PAGES 21–25

rce-wait-to-get-married-but-not-too-long/; Wolfinger, Nicholas H. 2015. "Replicating the Goldilocks Theory of Marriage and Divorce." *Institute for Family Studies.* Available at https://ifstudies.org/blog/replicating-the-goldilocks-theory-of-marriage-and-divorce/.

13. Wolfinger, Nicholas H. 2015. "Want to Avoid Divorce? Wait to Get Married, but Not Too Long." *Institute for Family Studies.* Available at https://ifstudies.org/blog/want-to-avoid-divorce-wait-to-get-married-but-not-too-long/; Wolfinger, Nicholas H. 2015. "Replicating the Goldilocks Theory of Marriage and Divorce." *Institute for Family Studies.* Available at https://ifstudies.org/blog/replicating-the-goldilocks-theory-of-marriage-and-divorce/. The effect of marriage age on divorce has changed appreciably over the past 40 years.

14. Twenty-seven represents the median maternal age at first birth in 2017, near the end of the CPS time series. Guzzo, Karen B. and Krista K. Payne. 2018. "Average Age at First Birth, 1970–2017." *Family Profiles, FP-18* 25. National Center for Family & Marriage Research, Bowling Green State University. Available at https://www.bgsu.edu/ncfmr/resources/data/family-profiles/guzzo-payne-age-first-birth-fp-18-25.html.

15. On trends in fertility, Guzzo, Karen B. and Krista K. Payne. 2018. "Average Age at First Birth, 1970–2017." *Family Profiles, FP-18* 25. National Center for Family & Marriage Research, Bowling Green State University. Available at https://www.bgsu.edu/ncfmr/resources/data/family-profiles/guzzo-payne-age-first-birth-fp-18-25.html; on median marriage ages, United States Census Bureau. 2019. *Median Age at First Marriage: 1890 to Present.* Decennial Censuses, 1890 to 1940, and Current Population Survey, Annual Social and Economic Supplements, 1947 to 2022. Available at https://www.census.gov/content/dam/Census/library/visualizations/time-series/demo/families-and-households/ms-2.pdf.

16. Fields, Jason and Lynne M. Casper. 2001. *America's Families and Living Arrangements: March 2000.* Current Population Reports, 20–537. Washington, DC: United States Census Bureau; on premarital fertility and marriage rates, Lichter, Daniel T. and Deborah Roempke Graefe. 2001. "Finding a Mate? The Marital and Cohabitation Histories of Unwed Mothers." 317–343 in Lawrence L. Wu and Barbara Wolfe *Out of Wedlock: Causes and Consequences of Nonmarital Fertility.* New York: Russell Sage Foundation. Upchurch, Dawn M., Lillard, Lee A. and Constantijn W. A. Panis. 2001. "The Impact of Nonmarital Childbearing on Subsequent Marital Formation and Dissolution." 344–380 in Lawrence L. Wu and Barbara Wolfe *Out of Wedlock: Causes and Consequences of Nonmarital Fertility.* New York: Russell Sage Foundation.

17. On children and wages, Budig, Michelle J. and Paula England, 2001. "The Wage Penalty for Motherhood," *American Sociological Review* 66: 204–225; Budig, Michelle J. and Melissa J. Hodges. 2010. "Differences in Disadvantage: Variation in the Motherhood Penalty across White Women's Earnings Distribution," *American Sociological Review* 75: 705–728; Waldfogel, Jane. 1997. "The Effect of Children on Women's Wages," *American Sociological Review* 62: 209–217; Avellar, Sarah and Pamela J. Smock. 2003 "Has the Price of Motherhood Declined Over Time? A Cross-Cohort Comparison of the Motherhood Wage Penalty," *Journal of Marriage and Family* 65: 597–607.

18. Waite, Linda J. and Lee A. Lillard. 1991. "Children and Marital Disruption," *American Journal of Sociology* 96: 930–953.

19. Goldstein, Joshua R. 1999. "The Leveling of Divorce in the United States." *Demography* 36: 409–414; Wang, Wendy. 2020. "The U.S. Divorce Rate Has Hit a 50-Year Low." Institute for Family Studies. Available at https://ifstudies.org/blog/the-us-divorce-rate-has-hit-a-50-year-low; Wolfinger, Nicholas H. 2023. "Family Change in the Context of Social Changes in the U.S." Pp. 97–118 in Mary Daly, Birgit Pfau-Effinger, Doug Besharov, and Neil Gilbert *The Oxford Handbook of Family Policy Over the Life-Course.* Oxford: Oxford University Press.

20. Lichter, Daniel T. and Deborah Roempke Graefe. 2001. "Finding a Mate? The Marital and Cohabitation Histories of Unwed Mothers." Pp. 317–343 in Lawrence L. Wu and Barbara Wolfe *Out of Wedlock: Causes and Consequences of Nonmarital Fertility.* New York: Russell Sage Foundation; Upchurch, Dawn M., Lillard, Lee A. and Constantijn W. A. Panis. 2001. "The Impact of Nonmarital Childbearing on Subsequent Marital Formation and Dissolution." Pp. 344–380 in Lawrence L. Wu and Barbara Wolfe *Out of Wedlock: Causes and Consequences of Nonmarital Fertility.* New York: Russell Sage Foundation. Both show that premarital fertility reduces the ultimate likelihood of marriage; Upchurch et al. further show that each additional premarital child makes marriage less likely. For a contrary finding, Wilcox, W. Bradford and Nicholas H. Wolfinger. 2007. "Then Comes Marriage? Religion and Marriage in Urban America." *Social Science Research* 36: 569–589. Also, the number of children does not appear to affect remarriage prospects for divorced women. See Martinson, Brian C. 1994. "Postmarital

NOTES TO PAGES 25-28   195

Union Formation: Trends and Determinants of the Competing Roles of Remarriage and Nonmarital Cohabitation among Women in the United States." Unpublished doctoral dissertation. Department of Sociology, University of Wisconsin-Madison.

21. Wu, Lawrence L., Larry L. Bumpass, and Kelly Musick. 2001. "Historical and Life Course Trajectories of Nonmarital Childbearing." Pp. 3–48 in L. L. Wu and B. Wolfe *Out of Wedlock: Causes and Consequences of Nonmarital Fertility*. New York: Russell Sage Foundation.

22. Miller, Brent C., Sage, Rayna A., and Bryan Winward. 2005. "Teen Childbearing and Public Policy." Pp. 47–72 in L. Kowaleski-Jones and N. H. Wolfinger *Fragile Families and the Marriage Agenda*. New York: Springer.

23. The impact of younger children is shown in much of the literature on mothers' earnings. For example, see Budig, Michelle J. and Melissa J. Hodges. 2010. "Differences in Disadvantage: Variation in the Motherhood Penalty across White Women's Earnings Distribution," *American Sociological Review* 75: 705–728.

24. On the long-term decline in fertility, United States Census Bureau. 1975. *Historical Statistics of the United States, Colonial Times to 1970*, Bicentennial Edition, Part 2, Washington, DC.

25. Bloome, Deirdre and Shannon Ang. 2020. "Marriage and Union Formation in the United States: Recent Trends Across Racial Groups and Economic Backgrounds." *Demography* 57: 1753–1786.

26. Martinson, Brian C. 1994. "Postmarital Union Formation: Trends and Determinants of the Competing Roles of Remarriage and Nonmarital Cohabitation among Women in the United States." Unpublished doctoral dissertation. Department of Sociology, University of Wisconsin-Madison.

27. United States Bureau of the Census. 2021. "CPS Historical Time Series Tables: Educational Attainment," Table A-2. Available at https://www.census.gov/data/tables/time-series/demo/educational-attainment/cps-historical-time-series.html. This figure is for adults 25 and over. Some observers suggest this estimate is too high, with true rates of high school completion below 80%. See Greene, Jay P. and Marcus A. Winters. 2005. "Public High School Graduation and College-Readiness Rates: 1991–2002." Education Working paper no. 8. Manhattan Institute. Available at https://docs.gatesfoundation.org/documents/manhattaninstitute0502.pdf. The most recent Census reports on educational attainment are Ryan, Camille L. and Kurt Bauman. 2016. *Educational Attainment in the United States: 2015*. Current Population Reports, 20–578. Washington, DC: United States Census Bureau. Available at https://www.census.gov/content/dam/Census/library/publications/2016/demo/p20-578.pdf; McElrath, Kevin and Michael Martin 2021. *Bachelor's Degree Attainment in the United States: 2005 to 2019*. American Community Survey Briefs, ACSBR-009. Washington, DC: United States Census Bureau. Available at https://www.census.gov/content/dam/Census/library/publications/2021/acs/acsbr-009.pdf.

28. We acknowledge that equivalency certificates and high school diplomas aren't the same thing. Cameron, Stephen V. and James J. Heckman. 1993. "The Nonequivalence of High School Equivalents." *Journal of Labor Economics* 11: Part 1: 1–47.

29. Georgetown Public Policy Institute. 2013. "Recovery: Job Growth and Education Requirements through 2020." Available at https://1gyhoq479ufd3yna29x7ubjn-wpengine.netdna-ssl.com/wp-content/uploads/2014/11/Recovery2020.FR_.Web_.pdf.

30. On marriage and education, Goldstein, Joshua R. and Catherine T. Kenney. 2001. "Marriage Delayed or Marriage Foregone? New Cohort Forecasts of First Marriage for U.S. Women." *American Sociological Review* 66: 506–519; Parker, Kim and Renee Stepler. 2017. "As U.S. Marriage Rate Hovers at 50%, Education Gap in Marital Status Widens." *Pew Research Center* 14. Available at https://www.pewresearch.org/fact-tank/2017/09/14/as-u-s-marriage-rate-hovers-at-50-education-gap-in-marital-status-widens/; Sweeney, Megan M. 2002. "Two Decades of Family Change: The Shifting Economic Foundations of Marriage." *American Sociological Review* 67: 132–47; Wolfinger, Nicholas H. 2023. "Family Change in the Context of Social Changes in the United States." Pp. 97–118 in Mary Daly, Birgit Pfau-Effinger, Doug Besharov, and Neil Gilbert *The Oxford Handbook of Family Policy Over The Life-Course*. Oxford: Oxford University Press. Parker, Kim and Renee Stepler. 2017. "As U.S. Marriage Rate Hovers at 50%, Education Gap in Marital Status Widens." *Pew Research Center* 14. Available at https://www.pewresearch.org/fact-tank/2017/09/14/as-u-s-marriage-rate-hovers-at-50-education-gap-in-marital-status-widens/).

31. Dronkers, Jaap. 2015. "The Changing Impact of Education on Divorce and Break-Up Risk." Institute for Family Studies. Available at https://www.researchgate.net/publication/353057709_

196 NOTES TO PAGES 29–37

Publishing_and_Parenting_in_Academic_Science_A_Study_of_Different_National_Conte xts; Raley, R. Kelly and Larry Bumpass. 2003 "The Topography of the Divorce Plateau: Levels and Trends in Union Stability in the United States after 1980." *Demographic Research* 8: 245–260.

32. Farley, Reynolds. 1996. *The New American Reality*. New York: Russell Sage Foundation.

33. United States Bureau of the Census. 2021. *CPS Historical Time Series Tables: Educational Attainment*, Table A-2. Available at https://www.census.gov/data/tables/time-series/demo/educ ational-attainment/cps-historical-time-series.html.

34. Belkin, Lisa. 2023. "The Opt-Out Revolution." *The New York Times*, October 26; for contrary evidence, *inter alia*, Goldin, Claudia. 2006. "Working it Out." *The New York Times*, March 15; Percheski, Christine. 2008. "Opting Out? Cohort Differences in Professional Women's Employment Rates from 1960 to 2005." *American Sociological Review* 73: 497–517. For a media overview of opting out, Young, Cathy. 2004. "Opting Out: The Press Discovers the Mommy Wars, Again." *Reason Online*, June. Available at https://reason.com/2004/06/01/opting-out-3/.

35. Edin, Kathryn, and Laura Lein. 1997. *Making Ends Meet: How Single Mothers Survive Welfare and Low-Wage Work*. New York: Russell Sage Foundation.

36. Hauser, Robert M. and John Robert Warren. 1997. "Socioeconomic Indexes for Occupations: A Review, Update, and Critique." Pp. 177–298 in A. E. Raftery *Sociological Methodology 1997*. Washington, DC: The American Sociological Association.

37. United States Bureau of the Census. 2020. *Poverty Thresholds 2018*. Available at https://www.cen sus.gov/data/tables/time-series/demo/income-poverty/historical-poverty-thresholds.html.

38. Albertini, Marco, Michael Gähler, and Juho Härkönen. 2018. "Moving Back to "Mamma"? Divorce, Intergenerational Coresidence, and Latent Family Solidarity in Sweden." *Population, Space and Place* 24: e2142; Sarkisian, Natalia and Naomi Gerstel. 2008. "Till Marriage Do Us Part: Adult Children's Relationships with Their Parents." *Journal of Marriage and Family* 70: 360–376; South, Scott J. and Lei Lei. 2015. "Failures-to-launch and Boomerang Kids: Contemporary Determinants of Leaving and Returning to the Parental Home." *Social Forces* 94: 863–890.

39. One paper identifies co-residence with relatives and others as a key component of the safety net for single mothers. Pilkauskas, Natasha V., Irwin Garfinkel, and Sara McLanahan. 2013. "Doubling Up as a Private Safety Net for Families with Children." Available at https://ffcws. princeton.edu/sites/g/files/toruqf4356/files/documents/wp13-13-ff.pdf.

40. On international variation in living with parents, and its continued importance for women in southern and eastern Europe, see Hogendoorn, Bran and Juho Härkönen. 2023 "Single Motherhood and Multigenerational Coresidence in Europe." *Population and Development Review* 49: 105–133.

41. McKeever, Matthew and Nicholas H. Wolfinger. 2006 "Shifting Fortunes in a Changing Economy: Trends in the Economic Well-Being of Divorced Women." Pp. 127–157 in L. Kowaleski-Jones and N. H. Wolfinger *Fragile Families and the Marriage Agenda*. New York: Springer; see also McKeever, Matthew and Nicholas H. Wolfinger. 2001. "Reexamining the Economic Consequences of Marital Disruption for Women." *Social Science Quarterly* 82: 202–217.

42. A note on terminology: unlike in most national data sets, the persons of interest in a CPS sample aren't always the respondents—sometimes the respondent is another family member. Throughout this book we'll call them respondents, because the alternatives—participants, subjects, includants, etc.—are all needlessly confusing.

43. Despite this limitation, our estimates are less problematic than is the case with most other datasets because for most multigenerational households either the parent or grandparent is the householder; more complicated family arrangements are less common in the U.S. On issues with identifying 'lone parents' in European data, see Bradshaw, Jonathan. 2016. The Well-Being of Children in the UK, 4th ed. Bristol: Bristol University Press.

44. On high cohabitation among divorcées, Bumpass, Larry L. and Hsien-Hen Lu. 2000. "Trends in Cohabitation and Implications for Children's Family Contexts in the United States." *Population Studies* 54: 29–41; on cohabitation supplanting remarriage, Brown, Susan L., and Matthew R. Wright. 2017. "Marriage, Cohabitation, and Divorce in Later Life." *Innovation in Aging* 1: 1–11; Martinson, Brian C. 1994. "Postmarital Union Formation: Trends and Determinants of the Competing Roles of Remarriage and Nonmarital Cohabitation among Women in the United States." Unpublished doctoral dissertation. Department of Sociology, University of Wisconsin-Madison.

45. Casper, Lynne M. and Philip N. Cohen. 2000. "How Does POSSLQ Measure Up? Historical Estimates of Cohabitation." *Demography* 37: 237–245. See Appendix D for more details.

On the historical resonance of the POSSLQ measure, Osgood, Charles. n.d. "My POSSLQ," available at https://archive.wikiwix.com/cache/index2.php?rev_t=20150221040428&url=http%3A%2F2000clicks.com%2Fgraeme%2FLangPoetryFunnyPOSSLQ.htm#federation=archive.wikiwix.com&tab=url.

46. On cohabitation stability, Bumpass, Larry L. and Hsien-Hen Lu. 2000. "Trends in Cohabitation and Implications for Children's Family Contexts in the United States." *Population Studies* 54: 29–41; Mernitz, Sara. 2018. A Cohort Comparison of Trends in First Cohabitation Duration in the United States. *Demographic Research* 38: 2073–2086. Available at https://www.demographic-research.org/volumes/vol38/66/; Musick, Kelly and Katherine Michelmore. 2018. "Cross-National Comparisons of Union Stability in Cohabiting and Married Families with Children." *Demography* 55: 1389–1421; on cohabitation stability for never-married mothers in particular, McLanahan, Sara. 2006. "Fragile Families and the Marriage Agenda." Pp. 1–21 in L. Kowaleski-Jones and N. H. Wolfinger *Fragile Families and the Marriage Agenda.* New York: Springer. It's worth noting that cohabiting relationships became shorter over the course of our study, as cohabitation became more common and increasingly attracted less committed partners.

47. McLanahan, Sara. 2006. "Fragile Families and the Marriage Agenda." Pp. 1–21 in L. Kowaleski-Jones and N. H. Wolfinger *Fragile Families and the Marriage Agenda.* New York: Springer.

48. Curtin, Sally C., Stephanie J. Ventura, and Gladys M. Martinez. 2014. "Recent Declines in Nonmarital Childbearing in the United States." NCHS Data Brief no 162. Hyattsville, MD: National Center for Health Statistics. Available at https://www.cdc.gov/nchs/products/databriefs/db162.htm.

49. Conversely, household income sometimes reflects the economic status of individuals who have no meaningful relationship to the householder, so household income can never be an accurate measure of how well-off families are.

50. Evans, Ann and Edith Gray. 2021. "Cross-National Differences in Income Pooling among Married and Cohabiting Couples." *Journal of Marriage and Family* 83: 534–550.

51. *Inter alia*, Brown, Susan L. 2002. "Child Well-Being in Cohabiting Families." Pp. 173–187 in Alan Booth and Ann C. Crouter *Just Living Together: Implications of Cohabitation for Children, Families, and Social Policy.* Mahwah, NJ: Lawrence Erlbaum; McLanahan, Sara S. and Gary Sandefur. 1994. *Growing Up with a Single Parent: What Hurts, What Helps.* Cambridge, MA: Harvard University Press.

52. Reese, Ellen. 2005. *Backlash Against Welfare Mothers: Past and Present.* Berkeley: University of California Press. On historically higher rates of single-parent African American families, Ruggles, Steve. 1994. "The Origins of African American Family Structure." *American Sociological Review* 59: 136–151.

53. Haney-Lopez, Ian. 2014. "The Racism at the Heart of the Reagan Presidency." *Salon*, January. Available at https://www.salon.com/2014/01/11/the_racism_at_the_heart_of_the_reagan_presidency/; Gilens, Martin. "Racial Attitudes and Opposition to Welfare." 1995. *The Journal of Politics* 57: 994–1014.

54. Younger readers will be excused for not knowing that America was a far less diverse country in 1980. Moreover, less diversity was presumed; the race/ethnicity variables at the beginning of our time series are much less sophisticated than they were in 2018. This is also reflected in the sampling. One sampling change in particular, from January of 1982, seems consequential: "The race categories in the second-stage ratio estimation adjustment were changed from White/Non-White to Black/Non-Black. . . [which] resulted in more variability for certain 'White,' 'Black,' and 'Other' characteristics." Page 16, United States Census Bureau. 2006. *Design and Methodology: Current Population Survey. Technical Paper 66.* Available at https://www2.census.gov/programs-surveys/cps/methodology/tp-66.pdf. This change is presumably responsible for the artificially large jump in African American nonmarital fertility between 1981 and 1982.

55. Martin, Teresa Castro and Larry L. Bumpass. 1989. "Recent Trends in Marital Disruption." *Demography* 26: 37–51.

56. Wikipedia has a useful compendium of Census data on the historical demography of the U.S. "Historical Racial and Ethnic Demographics of the United States." Available at https://en.wikipedia.org/wiki/Historical_racial_and_ethnic_demographics_of_the_United_States.

Chapter 3

1. Data were obtained from the Center for Economic and Policy Research, 2021, CPS ORG Uniform Extracts, Version 1.1. Washington, DC. Please consult Appendix D for additional information about the data and analysis.

198   NOTES TO PAGES 40–48

2. Blau, Peter M. and Otis Dudley Duncan. 1967. *The American Occupational Structure.* New York: Wiley.
3. Torpey, Elka and Audrey Watson. 2014. "Education Level and Jobs: Opportunities by State." U.S. Bureau of Labor Statistics. Available at https://www.bls.gov/careeroutlook/2014/article/education-level-and-jobs.htm.
4. Eika, Lasse, Magne Mogstad, and Basit Zafar. 2019. "Educational Assortative Mating and Household Income Inequality." *Journal of Political Economy* 127: 2795–2835; Mare, Robert D. 1991. "Five Decades of Educational Assortative Mating." *American Sociological Review* 56: 15–32; Schwartz, Christine R. 2013. "Trends and Variation in Assortative Mating: Causes and Consequences." *Annual Review of Sociology* 39: 451–470; Sweeney, Megan M. 2002. "Two Decades of Family Change: The Shifting Economic Foundations of Marriage." *American Sociological Review* 67: 132–147; for a contrary finding, see Gihleb, Rania and Kevin Lang. 2016. "Educational Homogamy and Assortative Mating Have Not Increased." National Bureau of Economic Research. Working paper 22927. Available at https://www.nber.org/system/files/working_papers/w22927/w22927.pdf.
5. Karoly, Lynn. 1993. "The Trend in Inequality among Families, Individuals, and Workers in the United States: A Twenty-Five Year Perspective." Pp. 19–97 in S. Danziger and P. Gottschalk *Uneven Tides.* New York: Russell Sage; Abel, Jaison R. and Richard Deitz. 2014. "Do the Benefits of College Still Outweigh the Costs?" *Current Issues in Economics and Finance* 20. New York Federal Reserve. Available at https://citeseerx.ist.psu.edu/viewdoc/download?doi=10.1.1.639.3807&rep=rep1&type=pdf.
6. McKeever, Matthew and Nicholas H. Wolfinger, 2011. "Thanks for Nothing: Income and Labor Force Participation for Never-Married Mothers since 1982." *Social Science Research* 40: 63–76.
7. Bartels, Larry M. 2016. *Unequal Democracy: The Political Economy of the New Gilded Age,* 2nd ed. Princeton, NJ: Princeton University Press; Stiglitz, Joseph E. 2012. *The Price of Inequality: How Today's Divided Society Endangers our Future.* New York: W. W. Norton & Company.
8. For trends, DeSilver, Drew. 2018. "For Most U.S. Workers, Real Wages Have Barely Budged in Decades." Pew Research Center. Available at https://www.pewresearch.org/fact-tank/2018/08/07/for-most-us-workers-real-wages-have-barely-budged-for-decades/; for a broad explanation, Noah, Timothy. 2012. *The Great Divergence: America's Growing Inequality Crisis and What We Can Do About It.* Camden: Bloomsbury Publishing U.S.A. To the usual explanations, David Leonhardt has recently proposed including cultural changes among the nation's employers. Leonhardt, David. 2023. *Ours Was the Shining Future: The Story of the American Dream.* New York: Random House.
9. Congressional Research Service. 2019. "Real Wage Trends, 1979 to 2019." Washington, DC: Congressional Research Service. https://fas.org/sgp/crs/misc/R45090.pdf
10. McKeever, Matthew and Nicholas H. Wolfinger, 2011. "Thanks for Nothing: Income and Labor Force Participation for Never-Married Mothers since 1982." *Social Science Research* 40: 63–76.
11. Shriver, Maria and Center for American Progress. 2009. *The Shriver Report: A Woman's Nation Changes Everything,* edited by Heather Boushey and Ann O'Leary: Washington, DC: Center for American Progress, 19.
12. And, in the U.S. single mothers are comparatively more likely to work than in other industrial societies: Biegert, Thomas, David Brady, and Lena Hipp. 2022. "Cross-National Variation in the Relationship between Welfare Generosity and Single Mother Employment." *Annals of the American Academy of Political and Social Science,* 702: 37–54. See also Zagel, Hannah. 2014. "Are All Single Mothers the Same? Evidence from British and West German Women's Employment Trajectories." *European Sociological Review* 30: 49–63.
13. Edin, Kathryn and Laura Lein. 1997. *Making Ends Meet: How Single Mothers Survive Welfare and Low-Wage Work.* Russell Sage Foundation.
14. As of 2017, about 8% of American households were composed of same-sex couples. Small numbers and limited data resources in earlier years prevented further analysis on this topic. Taylor, Danielle. 2019. *Male Couples Make up Majority of Same-Sex Households in Large Cities but Not Nationwide.* Washington, DC: United States Census Bureau. Available at https://www.census.gov/library/stories/2019/09/where-same-sex-couples-live.html.
15. A reminder: per the Census, a cohabiting couple comprises two separate families sharing a household, so a cohabiting partner's income doesn't contribute to family income. At the same time, examining household rather than family income isn't a viable strategy, as low-income individuals are disproportionately likely to live in households that contain multiple families.

NOTES TO PAGES 48–60   199

On Census definitions of families and households, United States Census Bureau. 2023. Subject Definitions. Washington, DC: United Sates Government Printing Office. Available at https://www.census.gov/programs-surveys/cps/technical-documentation/subject-definitions.html.

16. Smock, Pamela J. and Christine R. Schwartz. 2020. "The Demography of Families: A Review of Patterns and Change." *Journal of Marriage and Family* 82: 9–34.

17. Hamplová, Dana and Celine Le Bourdais. 2009. "One Pot or Two Pot Strategies? Income Pooling in Married and Unmarried Households n Comparative Perspective." *Journal of Comparative Family Studies* 40: 355–385; Hamplová, Dana, Céline Le Bourdais, and Évelyne Lapierre-Adamcyk. 2014. "Is the Cohabitation–Marriage Gap in Money Pooling Universal?" *Journal of Marriage and Family* 76: 983–997.

18. Mernitz, Sara. 2018. "A Cohort Comparison of Trends in First Cohabitation Duration in the United States." *Demographic Research* 38: 2073–2086; see also Musick, Kelly and Katherine Michelmore. 2018. "Cross-National Comparisons of Union Stability in Cohabiting and Married Families with Children." *Demography* 55: 1389–1421.

19. Brown, Susan L. and Wendy D. Manning. 2009. "Family Boundary Ambiguity and the Measurement of Family Structure: The Significance of Cohabitation." *Demography* 46: 85–101; Manning, Wendy D. and Pamela J. Smock. 2005. "Measuring and Modeling Cohabitation: New Perspectives from Qualitative Data." *Journal of Marriage and Family* 67: 989–1002.

20. Stanley, Scott M., Galena Kline Rhoades, and Howard J. Markman. 2006. "Sliding versus Deciding: Inertia and the Premarital Cohabitation Effect." *Family Relations* 55: 499–509.

21. Indeed, "[a]mong college-educated adults, the median adjusted household income of cohabiters ($106,400 in 2009) slightly exceeded that of married adults ($101,160) and was significantly higher than that of adults without opposite-sex partners ($90,067)." Fry, Richard and D. Cohn. 2011. "Living Together: The Economics of Cohabitation." Pew Research Center. Available at https://www.pewsocialtrends.org/2011/06/27/living-together-the-economics-of-cohabitation/.

22. Wolfinger, Nicholas H. 2003. "Parental Divorce and Offspring Marriage: Early or Late?" *Social Forces* 82: 337–353; Wolfinger, Nicholas H. 2005. *Understanding the Divorce Cycle: The Children of Divorce in Their Own Marriages.* New York: Cambridge University Press.

23. Losing your job is an understandably strong predictor of moving back with your parents. Kaplan, Greg. 2009. "Boomerang Kids: Labor Market Dynamics and Moving Back Home." *Federal Reserve Bank of Minneapolis.* Working paper 675.

24. Caputo, Jennifer. 2018. "Parental Coresidence, Young Adult Role, Economic, and Health Changes, and Psychological Well-Being." *Society and Mental Health* 10 (3).

25. McLanahan, Sara S. and Gary Sandefur. 1994. *Growing Up with a Single Parent: What Hurts, What Helps.* Cambridge, MA: Harvard University Press; but for a contrary finding, see Dunifon, Rachel. 2013. "The Influence of Grandparents on the Lives of Children and Adolescents." *Child Development Perspectives* 7: 55–60. One study found that the benefits of living with a grand-parent differed by race, with benefits for White kids but adverse consequences for African American offspring. Dunifon, Rachel and Lori Kowaleski-Jones. 2007. "The Influence of Grandparents in Single-Mother Families." *Journal of Marriage and Family* 69: 465–481.

26. Ventura, Stephanie J., T. J. Mathews, and Brady E. Hamilton. 2001. *Births to Teenagers in the United States 1940–2000.* Hyattsville, MD: National Center for Health Statistics.

27. Martin, Joyce A., Brady E. Hamilton, Michele J. K. Osterman, and Anne K. Driscoll. 2018. "Births: Final Data for 2017." National Vital Statistics Reports; vol 67 no 8. Hyattsville, MD: National Center for Health Statistics. Available at https://www.cdc.gov/nchs/data/nvsr/nvsr67/nvsr67_08-508.pdf.

28. CPS data do not allow us to determine whether married mothers were unwed when they gave birth as teenagers, but we suspect relatively few were: a nonmarital pregnancy reduces the likelihood of marriage. On this point, Lichter, Daniel T. and Deborah Roempke Graefe. 2001. "Finding a Mate? The Marital and Cohabitation Histories of Unwed Mothers." Pp. 317–343 in Lawrence L. Wu and Barbara Wolfe *Out of Wedlock: Causes and Consequences of Nonmarital Fertility.* New York: Russell Sage Foundation. In fact, at best 10% of never-married mothers marry within a year of a nonmarital birth. See Wilcox, W. Bradford and Nicholas H. Wolfinger. 2007. "Then Comes Marriage? Religion and Marriage in Urban America." *Social Science Research* 36: 569–589.

29. Hotz, V. Joseph, Susan Williams McElroy, and Seth G. Sanders. 1995. "The Costs and Consequences of Teenage Childbearing for Mothers," Working paper 9501, Harris School of Public Policy Studies, University of Chicago; Hotz, V. Joseph, Charles H. Mullin, and Seth G. Sanders. 1997. "Bounding Causal Effects Using Data from a Contaminated Natural

200 NOTES TO PAGES 60–68

Experiment: Analysing the Effects of Teenage Childbearing." *The Review of Economic Studies* 64: 575–603.

30. Avellar, Sarah and Pamela J. Smock. 2003 "Has the Price of Motherhood Declined Over Time? A Cross-Cohort Comparison of the Motherhood Wage Penalty," *Journal of Marriage and Family* 65: 597–607. Budig, Michelle J. and Paula England, 2001. "The Wage Penalty for Motherhood," *American Sociological Review* 66: 204–225; Budig, Michelle J. and Melissa J. Hodges. 2010 "Differences in Disadvantage: Variation in the Motherhood Penalty across White Women's Earnings Distribution," *American Sociological Review* 75: 705–728; Waldfogel, Jane. 1997. "The Effect of Children on Women's Wages," *American Sociological Review* 62: 209–217.

31. Avellar, Sarah and Pamela J. Smock. 2003 "Has the Price of Motherhood Declined Over Time? A Cross-Cohort Comparison of the Motherhood Wage Penalty," *Journal of Marriage and Family* 65: 597–607.

32. Budig, Michelle J. and Paula England, 2001. "The Wage Penalty for Motherhood," *American Sociological Review* 66: 204–225.

33. Noonan, Mary C. 2005. "The Long-Term Costs of Women's Work Interruptions." Unpublished paper, Department of Sociology, University of Iowa.

34. On trends in child support, Grall, Timothy, 2018. *Custodial Mothers and Fathers and Their Child Support: 2015.* Current Population Reports, 60–262. Washington, DC: United States Census Bureau. Available at https://www.census.gov/library/publications/2018/demo/p60-262.html.

35. The Moynihan Report is an obvious touchstone here. On the impact of race vs. poverty, see Duncan, Otis Dudley. 1969. "Inheritance of Poverty or Inheritance of Race?" Pp. 85–110 in Daniel P. Moynihan *On Understanding Poverty*. New York: Basic Books. For an updated look, see Brady, David, Ryan Finnigan, Ulrich Kohler, and Joscha Legewie. 2020. "The Inheritance of Race Revisited: Childhood Wealth and Income and Black–White Disadvantages in Adult Life Chances." *Sociological Science* 7: 599–627; Baker, Regina S. 2022. "Ethno-Racial Variation in Single Motherhood Prevalences and Penalties for Child Poverty in the United States." *The Annals of the American Academy of Political and Social Science* 702; and Williams, Dedric T. and Regina S. Baker. 2021. "Family Structure, Risks, and Racial Stratification in Poverty." *Social Problems* 68: 964–985.

36. Census Bureau reports provide contemporary and historical data on the relationship between race, family structure, and poverty. Semega, Jessica, Melissa Kollar, John Creamer, and Abinash Mohanty. 2020. *Income and Poverty in the United States: 2018.* Current Population Reports, 60–266, Washington, DC: United States Government Printing Office. (RV). The Black–White gap in single-parent families stems back to the nineteenth century. Ruggles, Steve. 1994 "The Origins of African American Family Structure." *American Sociological Review* 59: 136–151; Ruggles, Steve. 1997. "The Rise of Divorce and Separation in the United States, 1880–1990." *Demography* 34: 455–466. For a recent critique of the tendency to oversimplify this relationship, see Williams, Dedric T. and Regina S. Baker. 2021. "Family Structure, Risks, and Racial Stratification in Poverty." *Social Problems* 68: 964–985.

37. For the rest of the chapter we'll use "race" as shorthand for both race and ethnicity.

38. United States Census Bureau, 2023. "Historical Income Tables." Available at https://www.census.gov/data/tables/time-series/demo/income-poverty/historical-income-inequality.html. See People, Table P-1. In contrast, the gap in family income soared as the growth in African American single-parent families greatly outstripped the rate for Whites.

39. Crenshaw, Kimberlé. 1989. "Demarginalizing the Intersection of Race and Sex: A Black Feminist Critique of Antidiscrimination Doctrine, Feminist Theory and Antiracist Politics." *University of Chicago Legal Forum*: 139–167; Andersen, Margaret, L. and Patricia Hill Collins. 1992. *Race, Class and Gender: An Anthology*. Belmont, CA: Wadsworth.

40. A representative modern paean to intersectionality cited "race, gender, class, national origins, sexuality, normative gender, nonnormative gender, physical (dis)ability, religion, age, neocolonialism, xenophobic nationalism, heterosexism, transphobia, ableism, ageism, Islamophobia, 'and other social categories.'" Runyon, Anne Sisson. 2018. "What Is Intersectionality and Why Is It Important?" *Academe*, November-December. Available at https://www.aaup.org/article/what-intersectionality-and-why-it-important#YjvOBufMJM0.

41. Kearney, Melissa S. 2023. *The Two-Parent Privilege: How the Decline in Marriage Has Increased Inequality and Lowered Social Mobility, and What We Can Do About It.* Rugby, UK: Swift Press.

42. See King, Deborah K. 1988. "Multiple Jeopardy, Multiple Consciousness: The Context of a Black Feminist Ideology." *Signs* 14: 42–72; Kohlman, Marla H. 2006. "Intersection Theory: A More Elucidating Paradigm of Quantitative Analysis." *Race Gender & Class* 13: 42–59. One of the

NOTES TO PAGES 68–74   201

authors of this book has recently made the case for intersectionality as a hypothesis. Wolfinger, Nicholas H. 2019. "I Know What Intersectionality Is, and I Wish it Were Less Important." *Quillette*, February 20. Available at https://quillette.com/2019/02/20/i-know-what-intersecti onality-is-and-i-wish-it-were-less-important/.

43. Source: General Social Survey Data Explorer. We should note that these results are heavily dependent on how survey questions are worded. People tend to feel good about helping the poor just so long as the word "welfare" isn't used. See, for instance, Jacoby, William G. 2000. "Issue Framing and Public Opinion on Government Spending." *American Journal of Political Science*: 750–767.

44. The unemployment rate peaked at 9.6% in 2010.

45. Edin, Kathryn and H. Luke Shaefer. 2015. *$2.00 a Day: Living on Almost Nothing in America.* Boston, MA: Houghton Mifflin Harcourt.

46. Waring, Melody K. and Daniel R. Meyer. 2020. "Welfare, Work, and Single Mothers: The Great Recession and Income Packaging Strategies." *Children and Youth Services Review* 108: 1–10.

47. Edin, Kathryn and H. Luke Shaefer. 2015. *$2.00 a Day: Living on Almost Nothing in America.* Boston, MA: Houghton Mifflin Harcourt.

48. Fremstad, Shawn. 2013. "TANF and Two-Parent Families." Institute for Family Studies. Available at https://ifstudies.org/blog/tanf-and-two-parent-families.

49. Palimony first emerged as a playful portmanteau of "pal" and "alimony" after Michelle Triola sued the actor Lee Marvin for support in 1977. They'd lived together for five years, but never married. As of 2020, palimony has been awarded in only a few states. Others bar palimony on the grounds that it discourages marriage.

50. Grall, Timothy, 2018. *Custodial Mothers and Fathers and Their Child Support: 2015.* Current Population Reports, 60–262. Washington, DC: United States Census Bureau. Available at https://www.census.gov/library/publications/2018/demo/p60-262.html.

51. On fathers who can't afford to make support payments, one study writes, "70 percent of the arrears owed on child support are owed by people who reported less than $10,000 annual income. These people were expected to pay, on average, 83 percent of their income in child support." Makidis, Theonie. 2018. "Race, the Incarcerated Father, and Child Support Obligations." *The Federal Lawyer*: 42–54. Available at https://www.fedbar.org/wp-content/uploads/2018/09/Makidis-pdf-1.pdf. Brito, Tonya L. 2018. "The Child Support Debt Bubble." *University of California Irvine Law Review* 9: 953; Hakovirta, Mia, Daniel R. Meyer, and Christine Skinner. 2019. "Does Paying Child Support Impoverish Fathers in the United States, Finland, and the United Kingdom?" *Children and Youth Services Review* 106: 104485; Sorensen, Elaine and Chava Zibman. 2000. *A Look at Poor Dads Who Don't Pay Child Support. Discussion Papers. Assessing the New Federalism: An Urban Institute Program to Assess Changing Social Policies.* Washington, DC: The Urban Institute. Available at https://www.urban.org/sites/default/files/publication/62536/409646-A-Look-at-Poor-Dads-Who-Don-t-Pay-Child-Support.PDF; Sorensen, Elaine, Liliana Sousa, and Simon Schaner. 2007 *Assessing Child Support Arrears in Nine Large States and the Nation.* Washington, DC: The Urban Institute. Available at http://opnff.net/Files/Admin/Assessing%20Child%20Support%20Arrears.pdf. On in-kind aid, Kane, Jennifer B., Timothy J. Nelson, and Kathryn Edin. 2015. "How Much In-Kind Support Do Low-Income Nonresident Fathers Provide? A Mixed-Method Analysis." *Journal of Marriage and Family* 77: 591–611; Sariscsany, Laurel, Irwin Garfinkel, and Lenna Nepomnyaschy. 2019. "Describing and Understanding Child Support Trajectories." *Social Service Review* 93: 143–82; on child support more broadly, Grall, Timothy, 2020. *Custodial Mothers and Fathers and Their Child Support: 2015.* Current Population Reports, 60–262. Washington, DC: United States Census Bureau. Available at https://www.census.gov/content/dam/Census/library/publicati ons/2020/demo/p60-269.pdf.

52. Lamidi, Esther and Wendy D. Manning. 2016. "FP-16-17 Marriage and Cohabitation Experiences Among Young Adults." *National Center for Family and Marriage Research Family Profiles*: 60. Available at https://scholarworks.bgsu.edu/ncfmr_family_profiles/60.

53. Anderson, Kermyt G., Hillard Kaplan, and Jane B. Lancaster. 2001. "Men's Financial Expenditures on Genetic Children and Stepchildren from Current and Former Relationships. PSC Research Report." Available at https://files.eric.ed.gov/fulltext/ED463372.pdf.

54. On the growing acceptance of single parenthood, Livingston, Gretchen. 2018. "The Changing Profile of Unmarried Parents." Pew Research Center. Available at https://www.pewsocialtre nds.org/2018/04/25/the-changing-profile-of-unmarried-parents/; on legal developments, Breitenbach, Sarah. 2016. "Involving Dads in the Lives of Children Born out of Wedlock,"

202 NOTES TO PAGES 74–81

Stateline, September 29. Available at https://www.pewtrusts.org/en/research-and-analysis/blogs/stateline/2016/09/29/involving-dads-in-the-lives-of-children-born-out-of-wedlock.

55. Budig, Michelle J. 2003. "Are Women's Employment and Fertility Histories Interdependent? An Examination of Causal Order Using Event History Analysis." *Social Science Research* 32: 376–401.

56. The idea of regression decomposition, erroneously often referred to as Blinder–Oaxaca decomposition, was introduced by sociologist Evelyn Kitagawa. See Kitagawa, Evelyn M. 1955. "Components of a Difference Between Two Rates." *Journal of the American Statistical Association* 50: 1168–1194. On how the names attached to decomposition developed, Treiman, Donald. 2009. *Quantitative Data Analysis*. San Francisco: Wiley, 175.

57. We report the results of a modified decomposition based on income distributions rather than means. Family income is divided into percentiles, intervals each containing 1% of the income distribution. This provides sufficient categories to approximate the income distribution without spreading the sample too thin. The position in this distribution of income categories serves as a dependent variable predicted by ordered logistic regression models, which in turn facilitate a distributional decomposition. By decomposing entire income distributions via the ordered logistic regression models, we can examine distributional changes, instead of being restricted to reporting changes in the average return to labor force qualifications that the more standard mean log-income decomposition details. The analysis thus allows us to understand how changing individual characteristics and changing returns to individual characteristics have each affected married, divorced, and never-married mothers' location in the income distribution. For details, Fortin, Nicole M. and Thomas Lemieux. 1998. "Rank Regressions, Wage Distributions, and the Gender Gap." *Journal of Human Resources* 33: 610–643. We previously conducted rank-order decompositions of single mothers' incomes in two papers. McKeever, Matthew and Nicholas H. Wolfinger. 2006 "Shifting Fortunes in a Changing Economy: Trends in the Economic Well-Being of Divorced Women." Pp. 127–157 in L. Kowaleski-Jones and N. H. Wolfinger *Fragile Families and the Marriage Agenda*. New York: Springer; McKeever, Matthew and Nicholas H. Wolfinger. 2011. "Thanks for Nothing: Income and Labor Force Participation for Never-married Mothers since 1982." *Social Science Research* 40: 63–76.

Chapter 4

1. For a description of changes in inequality as measured by Gini coefficients, see United States Census Bureau, 2023. "Historical Income Tables." https://www.census.gov/data/tables/time-series/demo/income-poverty/historical-income-inequality.html. But Gini coefficients hardly tell the whole story. There are really two burgeoning forms of inequality. Better known is the eye-popping wealth of the top percentile—indeed, fraction of a percentile—highlighted most notoriously by the French scholar Thomas Pikkety (Pikkety, Thomas. 2014. *Capital in the 21st Century*, Cambridge MA: Harvard University Press.) There aren't a lot of single mothers in the top fraction of the income distribution and we suspect they have more in common with other wealthy Americans than with other single mothers. The second and more relevant form of inequality is what's transpiring in the rest of the income distribution, from the growing incomes of the educated and prosperous upper quartile to the immiserated bottom of the income distribution. For more on the second form of inequality, we point readers to several prominent monographs from the past decade: Edin, Kathryn and H. Luke Shaefer. 2015. *$2.00 a Day: Living on Almost Nothing in America*. Boston, MA: Houghton Mifflin Harcourt; Murray, Charles. 2012. *Coming Apart: The State of White America, 1960–2010*. New York: Forum Books; Putnam, Robert D. 2016. *Our Kids: The American Dream in Crisis*. New York: Simon and Schuster; Reeves, Richard V. 2018. *Dream Hoarders: How the American Upper Middle Class Is Leaving Everyone Else in the Dust, Why That Is a Problem, and What To Do about It*. Washington, DC: Brookings Institution Press.

2. Bernhardt, Annette, Martina Morris, and Mark S. Handcock. 1995. "Women's Gains or Men's Losses? A Closer Look at the Shrinking Gender Gap in Earnings." *American Journal of Sociology* 101: 302–328.

3. Garfinkel, Irwin and Sara S. McLanahan. 1986. *Single Mothers and Their Children: A New American Dilemma*. Washington, DC: The Urban Institute Press; Weitzman, Lenore J. 1985. *The Divorce Revolution: The Unexpected Social and Economic Consequences for Women and Children in America*. New York: The Free Press.

4. Roy, Avik and Aparna Mathur. 2014. "The Biggest Reason for Income Inequality is Single Parenthood." *Forbes Magazine*, November 19. Available at https://www.forbes.com/sites/

NOTES TO PAGES 81–82   203

theapothecary/2014/11/19/the-biggest-reason-for-income-inequality-is-single-parenthood/#d3adfcc2555c.

5. Eggebeen, David J. and Daniel T. Lichter. 1991. "Race, Family Structure, and Changing Poverty among American Children." *American Sociological Review* 56: 801–817; McLanahan, Sara and Christine Percheski. 2008. "Family Structure and the Reproduction of Inequalities." *Annual Review of Sociology* 34: 257–76.

6. Western, Bruce, Deirdre Bloome, and Christine Percheski. 2008. "Inequality among American Families with Children, 1975 to 2005." *American Sociological Review* 73: 903–920.

7. Lichter, Daniel T., Felicia B. LeClere, and Diane K. McLaughlin. 1991. "Local Marriage Markets and the Marital Behavior of Black and White Women." *American journal of Sociology* 96 (4): 843–867; Lichter, Daniel T., Diane K. McLaughlin, George Kephart, and David J. Landry. 1992. "Race and the Retreat from Marriage: A Shortage of Marriageable Men?" *American Sociological Review*: 781–799. Two recent important works have shined a much-needed light on regional inequality. Chetty, Raj, Nathaniel Hendren, Patrick Kline, and Emmanuel Saez. 2014. "Where is the Land of Opportunity? The Geography of Intergenerational Mobility in the United States." *Quarterly Journal of Economics* 129: 1553–1623; Edin, Kathryn J., H. Luke Shaefer, and Timothy J. Nelson. 2023. *The Injustice of Place: Uncovering the Legacy of Poverty in America.* Boston, MA: Mariner Books.

8. Fremstad, Shawn. 2016. "Partnered but Poor." Center for American Progress. Available at https://www.americanprogress.org/issues/poverty/reports/2016/03/11/131968/partnered-but-poor/.

9. Noah, Timothy. 2012. *The Great Divergence: America's Growing Inequality Crisis and What We Can Do about It.* Camden: Bloomsbury Publishing USA; Western, Bruce and Jake Rosenfeld. 2011. "Unions, Norms, and the Rise in U.S. Wage Inequality." *American Sociological Review* 76: 513–537.

10. Counsel of Economic Advisors. 2016. "Labor Market Monopsony: Trends, Consequences, and Policy Responses." Available at https://obamawhitehouse.archives.gov/sites/default/files/page/files/20161025_monopsony_labor_mrkt_cea.pdf.

11. Weissmann, Shoshana and C. Jarrett Dieterl. 2018. "Louisiana Is the Only State that Requires Occupational Licenses for Florists. It's Absurd." *USA Today*, March 28. Available at https://www.usatoday.com/story/opinion/2018/03/28/louisiana-only-state-requires-occupational-licenses-florists-its-absurd-column/459619002/.

12. Fortune tellers: Kaminer, Wendy. 2003. "The First Amendment Is for Fortune-tellers, Too." *Free Inquiry*. Available at https://secularhumanism.org/2003/06/the-first-amendment-is-for-fort une-tellers-too/; frog sellers: Minnesota Department of Natural Resources. N.d. "Commercial Frog Licenses." Available at https://www.dnr.state.mn.us/fishing/commercial/frogs.html.

13. Office of Economic Policy. 2016. "Non-compete Contracts: Economic Effects and Policy Implications." U.S. Department of the Treasury. Available at https://home.treasury.gov/sys tem/files/226/Non_Compete_Contracts_Econimic_Effects_and_Policy_Implications_MAR2 016.pdf.

14. Foroohar, Rana. 2016. *Makers and Takers: How Wall Street Destroyed Main Street.* New York: Crown Currency.

15. Pew Research Center. 2021. "The State of Gig Work in 2021." Available at https://www.pewresea rch.org/internet/2021/12/08/the-state-of-gig-work-in-2021/.

16. On historical numbers of single mothers. Bumpass, Larry L. and James A. Sweet. 1989. "Children's Experience in Single-Parent Families: Implications of Cohabitation and Marital Transitions." *Family Planning Perspective* 21: 256–260.

17. Whitehead, Barbara Dafoe. 1993. "Dan Quayle Was Right." *The Atlantic*, April. Available at http://www.theatlantic.com/magazine/archive/1993/04/dan-quayle-was-right/7015/.

18. Nevertheless, many authors have perpetuated the myth of the proliferation of middle-class professional single mothers. See, for example, Hertz, Rosanna. 2006. *Single by Chance, Mothers by Choice: How Women Are Choosing Parenthood Without Marriage and Creating the New American Family.* New York: Oxford University Press.

19. The World Bank. 2021. "Gini Index." Available at https://data.worldbank.org/indicator/SI.POV. GINI; downloadable data can be found at World Population Review. "Gini Coefficient by Country." 2021. Available at https://worldpopulationreview.com/country-rankings/gini-coef ficient-by-country. The nations closest to the U.S. in the rankings are Peru and Bulgaria.

20. Federal Reserve Bank of St. Louis. 2023. "Gini Index for the United States." Available at https://fred.stlouisfed.org/series/SIPOVGINIUSA.

21. There is an extensive literature demonstrating that inequality has adverse consequences for individuals irrespective of their own incomes. For examples, Kennedy, Bruce P., Ichiro Kawachi,

204 NOTES TO PAGES 82–108

Roberta Glass, and Deborah Prothrow-Stith. 1998. "Income Distribution, Socioeconomic Status, and Self Rated Health in the United States: Multilevel Analysis." *British Medical Journal* 317: 917; Levine, Adam Seth, Frank, Robert H., and Oege Dijk. 2010. "Expenditure Cascades." *Social Science Research Network*. Working paper. Available at http://ssrn.com/abstract=1690 612; for an overview, Stiglitz, Joseph E. 2012. *The Price of Inequality: How Today's Divided Society Endangers Our Future*. New York: W. W. Norton.

22. Martin, Molly A. 2006. "Family Structure and Income Inequality in Families with Children, 1976 to 2000." *Demography* 43: 421–45. See especially Figure 4.

23. Displaying confidence intervals would make this figure illegible. We computed these intervals via bootstrap and found that they range from 0.01 to 0.02, not enough to account for the differences by family structure.

24. Predictably this ignores income from informal employment, relied on by many single mothers. Edin, Kathryn and Laura Lein. 1997. *Making Ends Meet: How Single Mothers Survive Welfare and Low-Wage Work*. New York: Russell Sage Foundation.

25. Edin, Kathryn and H. Luke Shaefer. 2015. *$2.00 a Day: Living on Almost Nothing in America*. Boston, MA: Houghton Mifflin Harcourt.

26. Reeves, Richard V. 2018. *Dream Hoarders: How the American Upper Middle Class Is Leaving Everyone Else in The Dust, Why That Is a Problem, and What to Do About It*. Washington, DC: Brookings Institution Press.

27. On rates of child support receipt, see the regular Census reports by Timothy Grall and his colleagues. Grall, Timothy. 2006. *Custodial Mothers and Fathers and Their Child Support: 2003*. Current Population Reports, 60–230. Washington, DC: United States Census Bureau. Available at https://www2.census.gov/library/publications/2006/demo/p60-230.pdf; Grall, Timothy and Liza C. Valle. 2021. *The Regular Receipt of Child Support: 2017*. Current Population Reports, 70–176. Washington, DC: United States Census Bureau. Available athttps://www.census.gov/cont ent/dam/Census/library/publications/2022/demo/p70-176.pdf; see also Chapters 3 and 6. We provide citations for just two of these reports, but there are others.

28. United States Census Bureau. 2018. *Real Median Household Income by Race and Hispanic Origin: 1967 to 2017*. Available at https://www.census.gov/content/dam/Census/library/visuali zations/2018/demo/p60-263/figure1.pdf.

29. Smock, Pamela J. and Christine R. Schwartz. 2020. "The Demography of Families: A Review of Patterns and Change." *Journal of Marriage and Family* 82: 9–34.

30. It's not always possible to distinguish married CPS participants who move in with their own parents from those who move in their spouse's parents, but it doesn't matter for our analysis. Either spouse's parents can provide housing, income transfers, and childcare.

31. Wu, Lawrence L. 1996. "Effects of Family Instability, Income, and Income Instability on the Risk of a Premarital Birth." *American Sociological Review* 61: 386–406; Wu, Lawrence L. and Brian C. Martinson. "Family Structure and the Risk of a Premarital Birth." *American Sociological Review* 58: 210–232.

Chapter 5

1. On low returns to human capital for never-married mothers, see also McKeever, Matthew and Nicholas H. Wolfinger. 2011. "Thanks for Nothing: Income and Labor Force Participation for Never-married Mothers since 1982." *Social Science Research* 40: 63–76.

2. A reminder: women must have minor children at home to be considered mothers.

3. These averages are based on all 28 waves of NSFG data analyzed here, and therefore include many survey years, especially at the beginning and the end of the panel, when rates of motherhood were quite low.

4. Lichter, Daniel T. and Deborah Roempke Graefe. 2001. "Finding a Mate? The Marital and Cohabitation Histories of Unwed Mothers." Pp. 317–343 in Lawrence L. Wu and Barbara Wolfe *Out of Wedlock: Causes and Consequences of Nonmarital Fertility*. New York: Russell Sage Foundation; Lichter, Daniel T., Deborah Roempke Graefe, and J. Brian Brown. 2003. "Is Marriage a Panacea? Union Formation among Economically Disadvantaged Unwed Mothers." *Social Problems* 50: 60–86; Upchurch, Dawn M., Lee A. Lillard, and Constantijn W. A. Panis. 2001. "The Impact of Nonmarital Childbearing on Subsequent Marital Formation and Dissolution." Pp. 344–380 in Lawrence L. Wu and Barbara Wolfe *Out of Wedlock: Causes and Consequences of Nonmarital Fertility*. New York: Russell Sage Foundation.

5. Goldstein, Joshua R. 1999. "The Leveling of Divorce in the United States." *Demography* 36: 409–414.

NOTES TO PAGES 109–117   205

6. Martinson, Brian C. 1994. "Postmarital Union Formation: Trends and Determinants of the Competing Roles of Remarriage and Nonmarital Cohabitation among Women in the United States." Unpublished doctoral dissertation. Department of Sociology, University of Wisconsin-Madison; never-married mothers: McKeever, Matthew and Nicholas H. Wolfinger. 2011. "Thanks for Nothing: Income and Labor Force Participation for Never-married Mothers since 1982." *Social Science Research* 40: 63–76.

7. Income: Sweeney, Megan M. 2002. "Two Decades of Family Change: The Shifting Economic Foundations of Marriage." *American Sociological Review* 67: 132–147; wealth: Schneider, Daniel. 2011. "Wealth and the Marital Divide." *American Journal of Sociology* 117: 627–667.

8. Negative effect: "Finding a Mate? The Marital and Cohabitation Histories of Unwed Mothers." Pp. 317–343 in Lawrence L. Wu and Barbara Wolfe *Out of Wedlock: Causes and Consequences of Nonmarital Fertility*. New York: Russell Sage Foundation; no effect: Wilcox, W. Bradford and Nicholas H. Wolfinger. 2007. "Then Comes Marriage? Religion and Marriage in Urban America." *Social Science Research* 36: 569–589.

9. Bumpass, Larry, James Sweet, and Teresa Castro Martin. 1990. "Changing Patterns of Remarriage." *Journal of Marriage and Family* 52: 747–756; Martinson, Brian C. 1994. "Postmarital Union Formation: Trends and Determinants of the Competing Roles of Remarriage and Nonmarital Cohabitation among Women in the United States." Unpublished doctoral dissertation. Department of Sociology, University of Wisconsin-Madison. The predictors of remarriage have received surprisingly little research attention, but corroborating evidence can be found in a more recent Dutch study. See de Graaf, Paul M. and Matthijs Kalmijn. 2003. "Alternative Routes in the Remarriage Market: Competing-Risk Analyses of Union Formation after Divorce." *Social Forces* 81: 1459–1498. Yet another study suggests that the effects of employment may have changed over time. Sweeney, Megan M. 1995. "Remarriage of Men and Women: The Role of Socioeconomic Prospects." Working paper 95-08, Center for Demography and Ecology, University of Wisconsin-Madison.

10. For never-married mothers, McKeever, Matthew and Nicholas H. Wolfinger. 2011. "Thanks for Nothing: Income and Labor Force Participation for Never-married Mothers since 1982." *Social Science Research* 40: 63–76; Bramlett, Matthew D. and William D. Mosher. 2002. *Cohabitation, Marriage, Divorce, and Remarriage in the United States*. National Center for Health Statistics. Vital Health Stat 23. This study looks at all remarriages, not just among mothers.

11. Diekmann, Andreas and Peter Mitter. 1984. "A Comparison of the 'Sickle Function' with Alternative Stochastic Models of Divorce Rates." Pp. 123–153 in A. Diekmann and P. Mitter *Stochastic Modeling of Social Processes*. Orlando, FL: Academic Press; Goldstein, Joshua R. 1999. "The Leveling of Divorce in the United States." *Demography* 36: 409–414. Divorce rates are highest between two and four years after marriage, when couples are establishing compatibility. Thereafter, divorce rates decline as couples invest more in their relationship.

12. McKeever, Matthew and Nicholas H. Wolfinger. 2011. "Thanks for Nothing: Income and Labor Force Participation for Never-married Mothers since 1982." *Social Science Research* 40: 63–76, Wu, Lawrence L., Larry L. Bumpass, and Kelly Musick. 2001. "Historical and Life Course Trajectories of Nonmarital Childbearing." Pp. 3–48 in L. L. Wu and B. Wolfe *Out of Wedlock: Causes and Consequences of Nonmarital Fertility*. New York: Russell Sage Foundation.

13. Needless to say, widowhood is uncommon for young mothers. Only 57 women were widowed over the first 35 years of NLSY data. Loss of custody is also uncommon. Women still retain at least partial physical custody in 90% of divorce cases. Cancian, Maria, Daniel R. Meyer, Patricia R. Brown, and Steven T. Cook. 2014. "Who Gets Custody Now? Dramatic Changes in Children's Living Arrangements after Divorce." *Demography* 51: 1381–1396. Not surprisingly, this figure used to be even higher. Cancian, Maria and Daniel R. Meyer. 1998. "Who Gets Custody?" *Demography* 35: 147–57.The broader trends in custody have been chronicled by the late Mary Ann Mason: Mason, Mary Ann. 1994. *From Father's Property to Children's Rights: The History of Child Custody in the United States*. New York: Columbia University Press.

14. On the economic benefits of marriage for women who give birth out of wedlock, Lichter, Daniel T., Deborah Roempke Graefe, and J. Brian Brown. 2003. "Is Marriage a Panacea? Union Formation among Economically Disadvantaged Unwed Mothers." *Social Problems* 50: 60–86; on the economic benefits of remarriage for divorcées: Bachrach, Christine. 1983. "Children in Families: Characteristics of Biological, Step-, and Adopted Children." *Journal of Marriage and the Family* 45: 171–179; Morrison, Donna Ruane and Amy Ritualo. 2000. "Routes to Children's Economic Recovery after Divorce: Are Cohabitation and Remarriage Equivalent?" *American Sociological Review* 65: 560–580.

206 NOTES TO PAGES 117–119

15. McKeever, Matthew and Nicholas H. Wolfinger. 2001. "Reexamining the Economic Consequences of Marital Disruption for Women." *Social Science Quarterly* 82: 202–217; McKeever, Matthew and Nicholas H. Wolfinger. 2006 "Shifting Fortunes in a Changing Economy: Trends in the Economic Well-Being of Divorced Women." Pp. 127–157 in L. Kowaleski-Jones and N. H. Wolfinger *Fragile Families and the Marriage Agenda*. New York: Springer.
16. Figure 5.6 is based on life table estimates.
17. Diekmann, Andreas and Peter Mitter. 1984. "A Comparison of the 'Sickle Function' with Alternative Stochastic Models of Divorce Rates." Pp. 123–153 in A. Diekmann and P. Mitter *Stochastic Modeling of Social Processes*. Orlando, FL: Academic Press; Goldstein, Joshua R. 1999. "The Leveling of Divorce in the United States." *Demography* 36: 409–414. This having been said, divorce is less likely in the first few years of a child's life, and the effect diminishes for higher order births. Waite, Linda J. and Lee A. Lillard, 1991. "Children and Marital Disruption." *American Journal of Sociology* 96: 930–953.
18. A seeming discrepancy between the 31% statistic and the Figure 5.6 results can be attributed to data limitations. The figure shows that 40% of women have exited married motherhood after 15 years. This is confusing, in that after 15 years children cannot have attained majority. Presumably the limited exceptions—older stepchildren, older adoptees—aren't numerous enough to fully bridge the divide between 31% and 40%. The remaining difference reflects women who became married mothers prior to the first year of data collection. These respondents were identified from retrospective accounts, and the data are more limited and less reliable than the contemporaneous data. The same issue applies for pre-1979 exits from divorced and never-married motherhood. Finally, selective attrition may be affecting these results, despite the use of survey weights intended to account for non-response bias.
19. Edin, Kathryn and Maria Kefalas. 2005. *Promises I Can Keep: Why Poor Women Put Motherhood before Marriage*. Oakland: University of California Press; McLanahan, Sara, Irwin Garfinkel, and Ronald B. Mincy. 2001. "Fragile Families, Welfare Reform, and Marriage." Welfare Reform and Beyond: Policy Brief No. 10. Washington, DC: Brookings Institution; Wilcox, W. Bradford and Nicholas H. Wolfinger. 2007. "Then Comes Marriage? Religion and Marriage in Urban America." *Social Science Research* 36: 569–589.
20. Wilcox, W. Bradford and Nicholas H. Wolfinger. 2007. "Then Comes Marriage? Religion and Marriage in Urban America." *Social Science Research* 36: 569–589; also, Carlson, Marcia, Sara McLanahan, and Paula England. 2004. "Union Formation in Fragile Families." *Demography* 41: 237–261.
21. Lichter, Daniel T. and Deborah Roempke Graefe. 2001. "Finding a Mate? The Marital and Cohabitation Histories of Unwed Mothers." Pp. 317–343 in Lawrence L. Wu and Barbara Wolfe *Out of Wedlock: Causes and Consequences of Nonmarital Fertility*. New York: Russell Sage Foundation.
22. Martinson, Brian C. 1994. "Postmarital Union Formation: Trends and Determinants of the Competing Roles of Remarriage and Nonmarital Cohabitation among Women in the United States." Unpublished doctoral dissertation. Department of Sociology, University of Wisconsin-Madison. These figures include all remarriages, not just those involving minor children. That having been said, Martinson (1994) found that children had only a modest effect on remarriage rates. For other contemporaneous data, Bramlett, Matthew D. and William D. Mosher. 2002. *Cohabitation, Marriage, Divorce, and Remarriage in the United States*. National Center for Health Statistics. Vital Health Stat 23 (22).
23. On rebound marriages, Wolfinger, Nicholas H. 2007. "Does the Rebound Effect Exist? Time to Remarriage and Subsequent Union Stability." *Journal of Divorce & Remarriage* 46: 9–20.
24. On the myth of American intergenerational mobility, Reeves, Richard V. and Eleanor Krause. 2018. "Raj Chetty in 14 Charts: Big Findings on Opportunity and Mobility Se Should All Know." Washington, DC: Brookings Institute. Available at https://www.brookings.edu/blog/social-mobility-memos/2018/01/11/raj-chetty-in-14-charts-big-findings-on-opportunity-and-mobility-we-should-know/.
25. Blau, Peter M. and Otis Dudley Duncan. 1967. *The American Occupational Structure*. New York: Wiley.
26. Marriage: Goldstein, Joshua R. and Catherine T. Kenney. 2001. "Marriage Delayed or Marriage Foregone? New Cohort Forecasts of First Marriage for U.S. Women." *American Sociological Review* 66: 506–519; divorce: Bumpass, Larry L., Teresa Castro Martin, and James A. Sweet. 1991. "The Impact of Family Background and Early Marital Factors on Marital Disruption."

NOTES TO PAGES 119–127   207

Journal of Family Issues 12: 22–42; nonmarital fertility: Upchurch, Dawn M., Lee A. Lillard, and Constantijn W. A. Panis. 2002. "Nonmarital Childbearing: Influences of Education, Marriage, and Fertility." *Demography* 39: 311–329.

27. Wolfinger, Nicholas H. 2005. *Understanding the Divorce Cycle: The Children of Divorce in Their Own Marriages*. New York: Cambridge University Press.

28. McLanahan, Sara S. and Gary Sandefur. 1994. *Growing Up with a Single Parent: What Hurts, What Helps*. Cambridge, MA: Harvard University Press.

29. On parental divorce and offspring fertility, McLanahan, Sara S. and Gary Sandefur. 1994. *Growing Up with a Single Parent: What Hurts, What Helps*. Cambridge, MA: Harvard University Press; on out of wedlock parentage and offspring divorce: Wolfinger, Nicholas H. 2005. *Understanding the Divorce Cycle: The Children of Divorce in Their Own Marriages*. New York: Cambridge University Press.

30. McLanahan, Sara S. and Gary Sandefur. 1994. *Growing Up with a Single Parent: What Hurts, What Helps*. Cambridge, MA: Harvard University Press.

31. Amato, Paul R. and Alan Booth. 1997. *A Generation at Risk: Growing Up in an Era of Family Upheaval*. Cambridge, MA: Harvard University Press.

32. On the socializing benefits of parental employment, Hout, Michael. 1984. "Status, Autonomy, and Training in Occupational Mobility." *American Journal of Sociology* 89: 1379–1409.

33. This includes stepmothers and stepfathers.

34. United States Census Bureau. 1979. *Statistical Abstract of the United States: 1979* 99th ed. Washington, DC: United States Government Printing Office.

35. United States Bureau of the Census. 2021. "CPS Historical Time Series Tables: Educational Attainment." Available at https://www.census.gov/data/tables/time-series/demo/educational-attainment/cps-historical-time-series.html. See Table A-2.

36. Previous studies indeed show that women who give birth out of wedlock hail from parents with disproportionately low levels of education. An, Chong-Bum, Robert Haveman, and Barbara Wolfe. 1993. "Teen Out-of-Wedlock Births and Welfare Receipt: The Role of Childhood Events and Economic Circumstances." *The Review of Economics and Statistics* 75: 195–208.

37. Wolfinger, Nicholas H. 2005. *Understanding the Divorce Cycle: The Children of Divorce in Their Own Marriages*. New York: Cambridge University Press.

38. Blau, Peter M. and Otis Dudley Duncan. 1967. *The American Occupational Structure*. New York: Wiley.

39. Musick, Kelly and Robert D. Mare. 2006. "Recent Trends in the Inheritance of Poverty and Family Structure." *Social Science Research* 35: 471–499.

40. Amato, Paul R. and Alan Booth. 1997. *A Generation at Risk: Growing Up in an Era of Family Upheaval*. Cambridge, MA: Harvard University Press.

41. Amato, Paul R. and Alan Booth. 1997. *A Generation at Risk: Growing Up in an Era of Family Upheaval*. Cambridge, MA: Harvard University Press; Kearney, Melissa S. 2023. *The Two-Parent Privilege: How the Decline in Marriage Has Increased Inequality and Lowered Social Mobility, and What We Can Do about It*. Rugby, UK: Swift Press; McLanahan, Sara S. and Gary Sandefur. 1994. *Growing Up with a Single Parent: What Hurts, What Helps*. Cambridge, MA: Harvard University Press; Wolfinger, Nicholas H. 2005. *Understanding the Divorce Cycle: The Children of Divorce in Their Own Marriages*. New York: Cambridge University Press.

42. Teenage mothers: Geronimus, Arline T. and Sanders Korenman. 1992. "The Socioeconomic Consequences of Teen Childbearing Reconsidered." *Quarterly Journal of Economics* 107: 1187–1214; Grogger, Jeff T. and Stephen Bronars. 1993. "The Socioeconomic Consequences of Teenage Childbearing: Findings from a Natural Experiment." *Family Planning Perspectives* 25: 156–161, 174; Hoffman, Saul D. 1998. "Teenage Childbearing Is Not So Bad After All . . . Or Is It? A Review of the New Literature." *Family Planning Perspectives* 30: 236–239, 243; Hotz, V. Joseph, McElroy, Susan Williams, and Seth G. Sanders. 2002. "Teenage Childbearing and Its Life Cycle Consequences: Exploiting a Very Natural Experiment." *Journal of Human Resources* 40: 683–715; divorce: Bedard, Kelly and Olivier Deschênes. 2005. "Sex Preferences, Marital Dissolution, and the Economic Status of Women." *Journal of Human Resources* 40: 411–434; for a contrary finding: Smock, Pamela J., Wendy D. Manning, and Sanjiv Gupta. 1999. "The Effect of Marriage and Divorce on Women's Economic Well-Being." *American Sociological Review* 64: 794–812.

43. Heckman, James J. and George J. Borjas. 1980. "Does Unemployment Cause Future Unemployment? Definitions, Questions and Answers from a Continuous Time Model of Heterogeneity and State Dependence." *Economica* 47: 247–283; see also Brand, Jennie E.

208 NOTES TO PAGES 127–135

2015. "The Far-reaching Impact of Job Loss and Unemployment." *Annual Review of Sociology* 41: 359–375.

44. *Inter alia*, Bumpass, Larry L., Teresa Castro Martin and James A. Sweet. 1991. "The Impact of Family Background and Early Marital Factors on Marital Disruption." *Journal of Family Issues* 12: 22–42.

45. On the relationship between education and the chances of giving birth out of wedlock, Bronars, Stephen G. and Jeff Grogger. 1994. "The Economic Consequences of Unwed Motherhood: Using Twin Births as a Natural Experiment." *American Economic Review* 84: 1141–1156; Upchurch, Dawn M., Lee A. Lillard, and Constantijn W. A. Panis. 2002. "Nonmarital Childbearing: Influences of Education, Marriage, and Fertility." *Demography* 39: 311–29; Upchurch, Dawn M. and James McCarthy. 1990. "The Timing of a First Birth and High School Completion." *American Sociological Review* 55: 224–34. Upchurch and McCarthy find that the relationship teenage fertility and high school completion is more complicated than previously conceived. Although a teenage birth does not increase the chances of dropping out of school, teenage mothers who have already dropped out are less likely to return to school.

46. A study from 2010 showed that married mothers are most likely to attend college in the five years after childbirth, while rates of non-college school attendance (e.g., high school completion, vocational school) are higher for moms who aren't married. MacGregor, Carol Ann. 2010. "Education Delayed: Family Structure and Postnatal Educational Attainment." Fragile Families Working Paper 09-07-FF. Available at https://ffcws.princeton.edu/sites/g/files/toruqf4356/files/documents/wp09-07-ff.pdf.

47. Moynihan, Daniel Patrick. 1965. *The Negro Family: The Case for National Action*. Washington, DC: U.S. Department of Labor, Office of Policy Planning and Research.

48. There were insufficient members of other population groups in the NLSY to permit further classification.

49. See, *inter alia*, Fu, Vincent K., and Nicholas H. Wolfinger. 2011. "Broken Boundaries or Broken Marriages? Racial Intermarriage and Divorce." *Social Science Quarterly* 92: 1096–1117; Kreider, Rose M. and Jason M. Fields. 2001. *Number, Timing, and Duration of Marriages and Divorces: Fall 1996*. Current Population Reports, 70–80. Washington, DC: United States Census Bureau.

50. Teenage mothers: Geronimus, Arline T. and Sanders Korenman. 1992. "The Socioeconomic Consequences of Teen Childbearing Reconsidered." *Quarterly Journal of Economics* 107: 1187–1214; Grogger, Jeff T. and Stephen Bronars. 1993. "The Socioeconomic Consequences of Teenage Childbearing: Findings from a Natural Experiment." *Family Planning Perspectives* 25: 156–161, 174; Hoffman, Saul D., Foster, Michael E., and Frank F. Furstenberg, Jr. 1993. "Reevaluating the Costs of Teenage Childbearing." *Demography* 30: 1–13; Hotz, V. Joseph, Susan Williams McElroy, and Seth G. Sanders. 2002. "Teenage Childbearing and Its Life Cycle Consequences: Exploiting a Very Natural Experiment." *Journal of Human Resources* 40: 683–715; divorce: Bedard, Kelly and Olivier Deschênes. 2005. "Sex Preferences, Marital Dissolution, and the Economic Status of Women." *Journal of Human Resources* 40: 411–434.

51. Lino, Mark, Kevin Kuczynski, Nestor Rodriguez, and TusaRebecca Schap. 2017. *Expenditures on Children by Families, 2015*. Miscellaneous Publication No. 1528-2015. U.S. Department of Agriculture, Center for Nutrition Policy and Promotion. Available at https://cdn2.hubspot.net/hubfs/10700/blog-files/USDA_Expenditures%20on%20children%20by%20family.pdf?t=1520090048492.

Chapter 6

1. Albeit a declining majority: women are now the primary or exclusive breadwinner 42% of the time. Glynn, Sarah Jane. 2016. "Breadwinning Mothers Are Increasingly the Norm." Center for American Progress. Available at https://www.americanprogress.org/issues/women/reports/2016/12/19/295203/breadwinning-mothers-are-increasingly-the-u-s-norm/.

2. Fremstad, Shawn. 2016. "Partnered but Poor." Center for American Progress. Available at https://www.americanprogress.org/issues/poverty/reports/2016/03/11/131968/partnered-but-poor/.

3. This figure is limited to women who became single mothers in between 1984 and 1990, inclusive. The post-1994 move to a biennial survey precludes this analysis for later survey years.

4. On the relative timing of separation and divorce, Ono, Hiromi. 1995. "Expanding on Explanations of Recent Patterns in U.S. Divorce Rates." Unpublished doctoral dissertation, Department of Sociology, University of California, Los Angeles. It's exceedingly difficult to look at separated mothers' incomes: while separation describes a woman's marital status when

NOTES TO PAGES 135–142   209

she completes a survey, income is generally based on the previous year and therefore probably reflects her soon-to-be ex-spouse's earnings.

5. Sara McLanahan and her colleagues provide similar findings with data from a more recent cohort. Meadows, Sarah O., Sara McLanahan, and Jean T. Knab. 2009. "Economic Trajectories in Non-traditional Families with Children." Fragile Families. Working paper WP09-10-FF. Available at https://ffcws.princeton.edu/sites/g/files/toruqf4356/files/documents/wp09-10-ff.pdf.

6. Gao, George and Gretchen Livingston. 2015. "Working while Pregnant Is Much More Common Than it Used to Be." Pew Research Center. Available at https://www.pewresearch.org/fact-tank/2015/03/31/working-while-pregnant-is-much-more-common-than-it-used-to-be/.

7. We also demonstrated this in one of our papers. McKeever, Matthew and Nicholas H. Wolfinger. 2011. "Thanks for Nothing: Income and Labor Force Participation for Never-married Mothers since 1982." *Social Science Research* 40: 63–76. A reminder: cohabiting relationships span two families within a single household.

8. Figure 6.3 is based on a regression standardization of logged median peak family income. Independent variables are set at their means. The baseline model contains a control for survey attrition and race/ethnicity. The second model contains measures of whether respondents lived with both biological parents to age 18, mother's education, father's education, whether fathers were working when respondents were 14, and the two proxies for cultural capital described in Chapter 5 (having a library card, and regular newspapers at home). The third model includes a measure of the age at which women became mothers, and the number of children they've had prior to 2000. This year is chosen as a balance between allowing time for children and the attainment of income. The fourth model adds continuous measures of years spent in married, divorced, and never-married motherhood. The fifth model adds education at age 25, an age by which almost everybody has completed their formal schooling. Nonmothers are omitted from the analysis. N = 3,864. In the baseline model, continuously married mothers had significantly (p < .001) higher incomes than anyone who'd ever been a single mother; by the fifth model, only continuously never-married mothers had significantly (p < .001) different incomes. Ancillary models examined two additional variables, broad Census job classifications for both parents and respondent scores on the Armed Forces Qualifying Test. Neither offered a substantial unique contribution to the analysis, so are omitted on grounds of parsimony.

9. As noted in the previous chapter, researchers have identified separate mechanisms for the intergenerational transmission of family structure and income. Musick, Kelly and Robert D. Mare. 2006. "Recent Trends in the Inheritance of Poverty and Family Structure." *Social Science Research* 35: 471–499.

10. Another way of exploring sample selection is the naturally occurring experiment proposed by economist V. Joseph Hotz and his colleagues. They contrasted incomes for women who give birth to women who miscarry and found little difference. Hotz studied the effects of a teen-aged birth, not nonmarital fertility. We replicate their results for women who give birth out of wedlock. The results suggest that nonmarital fertility has little impact on women's incomes. Hotz, V. Joseph, Susan Williams McElroy, and Seth G. Sanders. 2002. "Teenage Childbearing and Its Life Cycle Consequences: Exploiting a Very Natural Experiment." *Journal of Human Resources* 40: 683–715. More recent research cast doubt on the validity of the miscarriage instrument: perhaps miscarriages are not randomly distributed. Fletcher, Jason M. and Barbara L. Wolfe. 2009. "Education and Labor Market Consequences of Teenage Childbearing Evidence Using the Timing of Pregnancy Outcomes and Community Fixed Effects." *Journal of Human Resources* 44: 303–325. A personal communication with Hotz (July 7, 2023), one of his previous articles, and a subsequent piece by other economists support the use of the miscarriage instrument, but contingent on bound parameters or weights to account for the differential selection into miscarriage. Ashcraft, Adam, Iván Fernández-Val, and Kevin Lang. 2013. "The Consequences of Teenage Childbearing: Consistent Estimates when Abortion Makes Miscarriage Non-random." *The Economic Journal* 123: 875–905; Hotz, V. Joseph, Charles H. Mullin, and Seth G. Sanders. 1997. "Bounding Causal Effects Using Data from a Contaminated Natural Experiment: Analysing the Effects of Teenage Childbearing." *The Review of Economic Studies* 64: 575–603.

11. We recognize that these are not entirely time-invariant attributes. A respondent could, for example, shift in their racial and ethnic identification, or obtain new information about their families of origin. These changes are rare and not easily measured in the NLSY, so these variables are excluded from fixed effects analyses.

210   NOTES TO PAGES 142–145

12. All models control for age, age squared, and panel attrition. A Hausman test verified the choice of fixed effects over random effects models. The income difference between married and single mothers is statistically significant ($p < .001$).

13. Upchurch, Dawn M. and James McCarthy. 1990. "The Timing of a First Birth and High School Completion." *American Sociological Review* 55: 224–34. Timely completion of a degree is likely more valuable in the labor market than eventual completion.

14. Avellar, Sarah and Pamela J. Smock. 2003 "Has the Price of Motherhood Declined Over Time? A Cross-Cohort Comparison of the Motherhood Wage Penalty," *Journal of Marriage and Family* 65: 597–607; Budig, Michelle J. and Paula England, 2001. "The Wage Penalty for Motherhood," *American Sociological Review* 66: 204–225; Budig, Michelle J. and Melissa J. Hodges. 2010 "Differences in Disadvantage: Variation in the Motherhood Penalty across White Women's Earnings Distribution," *American Sociological Review* 75: 705–728; Waldfogel, Jane. 1997. "The Effect of Children on Women's Wages," *American Sociological Review* 62: 209–217.

15. A full answer to this question entails qualitative data and is outside the scope of this book. One of the best accounts is provided by Edin, Kathryn and Laura Lein. 1997. "Work, Welfare, and Single Mothers' Economic Survival Strategies." *American Sociological Review*: 253–66; Edin, Kathryn and Laura Lein. 1997. *Making Ends Meet: How Single Mothers Survive Welfare and Low-Wage Work*. New York: Russell Sage Foundation. Among other things, some single mothers without visible employment make ends meet by relying on the informal economy.

16. Zill, Nicholas. 2023. "Food Stamps and Family: SNAP Recipients by Family Structure." Charlottesville, VA: Institute for Family Studies blog, April 25. Available at https://ifstudies.org/blog/food-stamps-and-family-snap-recipients-by-family-structure.

17. These and subsequent figures include both cash transfers and in-kind benefits. We refer to this aid collectively as "welfare," "public aid," or "government transfers." The spike in aid receipt for never-married mothers in 2012 is likely the consequence of a small sample size. Fifty-seven NLSY respondents were never-married mothers, an unsurprisingly low number given that NLSY respondents ranged in age from 47 to 55 that year. Alternately, the spike could represent residual effects of the Great Recession.

18. We're not aware of studies that formally test this hypothesis, but welfare shame is a theme that emerges in qualitative studies of single mothers. See, for instance, Seccombe, Karen, Delores James, and Kimberly Battle Walters. 1998. "They Think You Ain't Much of Nothing": The Social Construction of the Welfare Mother." *Journal of Marriage and Family* 60: 849–865.

19. Previously, we've noted the intergenerational transmission of family structure. Moreover, welfare receipt also appears to run in families. Pepper, John V. 2000. "The Intergenerational Transmission of Welfare Receipt: A Nonparametric Bounds Analysis." *Review of Economics and Statistics* 82: 472–488.

20. This distinction hasn't always been clear among public aid beneficiaries and some states have done little to disabuse would-be applicants of their misconceptions. Wiseman, Michael. 2002. "Food Stamps and Welfare Reform." Brookings, March 4. Available at https://www.brookings.edu/research/food-stamps-and-welfare-reform/.

21. After 2010, the sample sizes become too small to permit accurate estimates. In 2010, NLSY respondents range in age from 45 to 53, ages at which motherhood, especially single motherhood, is becoming increasingly less common.

22. Congressional Committee on Ways and Means. 2004. "Green Book." Background Material and Data on the Programs within the Jurisdiction of the Committee on Ways and Means. Available at https://www.govinfo.gov/app/details/GPO-CPRT-108WPRT108-6/.

23. It's worth noting that some single mothers give money to friends or family, even when it hurts them financially to do so. These transfers may be the product of the reciprocal relationships that allow struggling Americans to make ends meet. Pilkauskas, Natasha V., Colin Campbell, and Christopher Wimer. 2017. "Giving unto Others: Private Financial Transfers and Hardship among Families with Children." *Journal of Marriage and Family* 79: 705–722.

24. The NLSY data are atypically inconsistent across waves. Some years the data include both alimony and child support. In other years, they're limited to child support. Alimony has become uncommon in recent decades given the high likelihood of a dual-earner marriage. Finally, Figures 6.8 and 6.9 omit data from 1979 and subsequent to 2010 because of sample size limitations.

25. A divorce decree is ipso facto justification for support payments. In contrast, never-married mothers may need to first establish paternity before pursuing a support order.

NOTES TO PAGES 145–151   211

26. Grall, Timothy, 2018. *Custodial Mothers and Fathers and Their Child Support: 2015*. Current Population Reports, 60–262. Washington, DC: United States Census Bureau. Available at https://www.census.gov/library/publications/2018/demo/p60-262.html.

27. Lamidi, Esther. 2016. A Quarter Century of Change in Nonmarital Births. Family Profiles, FP-16-03. Bowling Green, OH: National Center for Family and Marriage Research. Available at https://www.bgsu.edu/content/dam/BGSU/college-of-arts-and-sciences/NCFMR/docume nts/FP/lamidi-nonmarital-births-fp-16-03.pdf. As of 2005, it was about half of unwed mothers. Sara McLanahan. 2005. "Fragile Families and the Marriage Agenda." Pp. 1–21 in L. Kowaleski-Jones and N. H. Wolfinger *Fragile Families and the Marriage Agenda*. New York: Springer; see also Livingston, Gretchen. 2018. "The Changing Profile of Unmarried Parents." Pew Research Center. Available at https://www.pewresearch.org/social-trends/2018/04/25/the-chang ing-profile-of-unmarried-parents/. On cohabitation rates more generally for never-married mothers, McKeever and Wolfinger, "Thanks for Nothing," 2011.

28. On the "magic moment," Edin, Kathryn and Maria Kefalas. 2005. *Promises I Can Keep: Why Poor Women Put Motherhood before Marriage*. Oakland: University of California Press. See also McLanahan, Sara. 2006. "Fragile Families and the Marriage Agenda." Pp. 1–21 in L. Kowaleski-Jones and N. H. Wolfinger *Fragile Families and the Marriage Agenda*. New York: Springer; on cohabitation rates more generally for never-married mothers, McKeever and Wolfinger, "Thanks for Nothing," 2011. The end of the magic moment also coincides with a decline in social support more broadly. Radey, Melissa and Karin Brewster. 2013. "Predictors of Stability and Change in Private Safety Nets of Unmarried Mothers." *Journal of Social Service Research* 39: 397–415.

29. Bumpass, Larry L. and Sheela Kennedy. 2008. "Cohabitation and Children's Living Arrangements: New Estimates from the United States." *Demographic Research* 19: 1663–1692; Casper, Lynne M. and Philip N. Cohen. 2000. "How Does POSSLQ Measure Up? Historical Estimates of Cohabitation." *Demography* 37: 237–245.

30. Bumpass, Larry L. and Hsien-Hen Lu. 2000. "Trends in Cohabitation and Implications for Children's Family Contexts in the United States." *Population Studies* 54: 29–41; Bumpass, Larry L. and Sheela Kennedy. 2008. "Cohabitation and Children's Living Arrangements: New Estimates from the United States." *Demographic Research* 19: 1663–1692 (see Table 5); Mernitz, Sara. 2018. "A Cohort Comparison of Trends in First Cohabitation Duration in the United States." *Demographic Research* 38: 2073–2086, 2073; Wolfinger, Nicholas H. 2001 "The Effects of Family Structure of Origin on Offspring Cohabitation Duration." *Sociological Inquiry* 71 (3): 293–313.

31. For an early review of the literature on adult co-residence with parents, White, Lynn. 1994. "Coresidence and Leaving Home: Young Adults and Their Parents." *Annual Review of Sociology* 20: 81–102. White writes relatively little about offspring family structure.

32. McKeever, Matthew and Nicholas H. Wolfinger. 2011. "Thanks for Nothing: Income and Labor Force Participation for Never-Married Mothers since 1982." *Social Science Research* 40: 63–76.

Chapter 7

1. Veght, Benjamin. 2015. *Social Security's Past, Present and Future*. Washington, DC: National Academy of Social Insurance. Available at https://www.nasi.org/discussion/social-securitys-past-present-and-future/; see also Reno, Virginia P. and Susan Grad. 1985. "Economic Security, 1935–85." *Social Security Bulletin* 48 (12): 5. Available at https://www.ssa.gov/policy/docs/ssb/ v48n12/v48n12p5.pdf.

2. Mather, Mark, Paola Scommegna, and Lillian Kilduff. 2016. "FactSheet: Aging in the United States." *Population Reference Bureau* 13. Available at https://www.prb.org/resources/fact-sheet-aging-in-the-united-states/.

3. Parolin, Zachary, Sophie Collyer, Megan A. Curran, and Christopher Wimer. 2021. *The Potential Poverty Reduction Effect of the American Rescue Plan*. Center on Poverty and Social Policy, Columbia University. Available at www.povertycenter.columbia.edu/news-internal/ 2021/presidential-policy/bideneconomic-relief-proposal-poverty-impact. Another recent study showed that public spending also helped to protect single mothers from the economic fallout of the Great Recession. Waring, Melody K. and Daniel R. Meyer. 2020. "Welfare, Work, and Single Mothers: The Great Recession and Income Packaging Strategies." *Children and Youth Services Review* 108: 1–10.

4. Chen, Yiyu and Dana Thomson. 2021. "Child Poverty Increased Nationally During COVID, Especially Among Latino and Black Children." Child Trends. Available at https://www.childtre nds.org/publications/child-poverty-increased-nationally-during-covid-especially-among-lat

212 NOTES TO PAGES 155–156

    ino-and-black-children#:~:text=We%20find%20that%20child%20poverty,million%20m
ore%20than%20in%202019.

5. Parolin, Zachary, Sophie Collyer, and Megan A. Curran. 2022. "Absence of Monthly Child Tax Credit Leads to 3.7 Million More Children in Poverty in January 2022." Poverty and Social Policy Brief 6 (2). Center on Poverty and Social Policy, Columbia University. Available at www. povertycenter.columbia.edu/publication/monthly-poverty-january-2022.

6. On rates of children living with single parents, Kramer, Stephanie. 2019. *U.S. Has World's Highest Rate of Children Living in Single-Parent Households.* Washington, DC: Pew Research. Available at https://www.pewresearch.org/short-reads/2019/12/12/u-s-children-more-lik ely-than-children-in-other-countries-to-live-with-just-one-parent/; for international data on single parenthood and income, Harkness, Susan. 2022. "Single Mothers' Income in Twelve Rich Countries: Differences in Disadvantage across the Distribution." *The Annals of the American Academy of Political and Social Science* 702: 164–187.

7. Kimberlin, Sara Elizabeth. 2013. *Metrics Matter: Examining Chronic and Transient Poverty in the United States Using the Supplemental Poverty Measure.* Doctoral dissertation University of California, Berkeley. Available at https://www.proquest.com/docview/1441350234?pqorigsite= gscholar&fromopenview=true.

8. Brito, Natalie H. and Kimberly G. Noble. 2014. "Socioeconomic Status and Structural Brain Development." *Frontiers in Neuroscience* 8 (276); Wagmiller, Robert L. Jr., Mary Lennon, L. Li Kuang, J. Lawrence Aber, and Philip Alberti 2006. "The Dynamics of Economic Disadvantage and Children's Life Chances." *American Sociological Review* 71: 847–866.

9. McLanahan, Sara S. and Gary Sandefur. 1994. *Growing Up with a Single Parent: What Hurts, What Helps.* Cambridge, MA: Harvard University Press. For a comprehensive review of research up to the start of the twenty-first century, see Brooks-Gunn, Jeanne and Greg J. Duncan. 1997. "The Effects of Poverty on Children." *The Future of Children* 7: 55–71. For an updated review, National Academies of Sciences, Engineering, and Medicine. 2019. *A Roadmap to Reducing Child Poverty.* Washington, DC: The National Academies Press. Available at https:// www.ncbi.nlm.nih.gov/books/NBK547361/pdf/Bookshelf_NBK547361.pdf.

10. Teachman, Jay D., Kathleen M. Paasch, Randal D. Day and Karen Price Carver. 1997. "Poverty During Adolescence and Subsequent Educational Attainment." Pp. 382–418 in Greg Duncan and Jeanne Brooks-Gunn *Consequences of Growing Up Poor.* New York: Russell Sage Press; Haveman, Robert and Barbara Wolfe. 1995. "The Determinants of Children's Attainments: A Review of Methods and Findings." *Journal of Economic Literature* 33: 1829–1878; Duncan, Greg, W. Jean Yeung, Jeanne Brooks-Gunn, and Judith Smith. 1988. "How Much Does Childhood Poverty Affect the Life Chances of Children?" *American Sociological Review* 63: 406–423; Ratcliffe, Caroline. 2015. "Child Poverty and Adult Success." Urban Institute. Available at https://www.urban.org/ sites/default/files/publication/65766/2000369-Child-Poverty-and-Adult-Success.pdf.

11. Brady, David, Ryan Finnigan, Ulrich Kohler, and Joscha Legewie. 2020. "The Inheritance of Race Revisited: Childhood Wealth and Income and Black–White Disadvantages in Adult Life Chances." *Sociological Science* 7: 599–627; Duncan, Greg, Kathleen M. Ziol-Guest, and Ariel Kalil. 2010. "Early-Childhood Poverty and Adult Attainment, Behavior and Health." *Child Development* 81: 306–325; Guo, Guang. 1998. "The Timing of the Influence of Cumulative Poverty on Children's Cognitive Ability and Achievement. *Social Forces* 77: 257–287; Korenman, Sanders and Jane E. Miller. 1998. "Effects of Long-Term Poverty on Physical Health of Children in the National Longitudinal Survey of Youth" Pp. 70–99 in Greg Duncan and Jeanne Brooks-Gunn. *Consequences of Growing Up Poor.* New York: Russell Sage Press; McLoyd, Vonnie C. 1998 "Socioeconomic Disadvantage and Child Development." *American Psychologist* 53: 185–204.

12. Schilbach, Frank, Heather Schofield, and Sendhil Mullainathan. 2016. "The Psychological Lives of the Poor." *American Economic Review* 106: 435–440.

13. Conger, Rand, Katherine Jewsbury Conger, and Glen H. Elder Jr. 1997. "Family Economic Hardship and Adolescent Adjustment: Mediating and Moderating Processes" Pp. 288–311 in Greg Duncan and Jeanne Brooks-Gunn *Consequences of Growing Up Poor.* New York: Russell Sage Press; Dearing, Eric. 2008. "Psychological Costs of Growing up Poor." *Annals of the New York Academy of Sciences* 1136: 324–332.

14. On emotional problems, McLanahan, Sara S. and Gary Sandefur. 1994. *Growing Up with a Single Parent: What Hurts, What Helps.* Cambridge, MA: Harvard University Press; on self-esteem, Whitbeck, Les B., Ronald L. Simons, Rand D. Conger, Frederick O. Lorenz, Shirley Huck, and Glenn H. Elder Jr. 1991. "Family Economic Hardship, Parental Support, and Adolescent Self-Esteem." *Social Psychology Quarterly*: 353–363; for a contrary finding, Axinn, William, Greg

NOTES TO PAGES 156–157 213

J. Duncan, and Arland Thornton. 1997. "The Effects of Parents' Income, Wealth, and Attitudes on Children's Completed Schooling and Self-Esteem." Pp. 518–540 in Greg Duncan and Jeanne Brooks-Gunn *Consequences of Growing Up Poor.* New York: Russell Sage Press.

15. Lipman, E. L., D. Offord, and M. H. Boyle. 1994. "Economic Disadvantage and Child Psychosocial Morbidity." *Canadian Medical Association Journal* 151: 431–437. The link seems especially strong for White children, per Costello, Elizabeth J., Gordon P. Keeler, and Adrian Angold. 2001. "Poverty, Race/ethnicity, and Psychiatric Disorder: A Study of Rural Children." *American Journal of Public Health* 91: 1494–1498; and Samaan, Rodney. 2000. "The Influences of Race, Ethnicity, and Poverty on The Mental Health of Children" *Journal of Health Care for the Poor and Underserved* 11: 100–110.

16. Haveman, Robert and Barbara Wolfe. 1995. "The Determinants of Children's Attainments: A Review of Methods and Findings." *Journal of Economic Literature* 33 (4): 1829–1878.

17. Kiker, B. F. and Carol M. Condon. 1981. "The Influence of Socioeconomic Background on the Earnings of Young Men." *Journal of Human Resources* 16: 94–105.

18. Haveman, Robert and Barbara Wolfe. 1995. "The Determinants of Children's Attainments: A Review of Methods and Findings." *Journal of Economic Literature* 33 (4): 1829–1878; Wagmiller, Robert Lee and Robert M. Adelman. 2009. "Childhood and Intergenerational Poverty: The Long-term Consequences of Growing Up Poor." National Center for Children in Poverty. Available at https://www.nccp.org/wp-content/uploads/2020/05/text_909.pdf; Chetty, Raj, Nathaniel Hendren, Patrick Kline, and Emmanuel Saez. 2014. "Where is the Land of Opportunity? The Geography of Intergenerational Mobility in the United States." *Quarterly Journal of Economics* 129: 1553–1623.

19. Remarriage is an effective route to raising family income, but otherwise its benefits to children are mixed. Stepparents do the work of biological parents, but myriad studies show that remarriage doesn't ameliorate the adverse consequences of parental divorce and sometimes even exacerbates them. On the parenting work stepparents do, Mason, Mary Ann, Sydney Harrison-Jay, Gloria Messick Svare, and Nicholas H. Wolfinger. 2002. "Stepparents: De Facto Parents or Legal Strangers?" *Journal of Family Issues* 23: 507–522; on the consequences of remarriage for offspring, McLanahan, Sara S. and Gary Sandefur. 1994. *Growing Up with a Single Parent: What Hurts, What Helps.* Cambridge, MA: Harvard University Press; Wolfinger, Nicholas H. 2005. *Understanding the Divorce Cycle: The Children of Divorce in Their Own Marriages.* New York: Cambridge University Press.

20. Baker, Regina 2015 "The Changing Association Among Marriage, Work, and Childhood Poverty in the U.S., 1974–2000." *Journal of Marriage and Family* 77: 1166–1178.

21. A high-profile recent example is the report jointly issued by two of America's premier think tanks, the center-left Brookings Institute and the center-right American Enterprise Institute: Working Group on Childhood in the United States. 2022. "Rebalancing: Children First." Available at https://www.aei.org/wp-content/uploads/2022/02/AEI-Brookings-Rebalancing-Children-First-FINAL-REPORT-FEB-8-2022.pdf?x91208.

22. Fremstad, Shawn. 2016. "Partnered but Poor." Center for American Progress. Available at https://www.americanprogress.org/issues/poverty/reports/2016/03/11/131968/partnered-but-poor/.

23. Moon, Dawne and Jaye Cee Whitehead. 2006. "Marrying for America." Pp. 23–45 in L. Kowaleski-Jones and N. H. Wolfinger *Fragile Families and the Marriage Agenda.* New York: Springer.

24. Schneider, Daniel 2015 "Lessons Learned from Non-Marriage Experiments." *Future of Children* 25: 155–178; Wood, Robert G., Quinn Moore, Andrew Clarkwest, and Alexandra Killewald. 2014. "The Long-Term Effects of Building Strong Families: A Program for Unmarried Parents." *Journal of Marriage and Family* 76: 446–463.

25. Perhaps the foremost expression of this sentiment is the Family Story Project (first sentence of its mission statement: "Family Story works to address and dismantle family privilege in America."). Fremstad, Shawn, Sarah Jane Glynn and Angelo Williams. 2019. "The Case Against Marriage Fundamentalism: Embracing Family Justice for All." *Family Story.* Available at https://familystoryproject.org/case-against-marriage-fundamentalism/; see also Brady, David, Ryan M. Finnigan, and Sabine Hübgen. 2018. "Single Mothers Are Not the Problem." *New York Times,* Feb. 10; Brady, David, Ryan M. Finnigan, and Sabine Hübgen. 2017. "Rethinking the Risks of Poverty: A Framework for Analyzing Prevalences (sic) and Penalties." *American Journal of Sociology* 123: 740–786; DePaulo, Bella M. 2006. *Singled out: How Singles Are Stereotyped, Stigmatized, and Ignored, and Still Live Happily Ever After.* New York: Macmillan.

26. Brady, David and Rebekah Burroway. 2012. "Targeting, Universalism, and Single-Mother Poverty: A Multilevel Analysis across 18 Affluent Democracies." *Demography* 49: 719–746.

214 NOTES TO PAGES 157–160

27. On Moynihan's understanding of family structure, Moynihan, Daniel Patrick. 1965. *The Negro Family: The Case for National Action.* Washington, DC: U.S. Department of Labor, Office of Policy Planning and Research. Available at https://www.dol.gov/general/aboutdol/history/webid-moynihan; Moynihan, Daniel Patrick. 1986. *Family and Nation.* San Diego, CA Harcourt Brace Jovanovich; Patterson, James T. 2010. *Freedom Is Not Enough: The Moynihan Report and America's Struggle Over Black Family Life—from LBJ to Obama.* New York: Basic Books. We survey the intellectual history of the Moynihan Report in Appendix B. Many of the concerns about the relationship between the labor market, family structure, and inequality were echoed by the Kerner report, published soon after the Moynihan Report. Kerner, Otto, et al. 1968. *Report of the National Advisory Commission on Civil Disorders.* Washington, DC: United States Government Printing Office. Available at https://belonging.berkeley.edu/sites/default/files/kerner_commission_full_report.pdf?file=1&force=1. The litany of policy recommendations in the Kerner report was generally left untouched by the federal government.

28. It's worth noting that the effects of welfare reform were starting to be felt even before 1996. Beginning in 1993, many states were granted waivers to experiment with AFDC term limits. Rosewater, Ann. 1997. "Setting the Baseline: A Report on State Welfare Waivers." Office of the Assistant Secretary for Planning and Evaluation, U.S. Department of Health and Human Services. Available at https://aspe.hhs.gov/reports/setting-baseline-report-state-welfare-waivers.

29. Turner, Douglas. 1996. "Moynihan Rips Clinton Welfare-Reform Plan." *The Buffalo News,* March 22,. Available at https://buffalonews.com/news/moynihan-rips-clinton-welfare-reform-plan/article_d8a6086b-3bd9-5579-abbb-2304ff49e40c.html.

30. Weiner, Greg. 2016. "On Welfare Reform, Moynihan Was Right." *Huffington Post,* March 23. Available at https://www.huffpost.com/entry/on-welfare-reform-moyniha_b_10083346.

31. Mahar, Maggie. 2009. *Bull!: A History of the Boom and Bust, 1982–2004.* New York: HarperCollins.

32. Clinton White House archives. 2000. Available at https://clintonwhitehouse4.archives.gov/WH/New/html/20000112_2.html#:~:text=OVER%20THREE%20DECADES-,In%201993%2C%20the%20President%20Signed%20Into%20Law%20the%20Largest%20EITC,cents%20for%20two%20plus%20children.

33. For example, Grogger, Jeffrey. 2003. "The Effects of Time Limits, the EITC, and Other Policy Changes on Welfare Use, Work, and Income Among Female-Headed Families." *Review of Economics and statistics* 85: 394–408; Grogger, Jeffrey T. and Lynn A. Karoly. 2005. *Welfare Reform: Effects of a Decade of Change.* Cambridge, MA: Harvard University Press. These are two exemplars drawn from a voluminous literature.

34. For an entertaining history of the crash, Cassidy, John. 2002. *Dot. con: The Greatest Story Ever Sold.* New York: HarperCollins.

35. Gitis, Ben and Curtis Arndt. 2016. "The 20th Anniversary of Welfare Reform." American Action Forum, August 22. Available at https://www.americanactionforum.org/insight/20th-anniversary-welfare-reform/.

36. Edin, Kathryn and H. Luke Shaefer. 2015. *$2.00 a Day: Living on Almost Nothing in America.* Boston, MA: Houghton Mifflin Harcourt. Other scholars have also observed the bifurcation in single mother's prospects after welfare reform. Moffitt, Robert A. and Stephanie Garlow. 2018. "Did Welfare Reform Increase Employment and Reduce Poverty?" *Pathways* 2018 (Winter): 17–21. Available at https://inequality.stanford.edu/sites/default/files/Pathways_Winter2018_Employment-Poverty.pdf. Some conservatives have taken issue with Edin and Shaefer's estimates of the prevalence of $2 a day poverty. Rector, Robert and Jamie Bryan Hall. 2016. "Did Welfare Reform Increase Extreme Poverty in the United States?" Heritage Foundation, Legal Memorandum# 84 on Welfare and Welfare Spending. Washington, DC: Heritage Foundation. Available at https://scholar.google.com/scholar?hl=en&as_sdt=0%2C5&q=Did+Welfare+Reform+Increase+Extreme+Poverty+in+the+United+States%3F&btnG=#d=gs_cit&t=1650334465693&u=%2Fscholar%3Fq%3Dinfo%3AzhT-aMioYIQJ%3Ascholar.google.com%2F%26output%3Dcite%26scirp%3D0%26hl%3Den; Winship, Scott. 2016. "Nobody in America Lives on $2 per Day." Manhattan Institute, originally published in *The Federalist,* August 26. Available at https://www.manhattan-institute.org/html/nobody-america-lives-2-day-9194.html. Above and beyond these competing claims, we view the falling incomes of never-married mothers in the bottom decile (Figure 4.4) and persistently low incomes in the lower quartile (Figure 2.14) as ipso facto evidence of enduring deep poverty in the United States. Finally, Matthew Desmond has recently pointed out that poverty rates are biased downwards by mass incarceration: many of the Americans most likely to be poor are locked

up and thereby excluded from official statistics. Desmond, Matthew. 2023. *Poverty, by America.* New York: Crown Publishing Group, 19. One hundred and sixty-eight thousand were women incarcerated as of 2023. Monazzam, Niki and Kristen M. Budd. 2023. "Incarcerated Women and Girls." Fact sheet, Sentencing Project. Available at https://www.sentencingproject.org/factsheet/incarcerated-women-and-girls/.

37. Recent research has also noted that the post welfare reform policy regime has increased income inequality among the poor. Parolin, Zachary, Matthew Desmond, and Christopher Wimer. 2023. "Inequality Below the Poverty Line since 1967: The Role of the U.S. Welfare State." *American Sociological Review* 88: 782–809.

38. Cammett, Ann. 2010. "Deadbeats, Deadbrokes, and Prisoners." *Georgetown Journal on Poverty Law & Policy* 18: 127–168; Maldonado, Solangel. 2005. "Deadbeat or Deadbroke: Redefining Child Support for Poor Fathers." *University of California Davis Law Review* 39: 991–1022.

39. Lino, Mark, Kevin Kuczynski, Nestor Rodriguez, and Tusa Rebecca Schap. 2017. "Expenditures on Children by Families, 2015." Miscellaneous Report No. 1528-2015. Washington, DC: U.S. Department of Agriculture, Center for Nutrition Policy and Promotion. Available at https://fns-prod.azureedge.us/sites/default/files/resource-files/crc2015-march2017.pdf.

40. For a recent review of universal basic income (UBI) scholarship, Mohammad Rasoolinejad. 2021. "Universal Basic Income: The Last Bullet in the Darkness." Unpublished paper. Available at https://arxiv.org/pdf/1910.05658.pdf#:~:text=The%20UBI%20is%20not%20g ood,makes%20the%20inflation%20problem%20worse; for a primer on universal basic incomes, Lowrey, Annie. 2018. *Give People Money: How a Universal Basic Income Would End Poverty, Revolutionize Work, and Remake the World.* Portland, OR: Broadway Books.

41. Matthews, Dylan. 2019. "Mitt Romney and Michael Bennet Just Unveiled a Basic Income Plan for Kids." *Vox*, December 16. Available at https://www.vox.com/future-perfect/2019/12/16/ 21024222/mitt-romney-michael-bennet-basic-income-kids-child-allowance; a press release for the bill can be found on Senator Romney's Senate web site: Romney, Mitt. 2019. "Romney, Bennet Offer Path to Bipartisan Compromise on Refundable Credits, Business Tax Fixes." Available at https://www.romney.senate.gov/romney-bennet-offer-path-bipartisan-comprom ise-refundable-credits-business-tax-fixes/.

42. Medicare and Social Security enjoy near universal public support because they're universal programs, not aid to a disadvantaged and stigmatized minority. One recent poll found 96% support for Social Security. Waggoner, John. 2020. "AARP Poll Finds Near-Universal Support for Social Security After 85 Years." AARP, August 14. Available at https://www.aarp.org/retirement/ social-security/info-2020/aarp-poll-finds-near-universal-support.html.

43. The question of price stabilization is beyond the scope of this book, but we will make a couple of observations. First, any negative income tax or universal basic income funded by increasing the money supply (i.e., by printing money) is likely to trigger inflation. The second way to fund a UBI, deficit spending, has in modern times been the most common way of spending the people's money. A better solution is to fund a UBI by increasing the tax burden of wealthier Americans. Income distribution downwards is fundamentally inflationary given that poorer people spend a larger share of their money than do the more fortunate. To some extent this could be offset if some of the increased tax revenues were spent on deficit reduction, as two former Treasury secretaries recently suggested. Rubin, Robert E. and Jacob J. Lew. 2022. "A Plan to Help Kids Without Increasing Inflation." *The New York Times*, May 2. Available at https://www.nytimes. com/2022/05/02/opinion/child-tax-credit.html?searchResultPosition=1. Finally, we're skeptical of "modern monetary theory," which holds that governments can print money with impunity. If the inflation of the early 2020s haven't disabused MMT's adherents of this fantasy, we offer this excellent critique from the socialist magazine *Jacobin*. Henwood, Doug. 2019. "Modern Monetary Theory Isn't Helping." *Jacobin*, February 2. Available at https://jacobin.com/2019/02/ modern-monetary-theory-isnt-helping.

44. Moynihan, Daniel Patrick 1973. *The Politics of a Guaranteed Income: The Nixon Administration and the Family Assistance Plan.* New York: Random House. A guaranteed income plan was resurrected during the Carter administration but died much sooner. Steensland, Brian. 2011. *The Failed Welfare Revolution.* Princeton, NJ: Princeton University Press. Between 1965 and 1980 the federal government did conduct several negative income tax field experiments, with contested results. Levine, Robert A. et al. "A Retrospective on the Negative Income Tax Experiments: Looking Back at the Most Innovative Field Studies in Social Policy." *The Ethics and Economics of the Basic Income Guarantee*, 205, 95–106. Available at https://works.swarthmore. edu/fac-economics/347.

216 NOTES TO PAGES 161–162

45. On the provisions of the bill, United States Congress. 2021. H.R. 5376, Build Back Better Act, 117th Congress, 2021–2022. Available at https://www.congress.gov/bill/117th-congress/house-bill/5376; on the legislation's failure, Thompson, Alex. 2021. "Biden Concedes Build Back Better Bill Won't Get Passed This Year." *Politico*, December 16. Available at https://www.politico.com/news/2021/12/16/biden-concedes-bbb-bill-wont-get-passed-this-year-525194.

46. Ananat, Elizabeth, Benjamin Glasner, Christal Hamilton, and Zachary Parolin. 2021. "Effects of the Expanded Child Tax Credit on Employment Outcome: Evidence from Real-World Data from April to September 2021." Poverty and Social Policy Discussion Paper. Center on Poverty and Social Policy, Columbia University. Available at https://www.povertycenter.columbia.edu/publication/2021/expanded-child-tax-credit-impact-on-employment. The absence of any effect on maternal employment is corroborated by a large, randomized control trial. Sauval, Maria, Greg Duncan, Lisa A. Gennetian, Katherine Magnuson, Nathan Fox, Kimbrely Noble, and Hirokazu Yoshikawa. 2022. "Unconditional Cash Transfers and Maternal Employment: Evidence from the Baby's First Years Study" November 30. Available at: https://ssrn.com/abstract=4297310 or http://dx.doi.org/10.2139/ssrn.4297310

47. Zippel, Claire. 2021. "9 in 10 Families with Low Incomes Are Using Child Tax Credits to Pay for Necessities, Education." Center on Budget & Policy Priorities, October 21. Available at https://www.cbpp.org/blog/9-in-10-families-with-low-incomes-are-using-child-tax-credits-to-pay-for-necessities-education.

48. We might reasonably point the finger at the Fed's decades of low interest rates and pandemic-snarled supply chains, in part because of an unprecedented shift from services to goods as Americans isolated themselves from COVID. Tariffs enacted by President Donald Trump, left in place by President Joe Biden, are also inflationary. Moreover, Europe is experiencing inflation despite a variety of strategies for funding COVID relief. International Monetary Fund, n.d. "Policy Responses to COVID-19: Policy Tracker." Available at https://www.imf.org/en/Topics/imf-and-covid19/Policy-Responses-to-COVID-19.

49. The canonical reference on the benefits of two-parent families is McLanahan, Sara S. and Gary Sandefur. 1994. *Growing Up with a Single Parent: What Hurts, What Helps.* Cambridge, MA: Harvard University Press. Their work is especially germane given that they show that the income gap between single and married parents can explain about half of the disparity in high school completion rates. For a recent review of this literature, Wasserman, Melanie. 2020. "The Disparate Effects of Family Structure." *The Future of Children* 30: 55–82. Economist Melissa Kearney recently authored a well-publicized update of McLanahan and Sandefur's findings. Kearney, Melissa S. 2023. *The Two-Parent Privilege: How the Decline in Marriage Has Increased Inequality and Lowered Social Mobility, and What We Can Do about It.* Rugby, UK: Swift Press. Gay or straight: ample research has confirmed no appreciable differences in offspring well-being between homosexual and heterosexual parents. For a review, Stacey, Judith and Timothy J. Biblarz. 2001. "(How) Does the Sexual Orientation of Parents Matter?" *American Sociological Review*: 159–183. An infamous study purporting to show differences by parental sexual orientation actually reflects the effects of parental family structure. Regnerus, Mark. 2012. "How Different Are the Adult Children of Parents Who Have Same-Sex Relationships? Findings from the New Family Structures Study." *Social Science Research* 41: 752–70. Finally, a caveat: children in high-conflict, two-parent families don't fare well and can benefit from divorce when it alleviates conflict. Amato, Paul R., Laura Spencer Loomis, and Alan Booth. 1995. "Parental Divorce, Marital Conflict, and Offspring Well-Being During Early Adulthood." *Social Forces* 73: 895–915; Jekielek, Susan M 1998. "Parental Conflict, Marital Disruption and Children's Emotional Well-Being." *Social Forces* 76: 905–936.

50. Schneider, Daniel. "Lessons Learned from Non-Marriage Experiments." 2015. *Future of Children* 25: 155–178. This finding shouldn't be read as a repudiation of the role of men's prosperity affecting their marriage rates. Indeed, elsewhere Schneider has shown that men's declining real wages have contributed to the retreat from marriage. Schneider, Daniel, Kristen Harknett, and Matthew Stimpson. 2018. "What Explains the Decline in First Marriage in The United States? Evidence from the Panel Study of Income Dynamics, 1969 to 2013." *Journal of Marriage and Family* 80: 791–811.

51. Ullrich, Volker. 2015. *Bismarck: The Iron Chancellor.* London: Haus Publishing.

52. Social Security Administration. N.d. "Social Security History: Otto von Bismarck." Available at https://www.ssa.gov/history/ottob.html.

53. A 2013 Gallup poll found that 78% of Americans want to get married. Gallup Poll. 2023. "Marriage." https://news.gallup.com/poll/117328/Marriage.aspx. Another survey found that

NOTES TO PAGES 162–163 217

only 14% of never-married adults hold no interest in getting married. Parker, Kim and Renee Stepler. 2017. "As U.S. Marriage Rate Hovers At 50%, Education Gap in Marital Status Widens." Pew Research Center 14. Available at https://www.pewresearch.org/fact-tank/2017/09/14/as-u-s-marriage-rate-hovers-at-50-education-gap-in-marital-status-widens/. Majorities of Americans believe marriage makes society better off, is needed in order to create strong families, and improves the lot of parents and children alike. Karpowitz, Christopher F. and Jeremy C. Pope. 2018. The American Family Survey. https://media.deseret.com/media/misc/pdf/afs/2018-AFS-Final-Report.pdf. Finally, sociologist W. Bradford Wilcox recently argued there's a disjuncture between popular and scientific opinions on the importance of marriage, on the one hand, and select columnists in prestige media and a rump of academics who argue to the contrary, on the other. Wilcox, W. Bradford. 2024. *Get Married: Why Americans Must Defy the Elites, Forge Strong Families, and Save Civilization*. New York: HarperCollins.

54. National Conference of State Legislatures. N.d. "Federal EITC: What Legislators Need to Know." Available at https://www.ncsl.org/print/wln/EITC.pdf. It's worth acknowledging at this juncture a critique of the EITC made by sociologist Matthew Desmond and others: the EITC subsidizes large employers. They can pay their employees less because they know the government will pick up the slack. This holds true for government transfers more generally: according to a 2020 Government Accountability Office report, 70% of adult Medicaid and food stamp recipients worked full-time. We don't see this dynamic as a reason to oppose the EITC and other redistributive programs, but as a rationale to foster unionization and other mechanisms of "predistribution." Desmond, Matthew. 2023. *Poverty, by America*. New York: Crown; on employment and use of means-tested benefits, U.S. Government Accountability Office. 2020. "Federal Social Safety Net Programs: Millions of Full-Time Workers Rely on Federal Health Care and Food Assistance Programs." GAO-21-45, October 19. Available at https://www.gao.gov/products/gao-21-45.

55. Cass, Oren. 2018. *The Once and Future Worker: A Vision for the Renewal of Work in America*. New York: Encounter Books.

56. The psychology of windfall gains has long been understood. Arkes, Hal R., Cynthia A. Joyner, Mark V. Pezzo, Jane Gradwohl Nash, Karen Siegel-Jacobs, and Eric Stone. 1994. "The Psychology of Windfall Gains." *Organizational Behavior and Human Decision Processes* 59: 331–347.

57. On the role of economic factors in the retreat from marriage, Wilcox, W. Bradford and Nicholas H. Wolfinger. 2016. *Soul Mates: Religion, Sex, Love and Marriage among African Americans and Latinos*. New York: Oxford University Press. And while men aren't the focus of this book, there is extensive research that men's economic precarity has undermined marriage. This is one reason why Moynihan's 1965 report advocated federal investment in jobs for African American men.

58. Schott, Liz, LaDonna Pavetti, and Ife Floyd. 2015. "How States Use Federal and State Funds under the TANF Block Grant." *Center on Budget & Policy Priorities*. Available at https://www.cbpp.org/research/family-income-support/how-states-use-federal-and-state-funds-under-the-tanf-block-grant. Project Censored, a media watchdog group, identified state hording of TANF funds to be one of the most underreported stories of 2021–2022. Project Censored. 2023. "States Hoard Federal Assistance Funding Amidst Record Poverty Levels." May 22, 2023. Available at https://www.projectcensored.org/20-states-hoard-federal-assistance-funding-amidst-record-poverty-levels/.

59. Edin, Kathryn and H. Luke Shaefer. 2015. *$2.00 a Day: Living on Almost Nothing in America*. Boston, MA: Houghton Mifflin Harcourt.

60. On Moynihan and the Great Society, Weiner, Greg. 2015. *American Burke: The Uncommon Liberalism of Daniel Patrick Moynihan*. Lawrence: University Press of Kansas.

61. Lowrey, Annie. 2018. *Give People Money: How a Universal Basic Income Would End Poverty, Revolutionize Work, and Remake the World*. Portland, OR: Broadway Books.

62. Rosignal, Will and Patrick McIlheran. 2024. "Single-parent Households by State." Badger Institute, January 24. Available at https://www.badgerinstitute.org/numbers/single-parent-households-by-state/.

63. Cooper, David, Sebastian Martinez Hickey, and Ben Zipperer. 2022. "The Value of the Federal Minimum Wage Is at Its Lowest Point in 66 Years." Working Economics Blog, Economic Policy Institute, July 14. Available at https://www.epi.org/blog/the-value-of-the-federal-minimum-wage-is-at-its-lowest-point-in-66-years/.

64. Brady, David, Regina S. Baker, and Ryan Finnigan. 2013. "When Unionization Disappears: State-level Unionization and Working Poverty in the United States." *American Sociological Review* 78: 872–896.

NOTES TO PAGES 163–165

65. Leonhardt, David. 2023. *Ours Was the Shining Future: The Story of the American Dream.* New York: Random House; Noah, Timothy. 2012. *The Great Divergence: America's Growing Inequality Crisis and What We Can Do About It.* Bloomsbury Publishing USA.

66. Leonhardt, David. 2023. *Ours Was the Shining Future: The Story of the American Dream.* New York: Random House.

67. We're not aware of social science research on this point, but anecdotes abound. Here's one: United Food and Commercial Workers International Union (UFCW). 2015. "Celebrating UFCW Moms: Single Mom Sought Education and Career for Better Life, Gives Back to Union and Community." Available at https://www.ufcw.org/celebrating-ufcw-moms-single-mom-sou ght-education-and-career-for-better-life-gives-back-to-union-and-community/.

68. Duncan, Greg J., Martha S. Hill, and Saul D. Hoffman. 1988. "Welfare Dependence within and across Generations." *Science* 239 (4839): 467–471; for a recent overview, Desmond, Matthew. 2023. *Poverty, by America.* New York: Crown Publishing Group.

69. Schneider, Daniel. 2015. "Lessons Learned from Non-Marriage Experiments." *Future of Children* 25: 155–178.

70. Biegert, Thomas, Brady, David, and Lena Hipp. 2022. "Cross-National Variation in the Relationship between Welfare Generosity and Single Mother Employment." *The Annals of the American Academy of Political and Social Science* 702: 37–54.

71. Edin, Kathryn and Laura Lein. 1997. *Making Ends Meet: How Single Mothers Survive Welfare and Low-wage Work.* New York: Russell Sage Foundation.

72. We presented data on the growing number of single fathers in a recent conference paper. McKeever, Matthew and Nicholas H. Wolfinger. 2023. "Economic Inequality and Single-Parent Families." Paper presented at the 2023 annual meeting of the American Sociological Association, Philadelphia.

73. The *New York Times* columnist David Brooks caused a stir in 2020 by conceding this point in a hotly debated article. Brooks' argument was surprising because the center-right intelligentsia has long comprised the strongest proponents of marriage. It produced responses from some of our most prominent marriage scholars, including Andrew Cherlin, Richard Reeves, and W. Bradford Wilcox. Brooks, David. 2020. "The Nuclear Family was a Mistake." *The Atlantic*, March. Available at https://www.theatlantic.com/magazine/archive/2020/03/the-nuclear-family-was-a-mistake/605536/; Cherlin, Andrew J. 2020. "David Brooks Is Urging Us To Go Forward, Not Backward." *The Family Studies Blog*, February 12. Available at https://ifstudies.org/blog/david-brooks-is-urging-us-to-go-forward-not-backward; Reeves, Richard V. 2020. "David Brooks Is Correct: Both the Quality and Quantity of Our Relationships Matter." *The Family Studies Blog*, February 11. Available at https://ifstudies.org/blog/david-brooks-is-correct-both-the-quality-and-quantity-of-our-relationships-matter; Wilcox, W. Bradford and Wendy Wang. 2020. "What Do We Know About Extended Families in America? A Response to David Brooks." *The Family Studies Blog*, February 10. https://ifstudies.org/blog/what-do-we-know-about-extended-famil ies-in-america-a-response-to-david-brooks.

74. On how historical forces shaped the 1950s family, Cherlin, Andrew J. 1992. *Marriage, Divorce, Remarriage*, revised ed. Cambridge, MA: Harvard University Press; Wolfinger, Nicholas H. 2023. "Family Change in the Context of Social Changes in the United States." Pp. 97–118 in Mary Daly, Birgit Pfau-Effinger, Doug Besharov and Neil Gilbert *International Handbook of Family Policy: A Life-Course Perspective.* Oxford: Oxford University Press.

Appendix A

1. Wilcox, W. Bradford and Nicholas H. Wolfinger. 2016. *Soul Mates: Religion, Sex, Love and Marriage among African Americans and Latinos.* New York: Oxford University Press.

2. Akerlof, George A., Janet L. Yellen, and Michael L. Katz. 1996. "An Analysis of Out-of-Wedlock Childbearing in the United States." *The Quarterly Journal of Economics* 111: 277–317; Edin, Kathryn and Maria Kefalas. 2005. *Promises I Can Keep: Why Poor Women Put Motherhood before Marriage.* Oakland: University of California Press.

3. Wu, Lawrence L., Steven P. Martin, and Paula England. 2017. "The Decoupling of Sex and Marriage: Cohort Trends in Who Did and Did Not Delay Sex Until Marriage for U.S. Women Born 1938–1985." *Sociological Science* 4: 151–175.

4. A recent study provided strong evidence that men's deteriorating economic prospects has contributed to the decline in marriage. So too did mass incarceration. However, the authors were careful to note that these factors cannot fully explain the decline. Schneider, Daniel, Kristen Harknett, and Matthew Stimpson. 2018. "What Explains the Decline in First Marriage

NOTES TO PAGES 165–169   219

in the United States? Evidence from the Panel Study of Income Dynamics, 1969 to 2013." *Journal of Marriage and Family* 80: 791–811.

5. On the strong prevalence of aspirations to marriage, Gallup Poll. 2023. "Marriage." https://news.gallup.com/poll/117328/Marriage.aspx; Parker, Kim and Renee Stepler. 2017. "As U.S. Marriage Rate Hovers at 50%, Education Gap in Marital Status Widens." *Pew Research Center* 14. Available at https://www.pewresearch.org/fact-tank/2017/09/14/as-u-s-marriage-rate-hovers-at-50-education-gap-in-marital-status-widens/.

6. Cherlin, Andrew J. 1992. *Marriage, Divorce, Remarriage*, revised ed. Cambridge, MA: Harvard University Press; Wolfinger, Nicholas H. 2023. "Family Change in the Context of Social Changes in the United States." Pp. 197–218 in Mary Daly, Birgit Pfau-Effinger, Doug Besharov and Neil Gilbert. *The Oxford Handbook of Family Policy Over The Life Course*. Oxford: Oxford University Press.

7. Wolfinger, Nicholas H. 2023. "Family Change in the Context of Social Changes in the United States." Pp. 197–218 in Mary Daly, Birgit Pfau-Effinger, Doug Besharov and Neil Gilbert. *The Oxford Handbook of Family Policy Over The Life Course*. Oxford: Oxford University Press.

8. Aberg, Yvonne. 2009. "The Contagiousness of Divorce." *The Oxford Handbook of Analytical Sociology*: 342–64; McDermott, Rose, James H. Fowler, and Nicholas A. Christakis. 2013. "Breaking Up Is Hard to Do, Unless Everyone Else Is Doing It Too: Social Network Effects on Divorce in a Longitudinal Sample." *Social Forces* 92: 491–519.

9. Ono, Hiromi. 1998. "Husbands' and Wives' Resources and Marital Dissolution." *Journal of Marriage and Family* 60: 674–689. Ono found that female earnings past a certain point raised the odds of divorce, but earning potential did not.

10. Cherlin, Andrew J. 2014. *Labor's Love Lost: The Rise and Fall of the Working-class Family in America*. New York: Russell Sage Foundation; Edin, Kathryn and Maria Kefalas. 2005. *Promises I Can Keep: Why Poor Women Put Motherhood before Marriage*. Oakland: University of California Press.

11. Data from the 2017–2019 National Survey of Family Growth (N = 2,878).

12. Wolfinger, Nicholas H. 2005. *Understanding the Divorce Cycle: The Children of Divorce in Their Own Marriages*. New York: Cambridge University Press; see also Vlosky, Denese A. and Pamela A. Monroe. 2002. "The Effective Dates of No-Fault Divorce Laws in the 50 States." *Family Relations* 51: 317–324; Wernick, Robert. 1996. "Where You Went if You *Really* Had to Get Unhitched." *Smithsonian* 27: 64–72

13. Glenn, Norval D. 1997. "A Reconsideration of the Effect of No-Fault Divorce on Divorce Rates." *Journal of Marriage and the Family* 59: 1026–1030; see also Wolfers, Justin. 2006. "Did Unilateral Divorce Laws Raise Divorce Rates? A Reconciliation and New Results." *American Economic Review* 96: 1802–1820; for a contrary finding, Gruber, Jonathan. 2004. "Is Making Divorce Easier Bad for Children? The Long-Run Implications of Unilateral Divorce." *Journal of Labor Economics* 22: 799–833.

14. Wang, Wendy. 2020. "The U.S. Divorce Rate Has Hit a 50-Year Low." Institute for Family Studies. Available at https://ifstudies.org/blog/the-us-divorce-rate-has-hit-a-50-year-low.

15. On the 1950s family and how it's shaped our discourse, Cherlin, Andrew J. 1992. *Marriage, Divorce, Remarriage*, revised ed. Cambridge, MA: Harvard University Press; Coontz, Stephanie. 1992. *The Way We Never Were: American Families and the Nostalgia Trap*. New York: Basic Books.

16. Cherlin, Andrew J. 1992. *Marriage, Divorce, Remarriage*, revised ed. Cambridge, MA: Harvard University Press.

17. Singh, Gopal K. 2010. "Maternal Mortality in the United States, 1935–2007: Substantial Racial/Ethnic, Socioeconomic, and Geographic Disparities Persist." *Health Resources and Services Administration / Maternal and Child Health Bureau*. Available at https://www.google.com/books/edition/Maternal_Mortality_in_the_United_States/9XZQ0ZfHPW8C?hl=en.

18. Bumpass, Larry L. and James A. Sweet. 1989. "Children's Experience in Single-Parent Families: Implications of Cohabitation and Marital Transitions." *Family Planning Perspective* 21: 256–260.

Appendix B

1. Moynihan, Daniel Patrick. 1965. *The Negro Family: The Case for National Action*. Washington, DC: U.S. Department of Labor, Office of Policy Planning and Research. Available at https://www.dol.gov/general/aboutdol/history/webid-moynihan. For the circumstances surrounding the authorship of the Report and its contemporary implications for the civil rights movement,

220 NOTES TO PAGES 169–172

see Patterson, James T. 2010. *Freedom Is Not Enough: The Moynihan Report and America's Struggle Over Black Family Life—from LBJ to Obama.* New York: Basic Books. This source is uniquely valuable in understanding the Moynihan Report's intellectual and political history. Also useful is Massey, Douglas S. and Robert J. Sampson. 2009. "Moynihan Redux: Legacies and Lessons." *The Annals of the American Academy of Political and Social Science* 621: 6–27; and Weiner, Greg. 2015. *American Burke: The Uncommon Liberalism of Daniel Patrick Moynihan.* Lawrence: University Press of Kansas.

2. Moynihan, Daniel Patrick. 1965. *The Negro Family: The Case for National Action.* Washington, DC: U.S. Department of Labor, Office of Policy Planning and Research, 30. The African American psychologist Kenneth Clark first introduced the phrase "tangle of pathology" in writing about Black communities. Clark, Kenneth B. 1965 *Dark Ghetto: Dilemmas of Social Power.* Middletown, CT: Wesleyan University Press.

3. Ryan, William. 1965. "Savage Discovery: The Moynihan Report." *The Nation*, November 22. Available at http://www.columbia.edu/itc/hs/pubhealth/p9740/readings/william_ryan.pdf; for a retrospective view, Gans, Herbert. 2011. "The Moynihan Report and Its Aftermaths: A Critical Analysis." *Du Bois Review* 8: 315–327.

4. Ryan, William. 1976. *Blaming the Victim*, revised ed. New York: Vintage Books.

5. Coates, Ta-Nehisi. 2015. "A Note on the Moynihan Report, Black Women, and 'Urbanology,'" *The Atlantic*, September 15. Just three years later, Coates praised the report in an interview featured in a documentary on Moynihan released in 2018. Dorman, Joseph and Toby Perl Freilich. 2018. *Moynihan*. First Run Features. 1 hr., 45 min. Available at https://www.amazon.com/Moynihan-Daniel-Patrick/dp/B07TLFQ749/ref=sr_1_1?crid=I3ZFBCLI4UKO&keywords=moynihan+documentary&qid=1702098308&sprefix=moynihan+documentary%2Caps%2C135&sr=8-1

6. Rustin, Bayard. 1966. "The Watts." *Commentary*, March. Available at https://www.comment ary.org/articles/bayard-rustin-2/the-watts/. For a modern critique from the left, Reed, Touré. 2015. "Why Moynihan Was Not So Misunderstood at the Time: The Mythological Prescience of the Moynihan Report and the Problem of Institutional Structuralism." *Nonsite.org*, Issue 17, September 4. Available at https://nonsite.org/why-moynihan-was-not-so-misunderstood-at-the-time/#foot_src_35-9142.

7. Interview with Elizabeth Moynihan. Dorman, Joseph and Toby Perl Freilich. 2018. *Moynihan*. First Run Features.

8. For a recent critique of this trend, Downey, Douglas B. 2020. *How Schools Really Matter: Why Our Assumption about Schools and Inequality Is Mostly Wrong.* Chicago: University of Chicago Press.

9. Carroll, Peter N. 1982. *It Seemed Like Nothing Happened: America in the 1970s.* New Brunswick, NJ: Rutgers University Press; Frum, David. 2008. *How We Got Here: The 70's: The Decade that Brought You Modern Life (for Better or Worse).* New York: Basic Books.

10. Rainwater, Lee and William L. Yancey. 1967. *The Moynihan Report and the Politics of Controversy.* Cambridge, MA: MIT Press. The most consequential contemporaneous critique appears in Ryan, William. 1965. "Savage Discovery: The Moynihan Report." *The Nation*, November 22. For a pro-Moynihan retrospective, see Hymowitz, Kay S. 2005. "The Black Family: 40 Years of Lies." *City Journal*. Available at https://www.city-journal.org/html/black-family-40-years-lies-12872. html. For overviews of how social science gradually came to grips with the Moynihan Report, Massey, Douglas S. and Robert J. Sampson. 2009. "Moynihan Redux: Legacies and Lessons." *The Annals of the American Academy of Political and Social Science* 621: 6–27; Wolfinger, Nicholas H. 2005. *Understanding the Divorce Cycle: The Children of Divorce in Their Own Marriages.* New York: Cambridge University Press, Chapter 2.

11. Wilson, William Julius.1997. *When Work Disappears: The World of the Urban Poor*, New York: Vintage Books, 171.

12. Massey, Douglas S. and Robert J. Sampson. 2009. "Moynihan Redux: Legacies and Lessons." *The Annals of the American Academy of Political and Social Science* 621: 6–27.

13. Wilson, William Julius. 1987. *The Truly Disadvantaged: The Inner City, the Underclass, and Public Policy.* Chicago: University of Chicago Press. Among Wilson's countless honors, he's one of only 25 Harvard faculty members to hold the über prestigious title of "university professor."

14. Wilson, William Julius. 2009. "The Moynihan Report and Research on the Black Community." *The Annals of the American Academy of Political and Social Science* 621: 34–46.

15. McLanahan, Sara and Christopher Jenks. 2015. "Was Moynihan Right? What Happens to Children of Unmarried Mothers." *Education Next* 15: 14–21.

16. Obama, Barack. 2006. *Audacity of Hope: Thoughts on Reclaiming the American Dream*, New York: Crown Publishers, 254.

NOTES TO PAGES 172–178   221

17. Geary, Daniel.2015. "The Moynihan Report: An Annotated Edition." *The Atlantic*, September 14. Available at https://www.theatlantic.com/politics/archive/2015/09/the-moynihan-report-an-annotated-edition/404632/. We have some quibbles with Geary's annotations, but that shouldn't detract from his overview of Moynihan's legacy.

18. On the contretemps between New York mayor Bill De Blasio and police commissioner Bill Bratton, Barkan, Ross. 2015. "'Society Has Changed': De Blasio Breaks With Bratton Over Moynihan Report." *Observer*, September 2. Available at https://observer.com/2015/09/society-has-changed-de-blasio-breaks-with-bratton-over-moynihan-report/.

Appendix C

1. A paean to the Nobel Laureate economist James Heckman's important 1993 essay. Cameron, Stephen V. and James J. Heckman. 1993. "The Nonequivalence of High School Equivalents." *Journal of Labor Economics* 11, Part 1: 1–47.

2. Per capita income is family income divided by the number of people in the family (here and elsewhere, we follow the Census definition of a family as two or more people linked by blood, marriage or adoption). Census Supplemental Poverty adjusted income is calculated as family income divided by x:

- Single parents: x = (number of adults + 0.8*first child + 0.5*other children)$^{0.7}$
- All other families: x = (number of adults + 0.5*number of children)$^{0.7}$

  United States Census Bureau. 2021. *Equivalence Adjustment of Income*. October 8. Washington, DC: United States Government Printing Office. Available at https://www.census.gov/topics/income-poverty/income-inequality/about/metrics/equivalence.html.

Appendix D

1. United States Census Bureau. 2023. "About the Current Population Survey." Available at https://www.census.gov/programs-surveys/cps/about.html.

2. What's a householder? Per the Census: "The person, or one of the people, in whose name the home is owned, being bought, or rented. If there is no such person present, any household member 15 years old and over can serve as the householder." United States Census Bureau. 2023. "Glossary." Available at https://www.census.gov/glossary/?term=Householder.

3. Income is converted to 2018 dollars using the Consumer Price Index, available at the United States Department of Labor. 2023. "Inflation Calculator." Bureau of Labor Statistics, https://www.bls.gov/data/inflation_calculator.htm. "Family income" reflects the U.S. definition of a family as two or more people linked by blood, marriage, or adoption. McFalls, Joseph A. Jr. 2023. "What's a Household? What's a Family?" Population Reference Bureau. Available at https://www.prb.org/resources/whats-a-household-whats-a-family/#:~:text=Under%20the%20U.S.%20Census%20Bureau,their%20residence%20with%20unrelated%20individuals. One implication of the Census definition concerns cohabiting couples, who comprise two families sharing a single household. A cohabiting mother's family income therefore excludes her partner's earnings.

4. For information on bootstrapped standard errors, Efron, Bradley and Robert J. Tibshirani. 1994. *An Introduction to the Bootstrap*. Boca Raton, FL: CRC Press.

5. Gurrentz, Benjamin. 2018. "Living with an Unmarried Partner Now Common for Young Adults." United States Census Bureau. Available at https://www.census.gov/library/stories/2018/11/cohabitation-is-up-marriage-is-down-for-young-adults.html.

6. Manning, Wendy D. and Pamela J. Smock. 2005. "Measuring and Modeling Cohabitation: New Perspectives from Qualitative Data." *Journal of Marriage and Family* 67: 989–1002.

7. National Longitudinal Survey Program. 2011. Washington, DC: Bureau of Labor Statistics, available at http://www.bls.gov/nls/nlsy79.htm.

8. "[N]on-Blacks and non-Hispanics" is what we nowadays call "White."

9. Winship, Christopher and Larry Radbill. 1994. "Sampling Weights and Regression Analysis." *Sociological Methods & Research* 23: 230–257.

10. Paul, Christopher, William M. Mason, Daniel McCaffrey, and Sarah A. Fox. 2008. "A Cautionary Case Study of Approaches to the Treatment of Missing Data." *Statistical Methods and Applications* 17: 351–372. Paul and his colleague did what none of the proponents of fancy missing data techniques actually did: they test how they perform. The results were indeed underwhelming.

11. How few widows are there in NLSY79? In 1990, when respondents were in prime childbearing ages (25–33), there were 28 widowed mothers, or 0.45% of all female respondents.

222 NOTES TO PAGES 178–181

12. While many scholars have written about fixed effects models, sociologist Paul Allison is a beacon of clarity. Allison, Paul D. 2009. *Fixed effects regression models*. Los Angeles: SAGE publications.
13. Hausman, Jerry A. 1978. "Specification Tests in Econometrics." *Econometrica: Journal of the Econometric Society* 46: 1251–1271. At over 25,000 citations, this paper is as close to economic canon as it gets, although it still pales before the 142,581 citations racked up by Kuhn, Thomas. 1962. *The Structure of Scientific Revolutions*. Chicago: University of Chicago Press.
14. On the relationship between age, age squared, and income, Thurow, Lester C., 1969. The Optimum Lifetime Distribution of Consumption Expenditures. *The American Economic Review* 59: 324–330.

References

Abel, Jaison R. and Richard Deitz. 2014. "Do the Benefits of College Still Outweigh the Costs?" *Current Issues in Economics and Finance* 20 (3): 1–12. New York Federal Reserve. Available at https://citeseerx.ist.psu.edu/viewdoc/download?doi=10.1.1.639.3807&rep=rep1&type=pdf. (accessed 8/13/21)

Aberg, Yvonne. 2009. "The Contagiousness of Divorce." *The Oxford Handbook of Analytical Sociology*: 342–364.

Abramovitz, Mimi. 1988. *Regulating the Lives of Women: Social Welfare from Colonial Times to the Present.* Boston: South End Press.

Akerlof, George A., Janet L. Yellen, and Michael L. Katz. 1996. "An Analysis of Out-of-Wedlock Childbearing in the United States." *The Quarterly Journal of Economics* 111 (2): 277–317. Berkeley: University of California Press.

Albertini, Marco, Michael Gähler, and Juho Härkönen. 2018. "Moving Back to "Mamma"? Divorce, Intergenerational Coresidence, and Latent Family Solidarity in Sweden." *Population, Space, and Place* 24 (6): e2142.

Allison, Paul D. 2009. *Fixed Effects Regression Models.* Los Angeles: SAGE Publications.

Amato, Paul R. and Alan Booth. 1997. *A Generation at Risk: Growing Up in an Era of Family Upheaval.* Cambridge, MA: Harvard University Press.

Amato, Paul R., Laura Spencer Loomis, and Alan Booth. 1995. "Parental Divorce, Marital Conflict, and Offspring Well-Being During Early Adulthood." *Social Forces* 73 (3): 895–915.

American Association of University Women. 2017. *The Simple Truth about the Gender Pay Gap.* Washington, DC. Available at https://web.archive.org/web/20170224051057/https://www.aauw.org/aauw_check/pdf_download/show_pdf.php?file=The-Simple-Truth. (accessed 12/26/20)

The American Presidency Project. N.d. Santa Barbara: University of California, Santa Barbara. Available at https://www.presidency.ucsb.edu. (accessed 6/26/21).

An, Chong-Bum, Robert Haveman, and Barbara Wolfe. 1993. "Teen Out-of-Wedlock Births and Welfare Receipt: The Role of Childhood Events and Economic Circumstances." *The Review of Economics and Statistics* 75 (2): 195–208.

Ananat, Elizabeth, Benjamin Glasner, Christal Hamilton, and Zachary Parolin. 2021. "Effects of the Expanded Child Tax Credit on Employment Outcome: Evidence from Real-World Data from April to September 2021." Poverty and Social Policy Discussion Paper. Center on Poverty and Social Policy, Columbia University. Available at https://www.povertycenter.columbia.edu/publication/2021/expanded-child-tax-credit-impact-on-employment.

Anderson, Kermyt G., Hillard Kaplan, and Jane B. Lancaster. 2001. "Men's Financial Expenditures on Genetic Children and Stepchildren from Current and Former Relationships. PSC Research Report." Ann Arbor, Michigan: Population Studies Center. Available at https://files.eric.ed.gov/fulltext/ED463372.pdf.

Andersen, Margaret, L. and Patricia Hill Collins. 1992. *Race, Class and Gender: An Anthology.* Belmont, CA: Wadsworth.

Arkes, Hal R., Cynthia A. Joyner, Mark V. Pezzo, Jane Gradwohl Nash, Karen Siegel-Jacobs, and Eric Stone. 1994. "The Psychology of Windfall Gains." *Organizational Behavior and Human Decision Processes* 59 (3): 331–347.

Ashcraft, Adam, Iván Fernández-Val, and Kevin Lang. 2013. "The Consequences of Teenage Childbearing: Consistent Estimates When Abortion Makes Miscarriage Non-random." *The Economic Journal* 123 (571): 875–905.

224 REFERENCES

Avellar, Sarah and Pamela J. Smock. 2003 "Has the Price of Motherhood Declined Over Time? A Cross-Cohort Comparison of the Motherhood Wage Penalty," *Journal of Marriage and Family* 65: 597–607.

Axinn, William, Greg J. Duncan, and Arland Thornton. 1997. "The Effects of Parents' Income, Wealth, and Attitudes on Children's Completed Schooling and Self-Esteem." Pp. 518–540 in Greg Duncan and Jeanne Brooks-Gunn *Consequences of Growing Up Poor.* New York: Russell Sage Press.

Bachrach, Christine. 1983. "Children in Families: Characteristics of Biological, Step-, and Adopted Children." *Journal of Marriage and the Family* 45 (1): 171–179

Baker, Regina S. 2022. "Ethno-Racial Variation in Single Motherhood Prevalences and Penalties for Child Poverty in the United States, 1995–2018." *The Annals of the American Academy of Political and Social Science* 702 (1): 20–36.

Baker, Regina S. 2015. "The Changing Association Among Marriage, Work, and Childhood Poverty in the U.S., 1974–2000." *Journal of Marriage and Family* 77: 1166–1178.

Barkan, Ross. 2015. "'Society Has Changed': De Blasio Breaks with Bratton Over Moynihan Report." *Observer*, September 2. Available at https://observer.com/2015/09/society-has-changed-de-blasio-breaks-with-bratton-over-moynihan-report/. (accessed 7/5/2022)

Barroso, Amanda and Anna Brown. 2021. "Gender Pay Gap in U.S. Held Steady in 2020." Pew Research Center. Available at https://www.pewresearch.org/fact-tank/2021/05/25/gender-pay-gap-facts/. (accessed 2/3/22)

Bartels, Larry M. 2016. *Unequal Democracy: The Political Economy of the New Gilded Age,* 2nd ed. Princeton University Press.

Bedard, Kelly and Olivier Deschênes. 2005. "Sex Preferences, Marital Dissolution, and the Economic Status of Women." *Journal of Human Resources* 40: 411–434.

Belkin, Lisa. 2023. "The Opt-Out Revolution." *The New York Times*, October 26.

Bernhardt, Annette, Martina Morris, and Mark S. Handcock. 1995. "Women's Gains or Men's Losses? A Closer Look at the Shrinking Gender Gap in Earnings." *American Journal of Sociology* 101: 302–328.

Biegert, Thomas, Brady, David, and Lena Hipp. 2022. "Cross-National Variation in the Relationship between Welfare Generosity and Single Mother Employment." *The Annals of the American Academy of Political and Social Science*, 702 (1): 37–54.

Blank, Rebecca M. 2002. "Evaluating Welfare Reform in the United States." Working paper 8983, Cambridge, MA: National Bureau of Economic Research.

Blankenhorn, David. 1995. *Fatherless America: Confronting Our Most Uurgent Social Problem.* Scranton, PA: HarperCollins Publishers.

Blasko, Andrew. 2004. "Reagan and Heritage: A Unique Partnership." Washington, DC: Heritage Foundation. Available at: https://www.heritage.org/conservatism/comment ary/reagan-and-heritage-unique-partnership (accessed 6/25/21).

Blau, Peter M. and Otis Dudley Duncan. 1967. *The American Occupational Structure.* New York: Wiley.

Bleiweis, Robin, Diana Boesch, and Alexandra Cawthorne Gaines. 2020. "The Basic Facts About Women in Poverty." Center for American Progress. Available at https://www.ameri canprogress.org/issues/women/reports/2020/08/03/488536/basic-facts-women-poverty/. (accessed 12/24/20)

Bloome, Deirdre and Shannon Ang. 2020. "Marriage and Union Formation in the United States: Recent Trends Across Racial Groups and Economic Backgrounds." *Demography* 57 (5): 1753–1786.

Bogle, Donald. 1989. *Toms, Coons, Mulattoes, Mammies, and Bucks: An Interpretive History of Blacks in American Films.* New York: Continuum

Bradshaw, Jonathan. 2016. *The Well-Being of Children in the UK*, 4th ed. Bristol: Bristol University Press, 2016.

Brady, David, Regina S. Baker, and Ryan Finnigan. 2013. "When Unionization Disappears: State-Level Unionization and Working Poverty in the United States." *American Sociological Review* 78 (5): 872–896.

REFERENCES   225

Brady, David and Rebekah Burroway. 2012. "Targeting, Universalism, and Single-Mother Poverty: A Multilevel Analysis across 18 Affluent Democracies." *Demography* 49 (2): 719–746.

Brady, David, Ryan M. Finnigan, and Sabine Hübgen. 2017. "Rethinking the Risks of Poverty: A Framework for Analyzing Prevalences (Sic) and Penalties." *American Journal of Sociology* 123 (3): 740–786.

Brady, David, Ryan M. Finnigan, and Sabine Hübgen. 2018. "Single Mothers Are Not the Problem." *New York Times*, February 10: 4.

Brady, David, Ryan Finnigan, Ulrich Kohler, and Joscha Legewie. 2020. "The Inheritance of Race Revisited: Childhood Wealth and Income and Black–White Disadvantages in Adult Life Chances." *Sociological Science* 7: 599–627.

Bramlett, Matthew D. and William D. Mosher. 2002. "Cohabitation, Marriage, Divorce, and Remarriage in the United States." National Vital Statistics Reports; vol 23 no22: 1–93. Hyattsville, MD: National Center for Health Statistics. Available at https://pubmed.ncbi. nlm.nih.gov/12183886/. (accessed 9/4/12)

Brand, Jennie E. 2015. "The Far-Reaching Impact of Job Loss and Unemployment." *Annual Review of Sociology* 41: 359–375. Available at https://www.ncbi.nlm.nih.gov/pmc/articles/ PMC4553243/.

Braver, Sanford L. 1999 "The Gender Gap in Standard of Living after Divorce: Vanishingly Small." *Family Law Quarterly* 33: 111.

Braver, Sanford L. and Diane O'Connell. 1998. *Divorced Dads: Shattering the Myths.* New York: Tarcher.

Breitenbach, Sarah. 2016. "Involving Dads in the Lives of Children Born out of Wedlock," *Stateline*, September 29. Available at https://www.pewtrusts.org/en/research-and-analysis/ blogs/stateline/2016/09/29/involving-dads-in-the-lives-of-children-born-out-of-wedlock. (accessed 3/24/2022)

Brito, Natalie H. and Kimberly G. Noble. 2014. "Socioeconomic Status and Structural Brain Development." *Frontiers in Neuroscience* 8: 276

Brito, Tonya L. 2018. "The Child Support Debt Bubble." *University of California Irvine Law Review* 9: 953.

Bronars, Stephen G. and Jeff Grogger. 1994. "The Economic Consequences of Unwed Motherhood: Using Twin Births as a Natural Experiment." *The American Economic Review* 84 (5): 1141–1156.

Brooks, David. 2020. "The Nuclear Family was a Mistake." *The Atlantic*, March. Available at https://www.theatlantic.com/magazine/archive/2020/03/the-nuclear-family-was-a-mist ake/605536/. (accessed 5/19/2022)

Brooks-Gunn, Jeanne and Greg J. Duncan. 1997. "The Effects of Poverty on Children." *The Future of Children* 7 (2): 55–71.

Brown, Susan L. 2002. "Child Well-Being in Cohabiting Families." Pp. 173–187 in Alan Booth and Ann C. Crouter *Just Living Together: Implications of Cohabitation for Children, Families, and Social Policy..* Mahwah, NJ: Lawrence Erlbaum.

Brown, Susan L. and Wendy D. Manning. 2009. "Family Boundary Ambiguity and the Measurement of Family Structure: The Significance of Cohabitation." *Demography* 46 (1): 85–101.

Brown, Susan L. and Matthew R. Wright. 2017. "Marriage, Cohabitation, and Divorce in Later Life." *Innovation in Aging* 1 (2): 1–11.

Brush, Lisa D. 1997. "Worthy Widows, Welfare Cheats: Proper Womanhood in Expert Needs Talk about Single Mothers in the United States, 1900 to 1988." *Gender & Society* 1: 720–746.

Budig, Michelle J. 2003. "Are Women's Employment and Fertility Histories Interdependent? An Examination of Causal Order Using Event History Analysis." *Social Science Research* 32: 376–401.

Budig, Michelle J. and Paula England, 2001. "The Wage Penalty for Motherhood," *American Sociological Review* 66: 204–225.

226 REFERENCES

Budig, Michelle J. and Melissa J. Hodges. 2010 "Differences in Disadvantage: Variation in the Motherhood Penalty across White Women's Earnings Distribution," *American Sociological Review* 75: 705–728.

Bumpass, Larry L. 1984. "Children and Marital Disruption: A Replication and Update." *Demography* 21 (1): 71–82.

Bumpass, Larry L. and Sheela Kennedy. 2008. "Cohabitation and Children's Living Arrangements: New Estimates from the United States." *Demographic Research* 19: 1663–1692.

Bumpass, Larry L. and Hsien-Hen Lu. 2000. "Trends in Cohabitation and Implications for Children's Family Contexts in the United States." *Population Studies* 54: 29–41.

Bumpass, Larry L., Teresa Castro Martin and James A. Sweet. 1991. "The Impact of Family Background and Early Marital Factors on Marital Disruption." *Journal of Family Issues* 12 (1): 22–42.

Bumpass, Larry L. and R. Kelly Raley. 1995. "Redefining Single-Parent Families: Cohabitation and Changing Family Reality." *Demography* 32: 97–109.

Bumpass, Larry L. and James A. Sweet. 1989. "Children's Experience in Single-Parent Families: Implications of Cohabitation and Marital Transitions." *Family Planning Perspective* 21: 256–260.

Bumpass, Larry L. and James A. Sweet. 1989. "National Estimates of Cohabitation." *Demography* 26: 615–625.

Bumpass, Larry, James A. Sweet, and Teresa Castro Martin. 1990. "Changing Patterns of Remarriage." *Journal of Marriage and Family* 52: 747–56.

Cameron, Stephen V. and James J. Heckman. 1993. "The Nonequivalence of High School Equivalents." *Journal of Labor Economics* 11 (1) Part 1: 1–47.

Cammett, Ann. 2010. "Deadbeats, Deadbrokes, and Prisoners." *Georgetown Journal on Poverty Law & Policy* 18: 127–168.

Campbell, Author A. 1968. "The Role of Family Planning in the Reduction of Poverty." *Journal of Marriage and the Family* 30: 236–245, 238.

Cancian, Maria and Daniel R. Meyer. 1998. "Who Gets Custody?" *Demography* 35 (2): 147–157. https://doi.org/10.2307/3004048.

Cancian, Maria, Daniel R. Meyer, Patricia R. Brown, and Steven T. Cook. 2014. "Who Gets Custody Now? Dramatic Changes in Children's Living Arrangements after Divorce." *Demography* 51: 1381–1396.

Caputo, Jennifer. 2018. "Parental Coresidence, Young Adult Role, Economic, and Health Changes, and Psychological Well-Being." *Society and Mental Health* 10 (3): 199–217.

Carlson, Marcia, Sara McLanahan, and Paula England. 2004. "Union Formation in Fragile Families." *Demography* 41 (2): 237–261.

Carroll, Peter N. 1982. *It Seemed Like Nothing Happened: America in the 1970s.* New Brunswick, NJ: Rutgers University Press.

Casper, Lynne M. and Philip N. Cohen. 2000. "How Does POSSLQ Measure Up? Historical Estimates of Cohabitation." *Demography* 37: 237–245.

Cass, Oren. 2018. *The Once and Future Worker: A Vision for the Renewal of Work in America.* New York: Encounter Books.

Cassidy, John. 2002. *Dot.con: The Greatest Story Ever Sold.* New York: HarperCollins.

Cha, Youngjoo and Kim A. Weeden. 2014. "Overwork and the Slow Convergence in the Gender Gap in Wages." *American Sociological Review.* 79 (3):457–484.

Center for Economic and Policy Research. 2019. March CPS Uniform Extracts, Version 1.1. Washington, DC. Available at https://ceprdata.org/cps-uniform-data-extracts/march-cps-supplement/march-cps-data/ (accessed 8/1/2021)

Chen, Yiyu and Dana Thomson. 2021. "Child Poverty Increased Nationally During COVID, Especially Among Latino and Black Children." Child Trends, Available at https://www.chil dtrends.org/publications/child-poverty-increased-nationally-during-covid-especially-among-latino-and-black-children#:~:text=We%20find%20that%20child%20poverty,mill ion%20more%20than%20in%202019. (accessed 2/15/2022)

REFERENCES 227

Cherlin, Andrew J. 2020. "David Brooks Is Urging Us To Go Forward, Not Backward." *The Family Studies Blog*, February 12. Available at https://ifstudies.org/blog/david-brooks-is-urging-us-to-go-forward-not-backward.

Cherlin, Andrew J. 2014. *Labor's Love Lost: The Rise and Fall of the Working-Class Family in America*. New York: Russell Sage Foundation.

Cherlin, Andrew J. 1992. *Marriage, Divorce, Remarriage*, revised ed. Cambridge, MA: Harvard University Press.

Chetty, Raj, Nathaniel Hendren, Patrick Kline, and Emmanuel Saez. 2014. "Where is the Land of Opportunity? The Geography of Intergenerational Mobility in the United States." *Quarterly Journal of Economics* 129 (4): 1553–1623.

Chevan, Albert, and Randall Stokes. 2000. "Growth in Family Income Inequality, 1970–1990: Industrial Restructuring and Demographic Change." *Demography* 37 (3): 365–380.

Clark, Kenneth B. 1965 *Dark Ghetto: Dilemmas of Social Power*. Middletown, CT: Wesleyan University Press.

Clinton White House Archives. 2000. Available at https://clintonwhitehouse4.archives.gov/WH/New/html/20000112_2.html#:~:text=OVER%20THREE%20DECADES-,In%201993%2C%20the%20President%20Signed%20Into%20Law%20the%20Largest%20EITC,cents%20for%20two%20plus%20children. (accessed 4/2/22)

Coates, Ta-Nehisi. 2015. "A Note on the Moynihan Report, Black Women, and 'Urbanology,'" *The Atlantic*, September 15.

Coggan, Philip. 2011. "Falling Short." *The Economist*. April 9. Available at https://www.economist.com/special-report/2011/04/09/falling-short?story_id=18502013&CFID=168408657&CFTOKEN=85722840. (accessed 2/22/2022)

Collins, Gail. 2009. *When Everything Changed: The Amazing Journey of American Women from 1960 to the Present*. New York: Little, Brown.

Conger, Rand, Katherine Jewsbury Conger, and Glen H. Elder Jr. 1997. "Family Economic Hardship and Adolescent Adjustment: Mediating and Moderating Processes." Pp. 288–311 in Greg Duncan and Jeanne Brooks-Gunn *Consequences of Growing Up Poor*. New York: Russell Sage Press.

Congressional Committee on Ways and Means. 2004. "Green Book." Background Material and Data on the Programs within the Jurisdiction of the Committee on Ways and Means. Available at http://www.gpoaccess.gov/wmprints/green/index.html. (accessed 9/7/12)

Congressional Research Service. 2019. "Real Wage Trends, 1979 to 2019." Washington, DC: Congressional Research Service. https://fas.org/sgp/crs/misc/R45090.pdf. (accessed 12/25/23).

Coontz, Stephanie. 1992. *The Way We Never Were: American Families and the Nostalgia Trap*. New York: Basic Books.

Cooper, David, Sebastian Martinez Hickey, and Ben Zipperer. 2022. "The Value of the Federal Minimum Wage Is at Its Lowest Point in 66 Years." Working Economics Blog, Economic Policy Institute, July 14. Available at https://www.epi.org/blog/the-value-of-the-federal-minimum-wage-is-at-its-lowest-point-in-66-years/ (accessed 12/13/2023).

Costello, Elizabeth J., Gordon P. Keeler, and Adrian Angold. 2001. "Poverty, Race/ethnicity, and Psychiatric Disorder: A Study of Rural Children." *American Journal of Public Health* 91: 1494–1498.

Counsel of Economic Advisors. 2016. "Labor Market Monopsony: Trends, Consequences, and Policy Responses." Washington, DC: Council of Economic Advisors. Available at https://obamawhitehouse.archives.gov/sites/default/files/page/files/20161025_monopsony_labor_mrkt_cea.pdf (accessed 12/29/21).

Crenshaw, Kimberlé. 1989. "Demarginalizing the Intersection of Race and Sex: A Black Feminist Critique of Antidiscrimination Doctrine, Feminist Theory and Antiracist Politics." *University of Chicago Legal Forum* 1989 (1): 139–167.

Current Population Survey: Annual Social and Economic Supplement. N.d. Washington, DC: United States Census Bureau. Available at https://www.census.gov/programs-surveys/saipe/guidance/model-input-data/cpsasec.html. (accessed 8/1/21)

228 REFERENCES

Curtin, Sally C., Stephanie J. Ventura, and Gladys M. Martinez. 2014. "Recent Declines in Nonmarital Childbearing in the United States." National Vital Statistics Reports; no 162. Hyattsville, MD: National Center for Health Statistics. Available at https://www.cdc.gov/nchs/products/databriefs/db162.htm. (accessed 7/18/21)

Day, Jennifer Cheeseman. 2019. "College Degree Widens Gender Earnings Gap." United States Census Bureau. Available at https://www.census.gov/library/stories/2019/05/college-degree-widens-gender-earnings-gap.html. (accessed 7/9/21)

Dearing, Eric. 2008. "Psychological Costs of Growing up Poor." *Annals of the New York Academy of Sciences* 1136 (1): 324–332.

de Graaf, Paul M. and Matthijs Kalmijn. 2003. "Alternative Routes in the Remarriage Market: Competing-Risk Analyses of Union Formation after Divorce." *Social Forces* 81 (4): 1459–1498.

Demby, Gene. 2013. "The Truth Behind The Lies Of The Original 'Welfare Queen'" National Public Radio. *All Things Considered*, December. Available at https://www.npr.org/sections/codeswitch/2013/12/20/255819681/the-truth-behind-the-lies-of-the-original-welfare-queen. (accessed 7/8/21).

DeNavas-Walt, Carmen, Bernadette D. Proctor, and Jessica C. Smith. 2011. *Income, Poverty, and Health Insurance Coverage in the United States: 2010*, United States Census Bureau, Current Population Reports, 60–239, Washington, DC: United States Government Printing Office. Available at http://www.census.gov/prod/2011pubs/p60-239.pdf. (accessed 9/22/11)

DePaulo, Bella M. 2006. *Singled Out: How Singles Are Stereotyped, Stigmatized, and Ignored, and Still Live Happily Ever After*. New York: Macmillan.

DeSilver, Drew. 2018. "For Most U.S. Workers, Real Wages Have Barely Budged in Decades." Pew Research Center. Available at https://www.pewresearch.org/fact-tank/2018/08/07/for-most-us-workers-real-wages-have-barely-budged-for-decades/.

Desmond, Matthew. 2023. *Poverty, by America*. New York: Crown Publishing Group.

Diekmann, Andreas and Peter Mitter. 1984. "A Comparison of the 'Sickle Function' with Alternative Stochastic Models of Divorce Rates." Pp. 123–53 in A. Diekmann and P. Mitter *Stochastic Modeling of Social Processes*. Orlando, FL: Academic Press.

Dorius, Cassandra. 2012. "Measuring Maternal Multi-partnered Fertility with the NLSY79." Paper presented at the annual meeting of the American Sociological Association, Denver, CO.

Dorman, Joseph and Toby Perl Freilich. 2018. *Moynihan*. First Run Features. 1 hr., 45 min. Available at https://www.amazon.com/Moynihan-Daniel-Patrick/dp/B07TLFQ749/ref=sr_1_1?crid=I3ZFBCLI4UKO&keywords=moynihan+documentary&qid=1702098308&sprefix=moynihan+documentary%2Caps%2C135&sr=8-1. (accessed 12/8/2023)

Downey, Douglas B. 2020. *How Schools Really Matter: Why Our Assumption about Schools and Inequality is Mostly Wrong*. Chicago: University of Chicago Press.

Dronkers, Jaap. 2015. "The Changing Impact of Education on Divorce and Break-Up Risk." Institute for Family Studies. Available at https://www.researchgate.net/publication/353057709_Publishing_and_Parenting_in_Academic_Science_A_Study_of_Different_National_Contexts. (accessed 7/15/21)

Duncan, Greg, Martha S. Hill, and Saul D. Hoffman. 1988. "Welfare Dependence within and across Generations." *Science* 239 (4839): 467–471.

Duncan, Greg, Kathleen M. Ziol-Guest, and Ariel Kalil. 2010. "Early-Childhood Poverty and Adult Attainment, Behavior and Health." *Child Development* 81 (1): 306–325.

Duncan, Greg, W. Jean Yeung, Jeanne Brooks-Gunn, and Judith Smith. 1988. "How Much Does Childhood Poverty Affect the Life Chances of Children?" *American Sociological Review* 63 (3): 406–423.

Duncan, Otis Dudley. 1969. "Inheritance of Poverty or Inheritance of Race?" Pp. 85–110 in Daniel P. Moynihan *On Understanding Poverty*. New York: Basic Books.

Dunifon, Rachel. 2013. "The Influence of Grandparents on the Lives of Children and Adolescents." *Child Development Perspectives* 7 (1): 55–60.

REFERENCES   229

Dunifon, Rachel and Lori Kowaleski-Jones. 2007. "The Influence of Grandparents in Single-Mother Families." *Journal of Marriage and Family* 69 (2): 465–481.

Edin, Kathryn. 2000. "What Do Low-Income Single Mothers Say about Marriage?" *Social Problems* 47: 112–133.

Edin, Kathryn and Laura Lein. 1997. *Making Ends Meet: How Single Mothers Survive Welfare and Low-Wage Work*. New York: Russell Sage Foundation.

Edin, Kathryn and Laura Lein. 1997. "Work, Welfare, and Single Mothers' Economic Survival Strategies." *American Sociological Review* 62(2): 253–266.

Edin, Kathryn and Maria Kefalas. 2005. *Promises I Can Keep: Why Poor Women Put Motherhood before Marriage*. Oakland,: University of California Press.

Edin, Kathryn and H. Luke Shaefer. 2015. *$2.00 a Day: Living on Almost Nothing in America*. Boston, MA: Houghton Mifflin Harcourt.

Edin, Kathryn J., H. Luke Shaefer, and Timothy J. Nelson. 2023. *The Injustice of Place: Uncovering the Legacy of Poverty in America*. Boston, MA: Mariner Books.

Efron, Bradley and Robert J. Tibshirani. 1994. *An Introduction to the Bootstrap*. Boca Raton, FL: CRC Press.

Eggebeen, David J. and Daniel T. Lichter. 1991. "Race, Family Structure, and Changing Poverty among American Children." *American Sociological Review* 56: 801–817.

Eika, Lasse, Magne Mogstad, and Basit Zafar. 2019. "Educational Assortative Mating and Household Income Inequality." *Journal of Political Economy* 127 (6): 2795–2835.

Ellwood, David. 2001. "Welfare Reform as I Knew It: When Bad Things Happen to Good Policies." *The American Prospect* 26 (May-June): 22–29. Available at https://prospect.org/economy/welfare-reform-knew-it-bad-things-happen-good-policies/. (accessed 6/27/21)

Ellwood, David.T. and Lawrence Summers, H. 1985. *Poverty in America: Is Welfare the Answer or the Problem?* National Bureau of Economic Research, Working paper no. 1711. Cambridge, MA: National Bureau of Economic Research.

Evans, Ann and Edith Gray. 2021. "Cross National Differences in Income Pooling among Married and Cohabiting Couples." *Journal of Marriage and Family* 83 (2): 534–550.

Fagan, Patrick F., Robert W. Patterson, and Robert E. Rector. 2022. "Marriage and Welfare Reform: The Overwhelming Evidence that Marriage Education Works." The Heritage Foundation Backgrounder 1606, October 25: 1–14. Available at http://www.heritage.org/research/reports/2002/10/marriage-and-welfare-reform. (accessed 9/2/12)

Farley, Reynolds. 1996. *The New American Reality*. NY: Russell Sage Foundation.

Federal Forum on Child and Family Statistics. 2004. "America's Children Key National Indicators of Well-Being 2004." ChildStats.gov. https://www.childstats.gov/pdf/ac2004/ac_04.pdf. (accessed 2/20/22)

Federal Reserve Bank of St. Louis. 2023. "Gini Index for the United States." Available at https://fred.stlouisfed.org/series/SIPOVGINIUSA. (accessed 12/25/2023)

Fields, Jason and Lynne M. Casper. 2001. *America's Families and Living Arrangements: March 2000*. Current Population Reports, 20–537. Washington, DC: United States Census Bureau.

Fischer, Claude S. and Michael Hout. 2006. *Century of Difference: How America Changed in the Last One Hundred Years*. New York: Russell Sage Press.

Fletcher, Jason M. and Barbara L. Wolfe. 2009. "Education and Labor Market Consequences of Teenage Childbearing Evidence Using the Timing of Pregnancy Outcomes and Community Fixed Effects." *Journal of Human Resources* 44 (2): 303–325.

Foroohar, Rana. 2016. *Makers and Takers: How Wall Street Destroyed Main Street*. Crown Currency. New York.

Fortin, Nicole M. and Thomas Lemieux. 1998. "Rank regressions, wage distributions, and the gender gap." *Journal of Human Resources* 33 (3): 610–643.

Foster, E. Michael, Damon Jones, and Saul D. Hoffman. 1997. "Non-Marital Births and Single Mothers: Cohort Trends in the Dynamics of Non-Marital Childbearing." *The History of the Family* 2: 255–275.

230 REFERENCES

Foster, E. Michael, Damon Jones, and Saul D. Hoffman. 1998. "The Economic Impact of Nonmarital Childbearing: How are Older, Single Mothers Faring?" *Journal of Marriage and the Family* 60: 163–174.

Frank, Robert H. 2007. *Falling Behind: How Rising Inequality Harms the Middle Class*. Berkeley: University of California Press.

Fremstad, Shawn. 2016. "Partnered but Poor." Center for American Progress. Available at https://www.americanprogress.org/issues/poverty/reports/2016/03/11/131968/partne red-but-poor/. (accessed 6/27/21)

Fremstad, Shawn. 2013. "TANF and Two-Parent Families." Institute for Family Studies. Available at https://ifstudies.org/blog/tanf-and-two-parent-families.

Fremstad, Shawn, Sarah Jane Glynn and Angelo Williams. 2019. "The Case Against Marriage Fundamentalism: Embracing Family Justice For All." *Family Story*. Available at https://fam ilystoryproject.org/case-against-marriage-fundamentalism/. (accessed 2/17/2022)

Frum, David. 2008. *How We Got Here: The 70's: The Decade That Brought You Modern Life (for Better or Worse)*. New York: Basic Books.

Fry, Richard and D. Cohn. 2011. "Living Together: The Economics of Cohabitation." Pew Research Center. Available at https://www.pewsocialtrends.org/2011/06/27/living-toget her-the-economics-of-cohabitation/.

Fu, Vincent K. and Nicholas H. Wolfinger. 2011. "Broken Boundaries or Broken Marriages? Racial Intermarriage and Divorce." *Social Science Quarterly* 92: 1096–1117.

Gallup Poll. 2023. "Marriage." https://news.gallup.com/poll/117328/Marriage.aspx. (accessed 12/25/23)

Gans, Herbert. 2011. "The Moynihan Report and Its Aftermaths: A Critical Analysis." *Du Bois Review* 8 (2): 315–327.

Gao, George and Gretchen Livingston. 2015. "Working while Pregnant Is Much More Common than It Used to Be." Pew Research Center. Available at https://www.pewresea rch.org/fact-tank/2015/03/31/working-while-pregnant-is-much-more-common-than-it-used-to-be/. (accessed 1/25/22)

Garfinkel, Irwin and Sara S. McLanahan. 1986. *Single Mothers and Their Children: A New American Dilemma*. Washington, DC: The Urban Institute Press.

Garfinkel, Irwin, Chien-Chung Huang, Sara S. McLanahan, and Daniel S. Gaylin. 2003. The Roles of Child Support Enforcement and Welfare in Non-Marital Childbearing. *Journal of Population Economics*. 16 (1): 55–70.

Geary, Daniel. 2015. "The Moynihan Report: An Annotated Edition." *The Atlantic*, September 14. Available at https://www.theatlantic.com/politics/archive/2015/09/the-moynihan-rep ort-an-annotated-edition/404632/. (accessed 7/5/2022)

Georgetown Public Policy Institute. 2013. "Recovery: Job Growth and Education Requirements through 2020." Available at https://1gyhoq479ufd3yna29x7ubjn-wpengine.netdna-ssl.com/ wp-content/uploads/2014/11/Recovery2020.FR_.Web_.pdf. (accessed 3/16/22)

Geronimus, Arline T. and Sanders Korenman. 1992. "The Socioeconomic Consequences of Teen Childbearing Reconsidered." *Quarterly Journal of Economics* 107: 1187–1214.

Gihleb, Rania and Kevin Lang. 2016. " Educational Homogamy and Assortative Nating Have Not Increased." National Bureau of Economic Research, Working paper 22927. Available at https:// www.nber.org/system/files/working_papers/w22927/w22927.pdf. (accessed 3/18/22)

Gilens, Martin. 1995. "Racial Attitudes and Opposition to Welfare." *The Journal of Politics* 57 (4): 994–1014.

Gitis, Ben and Curtis Arndt. 2016. "The 20th Anniversary of Welfare Reform." American Action Forum, August 22. Available at https://www.americanactionforum.org/insight/ 20th-anniversary-welfare-reform/ (accessed 12/10/23).

Glenn, Norval D. 1997. "A Reconsideration of the Effect of No-Fault Divorce on Divorce Rates." *Journal of Marriage and the Family*. 59 (4): 1026–1030.

Glynn, Sarah Jane. 2016. "Breadwinning Mothers Are Increasingly the Norm." Center for American Progress. Available at https://www.americanprogress.org/issues/women/repo

REFERENCES 231

rts/2016/12/19/295203/breadwinning-mothers-are-increasingly-the-u-s-norm/. (accessed 1/31/22)

Goldin, Claudia. 2006. "Working it Out." *The New York Times*, March 15.

Goldstein, Joshua R. 1999. "The Leveling of Divorce in the United States." *Demography* 36: 409–414.

Goldstein, Joshua R. and Catherine T. Kenney. 2001. "Marriage Delayed or Marriage Foregone? New Cohort Forecasts of First Marriage for U.S. Women." *American Sociological Review* 66: 506–519.

González, Libertad. 2007. "The Effect of Benefits on Single Motherhood in Europe." *Labour Economics* 14 (3): 393–412.

Gordon, Linda. 1994. *Pitied but Not Entitled: Single Mothers and the History of Welfare, 1890–1935*. New York: Free Press.

Gorman, Kathleen L. 2010-2023. "Civil War Pensions." Virginia Center for Civil War Studies at Virginia Tech. Available at https://www.essentialcivilwarcurriculum.com/civil-war-pensions.html. (accessed 7/9/21)

Grall, Timothy 2006. *Custodial Mothers and Fathers and Their Child Support: 2003*. Current Population Reports, P60–230. Washington, DC: United States Census Bureau. Available at https://www2.census.gov/library/publications/2006/demo/p60-230.pdf. (accessed 12/8/23)

Grall, Timothy and Liza C. Valle. 2021. *The Regular Receipt of Child Support: 2017*. Current Population Reports, P70–176. Washington, DC:, United States Census Bureau. Available at https://www.census.gov/content/dam/Census/library/publications/2022/demo/p70-176.pdf (accessed 12/8/23)

Grall, Timothy. 2018. *Custodial Mothers and Fathers and Their Child Support: 2015*. Current Population Reports, 60–262. Washington, DC: United States Census Bureau. Available at https://www.census.gov/library/publications/2018/demo/p60-262.html. (accessed 8/19/21)

Grall, Timothy. 2020. *Custodial Mothers and Fathers and Their Child Support: 2017*. Current Population Reports, 60–269. Washington, DC: United States Census Bureau. Available at https://www.census.gov/content/dam/Census/library/publications/2020/demo/p60-269.pdf. (accessed 3/24/22)

Greene, Jay P. and Marcus A. Winters. 2005. *Public High School Graduation and College-Readiness Rates: 1991–2002*. Education working paper no. 8. Washington, DC: Manhattan Institute. Available at https://docs.gatesfoundation.org/documents/manhattaninstitute0502.pdf. (accessed 7/15/ 21)

Grogger, Jeffrey. 2003. "The Effects of Time Limits, the EITC, and Other Policy Changes on Welfare Use, Work, and Income among Female-Headed Families." *Review of Economics and statistics* 85 (2): 394–408.

Grogger, Jeff T. and Stephen Bronars. 1993. "The Socioeconomic Consequences of Teenage Childbearing: Findings from a Natural Experiment." *Family Planning Perspectives* 25 (4): 156–161, 174.

Grogger, Jeffrey T. and Lynn A. Karoly. 2005. *Welfare Reform: Effects of a Decade of Change*. Cambridge, MA: Harvard University Press.

Gruber, Jonathan. 2004. "Is Making Divorce Easier Bad for Children? The Long-Run Implications of Unilateral Divorce." *Journal of Labor Economics* 22 (4): 799–833.

Guo, Guang. 1998. "The Timing of the Influence of Cumulative Poverty on Children's Cognitive Ability and Achievement. *Social Forces* 77: 257–287.

Gurrentz, Benjamin. 2018. *Living with an Unmarried Partner Now Common for Young Adults*. United States Census Bureau. Available at https://www.census.gov/library/stories/2018/11/cohabitation-is-up-marriage-is-down-for-young-adults.html. (accessed 7/17/21)

Guzzo, Karen B. and Krista K. Payne. 2018. "Average Age at First Birth, 1970–2017." *Family Profiles, FP-18* 25. Bowling Green, OH: National Center for Family & Marriage Research, Bowling Green State University. Available at https://www.bgsu.edu/ncfmr/resources/data/family-profiles/guzzo-payne-age-first-birth-fp-18-25.html. (accessed 7/13/21)

232 REFERENCES

Hacker, Jacob S. and Paul Pierson. 2010. *Winner-take-all Politics: How Washington Made the Rich Richer—and Turned its Back on the Middle Class*. New York: Simon and Schuster.

Hakovirta, Mia, Daniel R. Meyer, and Christine Skinner. 2019. "Does Paying Child Support Impoverish Fathers in the United States, Finland, and the United Kingdom?" *Children and Youth Services Review* 106: 104485.

Hamplová, Dana and Celine Le Bourdais. 2009. "One Pot or Two Pot Strategies? Income Pooling in Married and Unmarried Households in Comparative Perspective." *Journal of Comparative Family Studies* 40 (3): 355–385.

Hamplová, Dana, Céline Le Bourdais, and Évelyne Lapierre-Adamcyk. 2014. "Is the Cohabitation–Marriage Gap in Money Pooling Universal?" *Journal of Marriage and Family* 76 (5): 983–997.

Han, Jeehoon, Bruce D. Meyer, and James X. Sullivan. 2021. "The Consumption, Income, and Well-Being of Single Mother Headed Families 25 Years After Welfare Reform." Unpublished paper. Available at https://voices.uchicago.edu/brucemeyer/files/2017/05/Han_Meyer_S ullivan_NTJ_text_v2.5.pdf. (accessed 9/4/21)

Haney-Lopez, Ian. 2014. "The Racism at the Heart of the Reagan Presidency." *Salon*, January. Available at https://www.salon.com/2014/01/11/the_racism_at_the_heart_of_the_reagan _presidency/.(accessed 7/8/21)

Harkness, Susan. 2022. "Single Mothers' Income in Twelve Rich Countries: Differences in Disadvantage across the Distribution." *The Annals of the American Academy of Political and Social Science* 702 (1): 164–187.

Hauser, Robert M. and John Robert Warren. 1997. "Socioeconomic Indexes for Occupations: A Review, Update, and Critique." Pp. 177–298 in A. E. Raftery *Sociological Methodology 1997*. Washington, DC: The American Sociological Association.

Hausman, Jerry A. 1978. "Specification Tests in Econometrics." *Econometrica: Journal of the Econometric Society* 46 (6): 1251–1271.

Haveman, Robert and Barbara Wolfe. 1995. "The Determinants of Children's Attainments: A Review of Methods and Findings." *Journal of Economic Literature* 33 (4): 1829–1878.

Heckman, James J. and George J. Borjas. 1980. "Does Unemployment Cause Future Unemployment? Definitions, Questions and Answers from a Continuous Time Model of Heterogeneity and State Dependence." *Economica* 47: 247–283.

Henwood, Doug. 2019. "Modern Monetary Theory Isn't Helping." *Jacobin*, February 2. Available at https://jacobin.com/2019/02/modern-monetary-theory-isnt-helping. (accessed 12/10/23)

Hertz, Rosanna. 2006. *Single by Chance, Mothers by Choice: How Women Are Choosing Parenthood without Marriage and Creating The New American Family*. New York: Oxford University Press.

Hoffman, Saul D. 1998. "Teenage Childbearing Is Not So Bad After All … Or Is It? A Review of the New Literature." *Family Planning Perspectives* 30: 236–239, 243.

Hoffman, Saul D., E. Michael Foster, and Frank F. Furstenberg, Jr. 1993. "Reevaluating the Costs of Teenage Childbearing." *Demography* 30: 1–13.

Hoffman, Saul D. and E. Michael Foster. 1997. "Non-Marital Births and Single Mothers: Cohort Trends in the Dynamics of Non-Marital Childbearing." *The History of the Family* 2: 255–275

Hogendoorn, Bran and Juho Härkönen. 2023. "Single Motherhood and Multigenerational Coresidence in Europe." *Population and Development Review* 49 (1): 105–133.

Holbrook, Evans. 1910. "Divorce Laws and the Increase of Divorce." *Michigan Law Review* 8: 386–395. Available at https://repository.law.umich.edu/cgi/viewcontent.cgi?article= 2093&context=articles.

Hotz, V. Joseph, McElroy, Susan Williams, and Seth G. Sanders. 2002. "Teenage Childbearing and Its Life Cycle Consequences: Exploiting a Very Natural Experiment." *Journal of Human Resources* 40: 683–715.

Hotz, V. Joseph, Susan, Williams McElroy, and Seth G. Sanders, 1995. "The Costs and Consequences of Teenage Childbearing for Mothers." Working Papers 9501, Harris School of Public Policy Studies, University of Chicago.

REFERENCES 233

Hotz, V. Joseph, Charles H. Mullin, and Seth G. Sanders. 1997. "Bounding Causal Effects Using Data from a Contaminated Natural Experiment: Analysing the Effects of Teenage Childbearing." *The Review of Economic Studies* 64 (4): 575–603.

Hout, Michael. 1984. "Status, Autonomy, and Training in Occupational Mobility." *The American Journal of Sociology* 89: 1379–1409.

Hymowitz, Kay S. 2005. "The Black Family: 40 Years of Lies." *City Journal.* Available at https://www.city-journal.org/html/black-family-40-years-lies-12872.html. (accessed 7/18/21)

Institute for American Values and The National Marriage Project. 2010. *When Marriage Disappears:The New Middle America.* The State of Our Unions: Marriage in America. Available at http://www.virginia.edu/marriageproject/pdfs/Union_11_12_10.pdf. (accessed 2/13/12)

International Monetary Fund, n.d. "Policy Responses to COVID-19: Policy Tracker." Washington, DC. Available at https://www.imf.org/en/Topics/imf-and-covid19/Policy-Responses-to-COVID-19. (accessed 10/18/23)

Jacoby, William G. 2000. "Issue Framing and Public Opinion on Government Spending." *American Journal of Political Science* 44 (4): 750–767.

Jansson, Bruce S. 1992. *The Reluctant Welfare State: A History of American Social Welfare Policies,* 2nd ed. Belmont, CA: Wadsworth.

Jekielek, Susan M 1998. "Parental Conflict, Marital Disruption and Children's Emotional Well-being." *Social Forces* 76 (3): 905–936.

Joint Economic Committee. 2020. "Improving Family Stability for the Well Being of American Children." Hearing before the Joint Economic Committee, Congress of the United States, 2020, 2. Available at https://www.govinfo.gov/content/pkg/CHRG-116jhrg40561/pdf/CHRG-116jhrg40561.pdf. (accessed 2/2/22)

Kaminer, Wendy. 2003. "The First Amendment Is for Fortune-tellers, Too." Free Inquiry. Available at https://secularhumanism.org/2003/06/the-first-amendment-is-for-fortune-tellers-too/. (accessed 12/29/21)

Kane, Jennifer B., Timothy J. Nelson, and Kathryn Edin. 2015. "How Much In-Kind Support Do Low-Income Nonresident Fathers Provide? A Mixed-Method Analysis." *Journal of Marriage and Family* 77 (3): 591–611.

Kaplan, Greg. 2009. "Boomerang Kids: Labor Market Dynamics and Moving Back Home." *Federal Reserve Bank of Minneapolis.* Working paper 675.

Karoly, Lynn. 1993. "The Trend in Inequality among Families, Individuals, and Workers in the United States: A Twenty-Five Year Perspective." Pp. 19–97 in S. Danziger and P. Gottschalk *Uneven Tides.* New York: Russell Sage.

Karpowitz, Christopher F. and Jeremy C. Pope. 2018. The American Family Survey. https://media.deseret.com/media/misc/pdf/afs/2018-AFS-Final-Report.pdf. (accessed 12/9/23)

Kearney, Melissa S. 2023. *The Two-Parent Privilege: How the Decline in Marriage Has Increased Inequality and Lowered Social Mobility, and What We Can Do about It.* Rugby, UK: Swift Press.

Kennedy, Bruce P., Ichiro Kawachi, Roberta Glass, and Deborah Prothrow-Stith. 1998. "Income Distribution, Socioeconomic Status, and Self Rated Health in the United States: Multilevel Analysis." *British Medical Journal* 317 (7163): 917–921.

Kerner, Otto, et al. 1968. *Report of the National Advisory Commission on Civil Disorders.* Washington, DC: United States Government Printing Office. Available at https://belonging.berkeley.edu/sites/default/files/kerner_commission_full_report.pdf?file=1&force=1.

Kiker, B. F. and C. M. Condon. 1981. "The Influence of Socioeconomic Background on the Earnings of Young Men." *The Journal of Human Resources* 16 (1): 94–105.

Kimberlin, Sara Elizabeth. 2013. *Metrics Matter: Examining Chronic and Transient Poverty in the United States Using the Supplemental Poverty Measure.* Doctoral dissertation University of California, Berkeley. Available at https://www.proquest.com/docview/1441350234?pqo rigsite=gscholar&fromopenview=true. (accessed 4/18/22).

Kitagawa, Evelyn M. 1955. "Components of a Difference Between Two Rates." *Journal of the American Statistical Association.* 50 (272): 1168–1194.

234 REFERENCES

Kohlman, Marla H. 2006. "Intersection Theory: A More Elucidating Paradigm of Quantitative Analysis." *Race Gender & Class* 13 (3–4): 42–59.

Korenman, Sanders and Jane E. Miller. 1997. "Effects of Long-Term Poverty on Physical Health of Children in the National Longitudinal Survey of Youth." Pp. 70–99 in Greg Duncan and Jeanne Brooks-Gunn *Consequences of Growing Up Poor*. New York: Russell Sage Press.

Kramer, Stephanie. 2019. "U.S. Has World's Highest Rate of Children Living in Single-Parent Households." Washington, DC: Pew Research. Available at https://www.pewresearch.org/short-reads/2019/12/12/u-s-children-more-likely-than-children-in-other-countries-to-live-with-just-one-parent/. (accessed 11/3/23).

Kreider, Rose M. and Jason M. Fields. 2001. *Number, Timing, and Duration of Marriages and Divorces: Fall 1996*. Current Population Reports, 70–80. Washington, DC: United States Census Bureau.

Kuhn, Thomas. 1962. *The Structure of Scientific Revolutions* as of 2023. Chicago: University of Chicago Press.

Kymlicka, B. B. and Jean V. Matthews. 1988. *The Reagan Revolution?* Chicago: Dorsey Press.

Labrecque, Jeremy and Sonja A. Swanson. 2018. "Understanding the Assumptions Underlying Instrumental Variable Analyses: A Brief Review of Falsification Strategies and Related Tools." *Current epidemiology reports* 5: 214–20. Available at https://www.ncbi.nlm.nih.gov/pmc/articles/PMC6096851/. (accessed 10/20/23).

Lamidi, Esther. 2016. A Quarter Century of Change in Nonmarital Births. Family Profiles, FP-16-03. Bowling Green, OH: National Center for Family and Marriage Research. Available at https://www.bgsu.edu/content/dam/BGSU/college-of-arts-and-sciences/NCFMR/documents/FP/lamidi-nonmarital-births-fp-16-03.pdf.

Lamidi, Esther and Wendy D. Manning. 2016. "FP-16-17 Marriage and Cohabitation Experiences Among Young Adults." *National Center for Family and Marriage Research Family Profiles 60*. Available at https://scholarworks.bgsu.edu/ncfmr_family_profiles/60.

Lang, Kevin and Russell Weinstein. 2015. "The Consequences of Teenage Childbearing before Roe v. Wade." *American Economic Journal: Applied Economics* 7 (4): 169–197.

Lekachman, Robert. 1982. *Greed is Not Enough*. New York: Pantheon Books.

Leonhardt, David. 2023. *Ours Was the Shining Future: The Story of the American Dream*. New York: Random House.

Lepore, Jill. 2018. *These Truths: A History of the United States*. New York: Norton.

Levine, Adam Seth, Robert H. Frank, and Oege Dijk. 2010. "Expenditure Cascades." *Social Science Research Network*. Working paper. Available at http://ssrn.com/abstract=1690612 (accessed 8/15/11).

Lichter, Daniel T. and Deborah Roempke Graefe. 2001. "Finding a Mate? The Marital and Cohabitation Histories of Unwed Mothers." Pp. 317–343 in Lawrence L. Wu and Barbara Wolfe *Out of Wedlock: Causes and Consequences of Nonmarital Fertility*. New York: Russell Sage Foundation.

Lichter, Daniel T., Deborah Roempke Graefe, and J. Brian Brown. 2003. "Is Marriage a Panacea? Union Formation Among Economically Disadvantaged Unwed Mothers." *Social Problems* 50: 60–86.

Lichter, Daniel T., Felicia B. LeClere, and Diane K. McLaughlin. 1991. "Local Marriage Markets and the Marital Behavior of Black and White Women." *American Journal of Sociology* 96 (4): 843–867.

Lichter, Daniel T., Diane K. McLaughlin, George Kephart, and David J. Landry. 1992. "Race and the Retreat from Marriage: A Shortage of Marriageable Men?" *American Sociological Review* 57 (6): 781–799.

Lino, Mark, Kevin Kuczynski, Nestor Rodriguez, and TusaRebecca Schap. 2017. "Expenditures on Children by Families, 2015." Miscellaneous Publication No. 1528–2015. U.S. Department of Agriculture, Center for Nutrition Policy and Promotion. Available at https://cdn2.hubspot.net/hubfs/10700/blog-files/USDA_Expenditures%20on%20children%20by%20family.pdf?t=1520090048492. (accessed 5/21/22).

REFERENCES   235

Lipman, Ellen Louise, David Offord, and Michael H. Boyle. 1994. "Economic Disadvantage and Child Psychosocial Morbidity." *Canadian Medical Association Journal* 151: 431–437.

Livingston, Gretchen. 2018. "The Changing Profile of Unmarried Parents." Pew Research Center. Available at https://www.pewsocialtrends.org/2018/04/25/the-changing-profile-of-unmarried-parents/ (accessed 12/26/20).

Livingstone, Gretchen. 2014. "The Demographics of Remarriage." Pew Research Center. Available at https://www.pewresearch.org/social-trends/2014/11/14/chapter-2-the-demog raphics-of-remarriage/ (accessed 7/19/21).

Livingston, Gretchen and Deja Thomas. 2019. "Why is the Teen Birth Rate Falling?" Pew Research Center. Available at https://www.pewresearch.org/fact-tank/2019/08/02/why-is-the-teen-birth-rate-falling/ (accessed 7/12/21).

Lowrey, Annie. 2018. *Give People Money: How a Universal Basic Income Would End Poverty, Revolutionize Work, and Remake the World.* Portland, OR: Broadway Books.

MacGregor, Carol Ann. 2010. "Education Delayed: Family Structure and Postnatal Educational Attainment." Fragile Families. Working paper 09-07-FF. Available at https://ffcws.princeton. edu/sites/g/files/toruqf4356/files/documents/wp09-07-ff.pdf (accessed 10/20/23).

Mahar, Maggie. 2009. *Bull!: A History of the Boom and Bust, 1982–2004.* New York: HarperCollins.

Makidis, Theonie. 2018. "Race, the Incarcerated Father, and Child Support Obligations." *The Federal Lawyer* (September): 42–54. Available at https://www.fedbar.org/wp-content/uplo ads/2018/09/Makidis-pdf-1.pdf (accessed 3/24/22).

Maldonado, Solangel. 2005. "Deadbeat or Deadbroke: Redefining Child Support for Poor Fathers." *University of California Davis Law Review* 39: 991–1022.

Manning, Wendy. D., Susan L. Brown, Krista K. Payne, and Hsueh-Sheng Wu. 2014. "Healthy Marriage Initiative Spending and U.S. Marriage & Divorce Rates, A State-level Analysis (FP-14-02)." National Center for Family & Marriage Research. Available at http://www.bgsu. edu/content/dam/BGSU/college-of-arts-and-sciences/NCFMR/documents/FP/FP-14-02_HMIInitiative.pdf (accessed 7/9/21).

Manning, Wendy D. and Pamela J. Smock. 2005. "Measuring and Modeling Cohabitation: New Perspectives from Qualitative Data." *Journal of Marriage and Family* 67 (4): 989–1002.

Mare, Robert D. 1991. "Five Decades of Educational Assortative Mating." *American Sociological Review* 56: 15–32.

Martin, Joyce A., Brady E. Hamilton, Michele J. K. Osterman, and Anne K. Driscoll. 2018. "Births: Final Data for 2017." National Vital Statistics Reports 67 (8). Hyattsville, MD: National Center for Health Statistics. Available at https://www.cdc.gov/nchs/data/ nvsr/nvsr67/nvsr67_08-508.pdf (accessed 12/23/20).

Martin, Joyce A., Brady E. Hamilton, Michele J. K. Osterman, and Anne K. Driscoll. 2019 "Births: Final Data for 2018." National Vital Statistics Reports; vol 68, no 13. Hyattsville, MD: National Center for Health Statistics. Available at https://www.cdc.gov/nchs/data/ nvsr/nvsr68/nvsr68_13-508.pdf.

Martin, Joyce A., Brady E. Hamilton, Michele J. K. Osterman, and Anne K. Driscoll. 2021. "Births: Final Data for 2019." National Vital Statistics Reports; vol 70 no 2. Hyattsville, MD: National Center for Health Statistics. Available at https://www.cdc.gov/nchs/data/ nvsr/nvsr70/nvsr70-02-508.pdf (accessed 7/19/21).

Martin, Molly A. 2006. "Family Structure and Income Inequality in Families with Children, 1976 to 2000." *Demography* 43 (3): 421–445.

Martin, Steven P., Astone, Nan Marie, and H. Elizabeth Peters. 2014. "Fewer Marriages, More Divergence: Marriage Projections for Millennials to Age 40." Urban Institute. Available at https://www.urban.org/research/publication/fewer-marriages-more-divergence-marri age-projections-millennials-age-40 (accessed 7/15/21).

Martin, Teresa Castro and Larry L. Bumpass. 1989. "Recent Trends in Marital Disruption." *Demography* 26 (1): 37–51.

Martinson, Brian C. 1994. "Postmarital Union Formation: Trends and Determinants of the Competing Roles of Remarriage and Nonmarital Cohabitation among Women in the

236 REFERENCES

United States." Unpublished doctoral dissertation. Department of Sociology, University of Wisconsin-Madison.

Mason, Mary Ann. 1994. *From Father's Property to Children's Rights: The History of Child Custody in the United States.* New York: Columbia University Press.

Mason, Mary Ann, Sydney Harrison-Jay, Gloria Messick Svare, and Nicholas H. Wolfinger. 2002. "Stepparents: De Facto Parents or Legal Strangers?" *Journal of Family Issues* 23 (4): 507–522.

Massey, Douglas S. and Robert J. Sampson. 2009. "Moynihan Redux: Legacies and Lessons." *The Annals of the American Academy of Political and Social Science* 621 (1): 6–27.

Mather, Mark, Paola Scommegna, and Lillian Kilduff. 2016. "Fact Sheet: Aging in the United States." *Population Reference Bureau* 13. Available at https://www.prb.org/resources/fact-sheet-aging-in-the-united-states/ (accessed 2/15/2022).

Matthews, Dylan. 2019. "Mitt Romney and Michael Bennet Just Unveiled a Basic Income Plan for Kids." *Vox,* December 16. Available at https://www.vox.com/future-perfect/2019/12/16/21024222/mitt-romney-michael-bennet-basic-income-kids-child-allowance (accessed 4/3/22).

McDermott, Rose, James H. Fowler, and Nicholas A. Christakis. 2013. "Breaking Up Is Hard to Do, Unless Everyone Else Is Doing It Too: Social Network Effects on Divorce in a Longitudinal Sample." *Social Forces* 92 (2): 491–519.

McElrath, Kevin and Michael Martin 2021. *Bachelor's Degree Attainment in the United States: 2005 to 2019.* American Community Survey Briefs, ACSBR-009. Washington, DC: United States Census Bureau. Available at https://www.census.gov/content/dam/Census/library/publications/2021/acs/acsbr-009.pdf (accessed 11/27/23).

McFalls, Joseph A. Jr. 2023. "What's a Household? What's a Family?" Population Reference Bureau. Available at https://www.prb.org/resources/whats-a-household-whats-a-family/#:~:text=Under%20the%20U.S.%20Census%20Bureau,their%20residence%20with%20unrelated%20individuals (accessed 12/11/23).

McKeever, Matthew and Nicholas H. Wolfinger. 2001. "Reexamining the Economic Consequences of Marital Disruption for Women." *Social Science Quarterly* 82: 202–217.

McKeever, Matthew and Nicholas H. Wolfinger. 2006. "Shifting Fortunes in a Changing Economy: Trends in the Economic Well-Being of Divorced Women." Pp. 127–157 in L. Kowaleski-Jones and N. H. Wolfinger *Fragile Families and the Marriage Agenda.* New York: Springer.

McKeever, Matthew and Nicholas H. Wolfinger. 2011. "Thanks for Nothing: Income and Labor Force Participation for Never-married Mothers since 1982." *Social Science Research* 40: 63–76.

McKeever, Matthew and Nicholas H. Wolfinger. 2012. "Over the Long Haul: The Persistent Economic Consequences of Single Motherhood." Pp. 1–39 in S. L. Blair *Economic Stress and the Famil.* Bingley, UK: Emerald Publishing.

McKeever, Matthew and Nicholas H. Wolfinger. 2023. "Economic Inequality and Single-Parent Families." Paper presented at the 2023 annual meeting of the American Sociological Association, Philadelphia.

McLanahan, Sara. 2006. "Fragile Families and the Marriage Agenda." Pp. 1–21 in L. Kowaleski-Jones and N. H. Wolfinger *Fragile Families and the Marriage Agenda.* New York: Springer.

McLanahan, Sara and Christine Percheski. 2008. "Family Structure and the Reproduction of Inequalities." *Annual Review of Sociology* 34: 257–276.

McLanahan, Sara and Christopher Jenks. 2015. "Was Moynihan Right? What Happens to Children of Unmarried Mothers." *Education Next* 15 (2): 14–21. Available at https://go.gale.com/ps/i.do?id=GALE%7CA408917747&sid=googleScholar&v=2.1&it=r&linkaccess=fulltext&issn=15399664&p=AONE&sw=w&casa_token=RRS6a6sKFy4AAAAA:ceUtkm8BDfLP2vK7H0XNsqTlu0lB7TBdgez3UXJXmpKNhMUJyVDLdnWoTq5YHdMKgGaUGtfo9ixPE-ExoA. (accessed 5/15/22).

McLanahan, Sara S. and Gary Sandefur. 1994. *Growing Up with a Single Parent: What Hurts, What Helps.* Cambridge, MA: Harvard University Press.

REFERENCES   237

McLanahan, Sara, Irwin Garfinkel, and Ronald B. Mincy. 2001. "Fragile Families, Welfare Reform, and Marriage." Welfare Reform and Beyond: Policy Brief No. 10. Washington, DC: Brookings Institution.

McLoyd, Vonnie C. 1998 "Socioeconomic Disadvantage and Child Development." *American Psychologist* 53: 185–204.

Mead, Lawrence M. 2020. "Poverty and Culture." *Academic Questions* 34 (1): 101–111. New York: National Association of Scholars. Available at https://www.nas.org/academic-questions/34/1/poverty-and-culture. (accessed 3/29/22)

Mead, Lawrence M. 1992. *The Nonworking Poor in America.* New York: Basic Books.

Meadows, Sarah O., Sara McLanahan, and Jean T. Knab. 2009. "Economic Trajectories in Non-traditional Families with Children." Fragile Families. Working paper WP09-10-FF. Available at https://ffcws.princeton.edu/sites/g/files/toruqf4356/files/documents/wp09-10-ff.pdf. (accessed 10/20/23)

Mernitz, Sara. 2018. A Cohort Comparison of Trends in First Cohabitation Duration in the United States. *Demographic Research* 38 (66): 2073–2086. Available at https://www.demographic-research.org/volumes/vol38/66/. (accessed 7/18/21)

Meyer, Bruce D. and Dan T. Rosenbaum. 2001. "Welfare, the Earned Income Tax Credit, and the Labor Supply of Single Mothers." *The Quarterly Journal of Economics* 116: 1063–1114.

Meyer, Bruce D. and James X. Sullivan. 2008. "Changes in the Consumption, Income, and Well-being of Single Mother Headed Families." *The American Economic Review* 98: 2221–2241.

Miller, Brent C., Sage, Rayna A., and Bryan Winward. 2005. "Teen Childbearing and Public Policy." Pp. 47–72 in L. Kowaleski-Jones and N. H. Wolfinger *Fragile Families and the Marriage Agenda.* New York: Springer.

Mills, Curt. 2018. "U.S. Still Paying a Civil War Pension." *U.S. News and World Report* August 8. Available at https://www.usnews.com/news/articles/2016-08-08/civil-war-vets-pension-still-remains-on-governments-payroll-151-years-after-last-shot-fired#:~:text=Since%20the%20Civil%20War's%20conclusion,in%201914%20among%20European%20parties. (accessed 5/1/2024)

Minnesota Department of National Resources. N.d. "Commercial Frog Licenses." Available at https://www.dnr.state.mn.us/fishing/commercial/frogs.html. (accessed 12/29/21)

Moffitt, Robert A. 1992. Incentive Effects of the U.S. Welfare System: A Review. *Journal of Economic Literature* 30 (1): 1–61.

Moffitt, Robert A. and Stephanie Garlow. 2018. "Did Welfare Reform Increase Employment and Reduce Poverty?." *Pathways* 2018 (Winter): 17–21. Available at https://inequality.stanford.edu/sites/default/files/Pathways_Winter2018_Employment-Poverty.pdf. (accessed 11/2/23)

Monazzam, Niki and Kristen M. Budd. 2023. "Incarcerated Women and Girls." Fact sheet, Sentencing Project. Available at https://www.sentencingproject.org/fact-sheet/incarcerated-women-and-girls/. (accessed August 28, 2023)

Monte, Lindsay. 2017. *Multiple Partner Fertility Research Brief.* Current Population Reports, P70BR-146. Washington, DC: United States Census Bureau. Available at https://www.census.gov/content/dam/Census/library/publications/2017/demo/p70br-146.pdf. (accessed 7/8/21)

Moon, Dawne and Jaye Cee Whitehead. 2006. "Marrying for America." Pp. 23–45 in L. Kowaleski-Jones and N. H. Wolfinger *Fragile Families and the Marriage Agenda.* New York: Springer.

Morgan, Kimberly J. 2006. *Working Moms and Welfare State.* Stanford: Stanford University Press.

Morris, Martina and Bruce Western. 1999. "Inequality in Earnings at the Close of the Twentieth Century." *Annual Review of Sociology* 25: 623–657.

Morrison, Donna Ruane and Amy Ritualo. 2000. "Routes to Children's Economic Recovery after Divorce: Are Cohabitation and Remarriage Equivalent?" *American Sociological Review* 65 (4): 560–580

Moynihan, Daniel Patrick. 1986. *Family and Nation.* Harcourt Brace Jovanovich.

238 REFERENCES

Moynihan, Daniel Patrick. 1965. *The Negro Family: The Case for National Action*. Washington, DC: U.S. Department of Labor, Office of Policy Planning and Research, 1965. Available at https://www.dol.gov/general/aboutdol/history/webid-moynihan.

Moynihan, Daniel Patrick 1973. *The Politics of a Guaranteed Income: The Nixon Administration and the Family Assistance Plan*. New York: Random House.

Murray, Charles. 1984. *Losing Ground: American Social Policy, 1950–1980*. New York: Basic Books.

Murray, Charles. 2012 *Coming Apart: The State of White America, 1960–2010*. New York: Forum Books.

Musick, Kelly and Robert D. Mare. 2006. "Recent Trends in the Inheritance of Poverty and Family Structure." *Social Science Research* 35: 471–499.

Musick, Kelly and Katherine Michelmore. 2018. "Cross-National Comparisons of Union Stability in Cohabiting and Married Families with Children." *Demography* 55 (4): 1389–1421.

National Academies of Sciences, Engineering, and Medicine. 2019. *A Roadmap to Reducing Child Poverty*. Washington, DC: The National Academies Press. Available at https://www.ncbi.nlm.nih.gov/books/NBK547361/pdf/Bookshelf_NBK547361.pdf. (accessed 12/8/23)

National Conference of State Legislatures. 2013. "Postcard: Teen Pregnancy Affects Graduation Rates." Washington, DC. Available at https://www.ncsl.org/research/health/teen-pregnancy-affects-graduation-rates-postcard.aspx. (accessed 7/22/21)

National Conference of State Legislatures. N.d. "Federal EITC: What Legislators Need to Know." Washington, DC. Available at https://www.ncsl.org/print/wln/EITC.pdf. (accessed 4/7/22)

National Longitudinal Survey Program. 2011. Washington, DC: U.S. Bureau of Labor Statistics. Washington, DC. Available at http://www.bls.gov/nls/nlsy79.htm (accessed 9/27/11).

The New York Times. 1976. "'Welfare Queen' Becomes Issue in Reagan Campaign," *The New York Times*, February. Available at https://www.nytimes.com/1976/02/15/archives/welfare-queen-becomes-issue-in-reagan-campaign-hitting-a-nerve-now.html?auth=login-google1tap&login=google1tap.

Noah, Timothy. 2012. *The Great Divergence: America's Growing Inequality Crisis and What We Can Do about It*. Camden: Bloomsbury Publishing USA.

Noonan, Mary C. 2005. "The Long-Term Costs of Women's Work Interruptions." Unpublished paper, Department of Sociology, University of Iowa.

Obama, Barack. 2006. *Audacity of Hope: Thoughts on Reclaiming the American Dream*. New York: Crown Publishers.

Office of the Administration for Children & Families, Office of Family Assistance. 2021. "About Healthy Marriage & Responsible Fatherhood." U.S. Department of Health and Human Services. Available at https://www.acf.hhs.gov/ofa/programs/healthy-marriage/about. (accessed 7/9/21)

Office of the Administration for Children & Families, Office of Family Assistance. 2021. "About TANF." U.S. Department of Health and Human Services. Available at https://www.acf.hhs.gov/ofa/programs/tanf/about. (accessed 6/27/21)

Office of Economic Policy. 2016. "Non-compete Contracts: Economic Effects and Policy Implications." U.S. Department of the Treasury. Available at https://home.treasury.gov/system/files/226/Non_Compete_Contracts_Econimic_Effects_and_Policy_Implications_MAR2016.pdf. (accessed 12/29/21)

O'Neill, William L. 1967. *Divorce in the Progressive Era*. New Haven: Yale University Press.

Ono, Hiromi. 1995. "Expanding on Explanations of Recent Patterns in U.S. Divorce Rates." Unpublished doctoral dissertation, Department of Sociology, University of California Los Angeles.

Ono, Hiromi. 1998. "Husbands' and Wives' Resources and Marital Dissolution." *Journal of Marriage and Family* 60 (3): 674–689.

Osterman Michelle J. K., Brady E. Hamilton, Joyce A. Martin, Anne K. Driscoll, and Claudia P. Valenzuela. 2022. "Births: Final Data for 2020." National Vital Statistics Reports; vol 70 no

REFERENCES 239

17. Hyattsville, MD: National Center for Health Statistics. Available at https://dx.doi.org/10.15620/cdc:112078. (accessed 2/18/22)

Parker, Kim and Renee Stepler. 2017. "As U.S. Marriage Rate Hovers at 50%, Education Gap in Marital Status Widens." *Pew Research Center* 14. Available at https://www.pewresearch.org/fact-tank/2017/09/14/as-u-s-marriage-rate-hovers-at-50-education-gap-in-marital-status-widens/. (accessed 3/16/22)

Parolin, Zachary, Sophie Collyer, and Megan A. Curran. 2022. "Absence of Monthly Child Tax Credit Leads to 3.7 Million More Children in Poverty in January 2022." Center on Poverty and Social Policy Brief 6 (2), Columbia University. Available at www.povertycenter.colum bia.edu/publication/monthly-poverty-january-2022. (accessed 11/2/23)

Parolin, Zachary, Sophie Collyer, Megan A. Curran, and Christopher Wimer. 2021. "The Potential Poverty Reduction Effect of the American Rescue Plan." Center on Poverty and Social Policy, Columbia University. Available at www.povertycenter.columbia.edu/news-internal/2021/presidential-policy/bideneconomic-relief-proposal-poverty-impact. (accessed 2/15/22)

Parolin, Zachary, Matthew Desmond, and Christopher Wimer. 2023. "Inequality Below the Poverty Line since 1967: The Role of the U.S. Welfare State." *American Sociological Review* 88: 782–809.

Patterson, James T. 2010. *Freedom Is Not Enough: The Moynihan Report and America's Struggle Over Black Family Life—from LBJ to Obama*. New York: Basic Books.

Paul, Christopher, William M. Mason, Daniel McCaffrey, and Sarah A. Fox. 2008. "A Cautionary Case Study of Approaches to the Treatment of Missing Data." *Statistical Methods and Applications* 17 (3): 351–372.

Pear, Robert. 1984. "Reagan Signs Bill Forcing Payments for Child Support." *The New York Times*, August. Available at https://www.nytimes.com/1984/08/17/us/reagan-signs-bill-forcing-payments-for-child-support.html.

Pepper, John V. 2000. "The Intergenerational Transmission of Welfare Receipt: A Nonparametric Bounds Analysis." *Review of Economics and Statistics* 82 (3): 472–488.

Percheski, Christine. 2008. "Opting Out? Cohort Differences in Professional Women's Employment Rates from 1960 to 2005." *American Sociological Review* 73 (3): 497–517.

Perper, Kate, Peterson, Kristen, and Jennifer Manlove. 2010. "Diploma Attainment Among Teen Mothers. Child Trends, Fact Sheet," Publication 2010-01: Washington, DC: Child Trends. Available at https://cms.childtrends.org/wp-content/uploads/2010/01/child_tre nds-2010_01_22_FS_diplomaattainment.pdf. (accessed 7/22/21)

Peterson, Janice, Xue Song, and Avis Jones-DeWeever. 2002. "Life after Welfare Reform: Low-Income Single Parent Families, Pre- and Post-TANF." Research-in-Brief #D446. Washington, DC: Institute for Women's Policy Research. Available at http://citeseerx.ist.psu.edu/view doc/download?doi=10.1.1.15.6994&rep=rep1&type=pdf. (accessed 9/27/11).

Peterson, Richard R. 1996. "A Re-Evaluation of the Economic Consequences of Divorce." *American Sociological Review* 61: 528–536.

Pew Research Center. 2021. "The State of Gig Work in 2021." Available at https://www.pewr esearch.org/internet/2021/12/08/the-state-of-gig-work-in-2021/. (accessed 12/29/21)

Pikkety, Thomas 2014. *Capital in the 21st Century*, Cambridge MA: Harvard University Press.

Pilkauskas, Natasha V., Colin Campbell, and Christopher Wimer. 2017. "Giving unto Others: Private Financial Transfers and Hardship among Families with Children." *Journal of Marriage and Family* 79 (3): 705–722.

Pilkauskas, Natasha V., Irwin Garfinkel, and Sara McLanahan. 2013. "Doubling up As a Private Safety Net for Families with Children." Available at https://ffcws.princeton.edu/sites/g/files/toruqf4356/files/documents/wp13-13-ff.pdf. (accessed 10/19/23)

Project Censored. 2023. "States Hoard Federal Assistance Funding Amidst Record Poverty Levels." May 22, 2023.Available at https://www.projectcensored.org/20-states-hoard-fede ral-assistance-funding-amidst-record-poverty-levels/. (accessed 11/22/23)

Putnam, Robert D. 2016. *Our Kids: The American Dream in Crisis*. New York: Simon and Schuster.

240 REFERENCES

Quayle, Dan. 1992. "On Family Values." Address to the Commonwealth Club of California, May 19, 1992. Available at http://www.vicepresidentdanquayle.com/speeches_StandingFir m_CCC_1.html. (accessed 9/19/11)

Radey, Melissa and Karin Brewster. 2013. "Predictors of stability and change in private safety nets of unmarried mothers." *Journal of Social Service Research* 39 (3): 397–415.

Rainwater, Lee and William L. Yancey. 1967. *The Moynihan Report and the Politics of Controversy.* Cambridge, MA: MIT Press.

Raley, R. Kelly and Larry Bumpass. 2003 "The Topography of the Divorce Plateau: Levels and Trends in Union Stability in the United States after 1980." *Demographic Research* 8: 245–260. http://www.demographic-research.org/volumes/vol8/8/8-8.pdf. (accessed 7/15/21)

Rasoolinejad, Mohammad. 2021. "Universal Basic Income: The Last Bullet in the Darkness." Unpublished paper. Available at https://arxiv.org/pdf/1910.05658.pdf#:~:text=The%20 UBI%20is%20not%20good,makes%20the%20inflation%20problem%20worse. (accessed 4/19/22)

Ratcliffe, Caroline. 2015. "Child Poverty and Adult Success." Urban Institute. Available at https://www.urban.org/sites/default/files/publication/65766/2000369-Child-Poverty-and-Adult-Success.pdf. (accessed 3/25/22)

Rawlings, Steve W. and Arlene F. Saluter. 1994. *Household and Family Characteristics: March 1994.* Current Population Reports, 20–483. Washington, DC: United States Government Printing Office. Available at https://citeseerx.ist.psu.edu/viewdoc/download?doi= 10.1.1.204.322&rep=rep1&type=pdf. (accessed 2/18/22)

Reagan, Ronald. 1984. "Proclamation 5166—National Single Parent Day, 1984." The American Presidency Project. Available at https://www.presidency.ucsb.edu/documents/proclamat ion-5166-national-single-parent-day-1984.

Rector, Robert and Jamie Bryan Hall. 2016. "Did Welfare Reform Increase Extreme Poverty in the United States?" Heritage Foundation, Legal Memorandum #84 on Welfare and Welfare Spending. Washington, DC: Heritage Foundation. Available at https://scholar.goo gle.com/scholar?hl=en&as_sdt=0%2C5&q=Did+Welfare+Reform+Increase+Extreme+ Poverty+in+the+United+States%3F&btnG=#d=gs_cit&t=1650334465693&u=%2Fscho lar%3Fq%3Dinfo%3AzhT-aMioYIQJ%3Ascholar.google.com%2F%26output%3Dc ite%26scirp%3D0%26hl%3Den. (accessed 4/18/22)

Rector, Robert and Melissa Pardue. 2004. "Understanding the President's Healthy Marriage Initiative." Washington, DC: Heritage Foundation. Available at https://www.heritage.org/ marriage-and-family/report/understanding-the-presidents-healthy-marriage-initiative. (accessed 6/25/21)

Reed, Touré. 2015. "Why Moynihan Was Not So Misunderstood at the Time: The Mythological Prescience of the Moynihan Report and the Problem of Institutional Structuralism." *Nonsite.org,* Issue 17, September 4. Available at https://nonsite.org/why-moynihan-was-not-so-misunderstood-at-the-time/#foot_src_35-9142. (accessed 7/6/22)

Reese, Ellen. 2005. *Backlash Against Welfare Mothers: Past and Present.* Berkeley: University of California Press.

Reeves, Richard V. 2020. "David Brooks Is Correct: Both the Quality and Quantity of Our Relationships Matter." *The Family Studies Blog,* February 11. Available at https://ifstudies. org/blog/david-brooks-is-correct-both-the-quality-and-quantity-of-our-relationships-matter. (accessed 5/19/2022)

Reeves, Richard V. 2018. *Dream Hoarders: How the American Upper Middle Class Is Leaving Everyone Else in the Dust, Why That Is a Problem, and What to Do about It.* Washington, DC: Brookings Institution Press.

Reeves, Richard V. and Eleanor Krause. 2017. "Cohabiting Parents Differ from Married Ones in Three Big Ways." Brookings Institute. Available at https://www.brookings.edu/research/ cohabiting-parents-differ-from-married-ones-in-three-big-ways/. (accessed 12/26/20)

Reeves, Richard V. and Christopher Pulliam. 2019. "Tipping the Balance: Why Equivalence Scales Matter More Than You Think." Brookings, April 17. Available at https://www.brooki

ngs.edu/articles/whats-in-an-equivalence-scale-maybe-more-than-you-think/. (accessed 10/21/23)

Reeves, Richard V. and Eleanor Krause. 2018. "Raj Chetty in 14 Charts: Big Findings on Opportunity and Mobility We Should All Know." Washington, DC: Brookings Institute. Available at https://www.brookings.edu/blog/social-mobility-memos/2018/01/11/raj-che tty-in-14-charts-big-findings-on-opportunity-and-mobility-we-should-know/. (accessed 3/4/22).

Regnerus, Mark. 2012. "How Different Are the Adult Children of Parents Who Have Same-Sex Relationships? Findings from the New Family Structures Study." *Social Science Research* 41 (4): 752–70.

Reich, Robert B. 2020. *The System: Who Rigged It, How We Fix It.* New York: Vintage

Reno, Virginia P. and Susan Grad. 1985. "Economic Security, 1935–85." *Social Security Bulletin* 48 (12): 5. Available at https://www.ssa.gov/policy/docs/ssb/v48n12/v48n12p5.pdf. (accessed 2/15/22)

Reyes, Emily A. 2014. "Federal Funds to Foster Healthy Marriage Have Little Effect, Study Finds." *Los Angeles Times*, February 9.

Romney, Mitt. 2019. "Romney, Bennet Offer Path to Bipartisan Compromise on Refundable Credits, Business Tax Fixes." https://www.romney.senate.gov/romney-bennet-offer-path-bipartisan-compromise-refundable-credits-business-tax-fixes/. (accessed 4/3/22)

Rosenzweig, Mark R. 1999. "Welfare, Marital Prospects, and Nonmarital Childbearing." *Journal of Political Economy* 107 (S6): S3–S32.

Rosewater, Ann. 1997. "Setting the Baseline: A Report on State Welfare Waivers." Office of the Assistant Secretary for Planning and Evaluation, U.S. Department of Health and Human Services. May 31. Available at https://aspe.hhs.gov/reports/setting-baseline-report-state-welfare-waivers. (accessed 4/2/22)

Rosignal, Will and Patrick McIlheran. 2024. "Single-parent Households by State." Badger Institute, January 24. Available at https://www.badgerinstitute.org/numbers/single-parent-households-by-state/.

Rossen, Lauren M., Brady E. Hamilton, Joyce C. Abma, Elizabeth C. W. Gregory, Vladislav Beresovsky, Addriana V. Resendez, Anjani Chandra, and Joyce A. Martin. 2023. "Updated methodology to estimate overall and unintended pregnancy rates in the United States. National Center for Health Statistics." *Vital Health Stat* 2 (201). Available at https://www.cdc.gov/nchs/data/series/sr_02/sr02-201.pdf. (accessed 5/1/2024)

Roy, Avik and Aparna Mathur. 2014. "The Biggest Reason for Income Inequality is Single Parenthood." *Forbes Magazine*, November 19. Available at https://www.forbes.com/sites/theapothecary/2014/11/19/the-biggest-reason-for-income-inequality-is-single-parenth ood/#d3adfcc2555c. (accessed 12/25/23)

Rubin, Robert E. and Jacob J. Lew. 2022. "A Plan to Help Kids without Increasing Inflation." *The New York Times*, vol. CLXXII: 26. May 3. Available at https://www.nytimes.com/2022/05/02/opinion/child-tax-credit.html?searchResultPosition=1. (accessed 5/3/22)

Ruggles, Steve. 1994 "The Origins of African-American Family Structure." *American Sociological Review* 59 (1): 136–151.

Ruggles, Steve. 1997. "The Rise of Divorce and Separation in the United States, 1880–1990." Demography 34 (4): 455–466.

Runyon, Anne Sisson. 2018. "What Is Intersectionality and Why Is It Important?" *Academe*, 104 (6): 10–14. November–December. Available at https://www.aaup.org/article/what-intersectionality-and-why-it-important#.YjvOBufMJM0. (accessed 3/23/22)

Rustin, Bayard. 1966. "The Watts 'Manifesto' & The McCone Report." *Commentary* 41 (3): 29–35. March. Available at https://www.commentary.org/articles/bayard-rustin-2/the-watts/. (accessed 7/6/22)

Ryan, Camille L. and Kurt Bauman. 2016. *Educational Attainment in the United States: 2015.* Current Population Reports, 20–578. United States Census Bureau. Available at https://www.census.gov/content/dam/Census/library/publications/2016/demo/p20-578.pdf. (accessed 8/12/21)

242 REFERENCES

Ryan, William. 1976. *Blaming the Victim*, revised ed. New York: Vintage Books.

Ryan, William. 1965. "Savage Discovery: The Moynihan Report." *The Nation* 201 (17): 380–384. November 22. Available at http://www.columbia.edu/itc/hs/pubhealth/p9740/readings/william_ryan.pdf. (accessed 2/2/22)

Samaan, Rodney. 2000. "The Influences of Race, Ethnicity, and Poverty on the Mental Health of Children" *Journal of Health Care for the Poor and Underserved* 11 (1): 100–110.

Sariscsany, Laurel, Irwin Garfinkel, and Lenna Nepomnyaschy. 2019. "Describing and Understanding Child Support Trajectories." *Social Service Review* 93 (2): 143–182.

Sarkisian, Natalia and Naomi Gerstel. 2008. "Till Marriage Do Us Part: Adult Children's Relationships with Their Parents." *Journal of Marriage and Family* 70 (2): 360–376.

Sauval, Maria, Greg Duncan, Lisa A. Gennetian, Katherine Magnuson, Nathan Fox, Kimbrely Noble, and Hirokazu Yoshikawa. 2022. "Unconditional Cash Transfers and Maternal Employment: Evidence from the Baby's First Years Study." November 30. Available at SSRN: https://ssrn.com/abstract=4297310 or http://dx.doi.org/10.2139/ssrn.4297310.

Schilbach, Frank, Heather Schofield, and Sendhil Mullainathan. 2016. "The Psychological Lives of the Poor." *American Economic Review* 106 (5): 435–440.

Schneider, Daniel. 2015. "Lessons Learned from Non-Marriage Experiments." *Future of Children* 25 (2): 155–178.

Schneider, Daniel. 2011. "Wealth and the Marital Divide." *American Journal of Sociology* 117: 627–667.

Schneider, Daniel and Alison Gemmill. 2016. "The Surprising Decline in the Non-Marital Fertility Rate in the United States." *Population and Development Review* 42 (4): 627–649.

Schneider, Daniel, Kristen Harknett, and Matthew Stimpson. 2018. "What Explains the Decline in First Marriage in the United States? Evidence from the Panel Study of Income Dynamics, 1969 to 2013." *Journal of Marriage and Family* 80 (4): 791–811.

Schott, Liz, LaDonna Pavetti, and Ife Floyd. 2015. "How States Use Federal and State Funds Under the TANF Block Grant." *Center on Budget & Policy Priorities*. Available at https://www.cbpp.org/research/family-income-support/how-states-use-federal-and-state-funds-under-the-tanf-block-grant. (accessed 4/19/22)

Schwartz, Christine R. 2013. "Trends and Variation in Assortative Mating: Causes and Consequences." *Annual Review of Sociology* 39: 451–470.

Seccombe, Karen, Delores James, and Kimberly Battle Walters. 1998. "'They Think you Ain't Much of Nothing': The Social Construction of the Welfare Mother." *Journal of Marriage and Family* 60 (4): 849–865.

Segal, Elisabeth. 2006. *The Promise of Welfare Reform: Political Rhetoric and the Reality of Poverty in the Twenty-First Century*. New York: Routledge.

Semega, Jessica, Kollar, Melissa, Shrider, Emily A., and John F. Creamer. 2020. *Income and Poverty in the United States: 2019*. United States Census Bureau, Current Population Reports, 60–270, Washington, DC: United States Government Publishing Office. Table B-2. Available at https://www.census.gov/content/dam/Census/library/publications/2020/demo/p60-270.pdf. (accessed 12/24/20)

Semega, Jessica, Melissa Kollar, John Creamer, and Abinash Mohanty. 2020. *Income and Poverty in the United States: 2018*. United States Census Bureau, Current Population Reports, 60–266 (RV). United States Government Printing OfficeWashington, DC: United States Government Printing Office.

Shriver, Maria and the Center for American Progress. 2009. *The Shriver Report: A Woman's Nation Changes Everything*, edited by Heather Boushey and Ann O'Leary: Washington, DC: Center for American Progress. Available at http://www.americanprogress.org/issues/2009/10/pdf/awn/a_womans_nation.pdf.

Sigle-Rushton, Wendy and Sara McLanahan. 2002. "For Richer or Poorer? Marriage As an Anti-poverty Strategy in the United States." *Population* 57 (3): 509–26.

Singh, Gopal K. 2010. "Maternal Mortality in the United States, 1935–2007: Substantial Racial/Ethnic, Socioeconomic, and Geographic Disparities Persist." *Health Resources and*

REFERENCES 243

Services Administration / Maternal and Child Health Bureau. Available at https://www.hrsa. gov/sites/default/files/ourstories/mchb75th/mchb75maternalmortality.pdf.

Skocpol, Theda. 1992. *Protecting Soldiers and Mothers: the Political Origins of Social Policy in the United States*. Cambridge, MA: Harvard University Press.

Smock, Pamela J. 1993. "The Economic Costs of Marital Disruption for Young Women over the Past Two Decades." *Demography* 30: 353–371.

Smock, Pamela J., Wendy D. Manning, and Sanjay S. Gupta. 1999. "The Effect of Marriage and Divorce on Women's Economic Well-Being." *American Sociological Review* 64: 794–812.

Smock, Pamela J. and Christine R. Schwartz. 2020. "The Demography of Families: A Review of Patterns and Change." *Journal of Marriage and Family* 82 (1): 9–34.

Somers, Margaret R. and Fred Block. 2005. "From Poverty to Perversity: Ideas, Markets, and Institutions over 200 Years of Welfare Debate." *American Sociological Review* 70: 260–287.

Social Security Administration. N.d. "Social Security History: Otto von Bismarck." Available at https://www.ssa.gov/history/ottob.html. (accessed 7/5/23)

Sorensen, Elaine, Liliana Sousa, and Simon Schaner. 2007. "Assessing Child Support Arrears in Nine Large States and the Nation." Washington, DC: The Urban Institute. Available at http://opnff.net/Files/Admin/Assessing%20Child%20Support%20Arrears.pdf. (accessed 3/24/22)

Sorensen, Elaine and Chava Zibman. 2000. "A Look at Poor Dads Who Don't Pay Child Support. Discussion Papers. Assessing the New Federalism: An Urban Institute Program To Assess Changing Social Policies." Washington, DC: The Urban Institute. Available at https://www.urban.org/sites/default/files/publication/62536/409646-A-Look-at-Poor-Dads-Who-Don-t-Pay-Child-Support.PDF. (accessed 3/24/22)

South, Scott J. and Lei Lei. 2015. "Failures-to-launch and Boomerang Kids: Contemporary Determinants of Leaving and Returning to the Parental Home." *Social Forces* 94 (2): 863–90.

Stanley, Scott M., Rhoades, Galena Kline, and Howard J. Markman. 2006. "Sliding versus Deciding: Inertia and the Premarital Cohabitation Effect." *Family Relations* 55 (4): 499–509.

Steensland, Brian. 2011. *The Failed Welfare Revolution*. Princeton University Press.

Stiglitz, Joseph E. 2012. *The Price of Inequality: How Today's Divided Society Endangers Our Future*. New York: W. W. Norton.

Sweeney, Megan M. 1995. "Remarriage of Men and Women: The Role of Socioeconomic Prospects." Working paper 95-08, Center for Demography and Ecology, University of Wisconsin-Madison

Sweeney, Megan M. 2002. "Two Decades of Family Change: The Shifting Economic Foundations of Marriage." *American Sociological Review* 67: 132–47.

Taylor, Danielle. 2019. *Male Couples Make up Majority of Same-Sex Households in Large Cities hi Not Nationwide*. United States Census Bureau. Available at https://www.census.gov/libr ary/stories/2019/09/where-same-sex-couples-live.html.

Teachman, Jay D., Kathleen M. Paasch, Randal D. Day and Karen Price Carver. 1997. "Poverty During Adolescence and Subsequent Educational Attainment." Pp. 382–418 in Greg Duncan and Jeanne Brooks-Gunn *Consequences of Growing Up Poor*. New York: Russell Sage Press

The World Bank. 2021. "Gini Index." https://data.worldbank.org/indicator/SI.POV.GINI. (accessed 12/29/21)

Thompson, Alex. 2021. "Biden Concedes Build Back Better Bill Won't Get Passed his Year." Politico, December 16. Available at https://www.politico.com/news/2021/12/16/biden-concedes-bbb-bill-wont-get-passed-this-year-525194. (accessed 4/19/2022)

Thornton, Arland and Linda Young-DeMarco. 2001. "Four Decades of Trends in Attitudes toward Family Issues in the United States: The 1960s through the 1990s." *Journal of Marriage and Family* 63 (4): 1009–1037.

Thurow, Lester C., 1969. The Optimum Lifetime Distribution of Consumption Expenditures. *The American Economic Review* 59: 324–30.

244 REFERENCES

Torpey, Elka and Audrey Watson. 2014. "Education Level and Jobs: Opportunities by State." U.S. Bureau of Labor Statistics. Available at https://www.bls.gov/careeroutlook/2014/arti cle/education-level-and-jobs.htm. (accessed 8/12/21)

Treas, Judith. 1987. "The Effect of Women's Labor Force Participation on the Distribution of Income in the United States." *Annual Review of Sociology* 13: 259–288.

Treiman, Donald. 2009. *Quantitative Data Analysis.* San Francisco: Wiley.

Turner, Douglas. 1996. "Moynihan Rips Clinton Welfare-Reform Plan." *The Buffalo News,* March 22. Available at https://buffalonews.com/news/moynihan-rips-clinton-welfare-ref orm-plan/article_d8a6086b-3bd9-5579-abbb-2304ff49e40c.html. (accessed 4/2/22)

Ullrich, Volker. 2015. *Bismarck: The Iron Chancellor.* London: Haus Publishing.

United Food and Commercial Workers International Union (UFCW). 2015. "Celebrating UFCW Moms: Single Mom Sought Education and Career for Better Life, Gives Back to Union and Community." Available at https://www.ufcw.org/celebrating-ufcw-moms-sin gle-mom-sought-education-and-career-for-better-life-gives-back-to-union-and-commun ity/. (accessed 5/13/22)

United States Census Bureau. 1961. *Statistical Abstract of the United States: 1961*, 81st ed. Washington, DC: United States Government Printing Office, Table 268.

United States Census Bureau. 1975. *Historical Statistics of the United States, Colonial Times to 1970,* Bicentennial Edition, Part 2, Washington, DC.

United States Census Bureau. 1979. *Statistical Abstract of the United States: 1979*, 99th ed. Washington, DC: United States Government Printing Office.

United States Census Bureau. 2006. "Design and Methodology: Current Population Survey. Technical Paper 66". Washington, DC. Available at https://www2.census.gov/programs-surveys/cps/methodology/tp-66.pdf. (accessed 12/19/23)

United States Census Bureau. 2011. *Statistical Abstract of the United States: 2011*, 131st ed. Washington, DC: United States Government Printing Office.

United States Census Bureau. 2010. *America's Families and Living Arrangements: 2010.* Washington, DC: United States Government Printing Office. Available at ttps://www.cen sus.gov/population/www/socdemo/hh-fam/cps2010.html. (accessed 9/20/11)

United States Census Bureau. 2012. *Statistical Abstract of the United States: Statistical Abstract of the United States: 2012*, 132nd ed. Washington, DC: United States Government Printing Office, calculations from Table 599.

United States Census Bureau. 2018. "Real Median Household Income by Race and Hispanic Origin: 1967 to 2017." Available at https://www.census.gov/content/dam/Census/library/visualizations/2018/demo/p60-263/figure1.pdf. (accessed 1/8/22)

United States Census Bureau. 2019. "Median Age at First Marriage: 1890 to Present." Decennial Censuses, 1890 to 1940, and Current Population Survey, Annual Social and Economic Supplements, 1947 to 2022. Available at https://www.census.gov/content/dam/Census/library/visualizations/time-series/demo/families-and-households/ms-2.pdf. (accessed 7/24/21)

United States Bureau of the Census. 2020. "Poverty Thresholds 2018." Available at https://www.census.gov/data/tables/time-series/demo/income-poverty/historical-poverty-thr esholds.html.

United States Census Bureau. 2020. "America's Families and Living Arrangements: 2020." Available at https://www.census.gov/data/tables/2020/demo/families/cps-2020.html. (accessed 2/7/22)

United States Bureau of the Census. 2021. "CPS Historical Time Series Tables: Educational Attainment," Table A-2. Washington, DC. Available at https://www.census.gov/data/tables/time-series/demo/educational-attainment/cps-historical-time-series.html. (accessed 7/16/21)

United States Census Bureau. 2021. "Equivalence Adjustment of Income." October 8. Washington, DC: United States Government Printing Office. Available at https://www.census.gov/topics/income-poverty/income-inequality/about/metrics/equivalence.html. (accessed 10/21/23)

REFERENCES 245

United States Census Bureau. 2023. "Historical Living Arrangements of Children," Washington, DC. Available at https://www.census.gov/data/tables/time-series/demo/families/children. html. (accessed 2/19/22).

United States Census Bureau. 2023. "Subject Definitions." Washington, DC: United States Government Printing Office. Available at https://www.census.gov/programs-surveys/cps/technical-documentation/subject-definitions.html. (accessed 7/17/21).

United States Census Bureau, 2023. "Historical Income Tables." Washington, DC. Available at https://www.census.gov/data/tables/time-series/demo/income-poverty/historical-income-inequality.html.(accessed 11/1/23)

United States Census Bureau. 2023. "About the Current Population Survey." Washington, DC. Available at https://www.census.gov/programs-surveys/cps/about.html. (accessed 11/12/23)

United States Census Bureau. 2023. "Glossary." Washington, DC. Available at https://www.census.gov/glossary/?term=Householder. (accessed 12/14/23)

United States Children's Bureau. 1933. "Mothers' Aid, 1931." Bureau publication no. 220, Washington, DC: United States Government Printing Office. Available at https://archive.org/details/mothersaid193100unit. (accessed 5/1/24)

United States Congress. 2022. H. R. 5376, Build Back Better Act, 117th Congress, 2021–2022. Washington, DC. Available at https://www.congress.gov/bill/117th-congress/house-bill/5376. (accessed 4/19/22)

United States Department of Health and Human Services, Administration for Children & Families. 2012. "Premarital and Marriage Education." The Healthy Marriage Initiative. Washington, DC. (accessed 9/2/12)

United States Department of Labor. 2010. "Women in the Labor Force: A Databook." Washington, DC: Bureau of Labor Statistics. Available at http://www.bls.gov/cps/wlf-databook-2010.pdf. (accessed 10/6/11)

United States Department of Labor. 2023. "Inflation Calculator." Bureau of Labor Statistics. Available at https://www.bls.gov/data/inflation_calculator.htm. (accessed 11/11/23)

United States Government Accountability Office. 2020. "Federal Social Safety Net Programs: Millions of Full-Time Workers Rely on Federal Health Care and Food Assistance Programs." GAO-21-45, October 19. Washington, DC. Available at https://www.gao.gov/products/gao-21-45. (accessed 7/2/23)

Upchurch, Dawn M., Lee A. Lillard, and Constantijn W. A. Panis. 2002. "Nonmarital Childbearing: Influences of Education, Marriage, and Fertility." *Demography* 39: 311–29.

Upchurch, Dawn M., Lillard, Lee A. and Constantijn W. A. Panis. 2001. "The Impact of Nonmarital Childbearing on Subsequent Marital Formation and Dissolution." Pp. 344–380 in Lawrence L. Wu and Barbara Wolfe *Out of Wedlock: Causes and Consequences of Nonmarital Fertility*. New York: Russell Sage Foundation.

Upchurch, Dawn M. and James McCarthy. 1990. "The Timing of a First Birth and High School Completion." *American Sociological Review* 55 (2): 224–234.

Usdansky, Margaret. 2009. "A Weak Embrace: Popular and Scholarly Depictions of Single-Parent Families, 1900–1998." *Journal of Marriage and Family* 71: 209–25.

Usdansky, Margaret L. and Sara McLanahan. 2003. "Looking for Murphy Brown: Are College-Educated, Single Mothers Unique?" Working paper 03-05-FF, Center for Research on Child Wellbeing, Princeton University. Available at https://citeseerx.ist.psu.edu/viewdoc/download?doi=10.1.1.584.7060&rep=rep1&type=pdf. (accessed 2/19/22)

Veght, Benjamin. 2015. "Social Security's Past, Present and Future." Washington, DC: National Academy of Social Insurance. Available at https://www.nasi.org/discussion/social-securitys-past-present-and-future/. (accessed 2/15/2022)

Ventura, Stephanie J., T. J. Mathews, and Brady E. Hamilton. 2001. *Births to Teenagers in the United States 1940–2000*. Hyattville, MD: National Center for Health Statistics.

Veroff, Joseph, Douvan, Elizabeth, and Richard A. Kulka. 1981. *The Inner American: A Self Portrait from 1957–1976*. New York: Basic Books.

246 REFERENCES

Vlosky, Denese A. and Monroe, Pamela A. 2002. "The Effective Dates of No-Fault Divorce Laws in the 50 States." *Family Relations* 51 (4): 317–324.

Waggoner, John. 2020. "AARP Poll Finds Near-Universal Support for Social Security after 85 Years." AARP, August 14. Available at https://www.aarp.org/retirement/social-security/info-2020/aarp-poll-finds-near-universal-support.html. (accessed 4/19/22)

Wagmiller, Robert Lee and Robert M. Adelman. 2009. "Childhood and Intergenerational Poverty: The Long-term Consequences of Growing Up Poor." National Center for Children in Poverty. Available at https://www.nccp.org/wp-content/uploads/2020/05/text_909.pdf. (accessed 5/9/22)

Wagmiller, Robert Lee, Mary Clare Lennon, Li Kuang, Philip M. Alberti, and J. Lawrence Aber. 2006. "The Dynamics of Economic Disadvantage and Children's Life Chances." *American Sociological Review* 71 (5): 847–866.

Waite, Linda J. and Maggie Gallagher. 2000. *The Case for Marriage: Why Married People Are Happier, Healthier, and Better off Financially.* New York: Doubleday.

Waite, Linda J. and Lee A. Lillard. 1991. "Children and Marital Disruption." *American Journal of Sociology* 96: 930–953.

Waldfogel, Jane. 1997. "The Effect of Children on Women's Wages." *American Sociological Review* 62: 209–217.

Wang, Wendy. 2020. "The U.S. Divorce Rate Has Hit a 50-year Low." *Institute for Family Studies*, November. Available at https://ifstudies.org/blog/the-us-divorce-rate-has-hit-a-50-year-low. (accessed 6/25/21)

Waring, Melody K. and Daniel R. Meyer. 2020. "Welfare, Work, and Single Mothers: The Great Recession and Income Packaging Strategies." *Children and Youth Services Review* 108: 1–10.

Wasserman, Melanie. 2020. "The Disparate Effects of Family Structure." *The Future of Children* 30 (1): 55–82.

Weiner, Greg. 2015. *American Burke: The Uncommon Liberalism of Daniel Patrick Moynihan.* Lawrence: University Press of Kansas.

Weiner, Greg. 2016. "On Welfare Reform, Moynihan Was Right." *Huffington Post*, March 23. Available at https://www.huffpost.com/entry/on-welfare-reform-moyniha_b_10083346. (accessed 4/2/2022)

Weissmann, Shoshana and C. Jarrett Dieterl. 2018. "Louisiana Is the Only State That Requires Occupational Licenses for Florists. It's Absurd." *USA Today*, March 28. Available at https://www.usatoday.com/story/opinion/2018/03/28/louisiana-only-state-requires-occupational-licenses-florists-its-absurd-column/459619002/. (accessed 12/29/21)

Weitzman, Lenore J. 1985. *The Divorce Revolution: The Unexpected Social and Economic Consequences for Women and Children in America.* New York: The Free Press.

Wernick, Robert. 1996. "Where You Went if You *Really* Had to Get Unhitched." *Smithsonian* 27: 64–72.

Western, Bruce, Deirdre Bloome, and Christine Percheski. 2008. "Inequality among American Families with Children, 1975 to 2005." *American Sociological Review* 73 (6): 903–920.

Western, Bruce and Jake Rosenfeld. 2011. "Unions, Norms, and the Rise in U.S. Wage Inequality." *American Sociological Review* 76 (4): 513–537.

Whitbeck, Les B., Ronald L. Simons, Rand D. Conger, Frederick O. Lorenz, Shirley Huck, and Glenn H. Elder Jr. 1991. "Family Economic Hardship, Parental Support, and Adolescent Self-Esteem." *Social Psychology Quarterly* 54 (4): 353–363.

White, Lynn. 1994. "Coresidence and Leaving Home: Young Adults and Their Parents." *Annual Review of Sociology* 20: 81–102.

Whitehead, Barbara Dafoe. 1993. "Dan Quayle Was Right." *The Atlantic*, April. Available at http://www.theatlantic.com/magazine/archive/1993/04/dan-quayle-was-right/7015/. (accessed 9/21/11)

Wikipedia. 2021. "Historical Racial and Ethnic Demographics of the United States." https://en.wikipedia.org/wiki/Historical_racial_and_ethnic_demographics_of_the_United_States. (accessed 7/21/21)

REFERENCES   247

Wilcox, W. Bradford. 2011. *Why Marriage Matters: Thirty Conclusions from the Social Sciences*, 3rd ed. New York: Broadway Publications.

Wilcox, W. Bradford. 2024. *Get Married: Why Americans Must Defy the Elites, Forge Strong Families, and Save Civilization*. New York: HarperCollins.

Wilcox, W. Bradford and Wendy Wang. 2020. "What Do We Know About Extended Families in America? A Response to David Brooks." *The Family Studies Blog*, February 10. https://ifstud ies.org/blog/what-do-we-know-about-extended-families-in-america-a-response-to-david-brooks. (accessed 5/19/22)

Wilcox, W. Bradford and Nicholas H. Wolfinger. 2016. *Soul Mates: Religion, Sex, Love and Marriage among African Americans and Latinos*. New York: Oxford University Press.

Wilcox, W. Bradford and Nicholas H. Wolfinger. 2007. "Then Comes Marriage? Religion and Marriage in Urban America." *Social Science Research* 36: 569–589.

Williams, Dedric T. and Regina S. Baker. 2021. "Family Structure, Risks, and Racial Stratification in Poverty." *Social Problems*. 68 (4): 964–985.

Wilson, William Julius. 2009. "The Moynihan Report and Research on the Black Community." *The Annals of the American Academy of Political and Social Science* 621 (1): 34–46.

Wilson, William Julius. 1987. *The Truly Disadvantaged: The Inner City, the Underclass, and Public Policy*. Chicago: University of Chicago Press.

Wilson, William Julius. 1997. *When Work Disappears: The World of the Urban Poor*. New York: Vintage Books.

Wines, Michael. 1992. "Views on Single Motherhood Are Multiple at White House." *The New York Times*, May 21. Available at https://www.nytimes.com/1992/05/21/us/views-on-single-motherhood-are-multiple-at-white-house.html.

Winship, Scott. 2016. "Nobody in America Lives on $2 per Day." Manhattan Institute, originally published in *The Federalist*, August 26. Available at https://www.manhattan-institute.org/html/nobody-america-lives-2-day-9194.html. (accessed 4/18/22)

Winship, Christopher and Larry Radbill. 1994. "Sampling weights and regression analysis." *Sociological Methods & Research* 23 (2): 230–257.

Wiseman, Michael. 2002. "Food Stamps and Welfare Reform." Brookings, March 4. Available at https://www.brookings.edu/research/food-stamps-and-welfare-reform/. (accessed 2/4/22)

Wolfers, Justin. 2006. "Did Unilateral Divorce Laws Raise Divorce Rates? A Reconciliation and New Results." *American Economic Review* 96 (5): 1802–1820.

Wolfinger, Nicholas H. 2001 "The Effects of Family Structure of Origin on Offspring Cohabitation Duration." *Sociological Inquiry* 71 (3): 293–313.

Wolfinger, Nicholas H. 2003. "Parental Divorce and Offspring Marriage: Early or Late?" *Social Forces* 82 (1): 337–353.

Wolfinger, Nicholas H. 2005. *Understanding the Divorce Cycle: The Children of Divorce in Their Own Marriages*. New York: Cambridge University Press.

Wolfinger, Nicholas H. 2007. "Does the Rebound Effect Exist? Time to Remarriage and Subsequent Union Stability." *Journal of Divorce & Remarriage* 46: 9–20.

Wolfinger, Nicholas H. 2015. "Replicating the Goldilocks Theory of Marriage and Divorce." *Institute for Family Studies*. Available at https://ifstudies.org/blog/replicating-the-goldilocks-theory-of-marriage-and-divorce/. (accessed 2/22/22)

Wolfinger, Nicholas H. 2015. "Want to Avoid Divorce? Wait to Get Married, but Not Too Long." *Institute for Family Studies*. Available at https://ifstudies.org/blog/want-to-avoid-divorce-wait-to-get-married-but-not-too-long/. (accessed 7/12/21)

Wolfinger, Nicholas H. 2019. "I Know what Intersectionality Is, and I Wish it Were Less Important." *Quillette*, February 20. Available at https://quillette.com/2019/02/20/i-know-what-intersectionality-is-and-i-wish-it-were-less-important/. (accessed 7/7/21)

Wolfinger, Nicholas H. 2023. "Family Change in the Context of Social Changes in the United States." Pp. 97–118 in Mary Daly, Birgit Pfau-Effinger, Doug Besharov, and Neil Gilbert *The Oxford Handbook of Family Policy Over The Life-Course*. Oxford: Oxford University Press.

248   REFERENCES

Wood, Robert G., Quinn Moore, Andrew Clarkwest, and Alexandra Killewald. 2014. "The Long-Term Effects of Building Strong Families: A Program for Unmarried Parents." *Journal of Marriage and Family* 76 (2): 446–463.

Working Group on Childhood in the United States. 2022. "Rebalancing: Children First." Washington, DC. Available at https://www.aei.org/wp-content/uploads/2022/02/AEI-Brookings-Rebalancing-Children-First-FINAL-REPORT-FEB-8-2022.pdf?x91208. (accessed 2/17/22)

World Population Review. "Gini Coefficient by Country." 2021. https://worldpopulationrev iew.com/country-rankings/gini-coefficient-by-country. (accessed 12/29/21)

Wrong, Dennis H., 1992. "Why the Poor Get Poorer," Review of *The New Politics of Poverty*, by Lawrence M. Mead, *New York Times*, April 19, vol CXLI (48941, Section 7): 3. Available at https://www.nytimes.com/1992/04/19/books/why-the-poor-get-poorer.html.

Wu, Huijing. 2017. "Trends in Births to Single and Cohabiting Mothers, 1980–2014." Family Profile No. 04, National Center for Family & Marriage Research (NCFMR), Bowling Green State University. Available at https://www.bgsu.edu/ncfmr/resources/data/family-profiles/ wu-trends-births-single-cohabiting-mothers-fp-17-04.html#:~:text=The%20share%20 of%20births%20to%20cohabiting%20mothers%20has%20more%20than,born%20i nto%20a%20cohabiting%20union. (accessed 12/26/20)

Wu, Lawrence L. 1996. "Effects of Family Instability, Income, and Income Instability on the Risk of a Premarital Birth. *American Sociological Review* 61: 386–406.

Wu, Lawrence L. and Brian C. Martinson. 1993. "Family Structure and the Risk of a Premarital Birth." *American Sociological Review* 58 (2): 210–232.

Wu, Lawrence L., Steven P. Martin, and Paula England. 2017. "The Decoupling of Sex and Marriage: Cohort Trends in Who Did and Did Not Delay Sex Until Marriage for U.S. Women Born 1938-1985. *Sociological Science* 4: 151–175.

Wu, Lawrence L. and Kelly Musick. 2000. "Historical and Life Course Trajectories of Nonmarital Childbearing." Center for Demography and Ecology, University of Wisconsin-Madison.

Wu, Lawrence L. and Barbara Wolfe. 2001. *Out of Wedlock: Causes and Consequences of Nonmarital Fertility.* New York: Russell Sage Foundation.

Wu, Lawrence L., Larry L. Bumpass, and Kelly Musick. 2001. "Historical and Life Course Trajectories of Nonmarital Childbearing." Pp. 3–48 in Lawrence L. Wu and Barbara Wolfe *Out of Wedlock: Causes and Consequences of Nonmarital Fertility.* New York: Russell Sage Foundation.

Wu, Lawrence L. and Miodrag Stojnic. 2007. "Poverty among the Poorest-Poor in the United States: Trends for Never-Married Women and Their Children." Paper presented at the Inaugural Conference, Center for Research on Inequalities and the Life Course, Yale University.

Young, Cathy. 2004. "Opting Out: The Press Discovers the Mommy Wars, Again." *Reason Online*, June. Available at https://reason.com/2004/06/01/opting-out-3/. (accessed 7/16/21)

Zagel, Hannah. 2014. "Are All Single Mothers the Same? Evidence from British and West German Women's Employment Trajectories." *European Sociological Review* 30 (1): 49–63.

Zill, Nicholas. 2021. "Growing Up with Mom and Dad: New Data Confirm the Tide Is Turning." Charlottesville, VA: Institute for Family Studies blog, June. Available at https:// ifstudies.org/blog/growing-up-with-mom-and-dad-new-data-confirm-the-tide-is-turn ing#:~:text=The%20proportion%20of%20children%20living,between%204%20and%20 5%20percent. (accessed 2/8/22)

Zill, Nicholas. 2023. "Food Stamps and Family: SNAP Recipients by Family Structure." Charlottesville, VA: Institute for Family Studies blog. April 25. Available at https://ifstudies. org/blog/food-stamps-and-family-snap-recipients-by-family-structure (accessed 12/7/23).

Zippel, Claire. 2021. "9 in 10 Families with Low Incomes Are Using Child Tax Credits to Pay for Necessities, Education." Center on Budget & Policy Priorities, October 21. Available at https://www.cbpp.org/blog/9-in-10-families-with-low-incomes-are-using-child-tax-cred its-to-pay-for-necessities-education. (accessed 4/20/22)

Index

For the benefit of digital users, indexed terms that span two pages (e.g., 52–53) may, on occasion, appear on only one of those pages.

Figures are indicated by an italic *f* following the page number.

African American, x–xi, 40–42, 66, 67f, 101, 102–3, 132–33, 171, 172
age, 20, 22–23, 27–28, 54–55, 58–59, 60–61f, 75–77f, 93–95, 110, 116–17, 121f, 126f, 127–28, 138, 140–41, 146f, 178–79, 180
    effect of, 17
    first birth, 129–30, 143
    income, 75–76
    marital status, 27f, 93
    maternal, 22
Aid to Families with Dependent Children (AFDC), 8–9, 10, 69, 70f, 72, 144, 158–59, 180
Akerlof, George, 167–68
American income inequality, 15
American Rescue Plan, 155, 162
Asian Americans, 67f, 102
Auletta, Ken, ix

BBB. *See* Build Back Better
Bennet, Michael (Senator), 161–62
Biden, Joseph (President), 162, 167
Bismarck, Otto von, 162–63
Black. *See* African American
Blau, Peter, 45, 120
Brady, David, xiii–xiv, 3–4, 48, 66, 156, 157, 164–65
Brady Amendment, 73–74
Brown, Sherrod (Senator), 162
Budig, Michelle, 63
Build Back Better (BBB), 162
Bush, George H. W. (President), 1–2
Bush, George W. (President), 10, 173

Campbell, Arthur, 20

cash transfers, direct, 161–62
Cass, Oren, 163
census, 73f, 175, 177
Cherlin, Andrew, 165, 169
Child Health Insurance Program (CHIP), 158
child support, 4–5, 39–40, 63–64, 69, 72–74, 75, 98f, 133–34, 146–47f, 152
child tax credit (CTC), 155, 158, 161–62, 164–65
Clinton, William J. (Bill) (President), 1–2, 5, 69
Coates, Ta-Nehisi, 171–72
cohabitation, 15, 38–40, 50–56, 55f–56, 103–6f, 108, 142, 148–49
    economic implications, 55
college graduation, 45, 57, 131
consumption, as a measure of income, 8
Crenshaw, Kimberlé, 68–69
cultural capital, measures of, 110, 125
culture of poverty, 4
Current Population Survey (CPS), 17, 19–23f, 27f–31f, 32f–36f, 37–38f, 41f–42f, 51f–55f, 57f–58f, 61f–62f, 64f–66f, 70f–73f, 77f–79f, 84f–87f, 91f–94f, 96f–102f, 105f–6f, 175–76f, 177

deadbeat dads, 69, 73–74, 161
decomposition. *See* income decomposition
divorce boom, 2f, 2–3, 19–20, 168–69
Duncan, Dudley Otis, 120

Earned Income Tax Credit (EITC), 158, 159–60, 163
economic inequality, 153, 165
    inherited, 66
economy, gig, 50, 54, 82

250 INDEX

Edin, Kathryn (Kathy), 10, 69–70, 81–82, 87–88, 163–65, 167, 168, 169
education
  effects of, 44, 90–91, 108, 109
  inheritance of, 123–25
educational attainment, 12, 22, 28–31, 30f, 32–33, 120, 123f, 124f
Ellwood, David, 3–4, 10
employment, 10–11, 12, 31f–32, 48, 91, 91f–93, 120–21, 128–29, 142, 159–60, 162, 164–65
  effect of, 150
  full-time, 30–31, 92
  parental, 120–23
  part-time, 48, 91
employment data, 121, 129
endogeneity. See sample selection
England, Paula, 63, 143
entering single motherhood, 17–18
exiting single motherhood, 17–18

family background. See family structure
family size, 7, 24, 25–26, 44, 60–62, 63–66, 97, 98f, 142f, 175
family structure, ix, 6–7, 14–15, 19, 37, 47, 68–69, 80, 91–92, 108, 127f–28, 136, 140f–41, 153–54, 157–58, 172–73
  and inequality, x–xi
  and poverty, ix
  and race for understanding income inequality, 102–3
  and single motherhood, 172–73
family structure inheritance. See intergenerational transmission of family structure
fertility. See family size
fertility trends, 20–26
fixed effects models, 142, 150
food stamps. See Supplemental Nutrition Assistance Program (SNAP)

Garfinkel, Irv, ix
gender wage gap, 12
gig economy, 50, 54, 82
Gini coefficient, 84
government transfer, 69–71, 72–73, 161–62, 180
Great Recession, 5, 34f, 46–47, 48, 55, 70f, 74, 109, 111–12, 114

Healthy Marriage and Responsible Fatherhood initiative. See marriage promotion
Heritage Foundation, 3, 160
high school graduate, 29, 45, 89f, 122f, 123–25, 130f, 178, 180
Hispanic. See Latino/Latina
households, multigenerational, 37–39, 56–60, 106–8, 149–50
Hymowitz, Kay, 172

income decomposition, 78
income growth, age-related, 95
income inequality, 5, 12–13, 15, 17–18, 20, 47, 81, 84, 87, 103f
  understanding, 102–3
inequality
  causes of, 35–36, 131
  within marital structure, 83–88
  for married mothers, 88, 90–91
  trend, 46–47, 108
  understanding, xiii–xiv, 69
intergenerational transmission of family structure, 127f, 127, 140–41, 172
intersectionality, 68–69

jobs. See employment

Kearney, Melissa, 69, 162
Kefalas, Maria, 148–49, 167, 169
Kerner Commission, 2–3

labor market regulation, 82
labor unions, 47, 82
Latino/Latina, 41f, 42, 102, 132–33
Lee, Mike (Senator), 1–2, 4
Lein, Laura, 7, 32, 50, 87, 143–44, 164–65
library cards, 125, 180
Lichter, Daniel, 10, 24, 25–26, 60, 81–82, 114
living arrangements, 2, 14, 24, 37–38, 48, 50–51, 53f–54f, 103–4, 110, 180
living with parents, 37–38, 57f, 59, 107
  effect of, 59

magic moment, 148–49
marital status changes, 134
marriage promotion, 10, 157, 158–59, 161, 163, 173
Martin, Molly, 12–13, 84

INDEX 251

McLanahan, Sara, ix, 8, 9, 10, 39–40, 81–82, 156–57
Mead, Lawrence, 5
median regression, 44, 178
minimum wage, 160, 164
Moynihan, Daniel Patrick, x–xi, 40, 163–64, 171, 172–73
multi-partner fertility (MPF), 16
Murphy Brown, 1, 15–16
Murphy Brown mothers, 15–16, 86*f*
Murray, Charles, 4

National Longitudinal Survey of Youth (NLSY), 17–18, 109–10, 113*f*, 115–16*f*, 118*f*, 121*f*, 122*f*–23*f*, 126*f*–28, 130*f*–31*f*, 132–33*f*, 141–42, 145*f*–47*f*, 148–49, 153–54
newspapers, 125–26*f*, 180

Obama, Barack (President), 172, 173
occupational status. *See* Socio-Economic Index (SEI)
older mothers, 93, 94–95, 111–12, 114, 117, 134

parental death. *See* widowhood
peak income, 141
Personal Responsibility and Work Opportunity Reconciliation Act, (PRWORA). *See* welfare reform
Person of Opposite Sex Sharing Living Quarters (POSSLQ), 38–39, 178
poverty, 3–4, 8–9, 12–14, 60, 124*f*, 127–28, 155, 156–57, 159–60, 161–62, 163
structural explanation, 172
poverty line, 7, 34–35, 175
poverty rate, 5, 14, 155, 159–60
public assistance, 6, 7, 63–64, 65–66, 69, 98–99, 144, 145
effects of, 98–99
importance of, 144

Quayle, Dan (Vice-President), 1–2, 15–16, 83

race. *See* race and ethnicity
race and ethnicity, 40–42, 66–68, 101, 132–33
Reagan, Ronald (President), 3, 9, 40, 163, 169
Reeves, Richard, 95, 165
regression, 7, 178

remarriage, 24–26, 27, 27*f*, 29, 114–15, 118*f*, 118, 119–20, 168, 169
Romney, Mitt (Senator), 161–62, 163, 181
Roosevelt, Theodore (Teddy) (President), 2–3
Roy, Avik, 81
Rustin, Bayard, 171–72
Ryan, William, 171–72

sample selection, 13, 76, 95, 114–15, 136, 141–43
Schneider, Daniel, 2, 6–7, 114–15, 157, 162, 164–65, 168
Schwartz, Christine, 52–53
SEI. *See* Socio-Economic Index (SEI)
selection bias. *See* sample selection
Shaefer, H. Luke, 10, 14, 69–70, 81–82, 87–88, 160, 163–64
single motherhood
causes, x, 15, 164–65, 167–68
single parents as cause of inequality, 84
Smock, Pamela, 12–13, 19–20, 52–53, 63, 104, 127–28
SNAP. *See* Supplemental Nutrition Assistance Program
Social Security, 4, 155, 161–62
Socio-Economic Index (SEI), 32–34, 62–63
Supplemental Nutrition Assistance Program (SNAP), 144*f*, 145, 158, 180

tax code, 82, 162
teen motherhood. *See* teenage motherhood
teenage motherhood, 13–14, 20–22, 60, 61*f*, 96*f*, 127–28, 129–30, 135
Temporary Assistance for Needy Families (TANF), 10–11, 69, 70*f*, 70–72, 158–59, 163–64. *See also* welfare

UBI. *See* universal basic income
Uniform Interstate Family Support Act, 73–74
unions. *See* labor unions
United States Census. *See* census
universal basic income (UBI), 161–62, 163–64, 173

welfare, 4, 9, 69, 72, 160, 164–65, 167

252 INDEX

welfare culture, 4
welfare queen, 4, 9, 181
welfare reform, 9, 10, 12–13, 14, 72, 73–74, 144, 145, 159–60, 161–62
widowhood, 8, 14

Wilcox, Bradford, xiii–xiv, 119*f*, 163, 165, 167
work. *See* employment

Yellen, Janet, 167–68